CONTENTS

3702129769

2

Coping with
Life Challenges

Chris L. Kleinke

University of Alaska, Anchorage

FRANCIS CLOSE HALL
LEARNING CENTRE
UNIVERSITY OF GLOUCESTERSHIRE
Swindon Road
Cheltenham GL50 4AZ
Tel: 01242 532913

Brooks/Cole Publishing Company

I(T)P® An International Thomson Publishing Company

Pacific Grove • Albany • Belmont • Bonn • Boston • Cincinnati • Detroit • Johannesburg • London
Madrid • Melbourne • Mexico City • New York • Paris • Singapore • Tokyo • Toronto • Washington

To Anya and Alex and their grandparents

Sponsoring Editor: *Eileen Murphy*
Marketing Team: *Jean Thompson, Margaret Parks*
Marketing Representative: *Tammy Stenquist*
Editorial Assistants: *Lisa Blanton, Susan Carlson*
Production Editor: *Kirk Bomont*
Manuscript Editor: *Kay Mikel*
Permissions Editor: *May Clark*

Design Editor: *E. Kelly Shoemaker*
Interior and Cover Design: *Laurie Albrecht*
Interior Illustration: *Jennifer Mackres*
Typesetting: *Bookends Typesetting*
Printing and Binding: *Maple-Vail Book Manufacturing Company*

For more information, contact:

BROOKS/COLE PUBLISHING COMPANY
511 Forest Lodge Road
Pacific Grove, CA 93950
USA

International Thomson Publishing Europe
Berkshire House 168-173
High Holborn
London WC1V 7AA
England

Thomas Nelson Australia
102 Dodds Street
South Melbourne, 3205
Victoria, Australia

Nelson Canada
1120 Birchmount Road
Scarborough, Ontario
Canada M1K 5G4

International Thomson Editores
Seneca 53
Col. Polanco
11560 México, D.F., México

International Thomson Publishing GmbH
Königswinterer Strasse 418
53227 Bonn
Germany

International Thomson Publishing Asia
221 Henderson Road
#05-10 Henderson Building
Singapore 0315

International Thomson Publishing Japan
Hirakawacho Kyowa Building, 3F
2-2-1 Hirakawacho
Chiyoda-ku, Tokyo 102
Japan

Printed in the United States of America

10 9 8 7 6 5 4 3 2 1

Library of Congress Cataloging-in-Publication Data
Kleinke, Chris L.
    Coping with life challenges / Chris L. Kleinke. — 2nd ed.
        p.   cm.
    Includes bibliographical references and index.
    ISBN 0-534-34549-2
    1. Adjustment (Psychology)   2. Adjustment (Psychology—Case studies.   I. Title
BF335.K59   1998
158—dc21   97-15989
                                                      CIP

9   Coping with Conflicts in Close Relationships   150

10   Coping with Loss   172

11   Coping with Aging   190

12   Coping with Pain   207

13   Coping with Illness and Maintaining Health   224

14   Coping with Injury and Trauma   246

15   Coping as a Life Philosophy   263

PREFACE

We are all confronted at times in our lives with problems and challenges. During times of stress, it is comforting to know you have skills and resources that will help you make the best of difficult situations.

Researchers have collected a wealth of information about how people cope with life challenges. They have directed their efforts toward answering these questions: "Can different styles of coping be identified and measured?" "Are some coping strategies more useful for certain problems than for others?" "How can I learn to cope more effectively with challenges that confront me?"

My purpose in writing this book is to communicate the findings of these studies to people not trained in the scientific jargon contained in professional journals. In this book I will provide an overview of what researchers have discovered about coping. You will read about coping responses you already use and about ones you don't know much about but will want to learn. You will come to appreciate the fact that you, as a human being, are adaptable. Your ability to cope is not fixed at birth; it is developed and perfected throughout your life. You need not be a passive bystander. Living is not always easy, but knowledge *is* power. I hope this book will empower you to gain a greater sense of control over the challenges in your life.

This book can be roughly divided into three sections. Chapters 1 through 3 provide an introduction to the concept of coping and explain a number of important terms. Chapter 1 defines the concept of coping and two terms that will be used throughout the book: *primary appraisal* and *secondary appraisal*. Several important topics are discussed, including the distinction between self-blame and self-responsibility, the pros and cons of avoidance, and common self-defeating behaviors. Chapter 2 focuses on daily hassles and how they affect us. You are encouraged to develop an attitude of mastery and self-efficacy. Chapter 3 describes eight skills that should be added to your coping arsenal: building a support system, problem solving, self-relaxation, maintaining internal control, talking yourself through challenges, developing your sense of humor, exercising, and rewarding yourself for accomplishments.

Chapters 4 through 12 focus on challenges people face at various times in their lives. Each of these chapters includes a description of useful coping skills. Chapter 4 teaches skills for coping with failure. Chapter 5 teaches skills for coping with depression. Chapter 6 teaches skills for coping with loneliness, shyness, and rejection. Chapter 7 teaches skills for coping with anxiety. Chapter 8 teaches skills for coping with anger. Chapter 9 teaches skills for coping with conflicts in close relationships. Chapter 10 teaches skills for coping with loss. Chapter 11 teaches skills for coping with aging, and Chapter 12 teaches skills for coping with pain.

Chapters 13 through 15 take a somewhat different approach, describing the experiences of people who have borne up to difficult challenges. Chapter 13 focuses on illness, preventive medicine, and health. Examples are given of how people cope with illness and health problems ranging from headaches to cancer and AIDS. Suggestions are given for developing an attitude of hardiness and a low-stress personality. Chapter 14 offers a tribute to people who have undergone injury and trauma. You will learn about coping by appreciating the experiences of those who suffered harm from natural and human-caused disasters. Included in this chapter is a discussion of post-traumatic stress disorder. In Chapter 15 I reprise the theme of this book by discussing coping as a life philosophy. A distinction is made between the psychological effects of helplessness and hope. You are encouraged to become a well-rounded person and to develop an attitude of self-preservation. The chapter concludes by highlighting the benefits of perfecting your coping skills in this challenging and unpredictable world.

How to Use This Book

Here are some ideas about how to use this book. Chapters 1 through 3 are intended to provide knowledge about coping that will be useful for everyone. It is probably best to read these chapters first. Chapter 15 contains helpful ideas about how to incorporate coping into your life philosophy, and you might want to read it next. Chapters 4 through 14 focus on coping skills that are beneficial for dealing with specific life challenges. Even though you might not be facing some of the problems addressed in these chapters, you will learn how to develop an arsenal of skills you can rely on as you encounter challenges during the rest of your life. You can use chapters that address problems of greatest interest to you as guidelines for current life challenges. Other chapters may help you to understand people you know who are facing specific problems. Although this book suggests solutions to a range of problems, the focus of the discussion is on ideas you can use to make your life richer and more self-fulfilling.

Acknowledgments

Many people have contributed their talents to making this a better book, and I thank them for their assistance. In particular I would like to acknowledge the helpful comments of the following reviewers: William Cheney, Community College of Rhode Island; Terri Kaye Needle, Rockland Community College; Young Song, California State University—Hayward; and Mark Young, Stetson University.

Chris L. Kleinke

What Does It Mean to Cope?

This book is about dealing with the challenges, traumas, and hassles in our lives. It is about "keeping the faith," "hanging in," and managing our fears, hostilities, doubts, frustrations, and sadness. It is a tribute to people's adaptability and capacity to overcome adversity. My goal in writing this book is to teach you a number of useful coping skills that you can rely on when confronted with life challenges. I also want to communicate a philosophy—a coping skills attitude toward life—that no matter how tough things seem, you can make a plan and survive. If you apply a coping attitude in your life, you will enhance your own potential for personal growth. You can make your life more interesting by mastering new skills and taking on meaningful challenges.

I will begin with a definition of coping and a description of how the coping process works. A good place to start is with the process of *appraisal*. R. S. Lazarus and S. Folkman (1984) define two kinds of appraisal: *primary appraisal* and *secondary appraisal*. When humans are faced with a potential challenge or stress, we first determine whether we are in jeopardy or danger. We ask ourselves whether this is something worth getting upset about. This is primary appraisal. Primary appraisal is concerned with our physical as well as our psychological well-being. If we determine that we are in jeopardy or danger, we ask ourselves whether there is something we can do about it and, if so, what? This is secondary appraisal.

PRIMARY APPRAISAL

Let's say that a company executive, in a harsh tone of voice, tells three of her assistants that she wants to see them in her office "first thing next morning." What sorts of primary appraisals might the assistants make?

One, Tim, might think: "This means trouble. That harsh tone can only mean I did something wrong and that I'm in hot water. There's nothing I can do now. I probably won't sleep all night, and I'll be really tired and anxious tomorrow."

Another, Lisa, might think: "Sometimes when the boss uses that harsh tone it doesn't mean anything, and sometimes it does. I won't know until tomorrow if there is any trouble, but it will be in my best interest to be up on my facts and figures. And, just in case, I'll dress extra professionally tomorrow."

The third, Ed, might think: "If the boss sounds harsh, that's her problem. Her problems don't concern me, so I'll just pretend nothing happened and come in tomorrow just as I always do."

Note the different impact as well as the subjectivity of primary appraisals. Tim has appraised the director's harsh tone as a definite threat. Lisa has appraised it as a possible threat. Ed has appraised it as posing no threat. At this point we don't know whose appraisal is correct, but you would probably agree that Lisa's is most prudent. Tim is being a "catastrophizer," and by assuming the worst he will suffer a good deal of stress. Ed is being a "denier." He is not under any stress right now, but he may pay a price in the future. Lisa is taking the issue seriously but is managing her stress by making concrete plans.

SECONDARY APPRAISAL

If our primary appraisal tells us we are in jeopardy, we need to ask what we can do about it. This process is referred to as the secondary appraisal. In the example, each of the three employees decided on a different response. Tim's secondary appraisal tells him he is facing a threat that is beyond his control. Lisa concludes there is a possible threat, and she draws up a "battle plan." Because Ed assumes there is no threat, he feels no need for a secondary appraisal.

Primary and secondary appraisals have an impact on how you respond to a challenge or a threat. It is in your best interest to make a realistic primary appraisal. You don't want to fly off the handle and panic, but you don't want to ignore real problems either. If your primary appraisal indicates reason for concern, you want to make a secondary appraisal that is adaptive. Here is an example of this appraisal process: "This is a genuine problem. Things look tough. I've got to come up with some good plans. Let me dig into my bag of coping strategies and make plan A and plan B, and possibly plan C."

Most of the time your secondary appraisal will suggest some steps you can take to manage the situation. On other occasions, however, you may determine that the situation is beyond your control and that the best plan is to "exert control" by not fighting a battle you can't win. Sometimes it is better to be flexible and roll with the punches.

A DEFINITION OF COPING

Rose Kennedy was once asked about her adjustment to the many tragedies that have befallen her family. She replied, "I cope." Coping can be defined as *the efforts we make to manage situations we have appraised as being potentially harmful or stressful.* This definition of coping, which is adapted from Lazarus and Folkman (1984), has three key features: (1) it implies that coping involves a certain amount of effort and planning; (2) it does not assume that the outcome of a coping response will always be positive; and (3) it emphasizes coping as a process taking place over time.

These features are important in defining coping because they allow us to study different styles and strategies of coping and to evaluate which ones work best in different situations. The goal of researchers has been to find out whether specific personality traits, beliefs, or ways of viewing the world are more or less adaptive in various situations. Once you have looked at what has been learned about these questions, you will be able to distinguish effective coping strategies you can use in your life.

TWO GENERAL COPING STRATEGIES

Lazarus and Folkman (1984) identify two general forms of coping: *problem-focused* coping and *emotion-focused* coping. Problem-focused coping strategies can be outer-directed or inner-directed. Outer-directed coping strategies are oriented toward altering the situation or the behaviors of others. Inner-directed coping strategies include efforts we make to reconsider our attitudes and needs and to develop new skills and responses. Emotion-focused coping is oriented toward managing emotional distress. Emotion-focused coping strategies include physical exercise, meditation, expressing feelings, and seeking support.

You are more likely to engage in problem-focused coping when you feel there is something you can do about a problem or a challenge. However, when a problem or challenge appears to be beyond your control, you are more likely to rely on emotion-focused coping (Folkman & Lazarus, 1980; Vitaliano, DeWolfe, Maiuro, Russo, & Katon, 1990). In most situations, we probably benefit most by combining these coping strategies. For example, you can prepare for a job interview by practicing your responses to questions and choosing appropriate attire (problem-focused) and by being relaxed and maintaining a nondefensive attitude (emotion-focused). When you must face a difficult confrontation, you may cope by keeping your cool (emotion-focused) and using effective negotiation skills (problem-focused).

The distinction between problem-focused and emotion-focused coping provides a broad framework for understanding the concept of coping. More specific coping responses are discussed next.

RESEARCH ON COPING RESPONSES

Take a few minutes to think about the most stressful event that has happened to you during the past month. With this event in mind, check how often you did each of the following things.

	Never	Sometimes	Often
1. Tried to see the positive side.	_____	_____	_____
2. Took things one step at a time.	_____	_____	_____
3. Stepped back to be more objective.	_____	_____	_____
4. Took some positive action.	_____	_____	_____

	Never	*Sometimes*	*Often*
5. Exercised more.	___	___	___
6. Talked with friends.	___	___	___
7. Kept my feelings to myself.	___	___	___
8. Ate more, smoked cigarettes, or used drugs.	___	___	___
9. Refused to acknowledge the problem.	___	___	___

These nine coping responses were studied in a community survey (Billings & Moos, 1981; Holahan & Moos, 1987). You may have noticed that responses 1, 5, 7, 8, and 9 are emotion-focused, and responses 2, 4, and 6 are problem-focused. Another way to categorize these coping responses is according to whether they represent an *active-cognitive* method (1, 2, 3), an *active-behavioral* method (4, 5, 6), or *avoidance* (7, 8, 9). Results of the survey indicated that women used active-behavioral methods and avoidance more often than men. Men and women did not differ in their use of active-cognitive methods. People who used active-cognitive and active-behavioral coping responses tended to be easygoing and less anxious. They also had relatively high self-confidence. People who were avoiders tended to be more depressed and anxious, and they suffered greater physical stress. Avoiders also had fewer educational and financial resources and less family support.

In another survey of how people cope, married couples were questioned about their responses to four sources of stress: marriage, parenting, household finances, and work (Pearlin & Schooler, 1978). A number of coping responses were employed by people who suffered comparatively low levels of emotional stress. These coping responses included taking an active, self-reliant, problem-solving approach. Greater amounts of emotional distress were experienced by people who felt helpless, blamed themselves, and engaged in denial and avoidance.

A third group of researchers surveyed people on their experiences with various coping responses when faced with losses, threats, and challenges (McCrae & Costa, 1986). The most effective coping responses included seeking help, communicating feelings, taking rational action, drawing strength from adversity, using humor, and maintaining faith, self-confidence, and feelings of control. The least effective coping responses included hostility, indecisiveness, self-blame, and attempting to escape or withdraw from the situation.

A fourth example of effective and ineffective coping responses comes from a community survey in which people reported how they coped with a recent stressful experience, such as a loss of self-esteem, concern for a loved one, interpersonal conflict, financial strain, health problems, or lack of success at work (Folkman, Lazarus, Dunkel-Schetter, DeLongis, & Gruen, 1986). People who reported satisfactory resolution of their stressful experience tended to cope by maintaining their composure and working out a plan and by using the stressful experience as an opportunity for personal growth. Those who did not successfully resolve their problem responded by being impulsive, aggressive, or angry or by ignoring the problem and downplaying its importance.

In yet another study investigating the relationship between coping and emotions (Folkman & Lazarus, 1988), participants reported how often they used the following types of coping responses for a recent stressful event:

Confrontive coping: "I stood my ground and fought for what I wanted."

Distancing: "I went on as if nothing had happened."

Self-control: "I tried to keep my feelings to myself."

Seeking social support: "I talked to someone who could do something concrete about the problem."

Accepting responsibility: "I criticized or lectured myself."

Escape-avoidance: "I wished that the situation would go away or somehow be over with."

Planful problem solving: "I knew what had to be done, so I doubled my efforts to make things work."

Positive reappraisal: "I changed or grew as a person in a good way."

The respondents also reported which of the following emotions they experienced as a result of their response to the stressful situation: *worried/fearful, disgusted/angry, confident,* or *pleased/happy.*

After analyzing the correlation between the respondents' coping responses and their resulting emotions, the researchers reached the following conclusions: Planful problem solving appeared to be the most effective coping response because it was associated with the most positive emotions. Confrontive coping and distancing turned out to be the least effective coping responses because they were associated with the most negative emotions. Positive reappraisal was more effective for the types of problems faced by adults in their 30s and 40s. Seeking social support was more effective for adults who were 60 and older. Results for the remaining coping responses did not show a strong pattern, but there was no evidence that they were particularly effective.

COPING SCALES

Researchers have classified coping responses that are effective and not so effective for dealing with life problems by creating various kinds of coping scales. I have described some coping strategies that are measured on coping scales. In this section, I will give you a closer look at three coping scales that were constructed to assess people's strategies for responding to life challenges. On all of these coping scales, respondents are asked to state how often they rely on various coping responses in stressful situations on numerical scales ranging from *not at all* to *very much.*

It stands to reason that the coping strategies people choose will depend on the situation. However, people also develop certain styles in the kinds of coping strategies they prefer (Terry, 1994). Coping scales give a general idea of how people cope with stressful situations and whether or not these preferred coping strategies are in their best interest.

The Coping Strategy Indicator

The Coping Strategy Indicator measures people's preferences for three coping strategies that have been identified in the research literature: problem solving, seeking support, and avoidance (Amirkhan, 1990a, 1994).

Problem solving is assessed by items such as: "I formed a plan of action in my mind." "I tried to solve the problem." "I tried to carefully plan a course of action rather than acting on impulse." "I weighed my options carefully." The advantage of problem solving as a coping strategy is that it provides a feeling of control over your life.

Seeking support is assessed by items such as: "I let my feelings out to a friend." "I accepted help from a friend or relative." "I told people about the situation." "I went to a friend to help me feel better about the problem." Seeking support can be a useful coping strategy if other people can help you take active steps to solve your problems.

Avoidance is assessed by items such as: "I daydreamed about better times." "I watched TV more than usual." "I avoided being with people." "I fantasized about how things could be different." Avoidance is often not a good coping strategy because it is associated with passivity and an attitude of being stuck.

The Coping Inventory for Stressful Situations

The Coping Inventory for Stressful Situations was designed to measure three of the most commonly discussed coping strategies in the research literature: task coping, emotion coping, and avoidance coping (Endler & Parker, 1990, 1994).

Task coping is assessed by items such as: "I schedule my time better." "I focus on the problem and see how I can solve it." "I think about how I have solved similar problems." "I work to understand the situation." "I come up with several different solutions to the problem." Task coping is similar to the *problem solving* measure on the Coping Strategy Indicator.

Emotion coping is assessed by items such as: "I blame myself for not knowing what to do." "I become preoccupied with aches and pains." "I become very tense." "I focus on my general inadequacies." "I take it out on other people." Emotion coping is a somewhat broader coping strategy than the *social support* measure on the Coping Strategy Indicator. Emotion coping reflects a general style of reacting to a stressful event, which may or may not involve relying on other people.

Avoidance coping is assessed by items such as: "I phone or visit a friend." "I go to a movie or watch TV." "I go out for a snack or meal." "I take time off and get away from the situation." "I buy myself something." Avoidance coping is comparable to the measure of *avoidance* on the Coping Strategy Indicator.

Researchers have determined that task coping is the most adaptive coping strategy (Endler & Parker, 1990, 1994). People who use task coping tend to be satisfied with how they handle stressful events, and they are less anxious and depressed. Emotion coping and avoidance coping result in a less satisfactory adjustment to stressful events, and people who use these coping strategies tend to be anxious and depressed.

The COPE Scale

The COPE Scale was developed in an attempt to include a greater variety of coping styles than those assessed on other coping scales (Carver, Scheier, & Weintraub, 1989).* The 14 coping styles measured on the COPE Scale are based on conclusions from personality theories about how people handle stressful events. I have listed the 14 coping styles assessed on the COPE Scale, along with representative questions and the personality factors correlated with a preference for each of these coping styles.

Active coping *(personal correlates: optimism, confidence, self-esteem, low anxiety)*: "I take additional action to try to get rid of the problem." "I concentrate my efforts on doing something about it." "I do what has to be done, one step at a time."

Planning *(personal correlates: optimism, confidence, self-esteem)*: "I try to come up with a strategy about what to do." "I make a plan of action." "I think hard about what steps to take."

Suppression of competing activities *(personal correlates: none)*: "I put aside other activities so I can concentrate on this." "I focus on dealing with this problem and, if necessary, let other things slide a little." "I keep myself from getting distracted by other thoughts or activities."

Restraint coping *(personal correlates: optimism, low anxiety)*: "I force myself to wait for the right time to do something." "I hold off doing anything about it until the situation permits." "I make sure not to make matters worse by acting too soon."

Seeking social support for instrumental reasons *(personal correlates: optimism)*: "I ask people who have had similar experiences what they did." "I try to get advice from someone about what to do." "I talk to someone to find out more about the situation."

Seeking social support for emotional reasons *(personal correlates: none)*: "I talk to someone about how I feel." "I try to get emotional support from friends or relatives." "I discuss my feelings with someone."

Positive reinterpretation and growth *(personal correlates: optimism, confidence, self-esteem, low anxiety)*: "I look for something good in what is happening." "I try to see it in a different light, to make it seem more positive." "I learn something from the experience."

Acceptance *(personal correlates: optimism)*: "I learn to live with it." "I accept that this has happened and that it can't be changed." "I get used to the idea that it happened."

Turning to religion *(personal correlates: optimism)*: "I seek God's help." "I put my trust in God." "I try to find comfort in my religion."

Focus on and venting of emotions *(personal correlates: low confidence, anxiety)*: "I get upset and let my emotions out." "I let my feelings out." "I feel a lot of emotional distress, and I find myself expressing those feelings a lot."

*Carver, C. S., Scheier, M. F., & Weintraub, J. K. (1989). Assessing coping strategies: A theoretically based approach. *Journal of Personality and Social Psychology, 56,* 267–283. Copyright 1989 by the American Psychological Association. Adapted with permission.

Denial (*personal correlates: pessimism, low confidence, low self-esteem, anxiety*): "I refuse to believe that it has happened." "I pretend that it hasn't really happened." "I act as though it hasn't happened."

Behavioral disengagement (*personal correlates: pessimism, low confidence, low self-esteem, anxiety*): "I give up the attempt to get what I want." "I just give up trying to reach my goal." "I admit to myself that I can't deal with it and quit trying."

Mental disengagement (*personal correlates: pessimism, low confidence, anxiety*): "I turn to work or other substitute activities to take my mind off things." "I go to movies or watch TV so that I think about it less." "I daydream about things other than this."

Alcohol and/or other drugs (*personal correlates: pessimism*): "I use alcohol or drugs to make myself feel better." "I try to lose myself for a while by drinking alcohol or taking drugs." "I use alcohol or drugs to help me get through it."

What We Can Learn from Coping Scales

Research on coping scales leads to the conclusion that it is most adaptive to cope with life challenges by taking an active, self-reliant approach that includes planning and problem solving. It is advantageous to develop a reasonable amount of outgoingness and extraversion (Amirkhan, Risinger, & Swickert, 1995; Cooper, Okamura, & McNeil, 1995). This will help you when you need to respond actively to life challenges and when it is appropriate to seek assistance from others. It is least adaptive to cope by avoiding and denying the challenge or by responding in an impulsive manner.

Coping scales prompt us to consider our strategies for coping with stressful events and to ask ourselves if our coping responses are working in our best interest. Assessing your coping strategies helps in two ways. First, you want to be flexible enough to choose the coping response that will work best in a given situation. A second benefit of assessing your coping strategies is that this process will go a long way toward reinforcing your feelings of self-confidence and control. The goal is not so much to choose the "correct" coping response as it is to maintain a "coping attitude" characterized by thoughtfulness, problem solving, and self-confidence (Amirkhan, 1990b; Carver & Scheier, 1994).

UNDERSTANDING ADAPTIVE PERSONALITY STYLES

To cope successfully with life challenges, it is helpful to be aware of your own personality style. Because personality styles are intimately related to how a person perceives the world and reacts to stressful events, it is understandable that some personality styles are more flexible than others. People who have the most trouble coping with life challenges are those whose personality styles are not flexible and who are therefore unable to adapt their responses to fit the demands of a specific situation.

The study of personality styles is as old as the field of psychology. Countless theories of personality have been proposed, and it would require a large volume to catalog all the models of personality that have been developed. One model of personality that has been around in one form or another for more than 100 years, and that is widely recognized for its effectiveness in predicting adaptive and maladaptive behaviors, identifies five distinct personality styles: *neuroticism, extraversion, openness, agreeableness,* and *conscientiousness* (Costa & McCrae, 1992; Goldberg, 1993; McCrae & John, 1992). Research studies on these five personality styles have resulted in the following conclusions (Costa & McCrae, 1990, 1992; Marshall, Wortman, Vickers, Kusulas, & Hervig, 1994; McCrae, 1991; McCrae & Costa, 1991; Trull, 1992).

Neuroticism

The worldview of people with a neurotic personality style is characterized by these kinds of statements:

> "I often feel helpless and want someone else to tell me what to do."
> "I often worry and feel anxious."
> "I don't match up to other people."
> "I get angry at others because they don't respect me."
> "When things go wrong, I get depressed and give up."

Neuroticism is rarely, if ever, an adaptive personality style. It is associated with depression, anxiety, self-depreciation, poor mental health, difficulty getting along with others, pessimism, hopelessness, low self-esteem, unresolved anger, and lack of satisfaction with life. People with a neurotic personality style have a tendency to rely on maladaptive coping styles, such as wishful thinking and self-blame (Bolger, 1990).

Extraversion

The worldview of people with an extraverted personality style is characterized by these kinds of statements:

> "I like to be around people."
> "I like to laugh and joke with others."
> "I am cheerful, talkative, and energetic."
> "I am very active."
> "I spend most of my time with others."

Extraversion is an adaptive personality style, unless it becomes extreme. In moderation extraversion is associated with low levels of depression and anxiety and with a positive self-image, good mental health, good interpersonal relationships, optimism, hope, high self-esteem, and satisfaction with life. If extraversion becomes too rigid or extreme, however, it can be correlated with impulsivity, antisocial behavior, aggression, narcissism, and manic behavior.

Openness

The worldview of people with an open personality style is characterized by these kinds of statements:

"I am excited by literature, poetry, and the arts."
"I love playing with theories and abstract ideas."
"I am a curious person."
"I enjoy being exposed to new ideas."
"I experiment with new ways of solving problems."

Openness is a fairly neutral personality style. It is associated with positive self-image, optimism, and curiosity. If openness becomes too rigid or extreme, it can be correlated with impulsivity and manic behavior.

Agreeableness

The worldview of people with an agreeable personality style is characterized by these kinds of statements:

"I try to be courteous with everyone."
"I hardly ever get into arguments."
"I generally trust other people."
"I get along with others."
"I am seen by others as being fair and honest."

Agreeableness is associated with good interpersonal relationships, closeness with others, good mental health, optimism, good self-control, and satisfaction with life. If agreeableness becomes extreme, it can be associated with lack of individuality.

Conscientiousness

The worldview of people with a conscientious personality style is characterized by these kinds of statements:

"I take good care of things that belong to me."
"I am very reliable."
"I am well organized."
"I set high standards for myself."
"I take a lot of pride in my work."

Conscientiousness is associated with low levels of depression and anxiety, positive self-image, good self-control, good mental health, optimism, and satisfaction with life. If conscientiousness becomes too rigid or extreme, however, it can cause a person to become too dependent on the approval of others.

The Repressive Coping Style

In addition to the five personality styles described above, another personality style that is not very adaptive is repressive coping style (Weinberger & Davidson, 1994; Weinberger & Schwartz, 1990). This style can be understood by appreciating how children learn to deal with their emotions. On one hand, children are taught to control their feelings and to refrain from acting out and throwing temper tantrums. On the other hand, children need to learn to communicate with others about how they are feeling. They want to be open, alive, and spontaneous. When people become rigid about communicating *any* negative feelings, they can become so repressed that they don't even admit their negative feelings to themselves. People who use a repressive coping style say these kinds of things to themselves:

"I am always courteous, even to people who are disagreeable."

"I don't get upset or angry when people are rude to me."

"I'm surprised when people ask me if I get anxious before an exam, because I don't."

"When I'm under stress, I just stay calm and rational."

People with a repressive coping style have learned to look at the world, and at themselves, in a very biased way. They have repressed their "unacceptable" feelings for so long that they hardly know they have them anymore.

A repressive coping style has two major disadvantages. First, although people can deny on the outside that stress bothers them, living under too much stress without engaging in adaptive coping responses will take its toll. A second disadvantage of a repressive coping style is that it is very isolating. It is difficult to have meaningful relationships with others if you suppress your spontaneity and always act like you have everything under control.

The Costs of Interpersonal Dependency

In Chapter 3 you will learn that developing a good support system is a useful skill to add to your coping arsenal. It is advantageous to be able to form close relationships with others so you can lean on them during times of stress. It must be remembered, however, that having a good support system means giving as well as receiving support. It is not adaptive to let yourself become so dependent on others that you lose touch with your sense of internal control. The lives of people who are overly dependent on others are compromised in the following ways (Bornstein, 1993):

Motivational: It is difficult for dependent people to motivate themselves because they can't function without guidance, support, and approval from others.

Cognitive: Dependent people perceive themselves as being powerless and ineffectual because they assume that others have control over what happens to them.

Affective: Dependent people become anxious and fearful when they are required to take care of themselves.

Behavioral: Dependent people interact with others in a needy and helpless manner.

Because dependent people rely so much on other people, they suffer a considerable amount of stress. For one thing, dependent people have little confidence in their own ability to cope with life challenges because they have come to count on help from others. Compounding this problem is the fact that the interpersonal style of dependent people is often annoying and causes others to avoid or reject them. It is no wonder that dependent people are at higher risk for the physical and psychological detriments of stress (Bornstein, 1995).

The Possibility for Personal Growth

An individual's personality style is relatively stable and enduring (McCrae, 1993). However, this does not mean that you can't change. One of my major goals with this book is to help you become aware of your personality style so you can modify the perceptions and responses to challenging life events that are not in your best interest.

DISTINGUISHING BETWEEN SELF-BLAME AND SELF-RESPONSIBILITY

One insight you will gain from reading this book is that it is not helpful to cope with life challenges by engaging in self-blame. People who blame themselves when faced with threats and trauma tend to be less happy, less well-adjusted, and more depressed than those who don't employ this self-defeating coping style (Kleinke, 1988; Revenson & Felton, 1989; Vitaliano, Katon, Maiuro, & Russo, 1989). Compared with self-blame, self-responsibility is a very different kind of coping style. Self-responsibility is *not* blaming or derogating ourselves for negative and unhappy events in our lives. Self-responsibility means developing our sense of mastery and internal control and making the effort to learn and practice coping skills such as those described in Chapter 3. Self-responsibility requires that we honestly determine when we are responsible (and not responsible) for the causes and solutions of our problems (see Chapter 15).

THE PROS AND CONS OF AVOIDANCE

We are all tempted at times to respond to life challenges with avoidance. Here are some examples (Schmidt, 1994):

Social isolation: "I avoid getting close to others."

Avoidance of intimacy: "I avoid becoming involved in close, intimate relationships."

Avoidance of expressing negative emotions: "I avoid situations where I might have to express negative feelings."

Procrastination: "I avoid working on tasks that are dull and boring."

Avoidance of conflict through subjugation: "I avoid situations where I have to give in to the demands of others."

Avoidance of evaluation and competition: "I avoid situations where my performance will be evaluated and made public."

Emotional distancing: "I avoid situations where I would need to depend on others."

Avoidance of work and financial matters: "I avoid turning in my work." "I avoid dealing with financial matters."

Avoidance means not putting out the effort to cope when we should. Instead of heading off problems at their source, we ignore them and hope they will go away. Unfortunately, most challenges in life don't automatically disappear. Although avoidance may reduce immediate anxiety, it often results in greater stress in the long run because we never know when problems will catch up with us.

Avoidance is a useful strategy for coping with problems that don't have long-term consequences. It is often more adaptive to let brief irritations pass rather than to get upset about them. There is no point in suffering stress from problems that will resolve themselves. But avoidance is not a good strategy for coping with life challenges requiring involvement. Under these circumstances, you need to control your stress by taking a coping attitude and using coping skills such as those outlined in Chapter 3 (Suls & Fletcher, 1985).

A major disadvantage of avoidance as a coping strategy is that it prevents the constructive use of personal feedback (Bednar, Wells, & Peterson, 1989). It is inevitable that you will receive both positive and negative reactions from other people. People who avoid negative feedback are not able to use this information (much of which is accurate) to make effective changes in their ways of thinking and acting. Avoiders also miss out on the benefits of positive feedback. Because they are so used to putting up a false front, they can't distinguish when another person's compliments are believable. In this sense, avoidance is a form of denial that hinders the use of feedback from others for one's personal growth.

Monitoring and Blunting

The pros and cons of avoidance can be further appreciated by considering the concepts of *monitoring* and *blunting* (S. M. Miller, 1987). Monitoring concerns the importance we attach to being alert, vigilant, and prepared for potential threats. People who are monitors exert a lot of effort to gain information about threatening events. High monitors read warning labels and safety information and collect facts about illness and health. They expend high amounts of energy trying to anticipate what is going to happen to them. Low monitors live their lives without paying much attention to potential dangers. They wait until threats happen before reacting to them.

Blunting refers to our tendency to distract ourselves from feelings and emotions associated with danger and threat. Blunters are people who shield themselves from the emotional impact of negative experiences. They don't focus on what's happening inside their bodies. Nonblunters are sensitive to their emotions when faced with threat. They are in touch with their feelings during challenging situations.

Research studies have found that it is best to seek information (high monitoring) and be emotionally sensitive (nonblunting) when we are confronted with threats we can overcome (S. M. Miller, 1987; S. M. Miller & Birnbaum, 1988; S. M. Miller, Brody, & Summerton, 1988). When a potential danger is surmountable, it is advantageous to be vigilant and energized by heightened emotions. When faced with threats beyond our control, it is more adaptive to cope by allowing life to take its course. It is stressful to try to monitor every threat that might potentially affect us. People who do this are at risk of being hypertensive (S. M. Miller, Leinbach, & Brody, 1989). We need to direct our information seeking and emotional energies toward challenges where we believe we can be most effective.

Self-Escape

Another kind of avoidance is *self-escape* (Baumeister, 1991a). Self-escape can be harmful or beneficial, depending on the circumstances. Harmful self-escape occurs when the demands people place on themselves become so extreme that they find it intolerable to face their shortcomings. This kind of self-escape results in an evasion of self-responsibility through behaviors that are passive, rigid, or impulsive. The desire to avoid looking at oneself can become so intense that people will resort to self-harm, substance abuse, and binge eating. Beneficial self-escape occurs when people put aside their self-focus and allow themselves to be creative and achieve pleasurable experiences. To use self-escape beneficially, it is advisable to practice the following skills:

- Set realistic goals for yourself so that you can achieve success without a chronic fear of failure.
- Don't avoid problems that require your immediate attention, but take a break when you need one—don't burn yourself out.
- Learn how to take a "time out" from your problems by using your imagination and engaging in creative activities.

HOW PEOPLE DEFEAT THEMSELVES

People can defeat themselves by *primary self-destruction, tradeoffs, counterproductive strategies,* and *self-derogation* (Baumeister & Scher, 1988). Understanding these self-destructive tendencies can help you to avoid them.

Primary Self-Destruction

The most common primary self-defeating behaviors are outlined below. Check how much you agree or disagree with these statements.

	Strongly agree	Agree	Disagree	Strongly disagree
1. I have done dangerous things just for the thrill of it.	____	____	____	____
2. Sometimes I don't seem to care what happens to me.	____	____	____	____
3. Often I don't take very good care of myself.	____	____	____	____
4. I usually call a doctor when I'm sure I'm becoming ill.	____	____	____	____

	Strongly agree	Agree	Disagree	Strongly disagree
5. I seem to keep making the same mistakes.	———	———	———	———
6. I am frequently late for important meetings.	———	———	———	———
7. I do not believe in gambling.	———	———	———	———
8. I smoke more than a pack of cigarettes a day.	———	———	———	———
9. I usually eat breakfast.	———	———	———	———
10. I frequently fall in love with the wrong person.	———	———	———	———

These statements come from the Chronic Self-Destructiveness Scale (Kelley et al., 1985). People tend to be more self-destructive if they agree with statements 1, 2, 3, 5, 6, 8, and 10 and disagree with statements 4, 7, and 9. People with high scores on self-destructiveness do not take responsibility for their own well-being. They have low feelings of internal control (see Chapter 3) and often do things that are not in their best interest, such as cheating, driving unsafely, and ignoring their health.

Examples of primary self-destruction include masochism, eating disorders, drug abuse, recklessness, and suicide. People usually know they are in emotional pain when they engage in these harmful behaviors; unfortunately, they are not always ready or able to change.

Tradeoffs

Tradeoffs result in self-defeating behaviors when people choose immediate pleasure or relief despite the long-term costs of health risk or anxiety. Some examples of tradeoffs include smoking, drinking, failing to wear seat belts, engaging in unsafe sex, avoiding exercise, eating poorly, neglecting health care, and using recreational drugs. Tradeoffs also occur when people choose safe but nonchallenging goals and when they allow excuses to stand in the way of achieving gratifications they could enjoy from more effortful accomplishments. People often make poor tradeoffs when they have not learned how to cope with failure (see Chapter 4).

Counterproductive Strategies

Counterproductive strategies result from poor insight and lack of good judgment. These strategies are often not very effective and can be recognized by their rigidity. For example, when trying to solve a difficult problem or negotiate a sensitive issue, people sometimes hinder themselves by not considering all their options. They get stuck on one track and forget alternative solutions. Or they make demands from which they can't retreat. A successful solution or fruitful negotiation requires flexibility. In some situations it may be best to be firm. At other times more may be gained by compromising or even allowing others to have their way. People who avoid counterproductive strategies know how to use a problem-solving approach like the one outlined in Chapter 3.

Self-Derogation

Check whether you agree or disagree with the following statements.

	True	False
1. I wish I could have more respect for myself.	____	____
2. On the whole, I am satisfied with myself.	____	____
3. I feel I do not have much to be proud of.	____	____
4. I'm inclined to think I'm a failure.	____	____
5. I take a positive attitude toward myself.	____	____
6. At times I think I'm no good at all.	____	____
7. I certainly feel useless at times.	____	____

These statements come from the Self-Derogation Scale (Kaplan, 1970). People with a strong tendency to derogate themselves agree with statements 1, 3, 4, 6, and 7 and disagree with statements 2 and 5. People who derogate themselves are less well-adjusted. They are anxious and depressed and have a hard time adjusting to life challenges. They are also more likely to experience physical and psychological stress, to become suicidal, and to engage in drug abuse or violent behavior (Kaplan, 1970; Kaplan & Peck, 1992; Kaplan & Pokorny, 1969, 1976a, 1976b).

Self-derogation results from the experience of growing up in a family or social group where it is difficult to get credit for engaging in appropriate behaviors. People with a history of rejection and nonacceptance often feel like underdogs and identify themselves as members of outgroups. Because they have failed to gain self-esteem and recognition by following societal norms, they sometimes become antisocial. Over time, this antisocial orientation can become the only way for them to maintain identity and self-esteem (Kaplan, Johnson, & Bailey, 1986; Kaplan, Martin, & Johnson, 1986).

It is understandable that people with a history of rejection would have a harder time learning adaptive coping responses than those who had good role models as they were growing up. It is difficult to have a coping attitude toward life when positive rewards seem beyond your control. However, our own thoughts, feelings, attitudes, and behaviors are ours to manage in the best way we can. The coping skills discussed in this book are meant to increase your power over yourself. By increasing your personal sense of competence and effectiveness, you stand a chance of gaining more positive reactions from others

SOME CONCLUSIONS ABOUT SUCCESSFUL COPING STRATEGIES

Research studies on coping allow us to reach a number of useful conclusions. People who cope most successfully are those who are equipped with a battery of coping strategies and who are flexible in adapting their responses to the situation. Good copers have developed the following three skills (Atonovsky, 1979): (1) *flexibility*: being able to create and consider alternative plans; (2) *farsightedness*: anticipating long-range effects of coping responses; and (3) *rationality*: making accurate appraisals.

In this chapter we looked at a number of research studies analyzing the effectiveness of people's coping responses. Although these studies used somewhat different terms for their coping measures, they all agreed with these conclusions:

> *Successful copers* respond to life challenges by taking responsibility for finding a solution to their problems. They approach problems with a sense of competence and mastery. Their goal is to assess the situation, get advice and support from others, and work out a plan that will be in their best interest. Successful copers use life challenges as an opportunity for personal growth, and they attempt to face these challenges with hope, patience, and a sense of humor.
>
> *Unsuccessful copers* respond to life challenges with denial and avoidance. They either withdraw from problems or react impulsively without taking the time and effort to seek the best solution. Unsuccessful copers are angry and aggressive or depressed and passive. They blame themselves or others for their problems and don't appreciate the value of approaching life challenges with a sense of hope, mastery, and personal control.

We live in a society where people want easy answers to their problems—a pill, a quick fix, or a guaranteed solution that doesn't require much cost or effort. Successful coping is not the result of discovering a single, fail-proof response. It is an attitude and a life philosophy. Successful copers teach themselves to use primary and secondary appraisal to derive coping responses best suited to the particular life event they are facing. You will learn more about how this process works in Chapter 2.

SUGGESTIONS FOR FURTHER READING

Atonovsky, A. (1979). *Health, stress, and coping.* San Francisco: Jossey-Bass.

Baumeister, R. F. (1991). *Escaping the self.* New York: Basic Books.

Goleman, D. (1985). *Vital lies, simple truths: The psychology of self-deception.* New York: Simon & Schuster.

Lazarus, R. S., & Folkman, S. (1984). *Stress, appraisal, and coping.* New York: Springer.

Menninger, K. (1966). *Man against himself.* New York: Harcourt Brace Jovanovich. (Original work published 1938)

Teger, A. I. (1980). *Too much invested to quit.* New York: Pergamon.

2

The Process of Coping

In this chapter I build on the concepts introduced in Chapter 1 to develop a model for understanding the process of coping. To lay the groundwork for this model, consider how you respond to daily hassles. Daily hassles are minor aggravating events. When considered alone, daily hassles don't amount to much. However, they can take a toll if you are under a lot of pressure or when they all seem to pile up at the same time. It has been recognized for some time that major life crises can significantly influence our lives (Dohrenwend & Dohrenwend, 1974; Holmes & Rahe, 1967). More recently, psychologists have documented the stresses caused by daily hassles (Kanner, Coyne, Schaefer, & Lazarus, 1981; Monroe, 1983). Although not as dramatic as major life crises, daily hassles are an important cause of stress. We are often not aware of how much such daily hassles can wear us out.

MEASURING DAILY HASSLES

Take a moment and think about the issues, fears, or desires that are a daily frustration for you. People responding in a survey said that they most commonly experienced these daily hassles (Kanner et al., 1981): concerns about weight and physical appearance, health of a family member, rising prices, home maintenance, too many things to do, property, investments, taxes, and crime. Also listed were pollution, traffic, inclement weather, arguments, and rejections. Another hassle that is difficult to avoid, and that is a strain for almost everyone, is the experience of interpersonal conflict (Bolger, DeLongis, Kessler, & Schilling, 1989). Interpersonal conflicts are particularly stressful when they are consistent and chronic (Avison & Turner, 1988).

The daily hassles in your life can be assessed by considering your responses to common daily life events. At the end of each day, mark which of the daily life events listed on the next page happened to you. Then rate the events that happened on the following scale:

1 = *occurred but was not stressful*
2 = *caused very little stress*
3 = *caused a little stress*
4 = *caused some stress*
5 = *caused much stress*
6 = *caused very much stress*
7 = *caused me to panic*

Daily life events	Score
1. Performed poorly at a task	____
2. Was criticized verbally or verbally attacked	____
3. Was interrupted while talking	____
4. Was stared at	____
5. Was embarrassed	____
6. Argued with someone	____
7. Had car trouble	____
8. Had difficulty in traffic	____
9. Misplaced something	____
10. Bad weather	____
11. Money problems	____
12. Heard some bad news	____
13. Experienced narrow escape from danger	____
14. Was late for work/appointment	____
15. Was exposed to upsetting TV show, movie, book, news article	____

These incidents are selected from the 58 daily hassles contained in the Daily Stress Inventory (Brantley, Waggoner, Jones, & Rappaport, 1987). This inventory is designed to give a daily reading of the effects of daily hassles on a person's life. You can derive a stress score by adding up the points you score for each event. Because some days are more stressful than others, it's natural for your stress score to change from day to day. But if your stress scores are consistently very high (an average of 5 or above), chances are that daily hassles are getting the best of you.

HOW DAILY HASSLES AFFECT US

It has long been suspected that daily hassles can have a detrimental effect on our physical and emotional well-being. Recent studies indicate that this is true. There is indeed a correlation between the number of daily hassles people experience and their symptoms of health problems and psychological as well as physiological stress (Brantley, Dietz, McKnight, Jones, & Tulley, 1988; DeLongis, Coyne, Dakof, Folkman, & Lazarus, 1982; Kanner et al., 1981; Kohn, Lafreniere, & Gurevich, 1991; Monroe,

1983). There is even evidence that stress can have a negative impact on the immune system and can increase the risk of contracting infectious diseases (Cohen, Tyrrell, & Smith, 1991, 1993; Cohen & Williamson, 1991).

Researchers have found that the detrimental effects of daily hassles are more severe for people who are already stressed out (Monroe, 1982) and for people who are anxious and who do not cope well when their peace of mind is disturbed (Kohn et al., 1991). Daily hassles are less of a problem for people with high self-esteem and good support systems (DeLongis, Folkman, & Lazarus, 1988). Later in this chapter you will learn how you can strengthen your self-esteem by building up your sense of internal control and self-efficacy. Good self-esteem helps us bear up to the negative effects of daily stress. In Chapter 3 you will learn about the benefits of developing a good support system. Support from others helps to alleviate the negative effects of daily stress on our moods and psychological well-being.

The fact that daily hassles and stress reactions influence each other has important implications for successful coping. The diagram in Figure 2.1 demonstrates the process we go through when faced with a life event (Lazarus, 1984a). This diagram has three key features. First, a life event (boss's harsh voice, traffic jam, rejection) is not a problem unless we appraise it as such (primary appraisal). The lesson here is that we want our primary appraisals to be realistic so that we attend to legitimate problems and threats but don't overburden ourselves with events that must be accepted as part of life. Second, when a life event is appraised as a problem or threat and results in stress, the negative effects of this stress can be moderated with a secondary appraisal that results in a self-perception of efficacy and competence. Third, a successful coping response will serve to further control and minimize stress. An unsuccessful coping response should prompt us to reappraise the life event or to try a different coping strategy. Figure 2.1 shows that coping responses must be flexible and that new coping strategies can be learned. As suggested in Chapter 1, it is always desirable to have a plan A, a plan B, and a plan C.

APPRAISING STRESSFUL EVENTS

Potentially stressful events are likely to have a negative impact on your life when you appraise them as threatening, important, and uncontrollable (Peacock & Wong, 1990). The following appraisals will cause you to view a life event as *threatening*:

> This situation makes me feel anxious.
> The outcome of this situation will be negative.
> This situation is threatening.

The following appraisals will cause you to view a life event as *important*:

> This situation has important consequences for me.
> This situation will greatly affect me.
> This situation has long-term consequences for me.

The following appraisals will cause you to view a life event as *uncontrollable*:

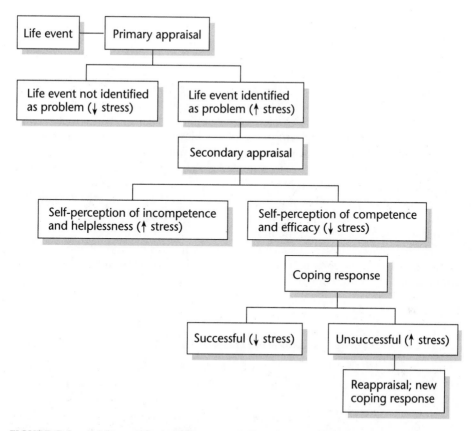

FIGURE 2.1   Primary and secondary appraisal in the coping process
Note: ↑ = increase in stress; ↓ = decrease in stress.

This is a totally hopeless situation.
It is impossible to do anything about this situation.
Neither I nor anyone else can change this situation.

You are better able to cope with potentially stressful life events when you appraise them as being *within your control*:

I have the ability to do well in this situation.
I can overcome this problem.
I have the necessary skills to succeed.

COPING WITH DAILY HASSLES

Two ways of coping with daily hassles that are associated with positive moods are distraction and relaxation (Stone, Kennedy-Moore, & Neale, 1995). *Distraction* involves diverting your attention away from the problem by thinking about other things or engaging in some activity. This does not mean avoiding problems that require your attention. Rather, distraction is a way of stopping yourself from dwelling or ruminating about something that you can't change, at least not right away. *Relaxation* means taking the time to engage in a self-relaxation exercise. Relaxation is a useful coping skill for many situations, and it will be discussed in greater detail in Chapter 3.

A response to daily hassles that is associated with negative moods is catharsis. *Catharsis* is a way of responding to daily hassles by "blowing off steam" and letting go of your emotions. As you will learn in Chapter 8, blowing off steam is not an effective way of coping unless it is done in conjunction with problem solving.

The use of support systems is recommended in Chapter 3 as a useful coping strategy. However, this depends on how support people are used. If you respond to daily hassles by complaining and ventilating to your support people, you may actually feel worse. If you use your support people to help with problem solving, however, it is likely that your mood will become more positive.

You now have a basic understanding of the concepts of primary appraisal, secondary appraisal, and coping. The remainder of this chapter is devoted to a more detailed analysis of these important processes.

PRIMARY APPRAISAL

How can you learn to make realistic primary appraisals? A good place to start is by understanding the insights offered by Albert Ellis in his *rational-emotive behavior therapy* (Ellis, 1962; Ellis & Harper, 1975). Ellis helps us appreciate the subjectivity of primary appraisals. He explains that people have more control over their primary appraisals than they might realize. Using rational-emotive theory, we can break up the process of primary appraisal into three steps (see Figure 2.2). Step 1 consists of a life event, which Ellis calls the *activating event*. Step 2 is the appraisal of this life event. This appraisal arises out of our subjective *belief system*. Step 3 consists of the feelings, emotions, and possible stresses that are a *consequence* of how the life event was appraised. To explain it another way, the manner in which we appraise a life event has a significant influence on our emotions and feelings. Ellis's theory is deceptively simple. It is easy to appreciate how it works, but it is often difficult to apply it in everyday life. For an example of how rational-emotive therapy applies to primary appraisal, consider a man who was just denied a promotion. What emotions would this person experience as he made the following appraisals?

> *Appraisal A:* "I lost the promotion and that means I'm a failure. I'm no good. My life is ruined. I can never be happy without that promotion." Resulting emotion: _____.
>
> *Appraisal B:* "So that's what I get for all my hard work. Stepped on! Those rotten executives think they are so high and mighty! They have no right to treat me this way." Resulting emotion: _____.
>
> *Appraisal C:* "I'm very disappointed about losing the promotion. It's a setback for me, and I'll probably be upset about it for some time. But now I have to pick myself up and find a new course of action." Resulting emotion: _____.

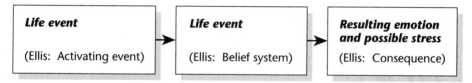

FIGURE 2.2 The process of primary appraisal

Appraisal D: "Not getting the promotion is no big deal. I don't care about what those executives think about me." Resulting emotion: _____.

Appraisal A would most likely result in depression. Appraisal B would probably cause anger. The consequence of Appraisal C is likely to be a combination of sadness and hope. The consequence of Appraisal D depends on its truthfulness. If the man really doesn't care about the promotion, the fact that he didn't get it won't have much effect on him. If he really wanted the promotion but is denying it, he will probably feel numbness in the short run and tension and stress in the long run.

The theory behind rational-emotive therapy is not new. In the first century A.D., the Greek philosopher Epictetus explained: "People feel disturbed not by things, but by the views they take of them" (cited in Ellis & Harper, 1975, p. 33). And William Shakespeare wrote in *Hamlet*: "There is nothing either good or bad, but thinking makes it so" (act II, scene 2).

Recognizing Irrational Appraisals

Primary appraisals are a product of an individual's belief system. If you demand that others be perfect, you will be disappointed when they're not. If you insist on unconditional attention from someone, you will be hurt and angry when it is not forthcoming. Ellis shows us that people can learn to recognize when they are making irrational appraisals and that they can take steps to correct them. Consider the following appraisals (Ellis, 1962; Ellis & Harper, 1975):

> "People who are important to me should always love me."
> "People should never treat me wrong, and they are bad people if they do."
> "It's awful when things are not the way I want them to be."
> "When things are uncertain, I have to keep worrying about them."
> "I must achieve success at all times."

Ellis points out that these appraisals are irrational because they are not realistic and are bound to result in negative experiences. Irrational appraisals tend to be absolute. They can be recognized by their "shoulds," "musts," and insistence on perfection. The following irrational beliefs were identified in a series of research studies (Lohr, Hamberger, & Bonge, 1988).

> *Demand for approval:* "I must be approved of and loved by all the significant people in my life."
> *High self-expectations:* "I must be thoroughly competent and adequate in all respects if I am to be worthwhile."

Blame-proneness: "If I (or others) am bad, wicked, or ignorant, then I (or others) should be blamed."

Emotional helplessness: "My unhappiness is caused by others or situations, and I have little or no ability to control my unhappiness."

Anxious overconcern: "If there's a chance that something dangerous or fearsome might happen, I should worry about it."

Problem avoidance: "It's easier to avoid than face certain difficulties and responsibilities."

Dependency: "I need someone stronger than myself to rely on."

Helplessness: "My past is an all-important determinant of my present behavior, and if something once strongly affected me, it will always affect me."

People who insist on these beliefs have problems in their lives because it is difficult for them to achieve satisfaction.

By learning to make more reasonable appraisals, we can moderate some of our negative emotions and reduce our stress. For example, assume that a woman's husband leaves her. How she manages this life event depends on her choice of one of the following kinds of appraisals:

"He is all that counts in my life. My life is worthless without him." (depression)

"I can't bear to have him leave me. I can't stand being without him." (desperation, panic)

"How can he do this to me? How could he be so thoughtless and irresponsible? He is a terrible person." (hurt, rage)

Any of these appraisals is likely to result in undue stress and suffering. The goal of rational-emotive therapy would be to help the rejected woman gain a stronger sense of control over her life by making a more adaptive assessment, such as:

"It hurts to have him leave me, and I'll really miss him. Right now I feel angry and also sad. But I know in time I'll be grateful for the life we had together, and then I'll be ready to move on with my life and find someone new." (anger, sadness, hope)

Recognizing Cognitive Distortions

Cognitive distortions are similar to irrational appraisals because they cause more unhappiness, dissatisfaction, and stress than we would experience if we learned to look at stressful life events as copers rather than as victims.

Aaron Beck and his colleagues have outlined the following examples of *cognitive distortions* (Beck, 1967, 1976; Beck, Freeman, et al., 1990; Bedrosian & Beck, 1980).

Selective abstraction involves focusing on a disturbing problem out of context. For example, a person may become depressed over a single failure while neglecting many other successes. Or a single unfriendly response from someone may override friendly responses that are received from others during the course of the day. The conclusion resulting from selective abstraction is: If one thing is bad, everything is bad.

Arbitrary inference refers to conclusions based on incomplete or inadequate information. For example, another person's frown "proves" that he doesn't like you. Or because the boss didn't say hello as she passed you in the hall, you can be certain that she is displeased with your performance. When we make arbitrary inferences, we are forgetting to balance the bad with the good.

Overgeneralizations are blanket judgments and inferences based on only one or two incidents. A single failure or rejection is taken to mean "I am an inadequate person." A negative response from one person proves that "Nobody likes me." Overgeneralizations occur when we don't take a deep breath, step back, and look at the whole picture.

Personalization is an inference that negative events are directed particularly toward oneself. "An impolite motorist in traffic is surely directing his aggression at me." "It is raining just to make my day miserable." "That policeman could have ticketed anybody. Why did he pick on me?" It is tempting to take things personally, but we must remind ourselves that we are one out of billions of people in this world.

Polarized thinking is black-and-white thinking. "You are either on my side, or you are my enemy." "If I don't get what I want, I can't be happy." "People who don't believe what I believe are stupid." Getting along in this world means learning to be flexible and recognizing all shades of gray.

Magnification and exaggeration is making minor displeasures into catastrophes. "You forgot my birthday. That means you don't love me." "I only got a B on the test. My academic career is shot." It is a useful coping skill to learn how to relax and keep one's peace of mind during times of frustration.

Assumption of excessive responsibility is unrealistic self-blame. "My girlfriend wouldn't have broken up with me if I were (more athletic, more musical, more charming, and so on)." "My husband gets angry when I don't do things right. I have to learn to make fewer mistakes so he won't get so upset." "My best friend is depressed, and she needs me to be with her at all times." Good adjustment requires the ability to set limits and boundaries.

Recognizing Maladaptive Schemas

Another way to understand irrational appraisals is by studying *maladaptive schemas* (Young, 1994). Schemas are patterns of thinking that determine how we perceive ourselves in relation to others around us. What kinds of roles do we play with others? Do we sometimes adopt beliefs about our interpersonal relations that are not in our best interest? All of the schemas described in Table 2.1 have disadvantages, and they are correlated with negative affect, depression, and anxiety (Schmidt, Joiner, Young, & Telch, 1995). People who use them would benefit by modifying them or giving them up.

Changing Maladaptive Schemas

Changing maladaptive schemas is not always easy, especially if you have been using them for a long time. It is often necessary to treat these schemas as enemies that must

TABLE 2.1   Maladaptive schemas

A. Autonomy
  1. Dependence
    a. Definition: Belief that one is unable to function on one's own and needs the constant support of others.
    b. Possible thoughts: "I can't function on my own." "I need someone else to help me." "I can't support myself."
    c. Potential problems: Being passive, alienating others, underachieving.
  2. Subjugation/lack of individuation
    a. Definition: The voluntary or involuntary sacrifice of one's own needs to satisfy others' needs, with an accompanying failure to recognize one's own needs.
    b. Possible thoughts: "If I do what I want, something bad will happen." "I must sacrifice myself for others." "My needs are not as important as those of others."
    c. Potential problems: Feeling stressed and worn out. Inner feelings of deprivation and anger.
  3. Vulnerability to harm or illness
    a. Definition: The fear that disaster is about to strike at any time.
    b. Possible thoughts: "Something terrible will happen to me." "I worry about things going wrong." "I feel anxious and fearful."
    c. Potential problems: Anxiety, panic, hypertension.
  4. Fear of losing control
    a. Definition: The fear that one will involuntarily lose control of one's own behavior, impulses, emotions, mind, body, and so on.
    b. Possible thoughts: "I'm losing control." "I can't control myself." "Am I becoming unbalanced?"
    c. Potential problems: Anxiety and tension or rigidity and overcontrol.
B. Connectedness
  5. Emotional deprivation
    a. Definition: The expectation that one's needs for nurturance, empathy, affection, and caring will never be adequately met by others.
    b. Possible thoughts: "No one is ever there to meet my needs." "I don't get enough love and attention." "No one really cares about me."
    c. Potential problems: Anger, resentment, manipulativeness.
  6. Abandonment/loss
    a. Definition: The fear that one will imminently lose significant others and then be emotionally isolated forever.
    b. Possible thoughts: "I'll be alone forever." "No one will be there for me." "I will be abandoned."
    c. Potential problems: Loneliness, fear of making commitments.
  7. Mistrust
    a. Definition: The expectation that others will willfully hurt, abuse, cheat, lie, manipulate, or take advantage of one.
    b. Possible thoughts: "People will hurt me, attack me, put me down." "I must protect myself." "I'll attack them before they get me."
    c. Potential problems: Hostility, mistrust, aggressiveness.
  8. Social isolation/alienation
    a. Definition: The feeling that one is isolated from the rest of the world, different from other people, and not a part of any group or community.
    b. Possible thoughts: "I don't fit in." "I'm different." "No one understands me."
    c. Potential problems: Isolation, loneliness.

TABLE 2.1   (continued)

C. Worthiness
  9. Defectiveness/unlovability
     a. Definition: The feeling that one is inwardly defective and flawed, that one is fundamentally unlovable.
     b. Possible thoughts: "No man/woman I desire will ever love me." "No one would want to stay close to me." "There's something inherently flawed and defective in me."
     c. Potential problems: Depression, low self-esteem.
  10. Social undesirability
     a. Definition: The belief that one is outwardly undesirable to others.
     b. Possible thoughts: "I'm a social outcast." "People don't like me." "I'm fat, I'm ugly, I'm boring."
     c. Potential problems: Loneliness, depression, low self-esteem.
  11. Incompetence/failure
     a. Definition: The belief that one cannot perform competently in areas of achievement, daily responsibilities, decision making.
     b. Possible thoughts: "Nothing I do is ever good enough." "I'm incompetent." "I screw up everything I try."
     c. Potential problems: Underachievement, rigidity, low self-esteem.
  12. Guilt/punishment
     a. Definition: The belief that one is morally or ethically bad or irresponsible and deserves harsh criticism or punishment.
     b. Possible thoughts: "I'm a bad person." "I deserve to be punished." "I don't deserve pleasure or happiness."
     c. Potential problems: Depression, low self-esteem.
  13. Shame/embarrassment
     a. Definition: Recurrent feelings of shame or self-consciousness.
     b. Possible thoughts: "I'm humiliated by my own failure and inadequacy." "I am too inferior to get close to someone." "If others found out about my defects, I couldn't face them."
     c. Potential problems: Anxiety, self-consciousness, low self-esteem.
D. Expectations and limits
  14. Unrelenting standards
     a. Definition: The relentless striving to meet extremely high expectations of oneself, at the expense of happiness, pleasure, sense of accomplishment, or satisfying relationships.
     b. Possible thoughts: "I must be the best." "I must be perfect." "I have to work harder."
     c. Potential problems: Hypertension, isolation.
  15. Entitlement/insufficient limits
     a. Definition: The insistence that one be able to do, say, or have whatever one wants immediately.
     b. Possible thoughts: "I should always get what I want." "I'm special and shouldn't have to accept restrictions placed on others." "I deserve immediate satisfaction."
     c. Potential problems: Impulsiveness, anger, alienation.

SOURCE: From *Cognitive Therapy for Personality Disorders: A Schema-Focused Approach* (Revised Edition) by J. E. Young, 1994, New York: Cognitive Therapy Center of New York. Copyright by Professional Resource Exchange, Inc., P. O. Box 15560, Sarasota, FL 34277. Adapted with permission.

be fought with a more realistic outlook on life. Some strategies for overcoming maladaptive schemas are suggested below (McMullin, 1986).

Counters.   Counters are things we can say to ourselves to avoid focusing on beliefs that are not in our best interest. Sometimes a counter can be a single word: "Nonsense!" "That's silly!" "Not true!" "Stop!" Or we can use a full sentence: "I don't need to be perfect as long as I do my best." "It is not realistic to expect everyone to love me." "Sometimes people don't treat me right, but that doesn't mean everyone is out to get me."

Alternative interpretations.   Maladaptive schemas often cause faulty interpretations of life events. It's useful to question our perceptions, particularly when facing stress and challenge. Here are some examples of how we can use alternative interpretations to make more adaptive primary appraisals of stressful life events:

1. A man is not hired for a job he really wants.
   a. *Maladaptive interpretations*
      "I'm not worthy of the job. I'm no good."
      "Those people are unfair. They were out to get me."
   b. *Alternative interpretations*
      "There was tremendous competition and only one opening."
      "My qualifications are good, but someone else fit their needs more closely."
2. A woman has suffered a recent loss.
   a. *Maladaptive interpretations*
      "I'm a weak person to let this bother me so much."
      "I'll never feel better."
      "Something is wrong with me."
   b. *Alternative interpretations*
      "It's natural to feel this way under the circumstances."
      "I need to give myself a break and not be too hard on myself."
3. Someone treats you rudely.
   a. *Maladaptive interpretations*
      "I'm no good. I deserve to be treated badly."
      "That person is rotten and deserves to be punished."
      "Everybody hates me."
   b. *Alternative interpretations*
      "That person was probably in a bad mood."
      "If people are nasty, that's their problem."
      "I know how to be tactful with all kinds of people."

Recognizing worst-case scenarios.   All of us sometimes blow things out of proportion and make them seem much worse than they really are. When this happens, we need to take a reality check by asking, "What's the worst thing that could happen?" This can be done by rating difficult life events from 1 to 10. The low end (1 up) includes those events that you consider unpleasant but that you know you would survive. The other end of the scale (8 to 10) represents events that you feel would be the end of the world. You want to use your coping skills to get your rating down to 5 or less.

Relabeling.   Relabeling helps us gain a more adaptive outlook on certain life events (McMullin, 1986, pp. 26–27). For example:

A *person who . . .*	*could be called . . .*	*or could be called . . .*
changes his or her mind a lot	wishy-washy	flexible
isn't orderly	sloppy, piggish	spontaneous, carefree
gets anxious	weak, cowardly	self-protective
is emotionally sensitive	sick, fragile	caring
isn't good at a task	stupid, inferior	inexperienced
pleases others	passive	likable
believes what others say	gullible	trusting
takes risks	impulsive	brave
gets excited	hysterical	exuberant
sticks to projects	compulsive	determined
gets depressed sometimes	neurotic	a normal human being
is sure of something	conceited	self-confident
expresses his or her opinion	egotistical	honest, assertive

Making Rational Appraisals

One way to alter your maladaptive schemas is to stop yourself when you are making them. A second approach is to practice making adaptive appraisals *before* you are confronted with life challenges. Think of the last time you were interviewed for a job. What did you say to yourself during the interview? How would you have felt if you responded to the interview with the following sorts of negative appraisals?

"I can't think of a thing to say."
"I'm being humiliated."
"The interviewer doesn't like me."
"I sound like I don't know what I'm talking about."
"I'm freezing up."

Compare the consequences of these negative appraisals with the consequences of the following positive appraisals.

"This is a job I want, and my attitude shows it."
"I would be really good at this job."
"This place needs someone like me."
"I'm dressed right and am well-prepared for this interview."
"Having a job interview is a good experience for me."

Researchers have found that people who experience low levels of anxiety about job interviews have more positive appraisals and fewer negative appraisals than job interviewees who are very anxious (Heimberg, Keller, & Peca-Baker, 1986). Throughout the book, many situations will be discussed in which it would be useful to practice adaptive appraisals.

A third way to manage the process of primary appraisal (see Figure 2.2) is to alter your life events. Later in this book you will learn how to gain more control over your life by developing social skills, assertiveness, and strategies for negotiation. Remember, however, that you can't control all life events and that many times you must rely on making realistic, rational, and adaptive appraisals.

The Value of Healthy Thinking

The above discussion was intended to reinforce the value of what Phillip Kendall (1992) calls *healthy thinking*. Two major components of thinking are content (what you think about) and process (the amount and accuracy of your thinking). When it comes to content, it is generally more fruitful to think positively and to believe in the power of possibilities than to think negatively and to lose hope and give up. You can help yourself by learning not to dwell on pessimistic and negative thoughts and by developing the skill of engaging in what Kendall refers to as the *power of nonnegative thinking*.

As far as the process of thinking is concerned, you need to examine whether your way of thinking about the world is characterized by deficiencies or distortions. People who behave impulsively often don't think enough about the consequences of their actions. They could help themselves by learning to consider their options before responding. People with an obsessive style who find it difficult to make choices or to take initiative sometimes think too much. They could benefit from learning to ruminate less and to avoid letting their thinking interfere with their spontaneity. It is a constant challenge to "keep in touch" with your thinking styles so that you can appraise your life experiences in an open-minded, flexible, and creative manner.

SECONDARY APPRAISAL

Secondary appraisal occurs when you ask yourself if there is anything you can do about a life event you have appraised as stressful. The process of secondary appraisal depends to a large degree on your sense of competence, mastery, and self-esteem.

Check how much you agree or disagree with the following statements.

	Strongly agree	Agree	Disagree	Strongly disagree
1. I believe my problem is controllable.	_____	_____	_____	_____
2. There is something that can be done about my problem.	_____	_____	_____	_____
3. My problem is very important to me.	_____	_____	_____	_____

	Strongly agree	Agree	Disagree	Strongly disagree
4. My problem is of serious concern to me.	_____	_____	_____	_____
5. I am quite familiar with these kinds of problems.	_____	_____	_____	_____
6. I have experienced this type of problem before.	_____	_____	_____	_____
7. I believe my problem is only temporary.	_____	_____	_____	_____
8. This is a short-lived problem.	_____	_____	_____	_____
9. My actions have contributed to my problem.	_____	_____	_____	_____
10. My problem is the result of my own behavior.	_____	_____	_____	_____
11. I know the course the problem will follow.	_____	_____	_____	_____
12. My problem is predict-able.	_____	_____	_____	_____

These statements come from the Dimensions of Distress Scale (Vitaliano, 1988; Vitaliano, Russo, Weber, & Celum, 1993). This scale measures six kinds of secondary appraisals:

Control: Statements 1 and 2. How much control do you feel you have over the problem? It is helpful when you can use your problem-solving skills to find some way of exerting control over stressful life events.

Importance: Statements 3 and 4. How important is this problem? How much does it concern you? Important problems cause more stress than unimportant problems. You want to accurately appraise the situation so that you don't overreact to unimportant problems and don't deny or avoid important problems.

Novelty: Statements 5 and 6. Have you experienced this kind of problem in the past or is it new to you? Novel problems challenge us because we are not used to them. However, you want to be flexible and creative when coping with problems that are novel as well as familiar.

Duration: Statements 7 and 8. Is the problem short-lived or something that will last a long time? Again, you want to be realistic by not suffering undue stress over problems that are short-lived while confronting and dealing with problems that won't go away by themselves.

Causality: Statements 9 and 10. Did you cause the problem or did it result for other reasons? You want to take responsibility for solving problems, but it is not particularly helpful to blame yourself for their cause.

Predictability: Statements 11 and 12. Can you predict the outcome of the problem? Problems with a predictable outcome are less stressful than problems
whose outcomes are unknown. Problems will appear more manageable if
you maintain your image as an effective coper.

As indicated in Figure 2.1, if you feel incompetent and helpless when facing a
threat or a challenge, you are not likely to come up with a suitable coping response.
Our sense of competence and mastery is a product of our knowledge and experience
in dealing with similar stresses in the past. It is also a state of mind. Two people with
the same knowledge and experience can differ widely in their feelings of competence.
Why is this so? To understand the secondary appraisal process more completely, it will
be useful to learn about the concept of *self-efficacy.*

SELF-EFFICACY

The concept of self-efficacy is based on a long tradition of research and theorizing
about the importance of people's expectations that they can cope successfully with difficult situations (Kirsch, 1986; Maddux, 1991). Much of our knowledge about the
process and development of self-efficacy comes from the research of Albert Bandura
(Bandura, 1977, 1989; Bandura, Adams, & Beyer, 1977). Self-efficacy has an important influence on a person's cognitions, motivation, and mood.

Cognitions.   Self-efficacy inspires people to set meaningful goals because they
have faith that they can reach them. People with feelings of self-efficacy perceive desirable outcomes in life as possibilities that can be achieved with planning, problem solving, and acquisition of necessary skills.

Motivation.   Self-efficacy inspires persistence, perseverance, and patience. People
with feelings of self-efficacy don't give up easily after failing. They seek alternative
ways of reaching their goals.

Mood.   Because people with high self-efficacy have confidence in their coping
skills, they are less prone to react to life challenges with anxiety or depression.
People with high self-efficacy are aware of their strengths and limitations. They set
realistic goals, and they have reasonable expectations. They are aware of the advantages of using problem-focused rather than emotion-focused coping (Chapter 1;
Chwalisz, Altmaier, & Russell, 1992). Because they have faith in their coping skills,
they don't avoid challenges that are difficult but that they know they can master. They
also know how to recognize unreasonable and unrealistic desires that, if rigidly pur-
sued, are bound to result in disappointment.
Three dimensions of self-efficacy are magnitude, strength, and generality
(Bandura, 1977, 1982).

Magnitude of self-efficacy.   Magnitude of self-efficacy refers to the difficulty of
challenges a person is willing to take on. Some people, for example, admit they need

to try something new but never get around to doing it. Others may take the risk to be assertive with their children, but not with other adults. A man or woman may feel confident about speaking to small groups but not about addressing a large convention.

Strength of self-efficacy.   Strength of self-efficacy refers to a person's convictions that she or he can perform a behavior in question. It is the difference between thinking "I *might* be able to do it" and thinking "I *know* I can do it."

Generality of self-efficacy.   Generality of self-efficacy refers to the extent to which a person feels confident about being able to perform specific behaviors in a wide variety of situations. It is a sense of being able to respond in the most appropriate manner on all kinds of occasions.

According to the self-efficacy model, the following three conditions must be met for a person to be willing to expend the effort to reach a goal or face a life challenge (Bandura, 1977).

1. The person believes that a particular goal is reachable. The person has the expectation that if he or she is willing to expend the effort, the goal can be achieved.
2. The person believes that she or he possesses the necessary skills to reach the goal.
3. The goal has enough value to be worth the effort.

Measuring Self-Efficacy

Check how much the following statements apply to you.

	Strongly agree	Agree	Disagree	Strongly disagree
1. If I can't do a job the first time, I keep trying until I can.	——	——	——	——
2. When I set important goals for myself, I rarely achieve them.	——	——	——	——
3. I give up easily.	——	——	——	——
4. When I have something unpleasant to do, I stick to it until I finish it.	——	——	——	——
5. If something looks too complicated, I will not not even bother to try it.	——	——	——	——
6. It is difficult for me to make new friends.	——	——	——	——

	Strongly agree	Agree	Disagree	Strongly disagree
7. I have acquired my friends through my personal abilities at making friends.	____	____	____	____
8. If I see someone I would like to meet, I go to that person instead of waiting for him or her to come to me.	____	____	____	____

These statements come from the Self-Efficacy Scale (Scherer & Adams, 1983; Scherer et al., 1982). People with high self-efficacy tend to agree with statements 1, 4, 7, and 8 and to disagree with statements 2, 3, 5, and 6. Statements 1 through 5 measure general self-efficacy, and statements 6 through 8 measure self-efficacy in social interactions. People with high scores on self-efficacy are more assertive and outgoing and have higher self-esteem and a greater sense of control over their lives. High self-efficacy is also related to job success and educational achievement.

Developing Self-Efficacy

Self-efficacy refers to our expectations and confidence that the responses we make to life challenges can have a meaningful effect. People with strong feelings of efficacy face life challenges with energy and persistence. They keep trying new alternatives until they succeed or at least survive.

How does self-efficacy develop? Why do some people have greater self-efficacy than others? Self-efficacy comes from life experiences and from people who serve as significant models (Bandura, 1977). That is, you develop self-efficacy by observing how other people deal successfully with life challenges and by the kinds of teaching and support you received as you were growing up. Self-efficacy is built up by responding to life challenges with *action, flexibility,* and *persistence*. Action is essential because you learn best by doing. Flexibility encourages you to try new alternatives and to avoid getting stuck. You might not always succeed, but persistence will give you an attitude of survival.

How can you increase the self-efficacy you bring to your life? Research by Bandura and his colleagues provides the following suggestions (Andersen & Williams, 1985; Bandura, 1977, 1989).

1. Live a life of goals. You can't develop self-efficacy unless you succeed at things, and you can't succeed if you don't have goals. Make it a practice to have goals and give yourself credit when you achieve them.
2. Set goals with reasonable standards. They should be challenging enough to provide a feeling of satisfaction but also realistic so you can reach them.
3. Seek out good role models. Role models don't have to be people you personally know, but they should be people who inspire a life attitude of competence and mastery.

4. Talk to yourself in a positive manner. If you are self-conscious about talking to yourself out loud, talk to yourself silently. Take time to "psych yourself up" and to think over good experiences and past successes.
5. Remember that success in reaching goals and overcoming life challenges depends on your willingness to exert sufficient energy and effort. Musicians, artists, and writers spend many hours mastering their craft. Athletes are well aware of this rule when they say, "Winning depends on how much you want it."

COPING

You have learned that coping involves keeping your composure when faced with life challenges and working out an appropriate course of action. You also learned that there are no guaranteed coping responses that can be applied in all situations. Coping is a process in which you use flexibility to respond with skills and strategies that best fit the demands of the situation. In Chapter 3 you will be introduced to eight coping strategies: using support systems, problem solving, self-relaxation, maintaining internal control, talking yourself through challenges, using your sense of humor, exercising, and rewarding yourself for accomplishments. These coping skills should be in everyone's coping arsenal. In the remainder of this book I will focus on specific life events that are potentially stressful in many people's lives. The knowledge you gain will help you to develop some useful strategies for holding your own when faced with these challenges, to feel good about yourself, and to make the challenge part of a growth-producing life experience.

SUGGESTIONS FOR FURTHER READING

Bandura, A. (1986). *Social foundations of thought and action.* Englewood Cliffs, NJ: Prentice-Hall.

Ellis, A., & Harper, R. A. (1975). *A new guide to rational living.* Englewood Cliffs, NJ: Prentice-Hall.

McMullin, R. E. (1986). *Handbook of cognitive therapy techniques.* New York: Norton.

Watzlawick, P. (1983). *The situation is hopeless but not serious.* New York: Norton.

Wegner, D. M. (1994). *White bears and other unwanted thoughts.* New York: Guilford.

Eight Skills to Add to Your Coping Arsenal

In this chapter you will learn how to use eight skills that should be added to your coping arsenal and practiced for the rest of your life. These coping skills include using support systems, problem solving, self-relaxation, maintaining internal control, talking yourself through challenges, using your sense of humor, exercising, and rewarding yourself for your accomplishments.

USING SUPPORT SYSTEMS

One coping skill neglected by many people is the constructive use of a support system. Support systems can help you cope with stressful events in many ways. It is useful to assess your support system, learn how support systems can help you, and consider some ideas for building a support system that will work for you.

Assessing Support Systems

A number of different questionnaires have been developed for assessing support systems (Heitzmann & Kaplan, 1988). Here is one commonly used measure of social support. Test your support system by answering the following questions.

1. Are there people you can really count on to listen to you when you need to talk? If so, list their names.
2. Are there people you can really talk with frankly, without having to watch what you say? If so, list their names.
3. Are there people you can really count on to be dependable when you need help? If so, list their names.
4. Are there people who really appreciate you as a person? If so, list their names.
5. Are there people you can really count on to care about you? If so, list their names.

6. Are there people you can really count on to support you in major decisions you make? If so, list their names.

These questions come from the Social Support Questionnaire (Sarason, Levine, Basham, & Sarason, 1983; Sarason, Sarason, Shearin, & Pierce, 1987). The Social Support Questionnaire is scored by tabulating the *number* of support people available for each problem. A second social support score is derived by rating on a scale from 1 (very dissatisfied) to 6 (very satisfied) how *satisfied* people are with their support systems for each problem.

We derive a sense of social support from knowing how much support we can expect to receive from specific people. Our sense of social support is also a function of developing an attitude that others will be there when we need them. In other words, we feel "supported" when we believe that we are a valuable, lovable, worthwhile, and desirable person (Pierce, Sarason, & Sarason, 1991).

The Benefits of Support Systems

Research studies indicate that people with good social support systems are less depressed and anxious and more optimistic about their lives than those with poor social support systems. Other studies show that people with good support systems are more successful at overcoming depression, adapting to injuries resulting from physical disability, maintaining self-esteem, and overcoming loneliness. There is also evidence that people with good support systems suffer fewer health complaints and have reduced levels of physiological stress (Billings & Moos, 1985; S. Cohen & Hoberman, 1983; D. R. Cohen, Sherrod, & Clark, 1986; S. Cohen & Syme, 1985; Lepore, Allen, & Evans, 1993; Mitchell, Billings, & Moos, 1982; Schulz & Decker, 1985).

Support systems can provide the following kinds of help (S. Cohen & Hoberman, 1983; Schaefer, Coyne, & Lazarus, 1981; R. S. Weiss, 1974):

Emotional support is useful when you need someone to confide in; when you seek reassurance that you are loved and cared about; when you want someone to lean on; or when you need a boost to your self-esteem.

Tangible support is useful when you need assistance with a job or a chore; when you require aid, a gift, or a loan; or when there is a problem you can't handle on your own.

Informational support is useful when you need information or advice, or when some feedback will help you with a problem or challenge.

Belonging support provides you with a sense of belonging; with a feeling that you "fit in" with other people; and with a belief that you are not alone and that you can have the company of other people when you need them.

A good support system provides many other benefits (Cobb, 1976; Heller, Swindle, & Dusenbury, 1986; B. R. Sarason, Shearin, Pierce, & Sarason, 1987; Thoits, 1986). First, support people can satisfy your need for nurturance and attachment and bolster your sense of self-worth, trust, and life direction. The knowledge that you have a good support system provides a boost to your self-confidence when you most need it. Second, a support system helps you become a better coper by inspiring you to do your best in dealing with life challenges. A third benefit of a good support system is the companionship it provides to make your life more enjoyable (Rook, 1987).

Building a Support System

How can you add an effective support system to your coping arsenal? Several points must be considered. First, it is important to understand that a strong support system has little to do with the number of people you know and a lot to do with developing special relationships that make you feel someone knows you and cares about you (Wethington & Kessler, 1986). Having a good support system is not related to being sociable and having many acquaintances. People who like to spend time alone can also have an effective support system to use when they need it.

Second, building a good support system is a coping skill because it requires personal effort (Dunkel-Schetter, Folkman, & Lazarus, 1987). It is not very effective to wait until others figure out that you need their support. You must be willing to take the initiative. In the following statements, check the alternative that best describes what you would do in each situation.

1. You are failing at a difficult task. Do you:
   a. Find someone who can teach you how to do it better?
   b. Keep working on your own?
2. When you are feeling lonely, do you call someone on the telephone to talk?
   a. Yes, I do call.
   b. No, I don't call.
3. If you are troubled by a personal problem, do you:
   a. Keep it to yourself?
   b. Discuss it with someone?
4. You need some important information. Do you:
   a. Look for it on your own?
   b. Ask someone for assistance?
5. After placing an order at a local sandwich shop, you realize you are 25 cents short. Do you:
   a. Cancel your order?
   b. Ask someone if you could borrow 25 cents?
6. You have to fill out some confusing official forms. Do you:
   a. Try to find someone who can help you?
   b. Work your way through them as best you can?
7. If you think you did badly on a project, do you:
   a. Wait and see how you did?
   b. Ask someone knowledgeable about it to give you feedback?
8. You are unsure about your career goals. Do you:
   a. Try to figure them out on your own?
   b. Seek someone who can help you clarify your goals?

These statements come from the SEEK Scale, which was developed to measure how actively people seek social support (Conn & Peterson, 1989). Those who are more willing to seek support choose alternative *a* for statements 1, 2, and 6 and alternative *b* for statements 3, 4, 5, 7, and 8. It is a mistake to view the use of social support systems as a sign of weakness. Willingness to seek support from others when you need it actually gives you an increased feeling of competence and self-esteem because you are taking action rather than passively waiting for things to get better.

A third fact to bear in mind when building a support system is that the benefits you receive from other people have a lot to do with your expectations and attitudes (Lakey & Cassady, 1990; Vinokur, Schul, & Caplan, 1987). A social support system is valuable only to the extent that you are able to open yourself up to it and take advantage of what it has to offer. It is desirable to view yourself as the kind of person who can take advantage of support from others.

A fourth guideline is to suit your support system to your individual needs (Bruhn & Phillips, 1984; S. Cohen, 1992; Cutrona, 1986). Some people prefer to have one or two individuals as their support system. Others find more value in support from groups. Some people are most comfortable with a nurturing support system that provides empathy and warmth. Others would rather have a support system that challenges and confronts them. Sometimes you need one support system for one kind of problem and a different support system for other kinds of problems. Our desire for social support and the kinds of support systems we favor undergo changes during the course of our lives. Keep in touch with yourself so you can maintain a social support system that is compatible with where you are in your life development.

Using Health Care Professionals

Of course, you want your support people to have a positive effect on your life by providing support, setting a good example, remaining calm, being reliable, and not making unreasonable demands (Suls, 1982). If it turns out that friends and family members are not able to provide the support you need, it is wise to seek help from *health care professionals.* The value of health care professionals is that they are in a position to provide support without being emotionally drained. It is unfortunate that many people don't appreciate the fact that gaining support from health care professionals is a coping skill and not a sign of weakness (Sibicky & Dovidio, 1986). These professionals can offer the following kinds of assistance (Wills, 1987):

1. *Enhance self-esteem.* The warmth, rapport, and sharing that take place when you work with a trained professional is a real morale booster. A good way to increase self-esteem is to take an active role in solving problems with the support of a person you trust.
2. *Help maintain self-confidence and motivation.* To confront life challenges successfully, it is necessary to maintain your confidence and motivation. A health care professional can give encouragement when you feel like giving up. Even though things may seem very discouraging at the moment, support from a professional will instill a feeling of confidence that you will find the best solution.
3. *Provide rational thinking.* A good deal of this book is devoted to the importance of rational thinking. Sometimes you need a trained professional to help analyze your perceptions and expectations in an objective manner. Are you telling

yourself things that are not in your best interest? Would some challenges in your life go more smoothly if you talked to yourself in a different way?

Another major focus of this book is the value of learning new coping skills. Health care professionals are teachers. They can help you increase your options when responding to difficult challenges.

Asking for Help When You Need It

There are real benefits in relying on your support systems when you are stuck. However, there are also some costs. One cost is that you have to be willing to reciprocate the assistance your support people give you. This is not too difficult if you carefully select your support people. Another cost of relying on support people is that asking for help sometimes causes us to feel dependent. Most people are more willing to accept help from others when the following conditions are met (S. Cohen & McKay, 1984; Wills & DePaulo, 1991):

1. When you do not feel embarrassed or guilty about the problems for which you are seeking help.
2. When asking for help does not require you to give up control over your life.
3. When the help received encourages development of skills rather than a passive role in which someone else fixes the problem.
4. When the help seeker is assured that she or he will have control over the duration of the help and the type of help that is offered.
5. When the potential support person is trusted and respected, and can provide support in a calm, unobtrusive, and reassuring manner.

Instead of rigidly refusing social support because of its potential costs, it is more fruitful to use your creativity to find support people who will allow you to maintain your sense of control and independence.

PROBLEM SOLVING

Check how much you agree or disagree with the following statements.

	Strongly agree	Agree	Disagree	Strongly disagree
1. I trust my ability to solve new and difficult problems.	____	____	____	____
2. Given enough time and effort, I believe I can solve most problems that confront me.	____	____	____	____
3. Many problems I face are too complex to solve.	____	____	____	____

	Strongly agree	Agree	Disagree	Strongly disagree
4. I make decisions and am happy with them later.	_____	_____	_____	_____
5. When confronted with a problem, I am unsure of whether I can handle the situation.	_____	_____	_____	_____
6. I have the ability to solve most problems even though no solution is immediately available.	_____	_____	_____	_____

These statements come from the Problem-Solving Inventory (Heppner & Peterson, 1982). If you agreed with statements 1, 2, 4, and 6 and disagreed with statements 3 and 5, you have relatively high confidence in your problem-solving ability. But no matter how high your problem-solving confidence is at the present time, there is a good chance you will raise it after reading this chapter.

Problem solving is the procedure you follow when developing plans for responding to life challenges. It is a practical coping skill, but it is also psychologically useful. The practice of good problem solving is a confidence builder. Your sense of competence and mastery will be bolstered when you know you have problem-solving skills at your disposal (Heppner & Hillerbrand, 1991). Effective problem-solving skills are correlated with good personal adjustment (D'Zurilla & Nezu, 1990; Haaga, Fine, Terrill, Stewart, & Beck, 1995). Researchers have found that good problem solvers accept the fact that overcoming life challenges requires personal effort (Baumgardner, Heppner, & Arkin, 1986).

Before I outline the process of problem solving, consider these three key points. First, people often get stuck because they rigidly apply a single solution to their problems. When this solution doesn't work, they end up doing *more of the same* (Watzlawick, Weakland, & Fisch, 1974). It is obvious that if we fail at fixing something with a hammer, then grabbing a sledgehammer might not be the best solution. However, we often lose sight of this fact when confronted with challenges in our everyday lives.

A second point to consider is that it is sometimes very effective to approach a problem with a solution that is unique and very different. This is especially true when dealing with other people. The next time you are stuck trying to work something out with another person, do something unexpected. I am not suggesting that you should act in a way that is dangerous or harmful. However, it is worthwhile to keep in mind that the best problem solvers are people who know how to be creative and to look at problems from all possible angles.

The third thing you should know about problem solving is that it requires you to take an active rather than a passive approach. Two styles of coping that are not very helpful are a *suppressive* or a *reactive* response to problems (Heppner, Cook, Wright, & Johnson, 1995). A suppressive response to problems is characterized by the following kinds of attitudes:

I don't sustain my actions long enough to really solve my problems.

I spend my time doing unrelated chores and activities instead of acting on my problems.

I avoid even thinking about my problems.

A reactive response to problems is characterized by the following kinds of attitudes:

I act too quickly, which makes my problems worse.

My old feelings get in the way of solving current problems.

I get preoccupied thinking about my problems and overemphasize some parts of them.

Instead of responding to problems with a suppressive or reactive style, it is more advantageous to maintain your self-confidence, keep your wits about you, and outline your options.

There are five stages of problem solving: self-perception, defining the problem, listing options, decision making, and testing (D'Zurilla & Nezu, 1982; Goldfried & Davison, 1976):

1. *Self-perception.* The first step in successful problem solving is developing the self-perception that you are a problem solver. Problem solvers realize that problem situations are part of life, and they are in touch with the fact that it is important to face such challenges calmly and rationally, and not impulsively. To develop a problem-solving orientation, you have to be able to say to yourself: "Part of life involves facing problems and hardships. When I'm in trouble, I know that I have to remain calm and rely on my problem-solving skills to decide on the best possible course of action."

2. *Defining the problem.* The first thing to do when faced with a threat or a challenge is to understand exactly what is happening. Take some time to figure out the critical issues and conflicts; then make a list of goals. This is a stage in problem solving when support people can be helpful by encouraging you to take an objective view and see all sides of the problem.

3. *Listing options.* This is the stage where you define plan A, plan B, and plan C. To develop good plans you have to remain open-minded. Before deciding on a course of action, it is important to consider *all* alternatives. Write down every possible plan — the more the better. Be creative. You need to come up with as many plans as possible so you will have plenty of ideas to work with. Again, support people can help you brainstorm and avoid getting stuck on one track.

4. *Decision making.* If you have taken sufficient time to define the problem and generate many alternatives, you are ready to decide on a course of action. The decision-making stage is much easier when you have a full grasp of the issues facing you and a flexible list of options. Run through the possible responses. Which are the most feasible? Which are most likely to get you what you want without causing other problems? After choosing the most appropriate response, it is a good idea to anticipate the possible outcomes. Remember, in most situations there is not one "correct" course of action. Responses to life challenges have drawbacks as well as advantages. You have to be flexible and have alternative plans if your first decision does not work out.

5. *Testing.* If your first course of action achieves success, grea
work through the stages of problem solving again. Have you defir
rectly? Did you consider all possible alternatives? You need to
options—always keeping in mind that you are a problem solver.

SELF-RELAXATION

Since prehistoric times, humans have faced threats and challenges by using the *fight-or-flight* response. The fight-or-flight response was described in the early 20th century by a famous physiologist of that time, Walter B. Cannon (1929). Cannon explained how humans learned to protect themselves by reacting with increased adrenalin, muscle tension, and blood flow so they could more energetically battle their adversaries or more quickly flee when faced with overwhelming danger. The fight-or-flight response was very useful during early human history because fighting or fleeing were the most adaptive responses to the kinds of threats people faced. In modern times the fight-or-flight response has lost much of its utility because the hassles and challenges that confront us now are often psychological. For example, while the fight-or-flight response might be adaptive for hunting and physical survival, it is not an appropriate method for coping with traffic jams, pollution, and interpersonal conflicts. If humans still inhabit the earth a million years from now, they very well may develop a natural relaxation response to daily frustrations and hassles. In the meantime, it is well worth your time to master the relaxation response. Fortunately, this response is not difficult to learn. It mainly requires patience and practice. Begin mastering self-relaxation as a coping skill by following the instructions suggested here. As you go along, you may wish to modify these statements to fit your individual tastes and needs.

Instructions for Self-Relaxation

Find a comfortable sitting or lying position. Take several slow, deep breaths. Feel the oxygen as it fills your lungs. Make your breathing slow and relaxed. Deep, slow breaths. Say to yourself, "Breathe deeply . . . hold . . . exhale." Let your mind rest. Put all of your thoughts and worries aside. There is plenty of time to attend to them later. This time is for you. If any distractions occur, let them pass. Just breathe deeply and slowly. As you continue to take slow, deep breaths, concentrate on your legs. Stiffen the muscles in your legs, either together or one at a time. Hold the tenseness for several seconds, and then relax. Let all the tension out of your muscles. As your leg muscles loosen, you will feel warmth as the blood in your legs flows more freely. As you alternate tensing and relaxing your leg muscles, you will learn to appreciate the difference between muscles that are tense and those that are relaxed. We all spend much of our days with tense muscles without even realizing it. This exercise will help you get in touch with your body so that you can learn how to control it better. After tensing and relaxing your leg muscles several times, let your legs relax completely. Allow all of the tension to go out of your muscles. Let the blood in your legs flow freely. Feel your legs as they get warmer and very comfortable. Imagine that your legs e floating in some nice warm water. You can hardly feel them because they are so comfortable and light.

Now focus on your arms and hands. Tense you hands, either together or one at a time. Then let them relax. Do the same with your arms. Learn to recognize the difference between tense and relaxed muscles in your arms and hands. After tensing and relaxing your hands and arms several times, let all the tenseness go out of them. Allow your hands and arms to get loose. As you release all of the tension in your hand and arm muscles, you will feel the blood flow more freely. Your hands and arms will feel warmer, relaxed, and comfortable, like they are floating, weightless, in nice warm water.

Now focus on your neck and shoulders. Lift your shoulders and make your shoulder and neck muscles tense. You can see that if you did this for very long you would end up with a stiff neck and a backache. This sometimes happens when we spend the day being tense and uptight without even realizing it. Relax the muscles in your shoulders and neck to become aware of the difference between tense and relaxed muscles. Try tensing and relaxing several times so you can learn how to recognize tenseness. Learning how to recognize tenseness is a valuable skill because it tells you when to put your relaxation exercise into effect. Now let all of the tension out of your neck and shoulder muscles. Say to yourself, "Relax . . . relax." Feel the muscles in your neck and shoulders get looser and looser, and appreciate the warm and relaxed sensation as the blood flows freely. Your neck and shoulders are getting more and more relaxed. You are floating on a cloud through the sky. There is no pressure on your neck and shoulders. Only a feeling of pure comfort.

Continue breathing deeply and slowly. Take slow, deep breaths. Let the oxygen flow into your body, replenishing your blood cells as you practice your self-relaxation exercise. Continue your slow, deep breathing. Now focus on the muscles in your face. Tighten your jaw muscles. You may be surprised to feel how strong these muscles are. Learn to recognize the difference between tight and loose jaw muscles. Close your eyes tightly, and make a strong grimace. You can easily tell that if you went through your day with tenseness in your facial muscles you would end up with a tension headache. Now let the muscles in your face get completely relaxed. Feel the blood flow into your face as it begins to get warm and comfortable.

Continue breathing deeply and slowly. While you were concentrating on your neck and shoulder muscles and facial muscles, you probably forgot completely about your legs and arms. Your legs and arms are now so relaxed they hardly feel like part of your body. You know they exist, but you are allowing them to be so relaxed that you barely feel them. You are floating on a cloud through the sky. You are lying on a beautiful beach in the warm sun. You are relaxing in the mountains by a refreshing waterfall.

Self-relaxation is a skill to use to do something good for yourself. It is your time to take a break from life's hassles. It is your time to find peace within yourself, to let your body do its miraculous work. As you breathe deeply and slowly, you are helping oxygen come into your blood. Your heart is working at a relaxed pace, pumping the enriched blood through your body. You can take time in your relaxed state to appreciate the inner workings of your body and the value of your relaxation skill for helping you put yourself in a positive state of being. Breathe slowly and deeply. Let all of your muscles get more and more relaxed as you float on a cloud to your favorite place. Take some time to be alone with yourself—far away from everything else in the world.

The relaxation response is made up of three components: environment, body, and mind (Benson, 1976; Jacobson, 1938; Wolpe, 1982).

1. *Environment.* The relaxation response is easiest to learn in a quiet environment. Place yourself in a comfortable posture in a place where there aren't too many distractions. As you improve your relaxation skills, you will find that you can relax even in distracting places.

2. *Body.* When you practice relaxation, your body slows down. Your breathing and blood pressure decrease, your heart beats more slowly, and your muscles are less tense. How can you get your body to respond this way? A good place to start is by slowing your breathing. Breathe deeply and slowly, hold, and exhale. Repeat this process for 5 minutes. Breathing deeply and slowly gets oxygen into your body with greater efficiency. When you are anxious and under stress, you tend to take quick, shallow breaths. Breathing is a crucial part of living, yet most of the time we pay little attention to how efficiently we are breathing. After a few moments of slow, deep breathing, you will begin to feel more relaxed.

A second way to teach your body to relax is to get in touch with your muscles using the self-relaxation procedure just described.

3. *Mind.* You can apply your mind power to relaxation in several ways. The relaxation response is enhanced when you distract yourself from daily thoughts and move into a relaxing frame of mind. One aid to overcoming distraction is repeating a word or phrase as you relax. In transcendental meditation, this is called a mantra. Herbert Benson (1976) suggests repeating the word "one" to yourself as you go through your relaxation exercise. I often like to say to myself, "Relax . . . relax." You can also use your mind creatively by practicing relaxing imagery. As you work on deep breathing and muscle relaxation, imagine you are in a special place, such as by a cool waterfall, on a warm beach near the ocean, or in a peaceful meadow. Use your mind power to enhance your feelings of peacefulness. Take your thoughts far away from your daily world.

Another way to apply your thinking process to relaxation is to suspend all judgment about how well you are doing. As you relax you are bound to be distracted from time to time by outside sounds or unpleasant thoughts. Be easy on yourself when this happens. Just let the distracting sounds or thoughts pass, and allow yourself to fall back into relaxation. The relaxation response requires an accepting attitude. Remind yourself to breathe deeply and slowly, to relax your muscles, and to see yourself again floating on a cloud to your special place, far removed from the activities of the world around you.

Even though the relaxation response is not automatic like the fight-or-flight response, it has been practiced by people for thousands of years. The important thing to remember is that relaxation is a skill that is learned through patience and practice.

MAINTAINING INTERNAL CONTROL

Check whether you agree or disagree with the following statements.

	Strongly agree	Agree	Disagree	Strongly disagree
1. I have little control over the things that happen to me.	_____	_____	_____	_____
2. There is really no way I can solve some of the problems I have.	_____	_____	_____	_____
3. There is little I can do to change many of the important things in my life.	_____	_____	_____	_____
4. I often feel helpless in dealing with the problems of life.	_____	_____	_____	_____
5. What happens to me mostly depends on me.	_____	_____	_____	_____
6. I can do just about anything I really set my mind to do.	_____	_____	_____	_____

If you disagreed with statements 1, 2, 3, and 4 and agreed with statements 5 and 6, you have a sense of mastery and control over your life. Researchers have found that people with strong feelings of mastery suffer fewer symptoms of physical and psychological stress than those who feel that much of their life is beyond their control (Folkman, Lazarus, Gruen, & DeLongis, 1986; Pearlin & Schooler, 1978).

The observation that people differ in their perceptions of how much control they have over their lives has been of interest to psychologists for many years. People who take responsibility for things that happen to them are called "internals" because they have an internal locus of control. Those who believe that most of what happens to them is beyond their control are called "externals" because they have an external locus of control. It is important to point out that we are not born as internals or externals. Your locus of control develops according to your learning and experiences as you grow up. Even more important is the fact that because locus of control is based on life perceptions it can be reevaluated and changed.

There are many areas in life where it is adaptive to have an internal locus of control. For example, internals often achieve more than externals because they react less negatively to failure and derive more personal satisfaction from success. Internals have a greater tendency to cope with stressful events with a problem-solving approach, especially when the stressful event is one over which they have some control (Parkes, 1984). Externals are more likely to respond to stressful events that are controllable with fantasy and wishful thinking. Internals are also more independent. Internals take more responsibility for events in their lives and for their mental and physical health (Lefcourt, 1976; Phares, 1976). Internals tend to hold the following beliefs (Rotter, 1966):

> In the long run, people get the respect they deserve in this world.
>
> Becoming a success is a matter of hard work, luck has little to do with it.
>
> People's misfortunes result from the mistakes they make.
>
> People who can't get others to like them don't understand how to get along with others.
>
> There is a direct connection between how hard I study and the grades I get.

Externals tend to hold the following beliefs (Rotter, 1966):

> Unfortunately, an individual's worth often passes unrecognized no matter how hard he or she tries.
>
> Getting a good job depends mainly on being in the right place at the right time.
>
> Many of the unhappy things in people's lives are partly due to bad luck.
>
> No matter how hard you try, some people just don't like you.
>
> There's not much use in trying too hard to please people, if they like you, they like you.
>
> Sometimes I can't understand how teachers arrive at the grades they give.

If you look back at the definition of coping in Chapter 1, you can appreciate the value of an internal locus of control. Coping involves planning, problem solving, and learning and practicing new skills. It is based on an attitude of self-responsibility and active mastery over your life. Externals often cope poorly because when they make primary appraisals of stressful life events they see little hope that they can do much to help themselves (Lefcourt & Davidson-Katz, 1991a). Secondary appraisals of externals are also stress-producing because externals don't recognize many options. Since externals have not developed a coping attitude toward life, they have difficulty reacting to life challenges in an active and self-reliant manner.

When internals make primary appraisals of stressful events, they view these situations as challenges to be solved rather than as threats to be suffered. The secondary appraisals of internals are more hopeful because internals know they have a number of useful coping skills at their disposal. Because internals view potentially stressful events as challenges rather than as threats, they aren't as prone as externals to react with emotionality or avoidance. Internals focus their energies on getting the information they need to solve their problems. People with an internal locus of control know they have to take care of themselves, and they take the responsibility to learn what they need to know to maintain their psychological and physical health.

Although developing an internal locus of control is a useful goal, don't push yourself past reality. There are many events in the world that you can't control, and it would be foolish to think otherwise. It doesn't serve a useful purpose to blame yourself for accidents, disasters, or even minor frustrations for which you are not responsible. Often, you have to live with life events you would like to control but can't. When this happens, your best course of action is to accept these life events as reality and use your internal locus of control to come up with the most adaptive ways to adjust to them.

TALKING YOURSELF THROUGH CHALLENGES

As human beings, we all have a special ability to talk to ourselves. Whether you talk to yourself out loud or silently, you can use this ability to coach yourself through difficult challenges. Although you probably talk to yourself during difficult situations already, three techniques will help you do this more effectively. These techniques include preparing for the challenge, confronting the challenge, and reflecting on what you learned (Meichenbaum, 1977, 1985).

Preparing for the Challenge

You can prepare for a challenge by talking to yourself in a way that will increase your feelings of control over the situation. Use your problem-solving skills to plan how you will get through this challenge. Think in terms of how you will cope and what you will gain from this experience, even though it may be stressful. Plan effective ways to utilize your support systems. And stop yourself from blowing things out of proportion and suffering before the challenge really happens. It helps to make a list of coping statements such as these:

"It won't help to sit and worry about it."
"I will not upset myself."
"I will use my problem-solving skills to make a plan."
"It might not be fun, but I can handle it."
"It will be a good learning experience."
"I'm feeling anxious, but that is natural."
"I can use my self-relaxation skills while I plan my strategy."

You can also prepare for a challenge by going over what it will be like in your mind. Picture yourself going through the situation as you use your problem-solving skills to cope when things become stressful. If you feel anxious or angry while rehearsing this challenge, use your self-relaxation skills to calm yourself down. Practice coping with the challenge over and over until you can get through the whole situation and still feel in control.

Confronting the Challenge

When the challenge is happening, give yourself a psychological boost so that you will feel satisfied about your performance. Tell yourself you are a coper who knows how to use the coping skills described in this chapter. Learn how to talk yourself through the challenge by telling yourself:

"I'm a coper, and I know I can handle this."
"This is tough, but I will survive."

"I'm getting uptight. It's time to relax."
"Stick to my plan. Don't let negative thoughts get me off track."
"Relax. I must concentrate on what I have to do."
"I won't let anxiety and anger get the best of me."
"If I act like I'm in control, I'll feel that way."

Use your creativity to think of things you can say to yourself when you are confronting challenges. Sometimes it helps to see the humor in difficult situations. Be easy on yourself. Use challenges as opportunities to test your coping skills. Be willing to make mistakes. Don't force yourself to be perfect.

Reflecting on What You've Learned

When the challenge is over, take some time to reflect on what you've learned. It's OK to notice your mistakes and ask yourself how you can improve as long as you're not too critical. We need to be willing to look at ourselves as fallible human beings who are always open to learning new things. But we must also be sure to look at what we did right. Take some time to visualize yourself as you were coping and getting through the situation. People often make the mistake of focusing on the negative side of their performance without taking credit for their successes. Our learning experiences are built up by appreciating what we did right as well as by correcting what we did wrong. Take some time to reflect on your performance by saying the following kinds of things to yourself:

"I survived and that's what counts."
"It wasn't as bad as I expected."
"I did pretty well and I can do even better next time."
"Life is full of difficult challenges. I might as well learn how to cope with them."
"It's gratifying to see myself as a coper."
"Life challenges give me an opportunity to practice my coping skills."

USING YOUR SENSE OF HUMOR

Which of the following statements describe the way you respond to challenges?

	Strongly agree	Agree	Disagree	Strongly disagree
1. I usually look for something comical to say when I am in tense situations.	_____	_____	_____	_____
2. I have often felt that if I am in a situation where I either have to cry or laugh, it is better to laugh.	_____	_____	_____	_____

	Strongly agree	Agree	Disagree	Strongly disagree
3. I often lose my sense of humor when I'm having problems.	____	____	____	____
4. I must admit my life would be easier if I had more of a sense of humor.	____	____	____	____
5. I can usually find some-thing to laugh or joke about even in trying situations.	____	____	____	____
6. It has been my experience that humor is often a very effective way of coping with problems.	____	____	____	____

These statements come from the Coping Humor Scale (Martin & Lefcourt, 1983). People who use humor as a coping skill tend to agree with statements 1, 2, 5, and 6 and to disagree with statements 3 and 4.

The value of humor as a coping skill has been recognized by psychologists for a long time. Freud described humor as the highest of the defense mechanisms. To Freud, humor is a "rare and precious gift" that allows us in the face of stress to say: "Look here! This is all that this seemingly dangerous world amounts to. Child's play—the very thing to jest about!" (quoted in Lefcourt & Davidson-Katz, 1991b, p. 43). Harry Stack Sullivan (1970, p. 182) described humor as a gift that provides the "capacity for maintaining a sense of proportion as to one's place in the tapestry of life." Arthur Brayfield (personal communication) often advised people to practice Rule 11: *Never take yourself too seriously.*

In a survey of literature on humor and health, researchers suggest the following conclusions about the value of humor as a coping skill (Lefcourt & Davidson-Katz, 1991b).

1. People with a good sense of humor are less likely to react with negative moods when faced with stressful experiences than are people whose sense of humor is lacking. Humor is particularly helpful when it allows people to cope with feelings of dissatisfaction by coming to terms with a negative event and putting it into perspective. However, humor does not necessarily decrease a person's anxiety in the face of a threatening experience.

2. Humor is an effective method for coping with negative emotions, such as anger, sadness, and depression. People with a good sense of humor are more likely to take an active stance toward their negative emotions and try to rise above them. A sense of humor allows us to carry on in the face of adversity. People who are lacking a sense of humor are more likely to be passive and to allow their negative emotions to control them.

3. People with a good sense of humor have a better chance of experiencing good physical health. Studies have linked humor to positive immune functioning and lowered physiological indices of stress.

Humor helps us cope with stress in several ways (Nezu, Nezu, & Blissett, 1988). First, humor enhances our feelings of self-efficacy. Instead of reacting with fear or panic, we can use our sense of humor to take a stressful event in stride and approach it as a challenge. Second, humor helps us "distance" ourselves from a problem, providing an opportunity to look at alternative solutions. A third advantage of humor is that others are more willing to be around us and lend support when we are mirthful and not depressed.

The kind of humor that appears to be most healthy is a gentle, self-directed form of jesting. This is, as suggested earlier, a sense of not taking yourself too seriously. This healthy kind of humor can be contrasted with a less healthy form of humor involving sarcasm and hostility.

Consider these four points about the value of humor as a coping skill. First, as Viktor Frankl (1967) explained, humor is paradoxical. You can't feel truly sorry for yourself and laugh at yourself at the same time. Second, humor is a uniquely human quality that provides a sense of choice and control by allowing people to detach themselves from their pain and suffering (Frankl, 1969, p. 17). Third, humor helps place problems into perspective by reminding us to take life in stride and not to exaggerate the gravity of our problems (Lefcourt et al., 1995). Finally, self-directed jesting is a form of self-affirmation. Laughing at yourself is a way of saying, "I like myself and I accept myself as a fallible person."

Albert Ellis, who has been a proponent of humor throughout his career, wrote a number of songs to help us put our problems into perspective. Here are some examples (Ellis, 1985, pp. 55–58).

"Whine, Whine, Whine"

(To the tune of "The Whiffenpoof Song," by Guy Schull)

I cannot have all of my wishes filled—
Whine, whine, whine!
I cannot have every frustration stilled—
Whine, whine whine!

Life really owes me the things that I miss,
Fate has to grant me eternal bliss!
And since I must settle for less than this—
Whine, whine, whine!

(Lyrics by Albert Ellis, copyright 1977 by the Institute for
Rational-Emotive Therapy. Reprinted by permission.)

"Love Me, Love Me, Only Me!"

(To the tune of "Yankee Doodle")

Love me, love me, only me or I'll die without you!
Make your love a guarantee, so I can never doubt you!

Love me, love me totally; really, really try, dear;
But if you must rely on me, I'll hate you till I die, dear!
Love me, love me all the time, thoroughly and wholly;
Life turns into slushy slime 'less you love me solely!
Love me with great tenderness, with no ifs or buts, dear:
For if you love me somewhat less, I'll hate your goddamned guts, dear!

(Lyrics by Albert Ellis, copyright 1977 by the Institute for
Rational-Emotive Therapy.Reprinted by permission.)

EXERCISING

Exercising has grown in popularity in recent years. More and more people are recognizing the benefits of a regular exercise program, and they are jogging, participating in exercise groups, and engaging in a variety of other physical activities. Exercising can help people in many ways and is therefore well worth including in your coping arsenal.

The Benefits of Exercising

Research studies comparing people who participated and did not participate in a regular exercise program have identified the following benefits of exercising (Clifford, Tan, & Gorsuch, 1991; Crews & Landers, 1987; Doyne, Chambless, & Beutler, 1983; Folkins & Sime, 1981; Freemont & Craighead, 1987; Jasnoski, Holmes, Solomon, & Aguiar, 1981; Keller & Seraganian, 1984; King, Taylor, Haskell, & DeBusk, 1989; Long, 1984; Long & Haney, 1988; Wilfley & Kunce, 1986):

- Reduced psychological tension
- Enhanced oxygen efficiency
- Increased satisfaction with one's physical appearance
- A greater sense of physical fitness
- Improved physiological recovery from stress
- Enhanced cardiovascular functioning
- Decreased percentage of body fat
- Reduced tension and anxiety
- Improved self-efficacy
- Heightened self-confidence
- Reduced depression
- Increased positive mood

Exercise has a direct beneficial effect on our bodies by getting us in better physical shape. Exercise also helps us psychologically by strengthening our sense of competence and self-efficacy (J. D. Brown, 1991). When you exercise, you know you are doing something good for yourself and you experience a sense of pride and accomplishment. Exercising is also psychologically useful because it provides an opportunity to take your mind off your troubles, offering an opportunity to work through your feelings of anger, depression, and anxiety (Bahrke & Morgan, 1978; Czajkowski et al., 1990; Simons, McGowan, Epstein, Kupfer, & Robertson, 1985).

Motivating Yourself

One of the most difficult challenges for people wanting to maintain an exercise program is sticking to it. How can you motivate yourself to exercise regularly? Here are some suggestions (Marcus & Owen, 1992; J. E. Martin & Dubbert, 1982; Wilfley & Kunce, 1986).

1. Set reasonable and obtainable goals. You want to put together an exercise program that is compatible with your level of motivation.
2. Avoid injuries. It is worthwhile to obtain instructions from professional trainers about appropriate exercise techniques.
3. Find an exercise environment that suits you. Some people prefer to use exercise as a time to be alone and to engage in their own thoughts. Others have more fun when they share their exercise sessions with friends or in groups and social settings.
4. Set up an exercise schedule. Make a log book to record your performance.
5. Remind yourself of the benefits you are receiving from your exercise program.
6. At first, people not used to exercising may find the experience of a sweaty body, a pounding heart, and shortness of breath unpleasant. However, regular exercisers have learned to associate these physical sensations with good health. Give yourself time to appreciate the hard work of exercise as making a valuable contribution to your well-being.
7. Find a type of exercise that suits you. There are many ways to get exercise, ranging from aerobics to swimming, running, bicycling, walking, and sports. Some people like lots of exercise. Others prefer to keep it to a minimum. Seek out an exercise program that matches your lifestyle and personality.

Three additional points about exercising are worth noting. First, if you have decided that exercise is a coping skill you wish to practice, it will help if you incorporate exercising into your personal identity (Kendzierski, 1990). Don't look at yourself as a "couch potato" or a sedentary person. Think of yourself as an "exerciser" who has decided to make physical fitness part of your life. Second, combine exercise with other coping skills, such as self-relaxation and talking yourself through challenges. This will give you a more balanced set of skills for coping with stress (Roskies et al., 1986). Finally, before you start an exercise program, be sure to consult your physician.

REWARDING YOURSELF
FOR ACCOMPLISHMENTS

One of the most striking experiences I have had as a clinical psychologist is to see how hard people can be on themselves. Check whether you agree or disagree with the following statements.

	Strongly agree	Agree	Disagree	Strongly disagree
1. When I succeed at small things, I am encouraged to go on.	____	____	____	____
2. When I do something right, I take time to enjoy feeling good about it.	____	____	____	____
3. Unless I do something absolutely perfectly, it gives me little satisfaction.	____	____	____	____
4. I don't often think positive thoughts about myself.	____	____	____	____
5. I get through hard times by planning things to enjoy afterwards.	____	____	____	____
6. The way I achieve my goals is by rewarding myself along the way.	____	____	____	____

These statements are adapted from the Frequency of Self-Reinforcement Scale (Heiby, 1982, 1983a). People who know how to feel good about themselves tend to agree with statements 1, 2, 5, and 6 and to disagree with statements 3 and 4. Who is your best friend? Your answer should be, "I am." How do athletes, artists, musicians, writers, and other people who accomplish things find the energy to reach their achievements? They do this to a large degree by setting up their goals in small steps so they can feel good about themselves as they go along. Achievers also understand the value of not being too hard on themselves. Small setbacks don't amount to much if you always have achievable goals that give you a feeling of satisfaction. It is amazing how reluctant many people are to give themselves credit and pat themselves on the back when they do something kind, good, or worthwhile. Of course, it is always nice to be acknowledged by others. Unfortunately, positive strokes from others are not always predictable or reliable. So, if you are going to accomplish anything with consistency, the rewards must come from yourself.

SOME THOUGHTS ABOUT
WHAT YOU LEARNED IN THIS CHAPTER

An important lesson in this chapter is that being a good coper is a skill. The positive part about this fact is that there is hope for all of us. However, it also means that coping doesn't always come easily. You have to work at it. Practice the eight coping skills described here while you read the rest of this book. Another important point is that emotional reactions are very much influenced by appraisals—and appraisals are subjective. In the following chapters, you will learn how to put your coping skills to work while confronting life challenges that most people, at one time or another, have to face.

SUGGESTIONS FOR FURTHER READING

Benson, H. (1976). *The relaxation response.* New York: Avon.
Goldfried, M. R., & Davison, G. C. (1976). *Clinical behavior therapy.* New York: Holt, Rinehart & Winston.
Meichenbaum, D. (1985). *Stress inoculation training.* New York: Pergamon.
Sachs, M. L., & Buffone, G. W. (Eds.). (1984). *Running as therapy: An integrated approach.* Lincoln: University of Nebraska Press.
Watson, D. L., & Tharp, R. G. (1989). *Self-directed behavior.* Pacific Grove, CA: Brooks/Cole.
Watzlawick, P., Weakland, J., & Fisch, R. (1974). *Change: Principles of problem formation and problem resolution.* New York: Norton.

4

Coping with Failure

The experience of failure provides a good opportunity for working through the processes of primary and secondary appraisal (Chapter 2). Referring back to Figure 2.1, we can identify a failure as a life event that we may or may not perceive as a problem (primary appraisal). Although failure is rarely a pleasant experience, we can often choose to take it in stride. Primary appraisal allows us to accept many of our failure experiences as part of life and to save our energy for coping with failures that we honestly feel are worth getting upset about.

Coping Skill 1: Saving Energy for Failures Worth Getting Upset About

Think of a time when you failed at something and became upset. What did you tell yourself? Check how much you used each of the following statements to explain your failure.

	Very true	Partly true	Slightly true	Not true
1. I failed because I lacked ability.	——	——	——	——
2. I failed because of bad luck.	——	——	——	——
3. I failed because I didn't try hard enough.	——	——	——	——
4. I failed because the challenge was too difficult.	——	——	——	——
5. I failed because of someone else.	——	——	——	——

TABLE 4.1   Feelings associated with explanations for success and failure

Secondary Appraisal	Resulting Feeling
I failed because I lack ability.	Incompetence, resignation
I succeeded because of my ability.	Competence, confidence
I failed because of bad luck.	Sadness, surprise
I succeeded because of good luck.	Suprise, thanks
I failed because I didn't try hard enough.	Guilt, shame
I succeeded because I tried hard.	Satisfaction, pride
I failed because the challenge was too difficult.	Inadequacy, anger
I succeeded because the challenge was easy.	Security, modesty
I failed because of someone else.	Anger, bitterness
I succeeded because of someone else.	Gratitude, appreciation

SOURCE: From "The Cognition-Emotion Process in Achievement-Related Contexts," by B. Weiner, D. Russell, and D. Lerman, 1979, *Journal of Personality and Social Psychology*, 37, pp. 1211–1220. Copyright 1979 by the American Psychological Association. Adapted with permission.

You may recognize that these explanations for failure are secondary appraisals that have a strong influence on your response to the failure experience (D. Russell, 1982). Secondary appraisals determine what you do after failing. They also have a bearing on how you feel. Researchers have identified feelings that commonly occur as a result of how we explain successes and failures (D. Russell & McAuley, 1986; Weiner, 1979, 1985; Weiner, Russell, & Lerman, 1979). Table 4.1 lists some examples of feelings associated with explanations for success and failure that will most likely match your experiences. These examples should remind you of the discussion in Chapter 2 about how much feelings are influenced by what you tell yourself. This fact has important implications for coping with failure that will be outlined in this chapter.

MAKING RATIONAL APPRAISALS

The first thing you want to ask yourself after deciding that a failure is worth getting upset about is, "How can I understand the reason for this failure in a rational way?" You might be surprised to know that you make appraisals, judgments, and decisions every day without really thinking about them. This is a good thing, because we would exhaust ourselves if we tried to stop and carefully weigh all of our options every time we moved. However, the ability we have to make quick appraisals can serve us wrong if these appraisals are not in our best interest. For example, most of us need to be realistic and accept the fact that we are not world-class athletes or geniuses. We would not be very happy if we went around being grandiose and expecting far more of ourselves than we could possibly deliver. Conversely, how often do you sell yourself short and write off a failure to bad luck or lack of ability when you could most likely succeed if you sacrificed the necessary time and effort?

An important part of coping with failure is developing the kind of coping attitude that was discussed in Chapter 1. When you fail at something worth getting upset about, you need to stop and make a rational appraisal. If your failure resulted because the challenge was beyond your *ability*, you might wish to reach your goal through a different route. If failure resulted because you didn't devote sufficient *effort*, or because you underestimated the *difficulty* of the task, you might wish to take the time to develop your skills and to learn new strategies. If you failed because of *bad luck*, you might want to try again. And if you failed because of *someone else*, you might wish to practice assertiveness and negotiation. Realistic appraisals help us feel less stuck after experiencing failure because they suggest a positive course of action.

Coping Skill 2: Using Rational Appraisals to Seek a Positive Course of Action

BEING PERSISTENT

It is apparent from the above discussion on making rational appraisals that you are most likely to persist and not give up after failing if you view your failure as resulting from lack of effort. This way of appraising failure allows us to use the problem-solving skills described in Chapter 3. When adopting a problem-solving attitude, it is up to you to take responsibility for your failure, to perfect your skills, and to expend greater effort next time. Persistence also involves focusing on achieving success rather than worrying about avoiding failure (Atkinson, 1957, 1964; Weiner et al., 1971).

It may help you appreciate the value of persistence if you consider the experiences of some of the world's most famous and productive people (Bandura, 1989; J. White, 1982):

- Gertrude Stein continued to submit poems to editors for 20 years before one was finally accepted.
- James Joyce's book *The Dubliners* was rejected by 22 publishers.
- Van Gogh sold only one painting during his lifetime.
- Rodin's sculptures were not accepted by major galleries.
- Stravinsky was run out of Paris when he first presented the *Rite of Spring*.
- The architecture of Frank Lloyd Wright was widely rejected during his career.
- Hollywood originally responded to Fred Astaire as a "balding skinny actor who can dance a little."
- Decca Records turned down a recording contract with the Beatles by saying: "We don't like their sound. Groups with guitars are on their way out."

Coping Skill 3: Being Persistent and Using Problem-Solving Skills to Seek Success

MAINTAINING PRIDE

What kind of self-concept would you have if you explained all of your successes as resulting from good luck and help from others? You might feel thankful, but it would be hard to experience much sense of pride. Pride comes from the feeling that you took time to develop your skills and that you devoted the effort necessary for achieving success. Pride comes from having a sense of internal control when you are confronted with a problem (Chapter 3).

Coping Skill 4: Maintaining Pride by Applying Effort and Talent

After considering how you can feel good about yourself when you succeed, you might want to ask how to maintain pride when you fail. One way to protect self-esteem after failing is to practice the kinds of adaptive appraisals discussed later in this chapter. Instead of blaming your failure on your "incompetence," you can use your problem-solving skills to figure out a strategy for doing better in the future. A second way to maintain self-esteem after failing is to follow the suggestions in this chapter for living with realistic expectations and seeking meaningful challenges. You can also maintain your self-esteem after failing by giving yourself a break and not being too hard on yourself. For example, if your hobby is playing the piano, remind yourself that you do not have to play as well as Horowitz. Or, if you are sick or under a lot of stress, remind yourself that your performance will be affected and that it's OK. We should be fair with ourselves when things beyond our control are preventing us from reaching ordinarily realistic goals. However, it is important to take responsibility when your performance could honestly be better. When you avoid taking responsibility for your performance, you are engaging in a *self-handicapping* strategy that is not always in your best interest.

SELF-HANDICAPPING

Check how much you agree or disagree with the following statements.

	Strongly agree	Agree	Disagree	Strongly disagree
1. When I do something wrong, my first impulse is to blame the circumstances.	____	____	____	____
2. I suppose I feel "under the weather" more often than most people.	____	____	____	____
3. Someday I might "get it all together."	____	____	____	____

	Strongly agree	Agree	Disagree	Strongly disagree
4. Sometimes I get so depressed that even easy tasks become difficult.	_____	_____	_____	_____
5. I would do a lot better if I tried harder.	_____	_____	_____	_____
6. I never let emotional problems in one part of my life interfere with other things in my life.	_____	_____	_____	_____
7. I tend to put things off until the last moment.	_____	_____	_____	_____
8. I always try to do my best, no matter what.	_____	_____	_____	_____

These statements come from the Self-Handicapping Scale (E. E. Jones & Rhodewalt, 1982; Rhodewalt, 1990). Self-handicappers tend to agree with statements 1, 2, 3, 4, 5, and 7 and to disagree with statements 6 and 8. People who engage in self-handicapping strategies don't have a great deal of confidence in their ability to succeed. Self-handicappers feel that their capabilities "are the way they are" and that there is not much they can do to improve their competence. For this reason, self-handicappers focus their efforts on avoiding failure. It is difficult for self-handicappers to have fun with challenging tasks because they don't see much opportunity to control their experiences of success. When they do well on a task, self-handicappers assume this was because the task was easy or because they got a break. This attitude prevents self-handicappers from taking pride in their performance. Self-handicappers don't appreciate the possibility that they can improve their chances of succeeding by learning new skills, working hard, and not getting discouraged by failure (Murray & Warden, 1992; Rhodewalt, 1994; Rhodewalt, Morf, Hazlett, & Fairfield, 1991).

People can handicap themselves by *behaving* in a way that will inhibit their chances of success or by *claiming* that something beyond their control compromised their performance (Arkin & Baumgardner, 1985). In both cases, the goal is to excuse poor performance by using the handicap as a reason why you could not do better.

Behavioral Self-Handicapping Strategies

Behavioral self-handicapping strategies are more drastic than claimed self-handicapping strategies because they involve engaging in behaviors that undermine your performance. People choose behavioral self-handicapping strategies when they feel a strong need to protect their self-esteem (Hirt, Deppe, & Gordon, 1991). Behavioral self-handicapping strategies are used when you feel it is too risky to attempt a challenge for which success is not guaranteed. You would rather sabotage your success and at least have an excuse for why you failed.

One behavioral self-handicapping strategy, with which you are most likely familiar, is the use of drugs or alcohol as an excuse for poor performance and undesirable behavior: "I can't be blamed because I was drunk" (Higgins & Harris, 1988; Tucker, Vuchinich, & Sobell, 1981). It is often easier to attribute your illegal or unacceptable behaviors to alcohol or drugs than to admit to poor impulse control or bad judgment. Politicians often use alcohol as an excuse when they break the law or behave in an unethical manner. People who engage in violent acts, such as spousal abuse, often get drunk first so they have an "explanation" for their behavior (Gelles, 1972).

The use of drugs for self-handicapping was examined in a study where participants worked on an intellectual task (Berglas & Jones, 1978). The study was set up to give some participants the idea that they succeeded because of their efforts. They were confident about their successes. Other participants succeeded, but weren't sure why. They were not confident about their successes. Before working on a second test, the participants were asked to choose between one of two drugs that were supposedly under investigation in the study. One drug was expected to help people perform better, and the other drug was expected to make them do worse. Which drug did participants choose? The majority of those who were confident about their previous success preferred the performance-enhancing drug. They wanted to see if they could do even better. In contrast, participants who were not confident about their previous success chose the drug that would hurt their performance. Because these participants were unsure of themselves, they handicapped themselves by taking a drug that they could blame for their future performance.

People also engage in behavioral self-handicapping by failing to prepare for a challenging task (Rhodewalt, Saltzman, & Wittmer, 1984), by not putting forth their best effort (Pyszczynski & Greenberg, 1983; Rhodewalt & Fairfield, 1991), by procrastinating (Ferrari, 1991, 1992), and by choosing to take on challenges in settings that are not conducive to good performance (Rhodewalt & Davison, 1986; Shepperd & Arkin, 1989). In all of these cases, the self-handicappers are undermining their chances of success so that they will have an excuse for why they failed. They are able to protect their self-esteem by offering the following kinds of explanations:

"I could have done better if I were more prepared."
"I didn't really put forth my best effort."
"I didn't have enough time to practice."
"I would do better in a different setting."

The obvious disadvantage of behavioral self-handicapping strategies is that, while they may protect our self-esteem in the short run, they prevent us from having many successful experiences.

Claimed Self-Handicapping Strategies

When people engage in claimed self-handicapping strategies, they don't behave in a way to hinder their performance. Instead, they find a mitigating factor they can claim as an excuse for their poor performance.

One claimed self-handicapping strategy is the use of an impairment over which we have no control, such as anxiety. An example of this self-handicapping strategy is seen in a study where students took an intellectual test and then rated the level of their anxiety (T. W. Smith, Snyder, & Handlesman, 1982). Students who were generally fearful of tests said they were more anxious than students who did not fear tests. This difference in self-reported anxiety was greatest when it was acceptable for students to use anxiety as an excuse for poor performance. When anxiety was not an acceptable excuse, students handicapped themselves by saying that they didn't take the test very seriously and that they hadn't bothered to prepare themselves (Harris & Snyder, 1986).

In Chapter 6 you will discover that most of us have experienced feelings of shyness. However, some people are "shy like a fox." They use shyness as an excuse for not putting themselves in certain social situations (Snyder & Smith, 1986; Snyder, Smith, Augelli, & Ingram, 1985). Other claimed self-handicapping strategies include attributing poor performance to health problems and bodily symptoms (Mayerson & Rhodewalt, 1988; T. W. Smith, Snyder, & Perkins, 1983), to obesity (Baumeister, Kahn, & Tice, 1990), to bad mood (Baumgardner, Lake, & Arkin, 1985), and to traumatic past experiences (DeGree & Snyder, 1985).

An example of blaming one's traumatic experience for an illegal act is seen in the following case:

> In 1980, Michael Tindall, who had served as a helicopter pilot in Vietnam, was charged with taking part in smuggling hashish from Morocco to Gloucester, Massachusetts. He insisted that he did it "because of a need to relive the excitement he experienced in combat" and that this need was a symptom of his illness, the "Vietnam Syndrome." In September 1980, a federal court jury in Boston acquitted Tindall of the charges against him. (Szasz, 1987, p. 287)

Psychiatric Symptoms

Psychiatric symptoms are also used as self-handicapping strategies. Studies of psychiatric patients have shown how they use psychiatric symptoms to obtain privileges and to maintain control over their protected environments (Braginsky, Braginsky, & Ring, 1969; Braginsky, Grosse, & Ring, 1966; Fontana, Klein, Lewis, & Levine, 1968). A more dramatic example of the use of psychiatric symptoms for self-handicapping is the insanity plea (Szasz, 1987).

One famous use of the insanity plea can be found in the trial of John Hinckley, Jr., who shot President Reagan and three others. Hinckley's parents offered the following explanation for his act: "How could anybody do such a horrible thing? The answer is schizophrenia, an overpowering mental illness that robbed John of his ability to control his thoughts and actions. . . . The disease is the culprit, not the person" (Szasz, 1987, p. 255).

Self-Handicapping as a Coping Strategy

There are times in life when you need to give yourself a break. It is not helpful to stress yourself out by trying to be a "superperson" and burdening yourself with too many difficult challenges at one time. You will experience higher self-esteem by limiting your challenges and succeeding than by taking on more than you can handle and failing (Tice, 1991). When used thoughtfully and in moderation, self-handicapping can be an effective coping strategy (Snyder & Higgins, 1988a).

Self-handicapping causes problems when it becomes a way of life. As with all coping styles, self-handicapping should be used in a flexible manner. When people rely too much on self-handicapping to cope with failure, they end up suffering a number of disadvantages.

One disadvantage of self-handicapping is that it often results in a negative impression (Higgins & Snyder, 1989; Rhodewalt, Sanbonmatsu, Tschanz, Feick, & Waller, 1995; D. S. Smith & Strube, 1991; Wallis & Kleinke, 1995). Most people can see through others' excuses, and they have unfavorable opinions of those who make them.

A second disadvantage of self-handicapping is that it reinforces people for being underachievers (Arkin & Baumgardner, 1985). By sticking with simple goals and never taking on risky but exciting challenges, we can protect ourselves from coming face to face with the limits of our competence. Underachievers face reduced stress and pressure because others never expect much from them. However, there is a cost to being an underachiever as it undermines self-esteem. It's hard to feel a sense of pride when we withhold our best talents and restrict ourselves to mediocre accomplishments.

A third disadvantage of self-handicapping is the risk of getting so used to practicing this coping style that we move from making excuses to "becoming the excuse" for unsatisfactory behaviors or unsuccessful endeavors (Snyder, 1990; Snyder & Higgins, 1988b). For example, instead of using anxiety to explain our behavior, we "become" an anxious person. As another example, we get so used to being easy on ourselves that we "become" underachievers. Other identities that people take on when their self-handicapping style becomes too rigid are "alcoholic," "depressed," "hypochondriac," and "mentally ill."

Some Useful Suggestions

We need to put other people's expectations of us into perspective (Higgins & Berglas, 1990). Although we all desire to please others, remind yourself that, in the final analysis, your goals, strivings, and accomplishments are *for you*. Don't allow your life to be ruled by the desire to satisfy others. Here are some points to consider about the constructive use of self-handicapping as a coping strategy.

1. Set goals that are stimulating.
2. Don't allow your goals to be compromised by a desire to please others.
3. Don't let fear of failing interfere with the pleasure of taking on challenges.
4. Remember that the efforts put into a challenge are as important as the outcome.

It is important to find the right balance between not being too hard on yourself and taking honest responsibility for your performance. You can keep this balance by making rational appraisals and living with realistic expectations.

Coping Skill 5: Finding the Right Balance Between Self-Handicapping and Self-Responsibility

SEEKING CHALLENGES

Seeking challenges has a lot to do with self-efficacy (Chapter 2). Self-efficacy is developed by living a life of goals, seeking out good role models, and exerting enough energy to experience meaningful accomplishments. What happens to people who don't cope well with failure? Researchers have found that they cop out either by sticking with simple challenges on which they are bound to succeed or by choosing impossible goals on which they are certain to fail (Atkinson, 1957, 1964; Weiner et al., 1971). Obviously, there is no reason to worry about failing when you stick with simple goals. And if you choose impossible goals and fail, nobody can blame you. But how much self-efficacy can you enjoy by achieving guaranteed success or by failing on an impossible task? You develop self-efficacy by seeking goals that challenge you to develop your skills and problem-solving abilities. When you do this, you will sometimes succeed and sometimes fail. Therefore, you have to learn how to savor successes and cope adaptively with failures. When it comes to savoring successes, you will want to practice the skill of rewarding yourself (Chapter 3). Research has shown that people who are "achievers" know how to feel pride and take credit for their accomplishments. Achievers seek challenges because they are not preoccupied with protecting themselves from failure (Weiner et al., 1971).

Coping Skill 6: Developing
Self-Efficacy by Seeking Meaningful Challenges

DEVELOPING COMPETENCIES

The concepts of self-efficacy and internal control are related to the desire to learn new things, to master challenges, and to develop competencies. This kind of life attitude is very useful in helping us cope with failure. People choose one of two different orientations when they are faced with problems. They become either *performance-oriented* or *mastery-oriented* (Dweck, 1991; Dweck & Leggett, 1988; Elliott & Dweck, 1988; Nicholls, 1984). These orientations are not fixed at birth. They are developed as a way of seeking the best method for coping with challenging situations.

Being Performance-Oriented

When you are performance-oriented, your focus is on proving your talents to others. You want to gain their approval and to avoid any possibility of being evaluated in a negative light. Performance-oriented people get frustrated and feel stuck when things don't come easily. When people take this attitude toward challenges, they become preoccupied with avoiding failure. Earlier in this chapter you learned how the motivation to avoid failure often leads people to set goals that are either too high or too low. Performance-oriented people tend to say the following kinds of things to themselves:

"What will people think of me?"

"Making a good impression is more important than enjoying myself or improving my skills."

"There is nothing to be gained from failure."

"Don't take risks. I should stay within my proven abilities."

Being performance-oriented is OK when you face simple challenges. However, when challenges become difficult, a performance orientation will hinder your problem-solving skills and prevent you from turning these challenges into useful learning experiences. When faced with tough problems, people who are performance-oriented tend to feel helpless and give up.

Another problem with being performance-oriented is that when you are too pre-occupied with pleasing others you lose your creativity. The following circumstances make it difficult to take a creative attitude toward a project or task (Amabile, 1990):

Evaluation: It is hard to be creative when you know you are being evaluated on your productivity and performance.

Surveillance: Creativity is undermined when you feel pressure from other people who are observing your performance.

Reward: Rewards can be detrimental to creativity if you focus on working for the reward rather than for the pleasure of exercising your competence.

Competition: It is harder to be creative when you are conscious of competing with others.

Restrictions: Creativity is more difficult when rules or limited resources restrict your options.

Sometimes these constraints on creativity are imposed by our environment. When this happens, the challenge is to find ways to rise above, work around, or alter these environmental restrictions. Other times, we limit our own creativity by taking on a performance orientation. When this happens, remind yourself of the benefits of being mastery-oriented.

Being Mastery-Oriented

People who are mastery-oriented focus on turning challenges into useful learning experiences. They don't demand that things come easily. It doesn't matter so much whether they succeed or fail as long as they feel they gain something from their efforts. Rather than being concerned about what others think of them, they are motivated by the chance to develop their skills and competencies. Mastery-oriented people tend to say the following kinds of things to themselves:

"What can I learn from this challenge?"

"People's judgments of me should not prevent me from having fun and improving my skills."

"Even if I fail, it can be a useful learning experience."

"It's OK to take risks and try new solutions."

Every child can benefit from learning how to develop new skills with a mastery-oriented approach.

Being mastery-oriented is adaptive for easy as well as difficult problems. Mastery-oriented people don't feel helpless when faced with tough challenges because their goal is to make the most of the experience, and they know they can learn from their failures.

A mastery orientation facilitates creativity because it emphasizes *intrinsic* motivation (Amabile, 1990; Deci & Ryan, 1985). It is easier to be creative when we take the following attitude toward jobs and tasks (Amabile, Hill, Hennessey, & Tighe, 1994):

"I enjoy tackling problems that are completely new to me."
"Curiosity is the driving force behind much of what I do."
"What matters most to me is enjoying what I do."
"No matter what the outcome of a project, I am satisfied if I feel I gained a new experience."

An important part of being mastery-oriented is to approach problems and tasks with a creative attitude that inspires you to put a piece of yourself into your efforts (Conti, Amabile, & Pollak, 1995).

Appreciating Your Ability to Learn

It is a valuable experience to be exposed to talented people. We sometimes assume that great scientists, athletes, musicians, artists, and writers were born with their skills, and we overlook their long hours of practice and self-discipline. It is also worth recognizing that the outstanding people in these fields had the courage to look at the world and to express themselves in ways that were never attempted or never believed to be possible.

One of the most serious mistakes you can make is to believe that your talents, intelligence, and abilities are fixed at birth and cannot be developed (Dweck, Chiu, & Hong, 1995; Dweck & Leggett, 1988). People who view their intelligence as a fixed entity hold the following kinds of beliefs:

"I have a certain amount of intelligence, and I can't do much about it."

"I am limited by my abilities in what I can pursue."

"When I fail at something, I know I have reached the limits of my competence."

If you take this kind of "fixed" position toward your abilities, you are bound to react to failure by saying the following kinds of things to yourself: "My failure proves that I'm not capable of solving this problem. I guess I'd better stick with easier challenges that I know I can handle."

People who view their intelligence as flexible hold the following kinds of beliefs:

"Intelligence has a lot to do with having good problem-solving skills."

"Even if I were born with a particular amount of 'intelligence,' I can always develop my capabilities by learning and mastering new skills."

"Intelligence has a lot to do with adapting to the world and having a flexible and creative way of solving my problems."

If you appreciate your ability to develop your skills and to learn new problem-solving strategies, you are more likely to react to failure by thinking: "My failure shows that I used the wrong approach. My challenge is to figure out how to do better next time."

Appreciating our capacity to learn does not mean that we can all be geniuses if we work at it. It is true that you must be realistic about the limits of your abilities. However, you won't know your limits until you test yourself. Think about how much more interesting your life will be if you view it as an opportunity to learn new things as opposed to playing it safe.

The Hidden Costs of Praise

Praise is a double-edged sword. We all enjoy being appreciated for our efforts and accomplishments. It is rewarding to be admired by others. However, we must bear in mind that our major focus in life must always be to please ourselves. If you get too used to relying on praise from others, you become trapped by their demands (Berglas, 1990). Instead of choosing your own goals and using your standards for judging your accomplishments, you allow your life to be dictated by others. It is worth taking some time to appreciate the writers, artists, and musicians who ended up destroying themselves when their self-identity was lost to the demands of the public.

Coping Skill 7: Using Failure as an Opportunity to Develop Competencies

You now have a good idea of how appraisals about failure can affect your moods and your decision to either persist or give up. You have also gained an understanding that coping successfully with failure involves making appraisals that are in your own best interest. Psychologists have conducted a large amount of research on how people learn to practice adaptive appraisals for successes and failures. I will consider some specific ideas about how to cope with failure in the remainder of this chapter.

LEARNING EFFECTIVE COPING

One important challenge for psychologists has been to teach people how to cope more effectively with failure. It will not come as a surprise to learn that children and adults who are low achievers often don't make adaptive appraisals for their successes and failures. Low achievers have not learned to savor their successes. They also tend to falsely blame many failures on lack of ability (C. I. Diener & Dweck, 1978; Dweck, 1975; Dweck & Gilliard, 1975).

How can we teach others (as well as ourselves) to seek challenges and to persist after experiencing failure? One important objective for low achievers is to stop blaming their failures on things beyond their control. It is important to recognize when failures can be avoided by expending more energy or by trying a different strategy or approach. We all need to set specific goals and ask for help with tough hurdles. Overcoming failure often means taking the responsibility to persist until you find the best solution. When you adopt such an attitude, your motivation increases, your expectations for success are greater, and you are more likely to succeed (Anderson, 1983; Peterson & Barrett, 1987).

Avoiding Self-Defeating Conclusions

Teaching programs have been developed where low achievers learn to stop after they fail and ask themselves the following questions before jumping to self-defeating conclusions (Chapin & Dyck, 1976; Dweck, 1975; Dweck & Reppucci, 1973): "Did I honestly fail because I lack ability? If not, what do I need to do to improve my performance? Do I need to try harder? Do I need to improve my skills and learn new strategies? Should I give up or can I succeed by being persistent?" As a result of learning how to talk to themselves adaptively, low achievers begin to set higher goals and to expend greater effort toward achieving success.

First-year college students often suffer self-doubts when they find themselves not doing as well as they did in high school. A self-defeating conclusion for this experience is: "I'm not as smart as I thought. Maybe I'm not cut out for college." As you can appreciate, a more realistic conclusion is: "The study skills I need for college are different from those I used in high school. If I give myself a year to master them, my grades will get better."

Research was conducted in which first-year college students were instructed that it is normal to experience a drop in grades during the first year in college and that grades improve as students adjust to the new style of learning (T. D. Wilson & Linville, 1982, 1985). As a result of these simple instructions, the students did significantly better during the following semester than a similar group of first-year students who weren't encouraged to understand their first semester "setback" in a realistic way.

Overcoming Perfectionism

People who are perfectionists have a difficult time with tasks because they are so worried about making mistakes that they have little energy left over for enjoying the challenge. Perfectionists approach problems by saying the following kinds of things to themselves (Frost, Marten, Lahart, & Rosenblate, 1990):

> "I should be upset if I make a mistake."
> "I hate being less than perfect at things."
> "If I do not do well all the time, people will not respect me."
> "If I fail on something, I am a failure as a person."
> "If I fail partly, it is as bad as being a complete failure."

These statements reflect the kinds of irrational appraisals and cognitive distortions discussed in Chapter 2. Perfectionists take a performance-oriented rather than a mastery-oriented approach toward tasks and problems. It should not be surprising to learn that people who demand perfection are more depressed and anxious than people who are less concerned with doing things perfectly (Frost et al., 1990). Perfectionists are under a great deal of physical and emotional stress. They are so preoccupied with avoiding mistakes that they take a rigid and uncreative approach toward problems. They often procrastinate rather than complete a project and risk imperfection. It is understandable that perfectionists react with self-doubts and lowered self-confidence when they experience failure (Frost et al., 1995). When the need for perfection becomes too extreme, experiences of failure can result in self-destructive behavior and suicide (Blatt, 1995). People who insist on being perfect need to practice the kinds of adaptive thinking skills that are outlined in Chapter 2.

Coping Skill 8: Overcoming Perfectionism

Enhancing Your Sense of Ability

Coping with failure is developed through experiencing success and learning to attribute success to your effort and ability. You can encourage yourself by saying: "I worked really hard. I didn't give up. I'm really good at this. I'm smart." When you appreciate your efforts, you are encouraged not to give up on a problem until you have explored all possible solutions. The appreciation of ability helps you realize that while some problems require a lot of work, many can be solved (Schunk, 1982, 1983, 1984).

Coping with failure is often learned from good role models. Children learn coping skills by observing how others talk themselves through problems. A good role model is a person with whom you can identify. You are not going to learn much from someone whose skills are far better or worse than your own. You will get your best lessons by watching people similar to you take on a problem, work it through without giving up, and take satisfaction for their success (Schunk & Hanson, 1985; Schunk, Hanson, & Cox, 1987).

Comparing Boys and Girls

Another insight about how people appraise failure comes from research showing that girls are more likely than boys to explain their experiences of failure in school as caused by lack of ability (Dweck & Gilliard, 1975). Girls suffer when they falsely blame their failures on lack of ability and become discouraged and give up. Boys, in contrast, explain their failures as caused by problems they can overcome. They say things such as: "Maybe I didn't try hard enough. Or maybe the teacher was being really hard. But I'm not dumb, and I can do better next time."

Why should boys and girls react to experiences of failure so differently? This question was explored by observing the responses of teachers to their students. The researchers found that teachers focus their criticisms of girls on poor intellectual performance. When teachers criticize boys, it is often for "goofing off" or breaking rules. Boys, therefore, learn to take teachers' criticisms with a grain of salt. They don't personalize a teacher's negative remarks as a reflection on their abilities. Even though teachers criticize girls less often than they criticize boys, girls suffer because they take the criticism to heart (Dweck & Bush, 1976; Dweck, Davidson, Nelson, & Enna, 1978; Dweck, Goetz, & Strauss, 1980).

Research showing that boys and girls react differently to failure emphasizes that coping with failure is very much influenced by how we learn to interpret our skills and abilities. Both men and women are challenged to evaluate the ways in which they have learned to react to failure and ask whether they might benefit from learning to take credit for their efforts and abilities.

Coping Skill 9: Taking Credit for Your Effort and Ability

LIVING WITH REALISTIC EXPECTATIONS

Coping successfully with failure means living a life of realistic expectations. If you set your goals too high, you will always fail, and that is discouraging. If you set your goals too low, you will never fail, but life will be boring. To live an interesting and challenging life, you must set your goals at a level where you sometimes succeed and sometimes fail. Disadvantaged children grow up with very few experiences of success. Because these children have not learned to savor success, they have no reason to set challenging goals for themselves. Advantaged children who grow up with nothing but success also suffer because they never learn how to cope with inevitable failures (Chapin & Dyck, 1976; Dweck, 1975).

Coping Skill 10: Setting Goals That Will Make Your Life Interesting and Rewarding

In addition to making your life more interesting, there is another reason for living with realistic expectations. The goals you seek and the explanations you give for success and failure have a strong impact on your attitude toward the future. If you convince yourself that you have no ability, that the world is against you, and that you are doomed to bad luck, you are in danger of falling victim to a self-fullfilling prophecy. People who *expect* to do poorly end up *doing* poorly. People who expect to do better than they possibly can also end up *doing* poorly. It is important to size up each challenge in a realistic way so you can prepare yourself to use the skill and effort required for success (Brickman & Hendricks, 1975; Sherman, Skov, Hervitz, & Stock, 1981). Here are some suggestions:

1. When faced with a simple task that verges on boredom, you have several options. You might appreciate having a chance to take it easy for a while. Or you can use your creativity to give this task a personal touch, or even to have some fun with it.
2. When pursuing challenges that are tough but within your grasp, "go for it." This is your chance to enjoy a feeling of accomplishment.
3. When faced with problems that appear insurmountable, you have two choices. You can protect yourself from failure by self-handicapping. Or you can decide that failure is not an issue and take on the problem as a learning experience. Instead of being performance-oriented, take on a mastery-oriented attitude. The goal is not a perfect outcome but rather an opportunity to practice your skills.

***Coping Skill 11: Matching
Expectations to the Difficulty of the Challenge***

COPING WITH FAILURE AS A MENTAL HEALTH SKILL

In Chapter 5 you will learn some techniques for coping when you are feeling down. As a way of leading into that chapter, let's explore how feeling down is related to experiences of failure. Earlier in this chapter, you read about how explanations for successes and failures can influence people's moods. Therefore, it will not come as a surprise to learn that depressed people are especially likely to perceive their failures as being beyond their control. Depressives usually explain their failures as caused by bad luck and poor ability. Because they underestimate the power of problem-solving skills for coping with failure, they often feel helpless and give up (Weary & Williams, 1990). Depressed people spend an inordinate amount of time focusing on their failures. They are so preoccupied with their failures that they have little energy left for appreciating what they have done successfully. It is no wonder that they suffer from such low self-esteem (Pyszczynski & Greenberg, 1987a, 1987b).

We all know that it is hard to motivate ourselves and to expend a lot of effort when we're feeling down. Feeling down makes us feel less ambitious. However, it is also important to understand that forcing ourselves to be ambitious and energetic will make us feel less down. Depressives feel better and start to accomplish things when they learn to talk themselves through challenges (Chapter 3) and begin to make realistic appraisals for their failures ("Failing doesn't prove I'm dumb or worthless." "Failing once doesn't mean I'll always fail." "I can tolerate failures because that's how I learn.") and to take appropriate credit for their successes ("I don't have to be perfect to feel good about my accomplishments." "Even if I fail, I can take pride in my efforts." "The challenge is as important to me as the outcome.") (Klein, Fencil-Morse, & Seligman, 1976; Klein & Seligman, 1976; Sweeney, Anderson, & Bailey, 1986). What was found in these treatment studies is relevant for everyone: To lead a challenging and productive life, we have to learn how to fail.

Coping Skill 12: Learning How to Fail

LIST OF SKILLS FOR COPING WITH FAILURE

- *Coping Skill 1:* Saving Energy for Failures Worth Getting Upset About
- *Coping Skill 2:* Using Rational Appraisals to Seek a Positive Course of Action
- *Coping Skill 3:* Being Persistent and Using Problem-Solving Skills to Seek Success
- *Coping Skill 4:* Maintaining Pride by Applying Effort and Talent
- *Coping Skill 5:* Finding the Right Balance Between Self-Handicapping and Self-Responsibility
- *Coping Skill 6:* Developing Self-Efficacy by Seeking Meaningful Challenges
- *Coping Skill 7:* Using Failure as an Opportunity to Develop Competencies
- *Coping Skill 8:* Overcoming Perfectionism
- *Coping Skill 9:* Taking Credit for Your Effort and Ability
- *Coping Skill 10:* Setting Goals That Will Make Your Life Interesting and Rewarding
- *Coping Skill 11:* Matching Expectations to the Difficulty of the Challenge
- *Coping Skill 12:* Learning How to Fail

SUGGESTIONS FOR FURTHER READING

Ellis, A., & Knaus, W. (1977). *Overcoming procrastination.* New York: New American Library.

Higgins, R. L., Snyder, C. R., & Berglas, S. (Eds.). (1990). *Self-handicapping: The paradox that isn't.* New York: Plenum.

Snyder, C. R., Higgins, R. L., & Stucky, R. J. (1983). *Excuses: Masquerades in search of grace.* New York: Wiley.

Szasz, T. S. (1987). *Insanity: The idea and its consequences.* New York: Wiley.

Weiner, B. (1995). *Judgments of responsibility: A foundation for a theory of social conduct.* New York: Guilford.

White, J. (1982). *Rejection.* Reading, MA: Addison-Wesley.

Coping
When You're Down

Everyone has ups and downs. As long as they are not too extreme, our ups and downs make life interesting and challenging. But when you feel exceptionally low, or when you are in the dumps for a long period of time, you need to appraise the situation and look for suitable coping responses.

SYMPTOMS OF DEPRESSION

To put this chapter into perspective, you need to understand the clinical term *depression* and how a diagnosis of depression is used by professional psychotherapists. The American Psychiatric Association (1994) states that the following symptoms may be experienced by people who are clinically depressed over a period of two or more weeks:

1. Change in appetite. Either poor appetite and weight loss or increased appetite and weight gain.
2. Inability to sleep, or sleeping more than usual.
3. Low energy and fatigue.
4. Loss of interest or pleasure in previously enjoyed activities.
5. Feelings of worthlessness, self-reproach, or excessive guilt.
6. Diminished ability to think or concentrate.
7. Recurrent thoughts of death. Suicidal thoughts.

A rough measure of the degree of depression you are experiencing can be obtained by rating the following ten items using this scale:

0 = this is not a problem for me
1 = this is sometimes a problem for me
2 = this is often a problem for me
3 = this is almost always a problem for me

1. Feeling sad   _____
2. Feeling depressed   _____
3. No hope for the future   _____
4. Feeling tired   _____
5. Poor appetite   _____
6. Feeling like a failure   _____
7. Thoughts of killing myself   _____
8. Crying spells   _____
9. Trouble sleeping   _____
10. Difficulty making decisions   _____

These items come from three widely used depression scales: the Beck Depression Inventory (Beck, Ward, Mendelson, Mock, & Erbaugh, 1961), the Zung Self-Rating Depression Scale (Zung, 1965), and the Center for Epidemiologic Studies Depression Scale (CES-D Scale) (Radloff, 1977). If your scores on the ten items average 2 or above, you are probably depressed enough to want to do something about it.

The coping skills discussed in this chapter are useful for clinically depressed people. Studying and practicing them can help you (Jamison & Scogin, 1995). However, people who are *clinically* depressed should also seek professional help. My purpose in this chapter is to offer you some tips for pulling yourself up when you're feeling sad, blue, low, or down.

FACTORS UNDERLYING DEPRESSION

A number of researchers have identified factors common to people who are most likely to get depressed (Barnett & Gotlib, 1988; G. P. Brown, Hammen, Craske, & Wickens, 1995; Burger, 1984; Pyszczynski & Greenberg, 1987a, 1987b). For people suffering from depression, the following styles have become habits they must learn to give up for the sake of their well-being (Hedlund & Rude, 1995):

Unrealistic dependency on others: Depressed people tend to tie their self-esteem too strongly to someone else's approval.

Lack of a social support system: People prone to depression tend to be introverted and withdrawn. They don't exert the social skills required to sustain supportive relationships.

Stress in close relationships: Feelings of depression are often intensified when there is disharmony in close relationships.

Depressive self-focusing style: Depressed people are preoccupied with negatives. They spend too much time ruminating on the bad things in their lives and never get around to implementing their coping strategies.

Perfectionistic vulnerability: Depressed people insist on being perfect. Because they are not, they view themselves as worthless and their lives as a waste.

External control: Depressed people feel that the important events in their lives are beyond their control.

When you feel down, it is usually because something has happened (an activating event) that is unacceptable or intolerable (belief system). In terms of the appraisal model described in Chapter 2 (see Figure 2.2), feeling down is the consequence of how you interpret the life event. One possible response is to alter the situation. A second response is to ask whether your primary appraisal is accurate. A third response is to ask whether your primary appraisal is rational. A fourth response is to use good coping skills. You will learn how to use each of these responses in this chapter.

ALTERING THE SITUATION

The most important rule about altering an unhappy situation is to be realistic. You must face the fact that many life events that lead you to feel down are beyond your control. It is not adaptive to burden yourself with these kinds of unrealistic thoughts:

"Why did it have to happen?"
"If only I had done things differently."
"It isn't fair."
"If only I had another chance."

Depressed people allow themselves to become overwhelmed because they see too many situations as being unpleasant (Rhodewalt & Zone, 1989). When an unhappy life event is beyond your control, it is in your best interest to acknowledge this fact (as unpleasant as it might be) and to focus your energies on your appraisals and coping responses. No purpose is served by brooding about life events you can't change. Reinhold Niebuhr summed up this first coping skill in his Serenity Prayer (Bartlett, 1982): "God, give us grace to accept with serenity the things that cannot be changed, courage to change the things which should be changed, and the wisdom to distinguish the one from the other."

Coping Skill 1: Acknowledging When Unpleasant Situations Are Beyond Your Control

Life events you sometimes can influence are those involving relations with other people. If you are feeling down because someone is not treating you right or is not meeting your needs, you may be able to alter the situation by negotiating, using social skills, and being assertive. A number of suggestions for using good social skills are given in Chapter 6. One important point is that you will usually get more favorable reactions from others if you are *responsive*. A natural reaction when other people don't meet our needs is to withdraw, get angry, and pout. The concept of responsiveness suggests that when you want something from others, you often have to be the first to give. Getting your needs met is a matter of pragmatics over pride. It is better to be assertive and ask directly for what you want than to seek attention "symptomatically" by trying to make others feel guilty. It is true that asking for something and being denied is not pleasant. However, when you are direct, others at least know where you stand. Even if you are denied, you can still control your life by making adaptive appraisals and using your coping skills. When taking a responsive and assertive approach toward others, it is important to recognize the value of negotiation (see Chapter 8). It is a fact of life that if you want good treatment from others, you have to give them something in return.

Coping Skill 2: Enhancing Personal
Relations with Social Skills, Assertiveness, and Negotiation

MAKING ACCURATE PRIMARY APPRAISALS
Listening to Your Accurate Self

Which of these two statements do you make to yourself when you try to accomplish a task and don't succeed?

"I failed, and this means I'm dumb."
"I failed because I didn't try hard enough, because I didn't approach the task correctly, or because I'm not good at that task, but not because I'm dumb."

It is obvious that the second statement is more accurate than the first. However, when you are feeling down, it is easy to make inaccurate appraisals by overgeneralizing and looking at unhappy life events as absolute and unchangeable (Coyne & Gotlib, 1983). When this happens, force yourself to question your faulty appraisals and to change them into appraisals that are more realistic. For example, assume that your best friend is abrupt with you. How would you feel if you made the following appraisal? "My friend doesn't like me anymore." This appraisal would most likely cause you to feel hurt, sad, or angry.

To pull yourself out of the dumps, you would have to argue with yourself in the following manner:

"That abrupt treatment means A doesn't like me anymore."
"How often is A abrupt with me?"
"Hardly ever."
"How often is A nice to me?"
"Most of the time."
"Is it possible that A's abruptness had nothing to do with me?"
"I guess so."
"Now let's assume that A was mad at me. Does that mean A dislikes me?"
"Not really."
"Friends can be abrupt with each other at times and still be friends, can't they?"

A valuable skill for coping with inaccurate primary appraisals is to listen to your accurate self. Train yourself to question and revise inaccurate primary appraisals that cause you to feel low. Here are some examples of common inaccurate primary appraisals and accurate revisions (Beck, Rush, Shaw, & Emery, 1979).

Self-blame

Inaccurate Self: Because I forgot my mother's birthday, I'm a bad person.

Accurate Self: Making a mistake is unfortunate, but it does not mean I am a bad person.

Irreversibility

Inaccurate Self: I am lonely and shy and will always be this way.

Accurate Self: I can learn how to overcome my loneliness and shyness.

Overgeneralization

Inaccurate Self: Person A was mean to me. Nobody likes me.

Accurate Self: Person A was mean to me, but there are many people who like me.

Absolutism

Inaccurate Self: My life is worthless without my lost love.

Accurate Self: My lost love doesn't constitute my whole life.

Personalization

Inaccurate Self: The boss is mad because my productivity is low.

Accurate Self: The boss is mad because our department's productivity is low.

Overreacting

Inaccurate Self: We had an argument, and our friendship is over.

Accurate Self: One argument does not end a friendship.

Managing Your "Shoulds" and "Musts"

People make themselves depressed when their desires become demands characterized by "shoulds" and "musts" (Ellis, 1987a).

> Instead of saying "I'm sorry I failed," depressed people say "I cannot stand failing."
> Instead of saying "I have some negative traits," depressed people say "I am a rotten person."
> Instead of saying "I will have both positive and negative experiences in the future," depressed people say "My future is bound to be negative and that's terrible."
> Instead of saying "I'm alone and need to seek out some friendships," depressed people say "People should like me, but they don't. I'm a loser."
> Instead of saying "I didn't do as well as I would have liked, but I can take credit for trying," depressed people say "I don't deserve credit because I should have done better."

Taking a Flexible View of the Future

Depressed people do not have a flexible view of the future. They are more likely than nondepressed people to believe that their futures will be negative and that their possibility of achieving happy experiences is limited (Andersen, 1990; Pyszczynski, Holt, & Greenberg, 1987). For this reason, depressed people focus more of their energies on avoiding unpleasant situations in the present than working toward potential rewards in the future (Wertheim & Schwartz, 1983). Depressed people feel stuck because they view their problems as *stable, global,* and *internal* (Heimberg, Vermilyea, Dodge, Becker, & Barlow, 1987; Peterson & Seligman, 1987; Raps, Peterson, Reinhard, Abramson, & Seligman, 1982; Sweeney et al., 1986):

Stability: Depressed people see negative events in their lives as stable, that is, as unlikely to change. Nondepressed people view negative experiences as temporary setbacks that won't last forever.

Globality: Depressed people are overwhelmed by their problems. Nondepressed people can put things in perspective. They balance the positives against the negatives in their lives.

Internality: Depressed people blame themselves for their problems. Nondepressed people take responsibility for things they can change but don't put themselves down for not being perfect.

Coping Skill 3: Questioning and Revising Inaccurate Primary Appraisals

MAINTAINING A SENSE OF CONTROL

Jerome Frank (1973) points out that one of the most important things psychotherapists can do for their clients is to help them overcome their feelings of hopelessness and demoralization. This is especially true for people who are depressed. When we are feeling down, we don't see any way to improve the situation, and we engage in negative patterns of thinking.

As you might expect, maintaining a sense of control, self-efficacy, and mastery over your life is an important skill when you are down (Anderson & Arnoult, 1985; J. D. Brown & Siegel, 1988; Marshall & Lang, 1990). Granted, it isn't always easy to be hopeful when all the odds appear to be against you. It is important to remember, however, that internal control and self-efficacy come from within and not from events in the outside world. Practice your skills for maintaining internal control (Chapter 3) and follow the philosophy of self-efficacy discussed in Chapter 2. A sense of control will reinforce your commitment to take responsibility for your problems and to use your problem-solving skills to find solutions for life challenges.

Coping Skill 4: Maintaining a Sense of Control

MAKING RATIONAL PRIMARY APPRAISALS

Even if you don't make an inaccurate primary appraisal such as those described in the previous section, a life event may still bring you down. What are you saying to yourself when this happens? Is your appraisal accurate and *rational?* For example, assume that someone is unfriendly to you. How would you feel if you made the following

When feeling down, it is helpful to take some time to balance happy thoughts against unhappy thoughts.

appraisal? "There must be something wrong with me." This appraisal would most likely cause you to feel down in the dumps because you are basing your self-worth on how others treat you. What if, however, you appraised the person's unfriendliness in a more rational manner? For example: "It's too bad that person was unfriendly, but my self-worth is not determined by how someone treats me." This appraisal would cause you to feel sorry or disappointed but wouldn't leave you in the dumps. When you are feeling too low for too long about something that happened, you have to question, and possibly revise, what you are saying to yourself about this life event.

To gain a useful perspective on how irrational appraisals bring us down, let's look at findings from research studies comparing appraisals made by depressed and non-depressed people (Eaves & Rush, 1984; Hammen & Cochran, 1981; Kanfer & Zeiss, 1983; Pietromonaco & Markus, 1985; Tabachnik, Crocker, & Alloy, 1983). For example:

Depressed people are preoccupied with sad thoughts about themselves.
Nondepressed people know how to get their minds off their sadness.

Depressed people don't give themselves the benefit of the doubt.
Nondepressed people give themselves a break when judging themselves.

Depressed people make unrealistic demands about what they need to be happy.
Nondepressed people have realistic expectations about what they need to be happy.

Depressed people allow unhappy life events to get the best of them.
Nondepressed people balance happy life events against unhappy life events.

Depressed people feel incapable.
Nondepressed people feel capable.

Coping Skill 5: Questioning and Revising Irrational Primary Appraisals

USING ADAPTIVE COPING SKILLS

Everyone is confronted with stressful life events, frustrations, and disappointments. Some people are subjected to even greater traumas and losses. No one can be expected to react favorably to misfortune, but some people are able to work through unhappy experiences while others get stuck being depressed. Why is this so? Those who can pull themselves out of depression have more effective resources (Billings & Moos, 1982). They know how to use the kinds of coping strategies outlined in Chapter 3.

Researchers have identified skills that are effective for coping with depression through two kinds of investigations. One approach involves comparing the coping strategies employed by depressed and nondepressed people. A second approach is to measure the correlation between people's preferred coping responses and their levels of depression.

Coping Strategies of Depressed and Nondepressed People

Researchers have found the following differences in the kinds of coping responses used by depressed and nondepressed people (Billings, Cronkite, & Moos, 1983; Billings & Moos, 1984; Coyne, Aldwin, & Lazarus, 1981; Holahan & Moos, 1987; Mitchell, Cronkite, & Moos, 1983; Monroe, Bellack, Hersen, & Himmelhoch, 1983; C. J. Taylor & Scogin, 1992):

- Depressed people engage in wishful thinking.
- Depressed people do not make sufficient use of problem-solving skills.
- Depressed people do not make sufficient use of social support.
- Depressed people engage in high amounts of avoidance.
- Depressed people don't make effective use of self-relaxation.
- Depressed people are not skillful at talking themselves through their problems.
- Depressed people are not good at pulling themselves up with humor.
- Depressed people are passive.
- Depressed people engage in an excessive amount of self-blame.
- Depressed people have less confidence in their ability to cope with depressing situations.

The Depression Coping Questionnaire

Check how often you do each of the following things when you are feeling down.

	Never	Rarely	Sometimes	Often
1. I seek out friends for support.	____	____	____	____
2. I blame myself.	____	____	____	____
3. I watch TV.	____	____	____	____
4. I work out a plan to make myself feel better.	____	____	____	____
5. I drink alcohol or take tranquilizers.	____	____	____	____
6. I sleep, daydream, or try to escape.	____	____	____	____
7. I engage in some sort of activity, such as reading, music, art, or sports.	____	____	____	____

The above list of coping responses is adapted from the Depression Coping Questionnaire (Kleinke, 1984a, 1988, 1991; Kleinke, Staneski, & Mason, 1982). This questionnaire was administered to hundreds of people of all ages and from a wide range of backgrounds. Respondents included people who were clinically depressed, moderately depressed, and nondepressed. Comparing the coping responses used by depressed people with the coping responses used by nondepressed people yielded some interesting findings. Nondepressed people tend to endorse items 1, 4, and 7. They make an active effort to get busy, to seek support, and to engage in problem solving when they are feeling down. Depressed people tend to endorse items 2, 3, 5, and 6. Depressed people are passive. They withdraw, and they blame themselves. They often use alcohol and tranquilizing drugs. This survey indicates that depression, passivity, and self-blame reinforce one another. Depressed people don't seem to have the energy to get out and engage in active coping responses. If they could force themselves to cope more actively, they would feel better.

Similar results were found when correlations were computed between respondents' preferred coping responses and their levels of depression. Lower levels of depression were correlated with a preference for the following coping responses:

- Seeking social support
- Problem solving
- Distracting oneself and getting busy with other things

Higher levels of depression were correlated with a preference for these coping responses:

- Self-blaming
- Using stimulants such as cigarettes and coffee

TABLE 5.1   Problem solving for parents

Problem	Possible Solutions
Family	
1. Taking care of children	Enlist help of in-laws
	Trade baby-sitting time with friends who have children
	Find a reputable day care program
	Share child-care responsibilities with spouse
	Arrange schedule to allow meaningful time with children
2. Having meaningful time with spouse	Set up regular schedule with spouse for meaningful time together
School	
1. Finding time to study	Schedule study time when others are available to care for children
2. Needing support	Contract with spouse to give encouragement about schoolwork, progress
3. Guilt	Schedule meaningful time with spouse and children
Job	
1. Fatigue	Enlist spouse's help with housework
	Hire part-time housekeeper

- Watching TV
- Becoming irritable and short-tempered
- Using drugs such as amphetamines and Valium

In the remainder of this chapter, I will focus on adaptive skills you can practice for coping with depression. These skills include problem solving, rewarding yourself for your accomplishments, controlling negative thinking, thinking adaptive thoughts, getting busy, and making effective use of support systems.

PROBLEM SOLVING

When a good friend was having a hard time, he said: "I was down for the count, but not out." Because my friend is a problem solver, he knew he would find a way to pull himself up. People who have good problem-solving skills are less likely to get depressed than people who do not (Nezu, Nezu, Saraydarian, Kalmer, & Ronan, 1986).

How can you apply the problem-solving skills outlined in Chapter 3 when you're down? As an example, consider a parent who is overwhelmed with the responsibilities of family, school, and a job. Table 5.1 indicates how the person could divide these problems into manageable parts and make a list of options and possible solutions. When a plan has been formulated, it can be tested to find out which solutions are working and which need to be revised.

There are several things to keep in mind when you use problem solving to pull yourself out of the dumps. First, it is important to break problems down into manageable parts so they don't seem so overwhelming. Second, remember to be creative when considering possible solutions. Don't forget to enlist support people to help you brainstorm and to provide encouragement. Combine your energies with the encouragement of your support people to bolster your self-efficacy and feelings of internal control. A third thing to keep in mind is to reward yourself for taking steps to get going. And, most of all, remember that you are a problem solver.

How well does problem solving work? A study was conducted in which clinically depressed people were given one of two therapy treatments (Nezu, 1986). Some of the depressed people were taught to use a problem-solving strategy similar to the one outlined in Chapter 3. Depressed people in a second group discussed their problems but did not learn about or practice a problem-solving strategy. Results of this study were very clear. Depressed people who learned and practiced problem solving experienced a significant decrease in their depression that was still present 6 months after the study was completed. In contrast, depressed people who discussed their problems without practicing problem solving experienced only a slight decrease in depression.

Two important conclusions are apparent. First, problem solving is an effective skill for coping when you are down. Second, it is necessary to push yourself into activity when you are feeling low.

Coping Skill 6: Making Active Use of Problem Solving

REWARDING YOURSELF FOR YOUR ACCOMPLISHMENTS

The coping skill of rewarding yourself for your accomplishments (Chapter 3) is particularly relevant for depressed people. Depressed people don't give themselves enough credit for their accomplishments. Because they focus on the negatives, they underestimate their achievements and see themselves as unworthy of appreciation. They don't make effective use of self-reinforcement (Heiby, 1982, 1983b). If you are depressed, you can benefit by (1) setting reasonable goals, (2) sticking with a schedule so you will accomplish things, (3) paying attention to your accomplishments, and (4) reinforcing yourself for your achievements (Fuchs & Rehm, 1977; Heiby 1986; Heiby, Ozaki, & Campos, 1984).

Coping Skill 7: Rewarding Yourself for Your Accomplishments

CONTROLLING NEGATIVE THINKING

In Chapter 2, you were introduced to the concept of *healthy thinking* and to the power of *nonnegative thinking*. Depressed people have a problematic thinking style because they focus on and ruminate about their negative feelings (Lyubomirsky & Nolen-Hoeksema, 1993, 1995; Nolen-Hoeksema, 1991; Nolen-Hoeksema, Morrow, &

Fredrickson, 1993; Pyszczynski & Greenberg, 1986). The act of obsessing and brooding over unpleasant events and unhappy feelings provides an illusion of "working
through" and finding solutions to these problems. However, unlike problem solving,
ruminating is not a creative process through which options are developed and tested
out. Ruminating tends to perpetuate feelings of depression. The more you focus on
how bad things are, the worse they seem. Ruminating also interferes with your
problem-solving abilities because it is difficult to think of creative solutions to problems when stewing over negative feelings. Depressed people *understand* that they
would feel better if they distracted themselves with pleasant thoughts and activities.
Unfortunately, they often get so caught up dwelling on their depression that they don't
have time or energy left for engaging in adaptive thinking.

Check how much you agree or disagree with the following statements about what
you can or cannot do when you are experiencing upsetting emotions or feelings.

	Strongly agree	Agree	Disagree	Strongly disagree
1. I can usually find a way to cheer myself up.	____	____	____	____
2. Wallowing in it is all I can do.	____	____	____	____
3. I can find a way to relax.	____	____	____	____
4. I can feel better by doing something creative.	____	____	____	____
5. I start to feel really down about myself.	____	____	____	____
6. I can find some humor in the situation and feel better.	____	____	____	____

These statements come from the Negative Mood Regulation Scale (Catanzaro &
Mearns, 1990). People who agree with statements 1, 3, 4, and 6 and disagree with
statements 2 and 5 have confidence in their ability to control their negative moods and
stop themselves from ruminating or obsessing about how bad they are feeling. An
important skill for coping with depression is learning how to stop yourself from ruminating on your unhappy feelings by thinking about other things. You can also distract
yourself from depressive ruminations by interacting with others or by getting involved
in meaningful activities (Lyubomirsky & Nolen-Hoeksema, 1995; Nolen-Hoeksema,
1991; Nolen-Hoeksema & Morrow, 1993).

People are less prone to getting depressed when they have learned to regulate
their negative moods and feel confident about their ability to do so (Catanzaro &
Greenwood, 1994; Kirsch, Mearns, & Catanzaro, 1990). Regulating your negative
moods does not mean ignoring your feelings. Acknowledge when you are feeling
down so you can respond appropriately. But avoid monitoring your negative moods so
carefully that they become a major focus in your life (Swinkels & Giuliano, 1995).
When you are down, it is to your advantage to get busy and overcome the temptation

to dwell on yourself and on your unhappy feelings (Nix, Watson, Pyszczynski, & Greenberg, 1995; Pyszczynski, Hamilton, Herring, & Greenberg, 1989).

Coping Skill 8: Controlling Negative Thinking

THINKING ADAPTIVE THOUGHTS

A number of years ago, researchers studied the effects of positive and negative moods (Velten, 1968). Negative moods were instilled in research participants by instructing them to repeat the following kinds of statements to themselves:

"I feel worn out."
"No matter how hard I try, things don't go my way."
"Sometimes I feel so alone that I could cry."
"Life often doesn't seem worth living."

As a result of making these statements, the participants' moods became more negative and their performance on various tests of concentration deteriorated. Most likely, you can see the connection between this study and your thoughts when you are feeling low. We perpetuate our blue moods by getting stuck on negative thoughts. When you catch yourself doing this, stop the negative thoughts and shift to thoughts that will make you feel better. For example, nondepressed as well as depressed people experienced more positive moods, and their performance on tests of concentration was enhanced, when they repeated these kinds of statements to themselves (Raps, Reinhard, & Seligman, 1980; Velten, 1968):

"I feel great!"
"I'm pleased that most people are so nice to me."
"There are so many things in life I enjoy."
"I feel energetic and happy."

Now let's consider some steps you can take to bolster your adaptive thinking.

Stopping Negative Thoughts

Depressed people are more likely than nondepressed people to occupy themselves with thoughts of *personal dissatisfaction, negative expectations, low self-esteem,* and *helplessness* (Hollon & Kendall, 1980; Ross, Gottfredson, Christensen, & Weaver, 1986):

Personal dissatisfaction: "Something has to change." "What's the matter with me?" "I wish I were a better person."
Negative expectations: "My future is bleak." "I'll never make it." "I'm a failure."
Low self-esteem: "I'm worthless." "I don't like myself."
Helplessness: "I can't finish anything." "It's just not worth it."

We often go through the day bringing ourselves down with negative thoughts without paying attention to what we are doing. To stop this from happening, train yourself to pay attention to what you are thinking. When you get stuck on negative thoughts, yell "Stop!" (If there are people around, you can "yell" to yourself.) Wear a rubber band on your wrist and snap it when you think negative thoughts. Don't permit yourself to get in the dumps with your thinking.

If you feel it is important to you to have some time each day to focus on "how awful things are," set up a schedule. Allow yourself to think negative thoughts during certain prearranged times (but *not* at any other time). Set aside a special chair or a place where you can make yourself feel blue. During your scheduled negative thinking times, try to exaggerate your negative thoughts to extremes. Maybe you can find humor in your propensity to make yourself miserable.

Practicing Positive Thoughts

It's helpful to keep track of what you tell yourself during the day. Try to balance thoughts that bring you down with thoughts that bring hope and satisfaction. For example, make a list of your accomplishments, like getting to work on time, reading a book, doing something healthy, or helping someone else. Value the people close to you and the things in your life (nature, art, music) you enjoy. Don't hold unrealistically high expectations for what must happen before you allow yourself to experience pleasure.

Four kinds of positive thoughts nondepressed people think more often than those who are depressed are thoughts about *life satisfaction, positive self-concept, acceptance by others,* and *positive expectations* (Ingram & Wisnicki, 1988):

Life satisfaction: "I am comfortable with life." "My life is running smoothly." "Life is exciting." "I am a lucky person."

Positive self-concept: "I have many good qualities." "I take good care of myself." "I deserve good things in life." "I have many useful skills."

Acceptance by others: "I am respected by my peers." "I have a good sense of humor." "I'm fun to be with." "I have a good way with others."

Positive expectations: "My future looks bright." "I will be successful." "I can look forward to many good things."

When you are feeling down, you may not feel like thinking these positive thoughts. However, the more you focus on them, the more automatic they become, and the better you will feel.

Taking Charge of Your Thinking

Don't just wait around passively for negative thoughts to go away and for positive thoughts to happen. Reinforce your feelings of self-efficacy and internal control by taking the initiative to balance your thoughts.

Coping Skill 9: Thinking Positive Thoughts

GETTING BUSY

There are three good reasons why it is important to get busy when you are down. First, to change how you are feeling, you have to change what you're doing. Second, getting busy is a useful way to bolster feelings of self-efficacy. Third, getting busy when you're down encourages positive responses from others.

Actions Change Feelings

Often when we're in the dumps we say to ourselves, "I feel too low to do anything. I'll get busy when I feel better." It is truly more difficult to be active when you're feeling low than when you're feeling great. However, if you insist on feeling better before you get busy, you'll waste a lot of time. Psychologists have verified through research and clinical practice something we all know from our life experiences: *Actions change feelings* (Kleinke, 1978, 1984b).

Psychological researchers have found that depressed people have a very low energy level (Christensen & Duncan, 1995) and that they engage in fewer pleasant activities than do nondepressed people. Researchers have also found that depressed people feel better when they are taught to bring more pleasant activities into their lives. For this reason, an important component in the psychotherapy of depression is the *daily activity schedule*. The purpose of this schedule is to help depressed people get busy with activities that will provide a sense of mastery and pleasure. To make an activity schedule, write down all hours of a given day and fill in these time slots with activities you promise to accomplish during that day. At the end of the day, record the activities you actually accomplished and rate them from 0 (low) to 5 (high) on how much mastery and pleasure they helped you experience (Beck, Rush, Shaw, & Emery, 1979; R. A. Brown & Lewinsohn, 1984; Lewinsohn, 1975).

Table 5.2 is an example of a daily activity schedule for a weekend or holiday. A daily activity schedule such as this serves three purposes. First, it commits you to being active. Second, it helps you see which activities are boring and nonfulfilling and which provide a sense of mastery and pleasure. You can use your activity schedule to plan more meaningful activities in the future. A third benefit of the daily activity schedule is providing an opportunity to reward yourself for your accomplishments.

The Value of Self-Efficacy

The value of self-efficacy in pulling ourselves up when we're down was demonstrated in a study that looked at factors related to successful therapy for depression (Steinmetz, Lewinsohn, & Antonuccio, 1983). The most important characteristic of people who got over their depression was how depressed they were in the first place. Not surprisingly, very depressed people did not pull themselves up as easily as moderately depressed people did. Two other factors related to improvement were people's expectations of success and their feelings of internal control. In other words, it was much easier for people to overcome depression when they were determined to feel better and when they took the responsibility to make this happen.

TABLE 5.2   Daily activity schedule for weekend or holiday

Time	Activity	Accomplished?	Mastery	Pleasure
8–9	Eat breakfast	Yes	2	4
9–10	Listen to music	Yes	2	4
10–11	Do laundry	Yes	3	2
11–12	Write letter	No—sat around	0	0
12–1	Meet friend for lunch	Yes	3	5
1–2	Relax with friend	Yes	3	5
2–4	Physical exercise	Yes	5	4
4–5	Relax at home—read newspaper	Yes	2	3
5–6	Housework	1/2	4	3
6–7	Cook special dinner	Yes	5	4
7–8	Eat dinner with friends or family	Yes	3	5
8–10	Watch TV	Yes	2	3
10–11	Read book	Sat around from 10–10:30	0	1
		Read from 10:30–11:30	4	4

Another research study demonstrating the value of self-efficacy involved a program where depressed people were divided into three therapy groups (Zeiss, Lewinsohn, & Munoz, 1979). Each therapy group emphasized a different coping skill: interpersonal relations, balanced thinking, or activities. The most interesting result of this study was that the *kind* of coping skill people learned was not as important as the fact that, as a result of their therapy, they felt a greater sense of self-efficacy and control over their lives. Even though the three therapy groups differed in content, they all provided the same message: *You can learn coping skills that will help you take control of your life.*

Coping Skill 10: Getting Busy and Controlling Your Life

Encouraging Positive Responses from Others

One good reason for getting busy when you are down is to encourage positive responses from others. Researchers have found that people don't usually like to be around someone who is depressed (Segrin & Dillard, 1992). For one thing, people get turned off by a depressed person because low moods are contagious. A depressed person also rubs others the wrong way because he or she doesn't engage in appropriate social interactions (Segrin, 1990). Compared with nondepressed people, those who are depressed engage in fewer social activities and have fewer high-quality relationships (Gotlib & Lee, 1989). People find it stressful and emotionally draining to live with a depressed person, and they report emotional reactions of annoyance, worry, distress, fatigue, discouragement, and strain from having to be the one in charge (Coyne et al., 1987).

A review of research studies comparing conversational responses of depressed and nondepressed people found that depressed people were weak in the following areas (Segrin & Abramson, 1994):

Style of speech: Depressed people speak slowly and softly. Their speech is characterized by many silences, pauses, and hesitations. Their tone of voice is monotonous, dull, and lifeless.

Content of speech: Depressed people make too many negative statements and not enough positive statements. They engage in too much self-disclosure about their problems, and the timing of these disclosures is often inappropriate.

Gaze: Depressed people often appear distant because they avoid eye contact.

Facial expression: The facial expressions of depressed people are sad and bland and lacking in vitality.

Gestures: Depressed people don't make effective use of gestures that add life and zest to what they have to say.

The communication style of depressed people comes across as unresponsive and impolite. Depressed people violate the social graces most people expect during conversations (Segrin & Abramson, 1994). Because depressed people are not much fun to be around, it is not surprising that they are avoided and rejected. Depressives are a burden and a strain on others. And to make matters worse, depressed people feel even more depressed because others dislike them.

The message from this research is loud and clear. If you want others to support you when you're down, you have to use appropriate social skills. This does not mean that you should never share your blue moods. To have close relationships, it is necessary to communicate feelings. The point is that you have to balance the amount of time you lean on others against the time they can lean on you. Depressed people are inordinately dependent and self-critical (Blatt, Quinlan, Chevron, & McDonald, 1982). Nobody likes being around someone like this for too long. So, let others know when you are down. It is valuable to have support people to lean on. But make an effort to be responsive so your support people can also lean on you.

Coping Skill 11: Using Appropriate Social Skills

MAKING EFFECTIVE USE OF SUPPORT SYSTEMS

The use of support systems (Chapter 3) is a valuable strategy for coping with depression. Having an effective support system is a significant factor related to overcoming depression (Billings & Moos, 1985; Monroe, Bromet, Connell, & Steiner, 1986). In addition, it is helpful for those who can't pull themselves up when they are depressed to take advantage of professional help (Robinson, Berman, & Neimeyer, 1990). Some of the difficulties depressed people have in appreciating the possibilities of working with a professional can be alleviated by considering the thoughts about professional help that are presented in Chapter 3 (Halgin, Weaver, Edell, & Spencer, 1987).

Coping Skill 12: Making Effective Use of Support Systems

HOPELESSNESS AND DESPAIR

In this chapter I have taken an upbeat tone to emphasize the value of taking charge when you are down. However, this discussion would not be complete without acknowledging the fact that people can have feelings of hopelessness and despair. Check whether the following statements are true or false descriptions of your current life.

	True	False
1. I look forward to the future with hope and enthusiasm.	_____	_____
2. I expect to get more of the good things in life than the average person.	_____	_____
3. I might as well give up because I can't make things better for myself.	_____	_____
4. All I can see ahead of me is unhappiness rather than pleasantness.	_____	_____
5. My future seems dark to me.	_____	_____
6. I can look forward to more good times than bad times.	_____	_____
7. I never get what I want, so it's foolish to want anything.	_____	_____
8. My past experiences have prepared me well for the future.	_____	_____

These statements come from the Hopelessness Scale (Beck, Weissman, Lester, & Trexler, 1974). When people are feeling hopeless, they agree with statements 3, 4, 5, and 7 and disagree with statements 1, 2, 6, and 8. When people feel hopeless and suicidal, they have no positive expectations about the future. They have lost faith that things will get better, and they are ready to give up. Some warning signs of suicide are: suicide threats, previous suicide attempts, sudden changes in behavior (withdrawal, apathy, moodiness), symptoms of depression (crying, sleeplessness, loss of appetite, hopelessness), and final arrangements (saying good-bye, giving away personal possessions).

Depressed people are less likely to be suicidal if they can report the following feelings that are measured on the Reasons for Living Inventory (Linehan, Goodstein, Nielsen, & Chiles, 1983):

Survival and coping beliefs
> I care enough about myself to live.
> I have the courage to face life.
> I believe I can find other solutions to my problems.

Responsibility to family
> My family depends on me and needs me.
> I love and enjoy my family too much and could not leave them.
> I have a responsibility and commitment to my family.

Child-related concerns
> The effect on my children could be harmful.
> It would not be fair to leave the children for others to take care of.
> I want to watch my children as they grow.

Fear of social disapproval
> Other people would think I am weak and selfish.
> I would not want people to think I did not have control over my life.
> I am concerned about what others would think of me.

Moral objections
> I consider it morally wrong.
> My religious beliefs forbid it.
> I believe only God has the right to end a life.

It is important to be aware of suicide signs so you can direct people at high risk toward professional help.

Coping Skill 13: Recognizing Hopelessness and Signs of Suicide Risk

A CONCLUDING THOUGHT

When you are feeling down, the last thing you need to do is engage in self-blame. Life is full of ups and downs, and you wouldn't be normal if you didn't experience both. It is challenging enough to cope with the downs of life without making things harder by expecting perfection and putting yourself down.

LIST OF SKILLS FOR COPING WHEN YOU'RE DOWN

■ *Coping Skill 1:* Acknowledging When Unpleasant Situations Are Beyond Your Control

■ *Coping Skill 2:* Enhancing Personal Relations with Social Skills, Assertiveness, and Negotiation

■ *Coping Skill 3:* Questioning and Revising Inaccurate Primary Appraisals

■ *Coping Skill 4:* Maintaining a Sense of Control

■ *Coping Skill 5:* Questioning and Revising Irrational Primary Appraisals

- *Coping Skill 6:*   Making Active Use of Problem Solving
- *Coping Skill 7:*   Rewarding Yourself for Your Accomplishments
- *Coping Skill 8:*   Controlling Negative Thinking
- *Coping Skill 9:*   Thinking Positive Thoughts
- *Coping Skill 10:* Getting Busy and Controlling Your Life
- *Coping Skill 11:* Using Appropriate Social Skills
- *Coping Skill 12:* Making Effective Use of Support Systems
- *Coping Skill 13:* Recognizing Hopelessness and Signs of Suicide Risk

SUGGESTIONS FOR FURTHER READING

Burns, D. D. (1980). *Feeling good: The new mood therapy.* New York: Signet/New American Library.

Emery, G. (1987). *Getting undepressed: How a woman can change her life through cognitive therapy.* New York: Touchstone Books.

Gordon, S. (1988). *When living hurts.* New York: Dell.

Greenberger, D., & Padesky, C. A. (1995). *Mind over mood: A cognitive therapy treatment manual for clients.* New York: Guilford.

Greist, J. H., & Jefferson, J. W. (1985). *Depression and its treatment.* New York: Warner Books.

LaHaye, T. (1985). *How to win over depression.* New York: Bantam.

Lewinsohn, P. M. (1984). *The coping with depression course: A psychoeducational intervention for unipolar depression.* Eugene, OR: Castalia.

Lewinsohn, P. M. (1985). *Control your depression.* Englewood Cliffs, NJ: Prentice-Hall.

Papolos, D. F., & Papolos, J. (1986). *Overcoming depression.* New York: Harper & Row.

Wright, H. N. (1988). *Beating the blues: Overcoming depression and stress.* Ventura, CA: Regal.

Coping with Loneliness, Shyness, and Rejection

THE EXPERIENCE OF LONELINESS

How often do you have the following feelings?

	Never	Rarely	Sometimes	Often
1. I lack companionship.	___	___	___	___
2. There is no one I can turn to.	___	___	___	___
3. I feel in tune with the people around me.	___	___	___	___
4. There are people I feel close to.	___	___	___	___
5. No one really knows me well.	___	___	___	___
6. I do not feel alone.	___	___	___	___
7. People are around me but not with me.	___	___	___	___

These statements come from the revised UCLA Loneliness Scale (Russell, Peplau, & Cutrona, 1980). People who feel lonely tend to agree with statements 1, 2, 5, and 7 and to disagree with statements 3, 4, and 6. Loneliness is viewed by most people as a negative experience. A survey by a university student health service determined that college students ranked loneliness as one of their most common health problems (Bradburn, 1969). In a national health survey, 26% of U.S. respondents said they recently felt "very lonely and remote from other people" (Peplau, Russell, & Heim, 1979). Two influential books, *The Lonely Crowd* (Riesman, Denny, & Glazer, 1961) and *The Pursuit of Loneliness* (Slater, 1970), describe how U.S. values of competition, independence, and individuality result in feelings of loneliness and alienation.

TABLE 6.1   Social and emotional loneliness

Social Loneliness	Emotional Loneliness
Common experiences	
Not feeling "in tune" with others	Having no one to turn to
Not having things in common with others	Not feeling close to anyone
Not feeling part of a group of friends	Not being understood as a person
Major need	
Reassurance of worth	Attachment and nurturance
Resulting emotions	
Depression	Depression, anxiety

SOURCE: From "Social and Emotional Loneliness: An Examination of Weiss's Typology of Loneliness," by D. Russell, C. E. Cutrona, J. Rose, and K. Yurko, 1984, *Journal of Personality and Social Psychology, 46,* 1313–1321. Copyright 1984 by the American Psychological Association. Adapted with permission.

Loneliness is an experience with which most of us can identify and one that is detrimental to many people (Jones, 1982).

Researchers have defined two kinds of loneliness: *social loneliness* and *emotional loneliness* (Russell, Cutrona, Rose, & Yurko, 1984; Weiss, 1973). As indicated in Table 6.1, social loneliness is caused by not feeling part of a group and not having people with whom to share activities. Social loneliness occurs when you are dissatisfied with your friendships and when you need reassurance about your worth. Emotional loneliness occurs when you are not satisfied with your personal attachments and when you don't have anyone to lean on for nurturance.

When people are lonely, they may experience any number of the following feelings (Mikulincer & Segal, 1990):

1. A focus on oneself with struggle and conflict, characterized by feelings of low self-confidence, anxiety, guilt, and alienation.
2. A focus on oneself with apathy, characterized by feelings of depression, boredom, and anguish.
3. A focus on others with struggle and conflict, characterized by feelings of anger and being rejected and misunderstood.
4. A focus on others with apathy, characterized by feelings of isolation and social estrangement.

Whether their loneliness is social or emotional, lonely people suffer from low self-esteem, and they are unhappy and often depressed (Peplau et al., 1979; Perlman & Peplau, 1981; Russell et al., 1984; Weeks, Michela, Peplau, & Bragg, 1980).

Loneliness occurs when there is a discrepancy between a person's desired and achieved social relations (Peplau et al., 1979). Loneliness is a subjective experience because it is governed by the appraisals we make when our social relations do not meet our expectations. The subjectivity of loneliness can be appreciated by looking at people's interpretations of this experience.

EXPLANATIONS FOR LONELINESS

Psychologists have conducted a large amount of research on people's explanations for life events. This research is called *attributional research* because it focuses on the causes and meanings we attribute to things that happen to us (Kleinke, 1978, 1986b). Attributions can influence our emotional and coping responses to loneliness (Michela, Peplau, & Weeks, 1982; Peplau et al., 1979; Rubenstein & Shaver, 1980, 1982; Shaver & Rubenstein, 1980). In Table 6.2, loneliness is categorized based on two factors. First, we ask whether our loneliness is caused by something about ourselves (personal cause) or whether our loneliness is due to our life situation (external cause). Second, we judge whether there is anything we can do to change the cause of our loneliness. This kind of analysis leads us to two very important points:

- The explanations we give for our loneliness have a strong influence on our emotional reactions and coping responses.
- The explanations we give for our loneliness are largely subjective.

It is advantageous to confront loneliness with self-responsibility rather than with self-blame. Lonely people often suffer because they believe their loneliness is due to shortcomings within themselves that they can't control (Anderson & Arnoult, 1985; Anderson, Horowitz, & French, 1983). It is useful to understand loneliness as a condition you can change. A good way to outline the skills for coping with loneliness is to follow the experience of loneliness through the appraisal process described in Chapters 1 and 2.

Coping Skill 1: Interpreting Loneliness as Changeable

PRIMARY APPRAISAL OF ALONENESS

In Chapter 2 you learned that your primary appraisal of a life event can affect your resulting emotions. Let's look at the life event of "aloneness" and examine the various ways we can appraise this experience. The example of making a primary appraisal of aloneness in Figure 6.1 is based on Figure 2.2 from Chapter 2.

What kinds of primary appraisals of being alone might lead to feelings of *depression*? Probably saying things to yourself like: "I'm all alone." "Nobody cares about me." "My life is worthless because I don't have anyone close to me." What kinds of appraisals might make you feel *anxious*? Probably saying things to yourself like: "I'm all alone, and I can't stand it." "I can't bear living without someone else close to me." What kinds of appraisals might cause feelings of *dissatisfaction*? Probably saying things to yourself like: "I'm all alone, and I'm not satisfied with my relationships. I have to look at what I need to do to improve this situation." What kinds of appraisals might engender feelings of *solitude*? Probably saying things to yourself like: "I'm all alone. This is a good time for me to do something for myself."

TABLE 6.2   Influence of attributions about loneliness on emotions and coping responses

Attribution About Cause and Changeability	Probable Emotions	Probable Response
Personal: unchangeable I am lonely because I'm unattractive and there's nothing I can do about it. I am lonely because I don't have an outgoing personality. I am lonely because people just don't seem to like me.	Depression, shame, self-depreciation	Passivity: cry, sleep, eat, take drugs, drink, watch TV
Personal: changeable I am lonely because I'm shy, but this is something I can work on. I am lonely because I haven't put enough energy into developing relationships. I am lonely because I haven't spent enough time learning how to get along with people.	Dissatisfaction, impatience	Active coping: self-mastery, self-motivation
External: unchangeable I am lonely because people don't ever try to get to know me. I am lonely because people where I live are too tied up with their own lives. I am lonely because I live in a place where it is impossible to meet people.	Anger, hostility	Solitude: walk, go to movie, exercise, read, listen to music
External: changeable I am lonely because I haven't taken the time to find out where I can meet people. I am lonely because I haven't asked enough people to do things with me. I am lonely because I don't belong to any social groups.	Dissatisfaction, impatience	Active coping: call or visit people, attend groups, attend social events

You may remember from Chapter 2 that Albert Ellis's rational-emotive therapy is deceptively simple. It's easy to see how emotional reactions to aloneness are affected by primary appraisals. However, teaching yourself to reconsider primary appraisals takes time and effort. You would probably agree that dissatisfaction and solitude are more desirable responses to the experience of being alone than anxiety and depression. How can you learn to achieve these appraisals?

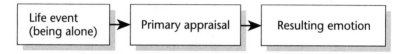

FIGURE 6.1 Primary appraisal of being alone

Appraising Aloneness as Solitude

People differ in how much time they spend with others and how much time they spend alone (Jones, Carpenter, & Quintana, 1985). However, it seems fair to say that everyone could benefit from learning to allow some solitary time for pursuing hobbies, interests, and other activities devoted to personal growth.

Philosopher Tom Wenzel has pointed out that creative people have learned to cherish times of aloneness as "solitude" where they work on self-fulfilling activities (personal communication, 1984). Numerous outstanding people have found their insights in solitude (Moustakas, 1961; Storr, 1988), and aloneness can indeed be a healing experience (Suedfeld, 1982).

It is unfortunate that many people are afraid of being alone and view aloneness as a stigma and a negative experience. The fact is that you are your own best friend. It is important to appreciate solitude as an opportunity to learn to like yourself. One of the best favors you can do for children is to help them develop creative ways for being alone (Rook, 1984; Young, 1982). We live in a fast-food society that encourages passivity and lack of initiative. When we're bored, we flip on the TV to be entertained by others rather than taking the effort to engage in a creative activity. When people get too used to seeking external sources of entertainment, they become helpless when they have to entertain themselves (Skinner, 1986). Consider the following quotations from writers who understood solitude as an opportunity for self-fulfillment (in Henry, 1959, pp. 212–213):

> "In solitude, when we are *least* alone" (Byron).
> "Solitude is as needful to the imagination as society is wholesome for the charac-
> ter" (James Russell Lowell).
> "I never found the companion that was so companionable as solitude" (Thoreau).

Clark Moustakas (1961) offers the following insight about the value of being alone:

> Loneliness keeps open the doors to an expanding life. In utter loneliness, one can find
> answers to living, one can find new values to live by, one can see a new path or direc-
> tion. Something totally new is revealed. (p. 102)

For each of the following pairs of statements, choose the one that best describes you.

1. a. I enjoy being around people.
   b. I enjoy being by myself.
2. a. I try to structure my day so that I always have some time to myself.
   b. I try to structure my day so that I am always doing something with someone.

It is a valuable skill to be able to appreciate the virtues of solitude.

3. a. One feature I look for in a job is the opportunity to interact with interesting
people.
   b. One feature I look for in a job is the opportunity to spend time by myself.
4. a. After spending a few hours surrounded by a lot of people, I usually find
myself stimulated and energetic.
   b. After spending a few hours surrounded by a lot of people, I am usually eager
to get away by myself.
5. a. Time spent alone is often productive for me.
   b. Time spent alone is often time wasted for me.
6. a. I often have a strong desire to get away by myself.
   b. I rarely have a strong desire to get away by myself.
7. a. I have a strong need to be around other people.
   b. I do not have a strong need to be around other people.

These statements come from the Preference for Solitude Scale (Burger, 1995). If you
chose statement *a* for pairs 2, 5, and 6 and statement *b* for pairs 1, 3, 4, and 7, you have
a strong preference for solitude. Some people prefer solitude because they are very
anxious in social situations or just don't get along with others. This is not particularly
healthy. Strive toward developing good social skills and comfort with others while also
learning to appreciate yourself and engage in creative activities when you are alone. If
you can do this, you are less likely to suffer from loneliness.

Coping Skill 2: Learning to Like Yourself by Using Solitude to Pursue Self-Fulfilling Activities

Appraising Aloneness as Dissatisfaction

Even people who are very good at using solitude have times when they say to themselves, "I've spent enough time right now doing things by myself. I'd like some closeness with others." When we appraise aloneness as dissatisfaction, it is time to make a *secondary appraisal* to settle on a course of action.

Secondary appraisal is when you recognize a problem and ask what, if anything, you can do about it. When you are dissatisfied with being alone, three issues should be considered. First, it is important to take a serious look at your social skills. Second, strive to overcome shyness and initiate personal contacts. Third, it is in your best interest to increase your tolerance for rejection. I will consider all of these issues in this chapter.

SOCIAL SKILLS DEFICITS OF LONELY PEOPLE

Lonely people are often deficient in social skills. Researchers have found that lonely people are hard to get to know because they don't disclose things about themselves in an appropriate manner. Lonely people are too cautious about revealing themselves to members of the opposite sex. At the same time, they sometimes make people of the same sex uncomfortable because their "need for a friend" causes them to share intimate details about themselves too soon (Jones, 1982; Solano, Batten, & Parish, 1982). Shy people lack the skill to seek and obtain help, especially from someone of the opposite sex (DePaulo, Dull, Greenberg, & Swain, 1989).

Another example of social skills deficits was seen in a study where college students were introduced to someone of the opposite sex with whom they could talk for 15 minutes (Jones, Hobbs, & Hockenbury, 1982). The conversations were videotaped, and each student was rated on social skills. Results showed that students with high scores on the revised UCLA Loneliness Scale had poorer social skills than students with low scores. Poor social skills were characterized by not showing interest in what the other person was saying and not following up the other person's statements with relevant questions and responses. A second phase of this study was especially interesting because it demonstrated that lonely students could be taught to increase their attention-showing skills by observing videotapes of successful conversations and by practicing their own skills with role playing. As a result of this training, lonely students demonstrated significant improvement in their conversational skills, and they experienced decreased feelings of loneliness.

Some researchers have concluded that lonely people are deficient in social skills not so much because they haven't learned what good social skills are but because they don't put good social skills into action (Vitkus & Horowitz, 1987). Lonely people take a passive and subordinate role with others because they are preoccupied with making a good impression and are doubtful about their ability to do so (Arkin, Lake, & Baumgardner, 1986; Carver & Scheier, 1986). Lonely people don't have a lot of interpersonal trust (Rotenberg, 1994). Because they feel vulnerable, they take a cautious and retiring approach toward others. They "play it safe" by sitting back, staying uninvolved, and remaining anonymous. Shy people are reluctant to take the initiative in social interactions. They let others do the work. And because they are nonresponsive and socially reticent, it is understandable that they don't make a particularly good impression on others (Gough & Thorne, 1986). Shy and lonely people disadvantage themselves in the following ways (Asendorpf, 1987, 1989; Bruch, Gorsky, Collins, & Berger, 1989; Frankel & Prentice-Dunn, 1990; Garcia, Stinson, Ickes, Bissonnette, & Briggs, 1991; Ickes, Robertson, Tooke, & Teng, 1986; Melchior & Cheek, 1990; Solano, 1989):

- They allow negative thoughts and self-doubts to distract them from being responsive in social interactions.
- They don't make effective use of positive self-talk.
- Their nonverbal behaviors keep them at a distance from others.
- They exaggerate their faults and give themselves too little credit for their strengths.
- They allow external factors to control their lives.
- Because they don't employ appropriate social skills, they come across as anxious, awkward, and inhibited in social interactions.

THE COSTS OF PLAYING IT SAFE

Playing it safe as a way of relating to others has all the disadvantages of avoidance that were discussed in Chapter 1. People who avoid taking the initiative in social interactions (*avoiders*) differ from those who are willing to put themselves out and take chances (*initiators*) in their perceptions, self-statements, actions, and internal control (Langston & Cantor, 1989). For example, avoiders have low expectations for experiencing success and pleasure. They tend to perceive social interactions as stressful and don't look forward to the possibility of positive outcomes. In contrast, initiators view social interactions as interesting and absorbing. They aren't preoccupied with negative thoughts, and they don't let themselves become overwhelmed. Avoiders tend to make self-deprecating statements. They feel that others are more appealing than they are, and they blame themselves for unsuccessful social interactions. Initiators are satisfied with their efforts in social interactions. They don't ruminate about unsuccessful social interactions; they move on to new challenges. They accept their strengths and weaknesses.

In terms of actions, avoiders are indecisive—they are too worried about failing. They don't effectively seek social support, and they feel like outsiders who don't fit in. Initiators, in contrast, focus on effective courses of action. They align themselves with others who can help them, and they put themselves out to become part of a group.

Avoiders are passive and follow the lead of others. They try to please others. In general, avoiders get lost in the crowd. But initiators are active and don't passively follow others. They gain self-worth from their own standards. They are willing to assert their individuality.

Because of their style, avoiders are anxious. They suffer from stress and dissatisfaction about their social interactions. However, there is hope. By practicing good social skills and learning to tolerate rejection, avoiders can turn themselves into initiators.

Coping Skill 3: Being an Initiator

SOCIAL SKILLS TRAINING

In recognition of the value of social skills, psychologists have developed training programs that teach people to improve their skills in social interactions. Participants in these programs usually sign a contract outlining their goals and their commitment to the program. Training groups are then set up. The group leader usually begins by describing effective social skills for various situations. He or she then models these behaviors in such a way that participants can adapt them to their personal styles and practice them in the group with the benefit of group feedback. Video recordings are often used. Group participants are also taught to use their imagination to prepare themselves for situations in which effective social skills are required. After sufficient practice and feedback, participants are given homework assignments for practicing effective social skills in their daily lives. Participants receive continued feedback from the group and are encouraged to enlist friends and family members for support. Participants are taught to work gradually from easy to more difficult social interactions, to monitor their progress, and to reward themselves for their efforts. When the training group ends, group members might agree to meet at a later date for a follow-up or "booster" session (Eisler & Frederiksen, 1980; L'Abate & Milan, 1985).

SOME USEFUL SOCIAL SKILLS

Researchers have identified the following factors as being associated with successful social interactions (Conger & Farrell, 1981; Greenwald, 1977; Kupke, Calhoun, & Hobbs, 1979; Kupke & Hobbs, 1979):

- Giving personal attention to what the other person is saying.
- Encouraging the other person to express his or her opinions.
- Holding up your end of the conversation, but balancing interest in the other person's statements against talking about yourself.
- Looking your best.

Other important social skills include engaging in a comfortable level of eye contact and self-disclosure. When it comes to eye contact, most people prefer potential friends to give them enough eye contact to feel "in contact" but not so much eye contact that they end up feeling stared at (Kleinke, 1986a). The same is true for self-disclosure (Kleinke, 1979, 1986b; Kleinke & Kahn, 1980). It is desirable to share enough about yourself with others so they can relate to you on a personal level. However, don't overwhelm new acquaintances with sensitive disclosures, and avoid boring them with long-winded accounts about yourself that are trivial. To have good social skills, you need to be in tune with the kinds of behaviors that are comfortable and uncomfortable for other people.

When developing your social skills, it is worthwhile to appreciate the value of being *immediate*. When you are immediate, you are actively engaged with others. You attend to them both verbally and nonverbally and communicate a sense that you are "with" them. The social skills outlined here all help to foster immediacy in interpersonal interactions. Other ways to communicate immediacy are by learning and using people's names and by using immediate language. When meeting people, it is a good policy to learn their names. We have a stronger sense that people are interested in us when they take the trouble to learn and use our names. In one research study, for example, it was found that engaged couples were viewed as being closer and better matched when they referred to one another by name during an interview than when they did not (Kleinke, Meeker, & LaFong, 1974). However, using people's names must be done with discretion (Kleinke, Staneski, & Weaver, 1972; Staneski, Kleinke, & Meeker, 1977). It leaves a bad impression when people call others by name too much. The best approach is to learn and use the name of someone you meet once or twice during your interaction. In this way you are able to communicate a personal interest in that person without coming across as phony or overbearing.

Immediate language is a way of communicating with people in a personal and direct manner (Wiener & Mehrabian, 1968). Nonimmediate language is distant and indirect. When you use nonimmediate language, you communicate a feeling of being distant and removed from the person to whom you are speaking. Here are some examples of nonimmediate language:

"That report was not bad."
"My primary feeling toward you is one of respect."
"It seems like you are a talented person."
"I kind of like the way you work with others."
"Our friendship is fairly close."
"I am, you know, kind of upset."
"That's a pretty sweater."

These statements would be more immediate if they were communicated in the following way:

"Your report was excellent."
"I respect you."
"I can see that you are a talented person."
"I have great respect for your skill in working with others."
"I feel a close friendship with you."
"I'm angry with you."
"Your sweater is pretty."

When you are immediate with others, you avoid distancing yourself and qualifying your feelings. Strive to be honest, forthcoming, and direct.

Coping Skill 4: Perfecting Your Social Skills

LEARNING TO BE RESPONSIVE

Of all the social skills taught in social skills training groups, probably the most important overall skill is that of being *responsive* (Davis & Perkowitz, 1979). The power of responsiveness was demonstrated in a study where college men were introduced to an attractive woman with whom they chatted for 5 minutes (Gold, Ryckman, & Mosley,

1984). For one group of men, the woman made a special effort to show interest, maintain eye contact, and hold up her end of the conversation. A second group of men met the same woman but were not given the opportunity to chat with her and receive her interest and attention. Because the woman was attractive, all the men liked her. However, the men who had received her attention were attracted to her even more. In fact, the 5 minutes of attention were enough to outweigh any disagreements that existed between the men and the woman about personal opinions and attitudes.

By being responsive, you can encourage others to like you and also help them to like themselves. When you are able to provide someone with the experience of a positive interaction, it makes that person feel good (Haemmerlie & Montgomery, 1984).

Responsiveness means being "with" another person by showing attention, maintaining eye contact, and hearing what he or she is saying. Carl Rogers (1961) has pointed out that we often respond to others by stating our own opinion without acknowledging their feelings. For example, assume someone says, "I liked that movie," or "I felt bad about what happened to so-and-so." A responsive reply would be, "What did you like about the movie?" or "I'm sorry you felt bad. Tell me about it." However, most of us would be more likely to simply state our own opinions by saying things like, "I didn't think the movie was so great," or "Yeah, I thought the movie was pretty good," or "I felt bad too, but in many ways what happened was to be expected." A responsive reply communicates empathy. It communicates an understanding of the other person's feelings (Davis & Holtgraves, 1984).

We can all understand why people like others who are responsive. Responsiveness communicates personal interest and positive feelings. Responsiveness also reinforces certainty and self-confidence. People like to know you are paying attention and taking them seriously.

What does it take to be responsive? Here are some suggestions (Davis & Perkowitz, 1979):

Motivation: Instead of simply expressing your own opinions, be willing to expend the energy to hear what the other person is saying.

Attentiveness: Maintain eye contact and listen carefully. What are the issues, feelings, and problems to which he or she desires a response?

Empathy: How is the other person feeling? If you are not sure, you need to ask.

Skill: Social skills should be practiced so you can respond in an appropriate manner.

One last point about responsiveness has a lot to do with the issue of internal versus external control discussed in Chapter 3. To be responsive, *you* have to take the initiative in social interactions. You can't just say, "That person didn't seem very interested in me, so I didn't respond." Instead, take the attitude that if you are responsive the other person will probably reciprocate. Research shows that people who are skillful at initiating interactions are willing to take the responsibility for getting a conversation started (Lefcourt, Martin, Fick, & Saleh, 1985). People who are good at getting others to "open up" have practiced their social skills to the point where they can answer yes to the following questions (L. C. Miller, Berg, & Archer, 1983; Pegalis, Shaffer, Bazzini, & Greenier, 1994):

- Are you a good listener?
- Are you accepting of others?
- Do you help people feel relaxed?
- Do you encourage people to tell you how they are feeling?
- Are you sympathetic to people's problems?

Of course, when you take the initiative to be responsive, there are times when you will be rejected. Some tips for tolerating rejection are presented later in this chapter.

Coping Skill 5: Practicing the Social Skill of Being Responsive

OVERCOMING SHYNESS

Shyness can be defined as being fearful about meeting people and suffering discomfort in their presence. An important thing to know about shyness is that it is an experience shared by most people. It may surprise you to learn that more than 80% of Americans in a survey by Philip Zimbardo (1977) said they knew what it means to feel shy. Only 7% claimed that they had never experienced shyness. Shy people describe themselves as having trouble making conversation and maintaining eye contact and as experiencing discomfort when attempting to initiate interactions with others. Shy people experience the following symptoms (Cheek, Melchior, & Carpentieri, 1986):

Physical discomfort: Upset stomach, pounding heart, sweating, and blushing
Self-consciousness: Self-deprecating thoughts, worries about being negatively evaluated by others
Poor social skills: Awkwardness, social inhibition

Shy people are likely to agree with the following statements (Cheek & Buss, 1981):

- I feel tense when I'm with people I don't know well.
- I am socially awkward.
- It is hard for me to act natural when I am meeting new people.
- I have doubts about my social competence.
- I feel inhibited in social interactions.
- I find it hard to talk to strangers.

People say they feel shy primarily when they are with strangers, members of the opposite sex, and authority figures. Zimbardo reports that feelings of shyness are common among some of the most seemingly outgoing television and movie personalities. To feel shy inside and still push yourself to be outgoing takes special coping skills. Let's look at what they are.

Adaptive Explanations for Shyness

Earlier in this chapter you learned the value of understanding loneliness as personal and changeable. An adaptive way to explain shyness is to say something like this: "It is natural to feel shy at times, but I can learn how to be outgoing in spite of these feelings." It is not adaptive to explain shyness with the following kinds of statements: "Being shy is part of my personality, and I'm not likely to change." "The reason I am shy is because other people don't understand me." Shy people take a pessimistic attitude by assuming they will always be shy and that their social life depends on the initiative of others (Teglasi & Hoffman, 1982). Shyness is overcome when people learn to take control over their social interactions (Bruch & Pearl, 1995).

The value of rational explanations for shyness was demonstrated in the following research study (Hoffman & Teglasi, 1982). People suffering from shyness were assigned to one of three different therapy groups. Shy people in one group were helped to understand their shyness as an outcome of their childhood experiences. Those in a second group learned to understand their shyness as a product of their thinking styles and self-perceptions. The third group of shy people received counseling that did not focus on finding explanations for shyness. Which therapy group was most successful? In general, the first two approaches, which helped the shy people find an explanation for their shyness, were more effective than the third approach, which did not. However, there is reason to argue that the approach taken in the second therapy group was most advantageous because it encouraged shy people to take responsibility for their shyness and to commit themselves to reevaluating their thinking styles and self-perceptions. Shy people in the first group might be tempted to cop out by "blaming" their shyness on their childhood experiences.

To have satisfactory interpersonal relations it is useful to work on your social skills. It is also important to take control of your thinking style and the interpretations you make about your social situation (C. R. Glass & Shea, 1986).

Coping Skill 6: Taking Control of Your Thinking Style

Opening Lines

You are probably aware that marriages in many societies are arranged by family elders. Sons and daughters have nothing to say about their future spouses. Although you probably prefer to choose your own romantic partners, you can appreciate the fact that arranged marriages avoid all the hassles of meeting people and the discomforts of dating until you find Mr. or Ms. "Right." But meeting people can be an adventure if you have the proper attitude.

My interest in opening lines began with the realization of their potential for expanding social networks. Most of the time, our social contacts are limited to people we meet at work, school, or through family members and friends. Although you may see people whom you would *like* to meet walking down the street, in stores, in parks, on buses, and in numerous other places, it might not occur to you that it is actually possible. In theory, your social marketplace is wherever you happen to be at a given time. How can you put this theory into practice? When you run across a person you would like to meet, you have to initiate social contact. To initiate contact, you must start a conversation, and to start a conversation, you have to say something—an opening line. An opening line is a negotiation. It is a way of expressing interest in another person in a nonthreatening way. The other person then has the opportunity to communicate whether she or he is willing to reciprocate. When using opening lines as a process of negotiation, you are faced with two challenges. First, you have to take a risk and say something. Second, you have to learn to tolerate rejection. In the remainder of this chapter, I will consider both of these challenges.

Preferred and Nonpreferred Opening Lines

More than a thousand people were surveyed about their attitudes toward opening lines for men meeting women and for women meeting men (Kleinke, Meeker, & Staneski, 1986). A statistical analysis was used to separate the opening lines into three categories: innocuous, direct, and cute/flippant. Some of the opening lines that were most preferred and least preferred are listed here:

Most preferred opening lines	Type of approach
"Hi."	Innocuous
"Can you give me directions to _____?"	Innocuous
"Can you help me with _____?"	Innocuous
"Did you see (a particular movie) or read (a particular book)?"	Innocuous
"I feel a little embarrassed about this, but I'd like to meet you."	Direct
"That's a very pretty (sweater, shirt, etcetera) you have on."	Direct
"You have really nice (hair, eyes, etcetera)."	Direct
"As we're both sitting alone, would you care to join me?"	Direct
"Is it OK if I sit with you?"	Direct

Least preferred opening lines	Type of approach
"I'm easy. Are you?"	Cute/flippant
"I've got an offer you can't refuse."	Cute/flippant
"What's your sign?"	Cute/flippant
"Didn't we meet in a previous life?"	Cute/flippant
"Your place or mine?"	Cute/flippant
"Is that really your hair?"	Cute/flippant
"You remind me of a woman (man) I used to date."	Cute/flippant
"Isn't it cold? Let's make some body heat."	Cute/flippant

When you examine these opening lines, two things will become clear. First, the respondents did not like opening lines that were cute/flippant. Second, innocuous and direct opening lines were both viewed as acceptable. However, two additional points must be considered. Although none of the respondents liked cute/flippant opening lines, women disliked cute/flippant lines even more than men did. In other words, the men underestimated how much women dislike cute/flippant opening lines. Also, although innocuous opening lines were generally viewed as acceptable, women liked this kind of approach more than men. Direct lines were equally liked by men and women.

People's reactions to opening lines have been tested in surveys, in studies where men and women were observed using various kinds of opening lines in videotapes, and in the "real-life" situation of a dating bar. Results from these studies suggest some specific advice for men and women (Cunningham, 1989; Kleinke & Dean, 1990; Kleinke et al., 1986).

Advice for Men

Men should be aware that most women prefer a soft, nonthreatening approach and that it is risky to come on too strong. They should realize that although the macho approach may work in the movies or on TV, this has little to do with real life. Men should also be aware of the fact that most stories about successful pickups they hear from friends or read about in magazines exist more in the realm of fantasy than in reality. Cute/flippant opening lines may help protect the user from admitting loneliness and the desire for a personal relationship, but they are likely to lose the woman. Men who have difficulty tolerating rejection are advised to stick with innocuous lines. Innocuous lines minimize vulnerability and give the woman an opportunity to respond without being turned off or driven away. For men who are willing to admit vulnerability, direct opening lines should be considered.

Advice for Women

The people surveyed said that they felt it is equally appropriate for women to approach men as it is for men to approach women. My first advice to women is to recognize this fact. Women don't need to sit and wait for a man to get up the nerve to approach them. After all, the man with the nerve might not be the right man. Women should seriously consider taking control of their social contacts. Of course, in taking the initiative for meeting men, women face some challenges. Many men are not used to being approached by women and don't know how to respond in a gracious manner. Women learn from a young age how to be polite and yet get away from men they don't like. Most men have not developed this skill. It is important for women to approach men in a nonthreatening manner. To do this takes sensitivity. The woman wants the man to know she is interested in him, but she does not want to come across as overbearing. Another challenge facing women is that men tend to interpret any interest shown by a woman as sexual (Abbey, 1982, 1987; Shotland & Craig, 1988). Women are advised to develop their self-esteem and confidence so they can deal with the discomfort experienced by some of the men they want to meet.

Coping Skill 7: Recognizing the Value of Opening Lines

MAKING CONVERSATION

A series of studies was conducted to find out how people are evaluated when they talk a small amount, a medium amount, or a large amount in a conversation with someone they have just met (Kleinke, Kahn, & Tully, 1979). Conversations between men and women were taped. In some of the tapes, the man talked 80% of the time and the woman talked 20% of the time. In other tapes, the woman talked 80% of the time and the man 20%. In a third group of tapes, the man and woman each talked 50% of the time. Research participants were asked to listen to these tapes and evaluate the men and women on a rating form. Although participants were not told that the study was about talking, the amount of talking had a strong effect on how the men and women were evaluated. Two findings were especially interesting. First, people talking 50% of the time were liked more than people who talked 20% or 80% of the time. Second, the 20% talkers were evaluated as being exceptionally submissive and introverted. The negative ratings given to men and women who spoke 20% of the time were surprising and suggested that people in first meetings are expected to hold up their end of the conversation. It seems that a good listener is not necessarily a person who is quiet but rather one who is responsive and adds to the other's statements.

You might think that men who talked 80% of the time would not be evaluated as unfavorably as women doing so. Men are often stereotyped as being more domineering than women, and a high amount of talking by men could be expected and taken for granted. This was not so. Research participants did not favor 80% talkers whether they were men or women.

The results of this study reinforce advice about being responsive. Getting along with others requires good conversational skills. Research has found that conversational skills of shy people are seriously lacking (Pilkonis, 1977). Shy people are reluctant to initiate conversations, they don't break silences, and they don't respond with enthusiasm to other people's statements.

Conversational Styles of Introverts and Extraverts

A study comparing conversational styles of extraverted and introverted women found very different styles when the women were getting acquainted with a new person (Thorne, 1987). Extraverted women came across as cheerful, enthusiastic, and sociable. They talked about activities and interests that were fun. Introverted women were more reserved. They asked questions and acted more as interviewers. When they did volunteer information, they tended to focus on their problems. Conversations between two introverts were the most uncomfortable because both people held back and waited for the other to take the initiative. Although such a study has not been conducted with men, the results would probably be similar.

When meeting new people, match your conversation to their style. When talking with introverts, you have to draw them out and not be put off by their reticence. With extraverts, you can spend more time being a good listener, but you still have to hold up your end of the conversation. Make the effort to be responsive, and share things about yourself so the other person gets to know you.

IMPROVING CONVERSATIONAL SKILLS

Fortunately, conversational skills can be learned and improved. People who have trouble making conversation often complain that it is hard to think of anything to say. There are three solutions to this problem. First, it is important to have realistic expectations. People who are "talkers" have learned not to censor many of their thoughts before they speak. They have also learned to reduce their expectations for "meaningful" conversations and to be satisfied with small talk. The purpose of small talk is to communicate to others that you are interested in them. When you first meet somebody, it is not so important *what* you say as long as you demonstrate your willingness to carry on a conversation. A deeper and more meaningful relationship will come later.

A second solution for improving conversational skills is to understand the characteristics of "high-quality" communication. Good interpersonal communication is made up of two components: *communication quality* and *depth and value of communication* (Sprecher & Duck, 1994). Communication quality is defined as talking in a way that gets across a sense of being relaxed, attentive, informal, smooth, open, understanding, and interesting. People who engage in communication with high quality know how to keep a conversation going by breaking silences when necessary and by giving the other person a sense that he or she is being understood. Depth and value of communication is characterized by a conversation that is personal, in-depth, and valuable. One way to help others experience their conversation with you as deep and valuable is to take a genuine interest in things that are meaningful and important to them.

The third solution for those with conversational difficulties is to *practice* talking with others. Here are some ideas for practicing talking skills (Zimbardo, 1977):

Use the telephone: Call the public library and ask the reference librarian for some information you would like to have. Call a theater and ask for show times. See if you can make the person on the telephone laugh. Call a radio talk show. Express an opinion and notice the announcer's reaction.

Say "hello": Say "hi" or "good morning" to people you see at work or school. Smile and say "hi" to people you pass on the street. Notice their reaction. If they don't respond, that's OK. It's still fun to see that you can do it.

Give compliments: Compliment someone standing in line at a bank or grocery store. Maybe the person is wearing some unusual jewelry or attractive clothing. Ask them where it came from.

Ask questions: Ask questions about a person's dog, running shoes, bicycle, or portable radio. Be open to learning new things. People love to talk about their activities and hobbies. Ask questions that require explanations rather than simple yes or no answers.

Share a common experience: Look for something you can share with a person you want to meet. Perhaps there is something unusual about the weather or the experience of standing in a long line or being in a crowd that you can talk about.

Read, ask, and tell: Read the newspaper, read movie and book reviews, learn about political situations in the world and events in your community. Ask people for their opinions on these issues, and share your knowledge with them.

Coping Skill 8: Developing the Ability to Make Conversation

LEARNING TO TOLERATE REJECTION

Lonely and shy people have difficulty tolerating rejection. One reason for this difficulty is that shy and lonely people take a different view of personal interactions than nonlonely people do. Nonlonely people take a *mastery-oriented* approach whereas lonely people take a *performance-oriented* approach toward social interactions (Chapter 4).

Research indicates that people who can handle rejection tend to look at social interactions as an opportunity to develop closeness with others and to share pleasant feelings (Goldfried, Padawer, & Robins, 1984). Shy and lonely people are more likely to view social interactions as a threatening experience where they are being judged and evaluated. This kind of attitude causes anxiety and defensiveness. Instead of relaxing and having fun with others, shy and lonely people tend to be uptight and negative (Goswick & Jones, 1981; Hansson & Jones, 1981; Jones, Sansone, & Helm, 1983). Stop yourself from becoming preoccupied with your own feelings of wanting acceptance and approval. Instead, focus your attention on the people with whom you are interacting and ask yourself what you can do to help *them* feel comfortable (Alden & Cappe, 1986).

Another reason shy and lonely people can't tolerate rejection is because they make negative primary appraisals. Referring back to Figure 2.2 in Chapter 2, we can define an experience of rejection as a life event. What are some of the worst things you can say to yourself when you are rejected? Some possible examples are: "If I'm rejected, it's just awful." "I can't stand it unless everyone likes me." "If I'm rejected, it means I'm unattractive, unlikable, and no good." These kinds of appraisals are likely to result in depression, anger, anxiety, and low self-esteem, which are exactly the kinds of feelings lonely people suffer. Weigh those unadaptive thoughts against the following more adaptive beliefs: "Even if I'm rejected, I can be proud for trying." "The more I can tolerate rejection, the more people I can meet." "Some people will like me and some people won't like me, but I feel I am accomplishing something when I can get out there and try."

How rational are the following expectations? "I can't be happy unless everyone I meet is responsive to me." "If every conversation I attempt doesn't lead to a good relationship, it is a failure." Can you substitute the following, more realistic expectations? "If I just say 'hi' to someone, I am achieving a goal." "I have to play the odds. The more people I talk to, the more people I will meet." "Some conversations go further than others. I must be patient and find satisfaction in making the attempt."

You can practice coping with rejection by using the self-relaxation skills described in Chapter 3. Sit down in a quiet, relaxing place, close your eyes, and imagine that you are approaching someone you would like to meet and are being rejected. What does it feel like? Start with mild thoughts of rejection, and counteract them with relaxation and with talking to yourself in a constructive manner. Work your way up slowly until you can imagine harder rejections while still remaining relaxed. Remember what it feels like to be relaxed when you are trying to meet people. Keep in touch with your feelings of self-doubt and anxiety, and use those feelings as cues to put your relaxation skills to work. Relaxation skills will help you realize that although being rejected is not fun you can stand it. Teach yourself that the mild inconvenience of being rejected is a worthwhile price to pay for the opportunity to meet many special and interesting people.

Coping Skill 9: Learning to Tolerate Rejection

LIST OF SKILLS FOR COPING WITH LONELINESS AND SHYNESS

- *Coping Skill 1:*   Interpreting Loneliness as Changeable
- *Coping Skill 2:*   Learning to Like Yourself by Using Solitude to Pursue Self-Fulfilling Activities
- *Coping Skill 3:*   Being an Initiator
- *Coping Skill 4:*   Perfecting Your Social Skills
- *Coping Skill 5:*   Practicing the Social Skill of Being Responsive
- *Coping Skill 6:*   Taking Control of Your Thinking Style
- *Coping Skill 7:*   Recognizing the Value of Opening Lines
- *Coping Skill 8:*   Developing the Ability to Make Conversation
- *Coping Skill 9:*   Learning to Tolerate Rejection

SUGGESTIONS FOR FURTHER READING

Gambrill, E., & Richey, C. (1985). *Taking charge of your social life.* Belmont, CA: Wadsworth.
Jones, W. H., Cheek, J. M., & Briggs, S. R. (Eds.). (1986). *Shyness: Perspectives on research and treatment.* New York: Plenum.
Kleinke, C. L. (1986). *Meeting and understanding people.* New York: W. H. Freeman.
Moustakas, C. E. (1961). *Loneliness.* Englewood Cliffs, NJ: Prentice-Hall.
Peplau, L. A., & Perlman, D. (Eds.). (1982). *Loneliness: A sourcebook of current theory, research, and therapy.* New York: Wiley-Interscience.
Storr, A. (1988). *Solitude: A return to the self.* New York: Free Press.
Zimbardo, P. G. (1977). *Shyness: What it is, what to do about it.* Reading, MA: Addison-Wesley.

7

Coping with Anxiety

We all feel anxious at various times in our lives. Because anxiety can be both objective and subjective, it is an interesting experience to understand in terms of the processes of primary appraisal discussed in Chapter 2. Some life events give us good reason to believe we are in jeopardy. Anxiety under these circumstances is a normal response. It works to mobilize the body for defense, and it signals us to pay attention and protect ourselves. When your primary appraisal of impending danger is realistic and accurate, the challenge is to come up with a suitable coping response. Anxiety here is helping to energize you during the coping process. It is when your primary appraisal of a life event is not accurate or realistic that anxiety can be undesirable. Anxiety causes trouble when you are tense and stressed for no good reason. Then you may suffer needlessly because your mind and body are keyed up to ward off a threat or danger you have falsely created.

SOME DEFINITIONS OF ANXIETY

I want to begin this discussion of anxiety with some definitions. The terms *fear* and *anxiety* are often used interchangeably. One distinction that can be made between these terms is that fear usually refers to the primary appraisal of actual peril or danger. Anxiety is related more to the resulting emotional state of tenseness and distress. *Phobias* are exaggerated and often disabling fears of specific events or objects. Phobias are characterized by the urge to avoid these fear-provoking experiences. *Panic* is a sudden overpowering fright accompanied by frantic attempts to find safety (Beck & Emery, 1990; Greist, Jefferson, & Marks, 1986). Some of the symptoms of a panic attack include palpitations, pounding heart, sweating, trembling or shaking, shortness of breath, feeling of choking, chest pain, nausea, feeling dizzy, and fear of losing control (American Psychiatric Association, 1994).

In this chapter you will learn how to analyze your appraisals of life events so you can ask yourself whether your feelings of anxiety are adaptive and self-protective or whether they are unnecessary and needlessly stressful. People whose lives are *seriously* debilitated by anxiety, phobias, or panic should seek professional help.

THE EXPERIENCE OF ANXIETY

The first step in coping with anxiety is learning to recognize the symptoms of anxiety and how they affect you. As noted above, anxiety can energize and prepare you to meet a challenge; anxiety can also be a distraction that gets in the way of normal functioning. You know when you are anxious by a combination of symptoms in your body, your thinking, and your sense of well-being (Beck & Emery, 1990).

The body: When you are anxious, your body reacts by heart palpitations, rapid breathing, shortness of breath, lump in throat, loss of appetite, nausea, insomnia, pressure to urinate, flushed face, sweating, trouble with speech, or restlessness.

Thinking: Anxiety can cause confusion, impaired memory, difficulty concentrating, distractibility, fear of losing control, self-consciousness, hypervigilance, and repetitive thoughts.

Well-being: When you are anxious, you might feel edgy, impatient, nervous, alarmed, terrified, jittery, jumpy, frightful, depressed, tense, or wound up.

It is important to be aware of these reactions so you can recognize when you are anxious. When you recognize these symptoms of anxiety, ask yourself whether they represent a natural reaction to a real threat or whether they are causing needless stress. How can you learn to do this? The first step is to look carefully at your primary appraisals.

Coping Skill 1: Recognizing Symptoms of Anxiety

You can get a measure of your anxiety by checking how much you are bothered by the following symptoms:

	Not at all	Moderately	Strongly
1. Feeling hot	____	____	____
2. Feeling dizzy or light-headed	____	____	____
3. Feeling unsteady	____	____	____
4. Having trembling hands	____	____	____
5. Having a flushed face	____	____	____
6. Fearing the worst happening	____	____	____
7. Being terrified	____	____	____
8. Feeling nervous	____	____	____
9. Fearing losing control	____	____	____
10. Being unable to relax	____	____	____

These items all come from the Beck Anxiety Inventory (Beck, Epstein, Brown, & Steer, 1988). Items 1 through 5 measure somatic symptoms, and items 6 though 10 measure subjective anxiety. This inventory was developed as an index of anxiety, independent of feelings of depression.

Accepting Anxiety as Part of Life

It is challenging enough to suffer anxiety that interferes with life functioning; you don't need to compound your problems by thinking badly about yourself (see Chapter 1) *because* you are anxious. If you do that, you will not only suffer from anxiety but also from self-imposed low self-esteem. When you catch yourself thinking irrational thoughts, such as "I'm weak," "I'm neurotic," "No one else gets anxious like I do," stop and think more rationally. Anxiety is part of life. Everyone knows what it is like to be anxious. You are not weak, foolish, or neurotic because you are anxious—you are human. You have enough work to do to master the skills for coping with anxiety; don't waste precious energy on self-imposed blame and punishment.

Coping Skill 2: Avoiding Self-Imposed Blame and Punishment

PRIMARY APPRAISAL

When faced with a problem or a challenge, your primary appraisal determines whether you are in jeopardy or danger. If you determine that you have good reason to be anxious, you should remember not to berate yourself for being anxious and to use the techniques for living with anxiety outlined later in this chapter.

If you determine that your anxiety is unnecessary and is causing needless suffering, you need to practice rational thinking (see Chapter 2) so that faulty thinking patterns don't cause you to feel miserable. Here are some examples of how we sometimes make ourselves suffer from anxiety (Beck, 1979; Beck & Emery, 1990; Deffenbacher, Demm, & Brandon, 1986):

> *Automatic thinking:* When you are preoccupied with something you are trying to avoid, you lose objectivity. You can't get this feared object or event out of your mind. Your preoccupation becomes involuntary and automatic and starts to consume your life.
>
> *Overgeneralization:* You see danger in things that only remotely resemble the object or event you are avoiding. You get anxious about sounds, sights, smells, and people's actions that remind you of these things you fear. You have fantasies about how a perfectly normal event could harm you.
>
> *Catastrophizing:* You blow things out of proportion, always thinking of the worst possible outcome. Everything seems terrible, awful, or horrible. You are beyond any possibility of reassurance because you have convinced yourself that the only possible outcome is disastrous.

Selective perception: You have an aptitude for picking out the negatives. There may be three positive aspects and one negative aspect of an event, and you will focus on the negative one. If you are feeling really anxious, you may even search for negative facts just to prove to yourself that it's right to be anxious.

Rigidity: You see things only in black and white. You can't tolerate uncertainty or ambiguity. Things are either good or bad, and because of your overgeneralization, selective perception, and lack of proportion, most things end up looking bad.

Perfectionism: You convince yourself that you must be perfect and feel anxiety and stress over the fear that you will not live up to your expectations.

Anxious overconcern: You ruminate about your fears. You dwell on negative events that could occur in your life.

Helplessness: You feel that the negative things that could happen to you are beyond your control. You lose track of the possibility of using your coping skills to manage your anxiety.

Circular reasoning: You say to yourself, "The fact that I'm not handling this proves that I can't handle it." You use your anxiety as evidence that something is wrong with you.

Unrealistic expectations: You demand perfection. You insist on a life free of challenges, tests, and traumas.

Coping Skill 3: Making Rational Primary Appraisals

UNDERSTANDING HOW ANXIETY CAN GET THE BEST OF YOU

Anxiety is compounded by irrational thinking. It is easy to get caught up in the kind of vicious cycle shown in Figure 7.1. An irrational appraisal of a life event makes you feel needlessly anxious. This anxiety then begins to "prove" that something must be wrong, and it reinforces your irrational appraisal. It can get to the point where the anxiety you are perpetuating with irrational thinking becomes an overriding problem that has nothing to do with reality. Anxiety gets the best of you when you blow things so far out of proportion that *fear of anxiety* is more debilitating than any realistic fear you could possibly have about the actual life event (Chambless & Gracely, 1989).

This vicious cycle is intensified by the fact that people who suffer from excess worry are in the habit of catastrophizing by thinking the worst. They become preoccupied with imagining all the horrible things that could occur, and they convince themselves that their apprehensions ("What if such-and-such happens?") will actually come true (Vasey & Borkovec, 1992). An important skill for coping with anxiety is not getting caught up in this vicious cycle.

Coping Skill 4: Preventing Anxiety from Getting the Best of You

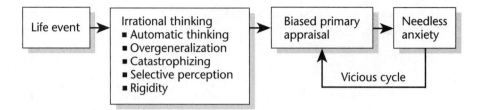

FIGURE 7.1 Vicious cycle where needless anxiety resulting from inaccurate primary appraisal provides "proof" for biased appraisal

FIVE RULES FOR COPING WITH ANXIETY

Before looking at techniques that can help you live with anxiety, it is worthwhile to learn five basic rules: don't be an avoider, use positive confrontation, be mastery-oriented, keep records, and be willing to work.

Don't Be an Avoider

In Chapter 1 you were advised of the pitfalls of avoidance. Avoidance is a particularly problematic coping style when it comes to anxiety. It does alleviate anxiety in the short run, but because it does not address the problem or issue, you end up paying a price in the long run. To put it another way, avoidance is a very tempting way of coping with anxiety because it provides immediate relief. It is very reinforcing to hide from people, places, and tasks that make life difficult. Unfortunately, these sources of anxiety will not go away until you confront them. As long as you avoid them, they will haunt you. You won't feel completely relaxed because you are constantly on guard. You never know when a source of anxiety might appear.

Another way to appreciate the disadvantages of being an avoider is by looking at what has been called the *repressive coping style* (see Chapter 1). Repressors are people who suffer from anxiety but deny it. They present themselves as rational, controlled, and undisturbed by stressors in their lives. Unfortunately, although denial might be a useful coping response in the short run, it has negative consequences. Repressors work so hard to convince themselves and others that life problems don't bother them that they don't have much energy left to take pleasure in things they find enjoyable. Their social relationships are often superficial because they don't fully experience and communicate their feelings. Repressors engage in few creative and stimulating activities. Repressors also pay a price with their health. They are vulnerable to symptoms of stress such as hypertension, aches and pains, and confusion.

Coping Skill 5: Not Being an Avoider

Use Positive Confrontation

If avoidance is not a good way of coping with anxiety, what is? You know the answer to this question from your life experience. How did you learn to swim, to give your first

Many skills discussed in this chapter can help you keep anxiety from getting the best of you.

speech, and to take risks in front of others? You gritted your teeth, took a deep breath, and did it. And you probably learned that it wasn't as hard as you expected.

A friend was having a hard time with his boss at work. I was struck by his response. Instead of avoiding his boss, he used every opportunity to put himself in the boss's presence. As he explained, "I'm going to throw myself into the fire until I master it."

There are two good reasons for using positive confrontation to cope with anxiety. First, confrontation is a way of desensitizing yourself to people, places, and tasks that make life difficult. Second, positive confrontation affects your self-concept. Think how differently you will feel when you see yourself taking an active response to your anxiety instead of being an avoider. There is plenty of psychological research to document a fact we all know from our own experience (Beck & Emery, 1990; Kleinke, 1978):

> *If you want to be,*
> *Act as if you are,*
> *And you will become.*

Coping Skill 6: Using Positive Confrontation

Be Mastery-Oriented

In Chapter 4 you learned that when you are mastery-oriented, your energies are focused on developing skills and turning challenges into learning experiences. This orientation toward life challenges was contrasted with being performance-oriented, where the primary goal is to avoid making mistakes. Someone who is performance-oriented finds it difficult to bounce back after failure. It is also hard for those people to overcome shyness and to take the initiative in developing personal relationships (see Chapter 6). Another area where a mastery orientation can help is when you are taking tests. Test anxiety and social anxiety will be discussed in greater detail later in this chapter.

To be mastery-oriented, you have to do two things. First, you must learn to focus your attention on the task in front of you. You must force yourself to avoid thinking about self-doubts and other negative ideas that interfere with good performance. Second, you must look at the task as a challenge. You can use the suggestions in Chapter 4 for maintaining a rational attitude toward failure. A combination of self-relaxation and self-talk (Chapter 3) will help you maintain your concentration (K. W. Collins, Dansereau, Garland, Holley, & McDonald, 1981).

Coping Skill 7: Being Mastery-Oriented

Keep Records

It is a good idea to keep records while you are working on your anxiety. The following information should be logged: (1) date, time of day, and situation; (2) a rating of your anxiety on a scale of 1 (moderate) to 5 (severe); (3) your appraisals (what you tell yourself); (4) the coping skills you employ; and (5) a rating of your anxiety on the same 5-point scale. Record keeping serves a number of useful purposes. First, it gives you an accurate idea of *when* and *where* you get anxious. This knowledge will help you plan your use of coping skills. Second, record keeping will help you identify which coping skills are working and which are not. By monitoring your progress, you can fine-tune the anxiety reduction techniques you are employing. Finally, if you keep records of your progress, you will be able to take pleasure at your improvement. Small improvements aren't always noticeable when you have high expectations. It is important to remember that large goals are reached in short steps.

Coping Skill 8: Keeping Records

Be Willing to Work

It would be nice (but boring) if everything in life were easy. If you want to live effectively with anxiety, you have to work at it. The skills for coping with anxiety described in this chapter have been found to be effective in scientific research. However, these skills were effective only when the participants in the research studies devoted the time and effort necessary to master them and put them into practice. You must be willing to practice your anxiety coping skills every day.

Coping Skill 9: Being Willing to Work

MANAGING ANXIETY-PRODUCING TRAITS

Four traits bring about anxiety: perfectionism, excessive need for approval, ignoring physical and psychological signs of stress, and excessive need for control (Bourne, 1995). You can do a lot to control your anxiety by managing these anxiety-producing traits.

Don't Be a Perfectionist

People get anxious when their expectations are unreasonably high and when they spend too much time worrying about small flaws and trivial mistakes. It is difficult to relax and enjoy life when you find too many things to be concerned about. You can put your perfectionism into perspective by observing the following suggestions (Bourne, 1995).

1. Don't allow your self-worth to be determined by your accomplishments. If you insist on basing part of your self-esteem on your achievements, be sure to set realistic goals.

2. Recognize and overcome perfectionist thinking styles. Try not to say the following kinds of things to yourself:

"I must not make mistakes."
"I should be able to do things right."
"I just can't do it."
"There is no point even trying."

Instead, practice the following kinds of self-statements:

"I'll do the best I can."
"I can learn from my mistakes."
"I need to break this down into small steps."
"I'll try it just for the heck of it."

3. Don't magnify the importance of small errors. Just about every small mistake you make will be long forgotten in a relatively short period of time. Why suffer needless stress about it? It is not fair to overwhelm yourself by insisting that all small details have to fall into place. Pick out the few very important things to worry about, and let the other things go. Don't sweat the little stuff.

4. Focus on the positives. When you are causing yourself needless anxiety, you need to distract yourself. A good way to do this is to shift your attention from negative thinking to a focus on the positives. Take some time to appreciate the good things you are doing with your life.

5. Work on goals that are realistic. Your goals should be high enough to be interesting and challenging but not so high that you can't reach them. Your goals don't have to be firm. You can adjust them as you assess how things are going.

6. Take some time to have fun. If you must be a perfectionist about *some* things, at least don't be a perfectionist about *everything*.

7. Take a mastery-oriented approach toward life. That way you can appreciate the process of meeting challenges without worrying so much about the outcome.

Cultivate Self-Acceptance

Albert Ellis has pointed out many times in his lectures and writing that we are making a big mistake if we base our feelings of self-worth on how others treat us. If people are not nice to us, we feel depressed and angry. If people are nice to us, we feel anxious. Why? Because we are concerned that even though they are nice to us now, they might not be nice to us in the future. As Ellis explains, the only way out of this trap is *self-acceptance*. We would *prefer* that others like us and treat us well, but we cannot base our personal value on their actions, which are often quite unpredictable.

Attend to Signs of Stress

An important part of controlling your anxiety is staying in touch with your physical and mental well-being. Try to catch yourself when you are feeling stressed out or anxious so you can put your coping skills to work. A good way to monitor yourself is by checking your feelings and experiences against the items on the Beck Anxiety Inventory outlined at the beginning of this chapter.

Be Flexible About Control

People with an excessive need for control are caught in the same trap as those with an excessive need for approval. When they don't have control, they feel frustration and panic. When they have control, they are anxious because they never know how long this control might last. Letting go of control is not easy, but it is an important step to take toward a more relaxed and enjoyable life. Here are some things that can help those of you who have difficulty relinquishing control (Bourne, 1995):

Acceptance: Learn to live with the fact that things will work out even if you are not in charge. Maybe they won't be as perfect as they would be if you had control, but the world will run *acceptably*.

Patience: Things may not be as efficient without you in control, but they *will* get done.

Trust: Most things will work out. It is better to relax and feel trust about the many positive events in life than to be stressed out and anxious about the threat of a few unpredictable negative events.

Humor: Use your sense of humor as a coping skill (Chapter 3). It can be terrifying when you stop trying to control things in your life. Using your sense of humor will help you maintain a warm and accepting perspective on this "terror."

Coping Skill 10: Managing Anxiety-Producing Traits

HOW TO LIVE WITH ANXIETY

The rules for coping with anxiety suggest that you must take active responsibility for coping when you are anxious. Coping skills reinforce your feelings of internal control and self-efficacy (see Chapters 2 and 3). When a primary appraisal tells you a life event is worth getting anxious about, you want to know you have good coping skills at your disposal when you make your secondary appraisal and ask, "What can I do about it?" In addition to living by the five rules described above, you can employ two general strategies for living with anxiety. The first strategy focuses on the body and includes the techniques of self-relaxation, systematic desensitization, flooding, and implosion. The second strategy focuses on brain power and includes testing your thinking, testing your perceptions, and talking yourself through challenges.

Controlling Your Body

Self-relaxation.   Self-relaxation is one of the skills you added to your coping arsenal after reading Chapter 3. Because anxiety causes you to feel tense, uptight, and generally worked up, it stands to reason that you can live more easily with anxiety if you relax. There are two ways to use self-relaxation for coping with anxiety. One generally effective method is to pay attention to your body. Monitor your breathing, your heart rate, and other signs of bodily arousal such as tense muscles and sweaty palms. When your body tells you it is anxious, it is time to use your self-relaxation skills. For example, let's say you are performing or giving a speech in front of an audience. Your body tells you it is getting anxious. Instead of going into a panic and losing control, tell yourself, "OK, I need to take a deep breath and relax." The advantage of using your bodily responses as a cue for self-relaxation is that you feel prepared for coping with anxiety in any situation. You are carrying your coping skill with you wherever you happen to be. Psychologists call this practicing self-relaxation *in vivo*—in your everyday life (Deffenbacher & Suinn, 1985; Goldfried, 1971).

Systematic desensitization.   You can also use self-relaxation to prepare yourself ahead of time for anxiety-producing situations. Let's say you are planning to ask your boss for a vacation or for a raise. You know you can use your self-relaxation skills to stay on top of your anxiety on the day of the meeting. You can also prepare yourself for this anxiety-producing event with *systematic desensitization*. This technique, which was pioneered by Joseph Wolpe (1958, 1982), works in the following way. Make a list of the events leading up to the actual meeting with your boss. An example of such a list is shown in Table 7.1. After making the list, rate each event on a scale from 0 to 100 according to how much anxiety it will cause. You can use this list to prepare your-

TABLE 7.1   Events preceding meeting with boss

Event (in order of difficulty)	Individual Anxiety Rating (0–100)
Riding to work a month before meeting	10
Riding to work a week before meeting	20
Seeing boss in lunchroom	40
Riding to work a day before meeting	45
Passing boss in hallway a day before meeting	60
Riding to work the day of meeting	80
Ten minutes before meeting	90
Knocking on boss's door	95
Entering boss's office	99

self for the meeting. First, relax yourself until your anxiety is at a level close to 0, then imagine riding to work a month before the meeting. You may feel your anxiety go up to 10. As you keep this event in mind, relax yourself again back down to 0. Then imagine the event repeatedly until you can keep your feelings of anxiety about that event close to 0. Then move on to the next event on your list. In this case, imagine that you are riding to work a week before the meeting. You may feel your anxiety rising up to 20. Again, keeping this event in mind, relax yourself back down to 0. Work through your list in this way until you can vividly picture yourself knocking on the boss's door and entering the office while keeping your anxiety level down to 20 or 30. It may take a while to work through your entire list of events while keeping your anxiety at a reasonable level. But if you give yourself enough time and practice, you will find a boost to your self-confidence and sense of preparation.

Flooding and implosion.   Another way to desensitize yourself from events that make you anxious is to throw yourself into them until they no longer disturb you. This technique is called *flooding*. The theory behind flooding is that when you force yourself to confront tasks, people, and places you previously avoided, you discover that they aren't so terrifying. You find out through direct experience that your reasons for anxiety were exaggerated. However, when you use flooding, you must be committed to stick with it and resist your temptation to escape. If you run away before forcing yourself to become desensitized, your immediate relief will reinforce the urge to be an avoider.

In addition to confronting physical events that cause anxiety, you can practice desensitization through your imagination. You can work through a list of anxiety-producing events such as those in Table 7.1. As you allow yourself to become anxious, remind yourself that even though anxiety is not pleasant it is not fatal. You will discover that you can live with it. The technique of desensitizing yourself with thoughts and imagination is called *implosion*. One advantage of implosion is that you can use this technique anytime to prepare yourself for the flooding day and to bolster your self-confidence.

If you are a chronic worrier, you should schedule your implosion sessions for specific times and places each day. During your scheduled time, you can allow yourself to feel as much anxiety as possible. However, you are not permitted to think anxiety-producing thoughts at any other time of the day. For the rest of the day, you must commit yourself to gaining satisfaction through activities that don't involve worrying. The technique of scheduling your worry time is called *stimulus control*. When you catch yourself worrying during nonscheduled times, tell yourself "Stop!" and force yourself to get involved in other activities. This is called *thought-stopping*.

When used together, the techniques described in this section provide an active coping skill that will bolster your feelings of internal control and self-confidence (Beck & Emery, 1990; Deffenbacher & Suinn, 1985; Stampfl & Lewis, 1967).

Coping Skill 11: Controlling Your Body

Using Your Brain's Power

As human beings, we are blessed with powerful brains. You can use your thinking powers to enhance your coping skills in three ways: by testing your thinking, testing your perceptions, and talking yourself through challenges.

Testing your thinking.   Earlier in this chapter, you learned about faulty thinking patterns that often cause unnecessarily high anxiety—automatic thinking, overgeneralizing, lack of proportion, selective perception, rigid thinking, circular reasoning, and unrealistic expectations. Human beings have a penchant for faulty thinking (Ellis, 1987b). It is therefore necessary to make a practice of testing your thinking, particularly when you are dissatisfied or unhappy. You have learned how your thoughts can influence your feelings. For this reason, analyzing what you tell yourself is an important coping skill. A good method for testing your thinking is to keep daily records such as the one shown in Table 7.2. On the daily log, record what was going on (the life event), what you were thinking (your primary appraisal), and your resulting feelings. You may recognize that these factors make up the process of primary appraisal outlined in Figure 2.2 (see Chapter 2). Also include a column where you analyze the logic of your thinking. If your thinking is faulty, fill in a more reasonable way of appraising the life event and conclude the log with the new feelings your corrected thinking will bring.

Coping Skill 12: Testing Your Thinking

Testing your perceptions.   At the beginning of this chapter you were advised not to blame yourself when you feel anxious. In addition to telling yourself that anxiety is part of life, you can use your thinking powers to look at anxiety in ways that will "psych you up" rather than bring you down. For example, let's say you are preparing

TABLE 7.2   Example of daily record

Life Event	Thoughts	Resulting Feelings	Analyzing the Logic	Revised Thinking	New Feeling
Taking an exam	"I'm going to fail."	Panic	Automatic thinking	"I may not do as well as I would like."	Concern
	"My life is ruined."	Desperation	Lack of proportion	"A low grade would be a setback, but it would not ruin my life."	Disappointment
At a job interview	"I can tell the interviewer doesn't like me."	Anxiety	Selective perception	"The interviewer seems to be having a bad day."	Concern
	"They'll never hire me."	Hopelessness	Rigid thinking	"The job market is tight, but I have as good a chance as anyone."	Hope
	"This is too hard. It's not fair."	Anger	Unrealistic expectations	"This interview is tough, but I'll give it my best shot."	Cautious optimism
Giving a speech	"My hands are sweating. I'm falling apart."	Panic	Overgeneralizing, lack of proportion	"I'm a bit nervous, but that is to be expected."	Temporary nervousness
	"That person looks bored. He doesn't like me."	Anxiety	Selective perception, overgeneralizing	"That person has something else on his mind, but most of the audience is with me."	Temporary distraction
	"I'm not relaxed and happy. I'm a failure as a speaker."	Depression	Unrealistic expectations, circular reasoning	"There is always room for improvement, but I'm getting through this satisfactorily."	Satisfaction

TABLE 7.3   Adaptive relabeling of perceptions

Life Event	Perception	Revised Perception
Giving a speech	Panic	Motivation to do well
Confrontation	"Freaked out"	"Pumped up"
Asking for a date	Doom	Excitement
Facing uncertainty	Terror	Nervousness, caution
Taking an exam	Panic	Challenge
Job interview	Anxiety	Enthusiasm

to give a speech in class. You can choose to perceive the emotions you are experiencing as panic or as proof of your motivation to do well. If you have to interact with someone who is very intimidating, you can perceive yourself as "freaked out" or you can say that the adrenalin you feel is pumping you up to meet this challenge. Feelings of doom at the prospect of asking someone for a date can be reinterpreted as excitement about the fact that you are finally going to do it (see Table 7.3). That is, you can label the emotions you are experiencing as either negative or positive. Obviously, when you label them as positive it helps you do your best in the anxiety-provoking situation. This procedure of redefining your perceptions is called *adaptive relabeling*. Remember the discussion of rational-emotive therapy in Chapter 2: "There is nothing either good or bad, but thinking makes it so" (Deffenbacher & Suinn, 1985; Goldfried, Decenteceo, & Weinberg, 1974).

Coping Skill 13: Relabeling Perceptions

Talking yourself through challenges.   A good strategy for getting through anxiety-provoking situations is to use the techniques of talking to yourself in an adaptive manner that were described in Chapter 3. You can use your thinking powers to coach yourself from the beginning to the end of a challenging life event. For example, before a job interview, you can say to yourself: "My goal is to have an interesting conversation with the interviewer. I can look at my nervousness as excitement about the challenge of showing my skills. I must remember to keep my expectations realistic. I am prepared to use my coping skills when I feel anxious." Then, during the interview, you can remind yourself:

"Don't think about being afraid, just focus on making clear statements."
"This is an opportunity to sell myself."
"Take a deep breath now and relax."

After the interview, take credit for your success by telling yourself: "That wasn't so bad after all. I was able to live up to the challenge, and that's what counts. It was good for me to get this practice. My goal was realistic, and I met it—I can be proud of myself."

This technique of coaching yourself through stressful experiences was developed by Donald Meichenbaum (1977, 1985). It is called *stress inoculation* because it is designed to provide a sense of readiness and preparation. Stress inoculation statements such as those above can be used in two ways. You can employ stress inoculation to coach yourself as you go through a challenging life event. You can also practice ahead of time for the life event by relaxing and taking yourself through the experience in your imagination. The more you practice, the more prepared you will be to cope with the challenge when it happens.

Coping Skill 14: Talking Yourself Through Challenges

MANAGING DIET AND EXERCISE

If you are suffering from excessive anxiety, it is a good idea to have a medical checkup. In addition to being screened for medical conditions that can raise anxiety, it is useful to obtain professional consultation on your diet. Some obvious things to look at are nicotine and caffeine. Both of these chemicals are stimulants that are likely to heighten feelings of anxiety. It is worth remembering that in addition to coffee and tea, many cola beverages contain caffeine. Recreational drugs such as cocaine can increase feelings of anxiety. Keeping a balance on sugar consumption is also important.

After working out a suitable diet, there is nothing better than getting into a good routine of physical exercise. Exercise is a great coping skill (Chapter 3) because it contributes to your physical as well as your mental well-being.

Coping Skill 15: Managing Diet and Exercise

SELF-MEDICATION

If anxiety is a problem that interferes with a major part of your life functioning, it is possible to receive medication from a qualified physician. However, you need to think very seriously about medicating yourself with drugs and alcohol. Sometimes a quick drink or drug dose will help numb you during a stressful life event. But often this self-medication reduces your mental powers and undermines your functioning. It's not going to help much to get stoned before an exam if you are not able to think clearly and work out coherent answers. And even though it may be less scary to interact with others while drunk, your social skills are severely diminished by alcohol. And your sense of self-efficacy is undermined when you are psychologically addicted to drugs to get through tough situations. Self-medication is tempting because it is much easier than learning, practicing, and working at the coping skills suggested in this chapter. But in the long run, enduring and mastering these coping skills will do more for your self-esteem than any quick fix from alcohol and drugs.

Coping Skill 16: Avoiding Self-Medication

TEST ANXIETY

Check whether you agree or disagree with the following statements.

	Strongly agree	Agree	Disagree	Strongly disagree
1. I feel distressed and uneasy before tests.	___	___	___	___
2. I feel jittery before tests.	___	___	___	___
3. I find myself becoming anxious the day of the test.	___	___	___	___
4. Before taking a test, I worry about failure.	___	___	___	___
5 During tests, I wonder how the other people are doing.	___	___	___	___
6. Before tests, I feel troubled about what is going to happen.	___	___	___	___
7. During tests, I think about recent events.	___	___	___	___
8. Irrelevant bits of information pop into my head during a test.	___	___	___	___
9. During tests, I find myself thinking of things unrelated to the material being tested.	___	___	___	___
10. I get a headache during an important test.	___	___	___	___
11. My stomach gets upset before tests.	___	___	___	___
12. My heart beats faster when the test begins.	___	___	___	___

These statements come from the Test Anxiety Scale (Sarason, 1984). It measures four kinds of anxious reactions to tests: *tension* (items 1–3), *worry* (items 4–6), *test-irrelevant thinking* (items 7–9), and *bodily symptoms* (items 10–12). When these reactions are severe, a person's test performance can be seriously impaired.

People suffer from test anxiety because they become so preoccupied with avoiding failure that they can't concentrate on the problems they have to solve (Deffenbacher, 1980; Hunsley, 1987; Sarason, 1984). Test anxiety is correlated with the *emotion coping* and *avoidance coping* styles outlined in Chapter 1 (Endler, Kantor, &

Parker, 1994). Emotion coping is characterized by the following kinds of responses toward tests:

"I blame myself for not knowing what to do."
"I become preoccupied with aches and pains."
"I become very tense."
"I focus on my general inadequacies."

Avoidance coping is characterized by the following kinds of responses when it is time to study for a test:

"I phone or visit a friend."
"I go to a movie or watch TV."
"I go out for a snack or meal."
"I take time off and get away from the situation."

People who suffer from test anxiety also make negative statements to themselves (Blankstein, Toner, & Flett, 1989), such as:

"My skills are not very good."
"I don't think I can do it."
"I'm not smart enough."

Such people don't approach problems with a mastery orientation by taking a problem-solving approach. They don't talk themselves through problems (see Chapter 3). They have not learned to coach themselves by saying such things as:

"Let's see, how should I begin?"
"I want to look for the correct pattern here."
"I'm going to stay open-minded until I find a good strategy."

Good grades are correlated with a *task coping* style characterized by the following kinds of responses toward tests (Endler et al., 1994):

"I schedule my time better."
"I focus on the problem and see how I can solve it."
"I think about how I have solved similar problems."
"I work to understand the situation."
"I come up with several different solutions to the problem."

These examples suggest that people are more likely to do well on tests when they use problem-solving skills and take a mastery-oriented approach. Two strategies are used by mastery-oriented people to motivate themselves. One is to take a realistic attitude toward strengths and weaknesses. With such a strategy it is usually possible to be optimistic because you are generally clear about surmountable versus insurmountable challenges. When faced with surmountable challenges, you can apply yourself, be persistent, and usually succeed. When faced with insurmountable challenges, you can give it your best shot, but you shouldn't feel devastated if you fail. With a realistic attitude, there isn't much need to be anxious because you know what you can and cannot accomplish.

A second strategy is to take a pessimistic attitude and expect the worst. You are probably familiar with people who do this. They are the ones who always say they're going to blow the test and end up getting A's. People who use a pessimistic strategy have the following kinds of thoughts (Norem & Cantor, 1986a):

"I go into academic situations expecting the worst, even though I know I'll probably do OK."

"I often think about what it will be like if I do poorly in an academic situation."

This pessimistic strategy serves as a motivator to work hard and overcome the challenge. It protects people from anxiety because they are so focused on covering all contingencies that the possibility of failure is considerably reduced. However, people who use a pessimistic strategy pay a price. They are so focused on avoiding the anxiety of possible failure that they can't enjoy the challenges of their work. Although realistic and pessimistic people who are mastery-oriented usually end up being successful, realistic people stand a better chance of feeling relaxed and enjoying the fruits of their labor (Cantor & Norem, 1989; Norem & Cantor, 1986a, 1986b).

A final suggestion if you suffer from anxiety during tests is to learn how to stop yourself from the following kinds of thoughts that can interfere with your creative thinking (Sarason, Sarason, & Pierce, 1995):

"I'm not doing very well."

"What will the teacher think of me?"

"I'm feeling confused."

"I'm running out of time."

"Other students are doing better than I am."

To turn off these interfering thoughts, the following solutions are recommended (Naveh-Benjamin, 1991; Sedikides, 1992):

- Practice self-relaxation. Calming down will help you keep your thoughts under control.
- Whenever your thoughts begin to wander, force yourself to focus on the test.
- Try to put yourself in a positive mood by looking forward to positive activities when the test is over.

SOCIAL AND AUDIENCE ANXIETY

Two kinds of anxiety are associated with interpersonal situations. *Social anxiety* is the anxiety you experience in social interactions. *Audience anxiety* occurs when you are anxious in the presence of groups or audiences. Social anxiety is assessed by the following items on the Interaction Anxiousness Scale (Leary, 1983):

1. I often feel nervous even in casual get-togethers.
2. In general, I am a shy person.
3. I am not at ease when speaking with someone of the opposite sex.
4. I wish I had more confidence in social situations.
5. Parties often make me feel anxious and uncomfortable.

Audience anxiety is defined by the following items on the Interaction Anxiousness Scale:

1. I usually get nervous when I speak in front of a group.
2. I do not enjoy speaking in public.
3. I tend to experience "stage fright" when I must appear before a group.
4. I get nervous when I must make a presentation at school or work.
5. I get "butterflies" in my stomach when I must speak or perform before others.

The skills outlined in this chapter for coping with anxiety are useful for managing social and audience anxiety. Social anxiety presents a particular challenge because people have an inborn need for interpersonal attachments (Baumeister & Leary, 1995). Because of our need for acceptance from others, we are vulnerable to feelings of social anxiety when we fear that this acceptance might not be forthcoming. The desire for approval from others is such an important part of our lives that it is strongly interwoven with our sense of self-esteem (Leary & Downs, 1995; Leary, Tambor, Terdal, & Downs, 1995). Your self-esteem is enhanced when others accept you, and your self-esteem is deflated when others reject you. The first challenge in managing social anxiety, therefore, is to develop social skills (see Chapter 6) that will maximize satisfying interpersonal interactions. It is also important to recognize that your social interactions will go more smoothly when you are feeling a strong sense of self-esteem. The coping attitude I promote in this book is designed to encourage you to develop your self-efficacy by taking a mastery-oriented approach toward life (see Chapter 15). When it comes to the challenge of social anxiety, the following thoughts are useful in helping you maintain your self-esteem when you feel dependent on acceptance and approval from others (Ishiyama, 1991):

- It is a normal human experience to desire acceptance from others.
- The experience of social anxiety indicates that we are sensitive to our fellow human beings.
- Anxiety in social situations motivates us to develop ourselves into socially skillful people.

As you work to manage your social anxiety, stop yourself from thinking the following kinds of thoughts (Ball, Otto, Pollack, Uccello, & Rosenbaum, 1995; Showers, 1992):

- Disapproval from others is my worst fear.
- I need to do whatever I can to avoid social rejection.
- I need to approach social interactions with caution and trepidation because there is a constant danger that someone won't like me.
- I would rather avoid rejection by doing things that might harm me than honor my self-identity and risk disapproval.
- My value as a person depends on the reactions I get from others.

When people are not able to cope with social anxiety, they become so desperate for social approval that they engage in the following kinds of harmful behaviors (Leary, Schreindorfer, & Haupt, 1995; Leary, Tchividjian, & Kraxberger, 1994):

- Risky sexual behavior
- Risking skin cancer for the sake of looking "tanned and healthy"

- Eating disorders focused on maintaining an attractive figure
- Alcohol, tobacco, and illegal drug use
- Engaging in hazardous, reckless, and dangerous behaviors
- Getting involved in illegal and antisocial activities

People who are engaging in self-destructive behaviors for the sake of social acceptance are in particular need of training in the use of effective skills for coping with social anxiety.

LIST OF SKILLS FOR COPING WITH ANXIETY

- *Coping Skill 1:*   Recognizing Symptoms of Anxiety
- *Coping Skill 2:*   Avoiding Self-Imposed Blame and Punishment
- *Coping Skill 3:*   Making Rational Primary Appraisals
- *Coping Skill 4:*   Preventing Anxiety from Getting the Best of You
- *Coping Skill 5:*   Not Being an Avoider
- *Coping Skill 6:*   Using Positive Confrontation
- *Coping Skill 7:*   Being Mastery-Oriented
- *Coping Skill 8:*   Keeping Records
- *Coping Skill 9:*   Being Willing to Work
- *Coping Skill 10:*   Managing Anxiety-Producing Traits
- *Coping Skill 11:*   Controlling Your Body
- *Coping Skill 12:*   Testing Your Thinking
- *Coping Skill 13:*   Relabeling Perceptions
- *Coping Skill 14:*   Talking Yourself Through Challenges
- *Coping Skill 15:*   Managing Diet and Exercise
- *Coping Skill 16:*   Avoiding Self-Medication

SUGGESTIONS FOR FURTHER READING

Beck, A. T., & Emery, G. (1990). *Anxiety disorders and phobias: A cognitive perspective.* New York: Basic Books.

Bourne, E. J. (1995). *The anxiety & phobia workbook.* Oakland, CA: New Harbinger Publications.

Emery, G., & Campbell, J. (1987). *Rapid relief from emotional distress.* New York: Fawcett.

Greist, J. H., Jefferson, J. W., & Marks, I. M. (1986). *Anxiety and its treatment.* New York: Warner Books.

Leary, M. R., & Kowalski, R. M. (1995). *Social anxiety.* New York: Guilford.

Sarason, I. G. (Ed.). (1980). *Test anxiety: Theory, research and applications.* Hillsdale, NJ: Erlbaum.

Wilson, E. R. (1985). *Don't panic: Taking control of anxiety attacks.* New York: Harper & Row.

8

Coping with Anger

Anger is one of the most complex human emotions. It is a common reaction to frustration and mistreatment. We are all destined to face occasions for anger throughout our lives. The problem with anger is that although it is part of life it can hinder us from reaching our goals. This is why people have such a conflict about anger. On one hand, it is a natural human response. On the other hand, it can interfere with interpersonal relationships and keep us from getting what we want.

A HISTORICAL PERSPECTIVE

A good way to appreciate our ambivalence toward anger is to look at how anger has been regarded throughout U.S. history. Carol and Peter Stearns (1986) analyzed American attitudes toward anger in three areas of life: child rearing, work, and marriage.

Child Rearing

The prime focus of child rearing in early U.S. history was on obedience and will-breaking. If children felt angry, it was their problem. By the early 1800s, the emphasis shifted toward character building, and children were encouraged to manage their anger as a way of showing maturity and self-control. In the late 1800s and early 1900s, anger was disapproved of, and attempts were made to teach children (especially boys) to channel their anger through sports and other activities. The influence of Freud led to an increased permissiveness toward anger in the 1940s, and this more tolerant attitude lasted into the 1960s, when anger was again viewed as a negative emotion that needed to be disciplined and controlled.

Work

Expressing anger in the workplace has become less acceptable in modern times. Companies have adopted psychological testing to screen out "undesirable" workers. Companies have also employed counselors to help workers "manage their feelings" and have set up training groups where workers are taught how to get along better.

Marriage

In early U.S. history, expressing anger in the home was banned. The home was viewed as a sacred retreat, and quarrels between husbands and wives were tantamount to a failed marriage. This restriction on expressing anger changed over time, and by the 1960s psychologists were advising husbands and wives to express their anger and to learn how to "fight" with each other in a constructive manner.

Men have generally been permitted more freedom to express anger than women. Women have been urged to take the role of martyrs, never to complain, and to suffer frustrations and mistreatment in silence. Also, Americans have typically viewed anger as something that happens to them rather than as an emotion they choose to experience. In earlier chapters, you learned that your emotions are determined by your appraisals of life events. Individuals have the power and also the responsibility to react to life events with coping skills that are in their best interest. In this chapter I will focus on how you can use these coping skills to live effectively with feelings of anger.

DEFINING ANGER

It is difficult to give a definition of anger because people vary so widely in when they get angry, why they get angry, and how they respond to anger (Russell & Fehr, 1990). Some emotions often associated with anger are: fury, outrage, hostility, vengefulness, rage, hate, irritation, aggravation, jealousy, resentment, bitterness, wrath, spite, scorn, and annoyance (Shaver, Schwartz, Kirson, & O'Connor, 1987). Because we all differ in the ways we define and experience these feelings, it is impossible to state precisely what they all mean. What is important is knowing when your experiences with anger are causing you problems and compromising your life in a significant way. Although we have varying ideas and perceptions about anger and different thresholds for getting angry, we can all benefit from the suggestions given in this chapter for coping with anger when it is causing us difficulties.

THE EXPERIENCE OF ANGER

Everyone is confronted at some time with mistreatment and frustration, therefore it is instructive to see how people's experiences with anger compare. Researchers have conducted surveys in which people were asked about their experiences of anger. Here are some of the findings (Averill, 1979, 1983):

1. *Who causes anger?* Most respondents said that other people provoked their anger. In a large number of cases, anger was felt toward a loved one. Close friends and acquaintances were also common sources of anger. Disliked people and strangers comprised a relatively small proportion of people who made respondents angry.

2. *What makes people angry?* Because anger is usually experienced toward friends and loved ones, it is not surprising that causes of anger revolve around frustrations of needs and desires. The most commonly reported cause of anger was thwarting or interrupting plans. Other causes of anger were failure by someone to satisfy the respondent's expectations, and wishes and actions resulting in loss of pride or self-esteem. Respondents also reported feelings of anger toward others who did not act in a socially appropriate manner. A survey of people from a wide range of ages and backgrounds identified ten circumstances that cause people to get angry (Mabel, 1994):

- Interruption of a goal-directed behavior
- Being degraded personally or treated unfairly
- Someone being prejudiced, unfair, or unkind
- Being the object of dishonesty or broken promises
- One's proper authority, property, or feelings being disregarded by others
- Being ignored or treated badly by a significant other
- Experiencing harm due to being negligent toward oneself
- People demonstrating by their behavior a lack of personal care
- Being verbally or physically assaulted
- Being a helpless victim

When people appraise anger-provoking life events, they base the amount of anger they experience on the following factors (Ben-Zur & Breznitz, 1991; C. A. Smith, Haynes, Lazarus, & Pope, 1993; C. A. Smith & Lazarus, 1993):

The extent of the harm or damage. People are more likely to react with anger if they experience actions from others that are harmful, that interfere with their wishes and goals, and that are not easily corrected.

The cause of the harm or damage. People are more likely to react with anger if they are subjected to harmful life events that are intentional or that could have been prevented.

Whether the harm or damage was expected. People are more likely to react with anger if the harm or damage they experience was not expected.

Whether the harm or damage was caused by oneself or by others. People are more likely to react with anger if the harm or damage they experience was caused by others rather than by their own actions.

3. *Why do people get angry?* The most commonly reported reason for getting angry was to assert one's authority and independence. The second and third most commonly reported motives for anger were to strengthen the relationship with the anger-provoking person and to influence that person to change "for his or her own good." Getting revenge and "letting off steam" were also reported as reasons for getting angry.

4. *How do others react to expressions of anger?* Most respondents reported that they experienced negative consequences for their anger. The most commonly reported reactions to anger were: indifference or lack of concern, defiance, apology or

other signs of contrition, anger or hostility, denial of responsibility, hurt feelings, surprise, rejection, jokes, frivolity, or silliness. It is striking that these responses to anger are largely not in the angry person's best interest.

5. *How do angry people react to their own expressions of anger?* After recognizing that others generally respond negatively to expressions of anger, it is not surprising to learn that people often experience their own expression of anger in an unpleasant manner. The most commonly reported reactions to one's own expression of anger were: feeling irritable, hostile, and aggravated; feeling depressed, unhappy, and gloomy; feeling ashamed, embarrassed, and guilty; feeling relieved, calm, and satisfied; feeling good, pleased, and glad; and feeling triumphant, confident, and dominant.

Several important conclusions can be made from these surveys of people's anger:

1. Anger is a common emotion that is often felt toward friends and loved ones who fail to live up to our wishes and desires.
2. Anger is often motivated by the desire to get what we want.
3. People's reactions to expressions of anger are often negative.
4. Although we sometimes feel satisfaction after expressing anger, we don't necessarily achieve our goals in the long run.

These conclusions strongly suggest that we have to use other skills in addition to anger to get our needs met. That's what this chapter is about—how you can constructively live with anger.

COMPARING THE PERCEPTIONS OF VICTIMS AND PERPETRATORS

Another way to understand the experience of anger is by comparing people's perceptions when they cause others to get angry versus when others cause them to get angry. A survey was conducted in which participants explained situations in which they angered someone else as well as situations in which someone else angered them (Baumeister, Stillwell, & Wotman, 1990). It turned out that the people's perceptions were very different when they were perpetrators rather than victims of anger. When people angered someone else, they believed they had good reasons for their actions. They often felt regret over the incident, but they also believed they had duly apologized and that the problem was over. In other words, perpetrators of anger saw their provocation as an isolated event that was unfortunate, but understandable. They were ready to let the issue drop and continue their relationship with the person they angered.

When people were angered by someone else, they often could find no good reason for that person's behavior. Therefore, they perceived the provocation as unjustified and unfair. They felt harmed by the person who made them angry, and they ruminated about being mistreated. They did not view the actions of the person who angered them as an isolated incident that could be easily forgotten.

It is apparent that the disparate interpretations made by victims and perpetrators of anger can result in some serious misunderstandings. In many cases, people who are angered by others keep their negative reactions to themselves. The person who caused the anger assumes everything is OK and, inevitably, angers the victim again. Sooner or later, the victim blows up at the person who has been causing "so much anger" and accuses the anger-provoking person of being unkind, insensitive, and uncaring. The perpetrator is taken aback by this outburst, viewing it as an overreaction to provocations that, in the perpetrator's perception, have already been put to rest. If the victim's complaints are particularly vociferous, the perpetrator might even feel angry about being so unjustly attacked.

It is clear that many problems could be avoided if people could assert themselves when someone angers them and negotiate with the anger-provoking person so that these provocations are less likely to occur in the future. The skills of assertiveness and negotiation will be outlined later in this chapter.

ASSESSING ANGER

Before looking at ways to cope with anger, it might be useful to measure your feelings of anger. Check how much you agree or disagree with the following statements.

	Strongly agree	Agree	Disagree	Strongly disagree
1. I tend to get angry more frequently than most people.	____	____	____	____
2. It is easy to make me angry.	____	____	____	____
3. I am surprised at how often I feel angry.	____	____	____	____
4. I get angry when something blocks my plans.	____	____	____	____
5. I get angry when I am delayed.	____	____	____	____
6. I get angry when people are unfair.	____	____	____	____
7. People can bother me just by being around.	____	____	____	____
8. When I get angry, I stay angry for hours.	____	____	____	____
9. I get angry when I have to work with incompetent people.	____	____	____	____

These statements come from the Multidimensional Anger Inventory (Siegel, 1986). Statements 1, 2, and 3 measure *anger arousal*. Anger arousal refers to the intensity, duration, and frequency of your anger. Statements 4, 5, and 6 measure the *range of* things you get angry about. Statements 7, 8, and 9 measure your tendency to have a *hostile outlook*. Another dimension measured by the inventory is the ease with which you express your anger. People who express their anger very readily tend to agree with these statements:

- When I am angry with someone, I let that person know.
- It is not difficult for me to let people know I'm angry.

Those who keep their feelings of anger to themselves tend to agree with these statements:

- I feel guilty about expressing my anger.
- I harbor grudges that I don't tell anyone about.

Later in this chapter you will learn about the virtues of communicating your feelings of anger in a way that is assertive but not aggressive. First, let's consider the kinds of appraisals we make when faced with anger-provoking situations.

THE COSTS OF ANGER

Because anger is a predictable reaction to mistreatment, it is understandable that we will all get angry from time to time. There is no point in putting yourself down when you become angry about things that upset you. Don't adopt a repressive coping style (see Chapter 1) and deny your feelings to the point that you don't do anything about them. Instead, evaluate whether or not your ways of coping with anger are working in your best interest. Anger can have significant physical and interpersonal costs (McKay, Rogers, & McKay, 1989). The physical costs of anger include physiological stress and hypertension and the bodily ailments that go along with these problems. Interpersonal costs of anger are feelings of helplessness, loneliness, and isolation.

Rate the degree of impact your anger has on your life using the following scale:

0 = *no effect*
1 = *minor effect*
2 = *moderate effect*
3 = *strong effect*
4 = *major effect*

Rating

1. Relationships to authorities (teachers, bosses, police, and so forth) _____

2. Relationships to peers and colleagues at work _____

3. Relationship to subordinates at work _____

4. Relationships to children _____

5. Relationships to spouse or lover _____

6. Relationships to parents _____

7. Relationships to other family members _____

Rating

8. Relationships to friends   _____

9. Time lost to angry feelings   _____

10. Anger intrusion into relaxing or pleasurable activities
    (sex, sports, hobbies, and so forth)   _____

11. Effect of anger on drinking or drug abuse   _____

12. Effect of anger on creativity or productivity   _____

13. Accidents, errors, and mistakes   _____

These statements come from the Anger Impact Inventory (McKay et al., 1989). If your ratings on some or all of the items are 3 or 4, you should seriously consider learning ways to keep your anger from interfering so much with your life.

A SURVEY OF COPING RESPONSES

University students who participated in a survey reported that the following responses helped to make them feel better when they were angry (M. B. Harris, 1992):

- Yelling at the person who made them angry
- Exercising
- Treating themselves to something
- Trying to think of something else

Students indicated that they would feel worse if they did the following things when they were angry:

- Steal something from the person who made them angry
- Brood about what made them angry
- Physically hurt the person who made them angry

On the whole, men did not feel that aggressive responses to anger would make them feel better. However, men were more likely than women to favor aggressive responses to anger. Women were more likely than men to believe that hurting, stealing from, or insulting the person who made them angry would make them feel worse. Women were also more likely than men to say that they would feel better when they were angry if they did something nice for someone, treated themselves to something, or tried to think of something else.

BEING EMOTIONALLY CREATIVE

When you experience emotions that are getting the best of you, take a coping attitude by saying to yourself, "I am feeling _____. This is getting the best of me. How can I deal with my feelings in a way that is helpful?" More often than not, your immediate response to a problematic feeling is not the best possible choice. Take a moment and use your problem-solving skills (see Chapter 3) to come up with a way of responding that is adaptive. This task is usually easier if you can use your creativity (Averill & Thomas-Knowles, 1991). Instead of allowing your emotions to control you, you can use your emotions as an opportunity to come up with new and creative experiences.

When you are angry, go through the following steps. First, acknowledge and accept the fact that you are angry. Second, decide what to do about it. Sometimes you may decide it is in your best interest to respond aggressively. Other times you may opt for a passive or nonassertive response. More often than not, you will want to choose an assertive course of action. These possibilities will be outlined in more detail later in this chapter. What is important to understand here is that you have a choice—and a responsibility—in deciding on an appropriate way of responding when you are angry. It does not make sense to use anger as a reason or *excuse* for acting aggressively. In other words, to say "I acted out and (broke something or hurt someone) *because* I was angry" is an unreasonable way of avoiding responsibility (Averill, 1993, 1994). Anger does not *cause* us to act in certain ways. Rather, we get angry (which is acceptable) and *choose* to respond in a socially appropriate manner (which is acceptable) or in a socially deviant manner (which is unacceptable).

Coping Skill 1: Being Emotionally Creative

MAKING RATIONAL PRIMARY APPRAISALS

A good place to start learning how to cope with anger is by analyzing your primary appraisals. When you make a primary appraisal of a frustrating or difficult life event, you must decide whether it is something worth getting angry about. This is the time to put your rational thinking skills (Chapter 2) into practice. If you find yourself suffering from needless anger, you are probably making the following kinds of irrational demands:

> Because I strongly desire people to treat me considerately and fairly, they *absolutely must* do so, and they are evil, damnable people who deserve to be severely condemned and punished if they don't.
>
> Because I strongly desire people to treat me considerately and fairly, and because I AM A SPECIAL KIND OF PERSON, they *absolutely must* treat me well.
>
> Because I strongly desire people to treat me considerately and fairly, they *absolutely must* AT ALL TIMES AND UNDER ALL CONDITIONS DO SO.

These examples of irrational beliefs were collected by Albert Ellis (1987b) during his psychotherapeutic work with thousands of people. Although these statements might strike you as unrealistic, the fact is that we all make unrealistic demands of life. Because it is a natural human tendency to want the best out of life, we are predisposed toward holding expectations and making demands that are not always reasonable. Make it a habit to test the rationality of your appraisals. If you insist that things should *always* go your way, that others must *always* treat you right, and that you should *never* suffer frustration, you are certain to become angry. A useful coping skill is to catch yourself and change your demands to ones that are more realistic. For example, instead of retaining these irrational demands, talk to yourself in a more rational manner: "I strongly desire that people treat me considerately and fairly. When they do, it makes me happy, and when they don't, I don't like it. However, because the world does not revolve around my wishes and desires, I have to learn effective skills for coping when I am frustrated and mistreated." This kind of appraisal will still lead to feelings of disappointment or frustration when things don't go your way, but it will not result in needless anger.

Coping Skill 2: Testing the Rationality of Your Primary Appraisals

HOW TO CONTROL ANGER

When you experience mistreatment and frustration, remember that you are a coper who knows how to use the coping skills outlined in Chapter 3. Because anger gets the best of all of us at various times in our lives, psychologists have developed programs to help people cope with their anger more effectively (Novaco, 1975, 1985). A number of skills have been found to be effective in helping to cope with anger (Deffenbacher, Demm, & Brandon, 1986; Deffenbacher & Stark, 1992; Deffenbacher, Thwaites, Wallace, & Oetting, 1994; Hazaleus & Deffenbacher, 1986; Novaco, 1976).

Self-Relaxation

Self-relaxation (see Chapter 3) is a very useful skill to employ when anger gets the best of you. There is truth to the saying that you should count to 10 before responding when you are provoked. This gives you time to use your problem-solving skills to decide on the best course of action. You can also use your feelings of anger as a cue to tell yourself to relax. You can use deep-breathing and muscle-relaxation skills right there on the spot to calm yourself down. Then you will be in a better condition to weigh your options. If you feel that shouting or being aggressive is in your best interest, you can do so, but you will be acting *out of choice* and not as a result of uncontrolled anger.

Self-relaxation can also be used to prepare yourself for an anger-provoking situation. You can desensitize yourself (see Chapter 7) by rehearsing how you will respond when this situation occurs. Relax and imagine that you are confronted with frustration and mistreatment. When you feel your blood pressure rise, score your anger on a scale of 0 to 100. Then relax until your anger level is back down to a lower level (30 or below). Now imagine that the frustration and mistreatment is even worse. Again, score your anger and bring it under control with self-relaxation. If you give yourself enough practice, you will feel prepared to cope successfully when the frustration and mistreatment actually occur.

Coping Skill 3: Using Self-Relaxation to Maintain Control When You Are Frustrated and Mistreated

Stress Inoculation

In Chapter 7 you learned how to use stress inoculation as a skill for coping with anxiety. Stress inoculation is designed to give people a sense of readiness and preparation for difficult life events. This is done by learning how to coach yourself through challenges. You can prepare yourself by making a list of adaptive self-statements (Meichenbaum, 1985). For example, before the event, say to yourself:

"This is going to upset me, but I know how to handle it."
"It's not going to be fun, so I have to be prepared."
"I can use my coping skills to maintain control."
"Take it easy. This can be a good learning experience."
"When I find myself getting angry, I'll relax and calm myself down."
"I can coach myself through this challenge."

During the event remind yourself:

"Stay calm. Just continue to relax."
"As long as I keep cool and use my coping skills, I'm in control."
"Don't blow this out of proportion."
"Think of this as a useful experience."
"It's not fun, but I can roll with the punches."
"Take a deep breath, stay cool, and use your head."
"I have a right to be annoyed, but I need to concentrate on my goals."
"I can gain more by not blowing my top."
"I don't have to let the other person's anger get to me. I have more self-control."

Afterward, remember to give yourself credit for your efforts:

"I'm not perfect, but I handled it pretty well."
"It wasn't as hard as I thought."
"I'm getting better every time."
"These situations aren't fun, but they are part of life."
"I feel a lot better about myself when I use good coping skills."

These stress-inoculation statements can be used in two ways. They can be used as you go through the anger-provoking life event, and you can practice ahead of time by relaxing and talking yourself through the anger-provoking experience in your imagination. Use self-relaxation and adaptive self-statements as you rehearse and practice maintaining your self-control and feelings of self-efficacy (Meichenbaum, 1977, 1985; Novaco, 1980; Schlichter & Horan, 1981).

Coping Skill 4: Using Stress Inoculation
to Coach Yourself Through Anger-Provoking Life Events

Blowing Off Steam

When anger does get the best of us, it can help to blow off steam by getting busy with a physical or creative activity. The value of "working off" anger is that it will put you in a more relaxed frame of mind to solve the problem that made you angry in the first place. It is important to understand that blowing off steam as a skill for coping with anger is a two-stage process. The first stage involves getting the tenseness and arousal out of your system. The second stage involves working out the problem. Blowing off steam is often misunderstood as a coping skill because people don't recognize the importance of the second stage. Blowing off steam won't make the source of frustration or mistreatment go away. It will just give you more self-control so you can deal with it. Don't get in the habit of blowing off steam without taking the second step — solving the problem (Konecni, 1984; Novaco, 1986).

Coping Skill 5: Recognizing
That Blowing Off Steam Is a Two-Stage Process

Believing in Yourself as a Coper

When you start to believe in yourself as a coper, you no longer ask whether anger is a good or bad emotion. Instead, you focus on taking care of yourself and getting your needs met without harming others. At times it may be very useful and appropriate to express anger. On other occasions, expressing anger will only make things worse. As a coper, you decide whether expressing anger is in your best interest or whether other tactics will serve you better. Because relating to others with anger is not always an optimal strategy, how else can you protect yourself? You certainly don't want to be a passive person who is controlled by others. The answer to this question lies in understanding the difference between nonassertiveness, aggression, and assertiveness (Lange & Jakubowski, 1976).

Coping Skill 6: Believing in Yourself as a Coper

NONASSERTIVENESS

People are nonassertive when they fail to stand up for themselves. To be nonassertive is to be passive, apologetic, timid, and self-effacing. Nonassertiveness gives the message that your needs are not important and that you are willing to go along with what others want, even when what they want is not in your best interest. Nonassertiveness indicates a lack of respect for your own needs. It also communicates to others that you are not willing to hold up your end of an interpersonal relationship, which, by definition, requires bargaining and negotiation.

One reason people fall into the trap of being nonassertive is that they don't acknowledge their personal rights. You want to be helpful and polite, so you give in to other people's wishes. Sometimes people mistake assertiveness for being pushy and aggressive. You may feel that it is inappropriate or impolite to say what's on your mind and to stand up for yourself. It is also tempting to be nonassertive to avoid negative responses.

If you are going to take care of your needs, you are bound to come into conflict with others. You must learn to tolerate the frowns, criticisms, pouts, and other punishments that come when you refuse to be passive. It is often easy to be nonassertive because it is the course of least resistance. But when you get used to being nonassertive, it is difficult to see how you can act any other way. Some hints about how to develop assertiveness are given later in this chapter.

Coping Skill 7: Taking Responsibility to Overcome Nonassertiveness

AGGRESSION

Aggression involves standing up for your rights in a *hostile* manner. Aggression is often directed toward taking advantage of others. When people are aggressive, they try to get their needs met by overpowering, belittling, humiliating, or degrading others. Aggression communicates that you are concerned only about yourself. When you are aggressive, other people's rights, needs, and desires don't matter to you.

People often fall into the trap of being aggressive when they feel threatened and vulnerable or mistreated. Anger builds up until it is expressed as aggression. Another reason for choosing aggression is that we are bombarded in movies and television with examples of "heroes" who come out on top with aggressive actions. However, in real life these "heroes" would be lonely and isolated people, unable to sustain long-term relationships. Aggressive behavior may look successful within the confines of television and movie scripts oriented toward a "quick fix" and immediate gratification, but in the long run, aggression alienates us from others and turns us into hostile, fearful, and suspicious people.

Coping Skill 8: Understanding the Limits of Aggression

ASSERTIVENESS

Assertiveness means standing up for your rights and expressing your thoughts and feelings in a direct, honest, and appropriate manner. When you are being assertive, you show respect for yourself and for others. On one hand, you are not passive and don't allow people to take advantage of you. On the other hand, you acknowledge other people's needs and attempt to relate to them in a tactful manner.

There are a number of advantages to being assertive. Assertiveness gives us a feeling of self-efficacy and internal control. This helps boost self-esteem and confidence when interacting with others. Because assertiveness requires tact and negotiation, you have to be flexible, and you won't always get everything you want. However, because other people also have needs, wishes, and desires, assertiveness provides the best approach for achieving mutually satisfying interpersonal relationships.

Coping Skill 9: Appreciating the Benefits of Being Assertive

EXAMPLES OF ASSERTIVENESS, NONASSERTIVENESS, AND AGGRESSION

A salesman is putting pressure on you to buy something:

Salesperson:	OK, are you ready for me to write up the sale?
Nonassertive Response:	Well, I guess so, if you think it's a good deal.
Aggressive Response:	Stop being so pushy! I'm not buying anything from you!
Assertive Response:	I'm sorry, but I'm not ready to make a purchase.

Someone tries to cut in front of you in a supermarket line:

Person:	You don't mind if I cut in here do you? I'm in a hurry.
Nonassertive Response:	Well, OK.
Aggressive Response:	Hey! What are you trying to do? Get the hell back in line!
Assertive Response:	I'm sorry, but I do mind. I'm in a hurry also.

Your supervisor gives you a questionable evaluation:

Supervisor:	Here is your evaluation. You need to sign it.
Nonassertive Response:	There are some things here that I'm not sure about, but I guess I can do better next time.
Aggressive Response:	This is a lousy evaluation! If you are not willing to change it, I'm going to the grievance committee.
Assertive Response:	I'm having trouble with some of the things you've written here. I'd like to talk with you about them.

A friend asks to borrow your car for the weekend:

Friend:	You don't mind if I borrow your car for the weekend, do you?
Nonassertive Response:	I did have some other plans, but OK. Try to let me know sooner next time.
Aggressive Response:	You've got a lot of nerve asking me on such short notice. Forget it!
Assertive Response:	I've already planned to use my car this weekend. I'd be happy to lend it to you in the future if you give me enough notice.

A relative calls and says she wants to visit next weekend:

Relative:	I know this is late notice, but you don't mind if I come visit next weekend, do you?
Nonassertive Response:	Well, we did have some plans. But, OK, I guess we can work around them somehow.

Aggressive Response:	Look, you can't just come and visit whenever you feel like it! We have plans, too, you know.
Assertive Response:	Next weekend is not a good time for you to visit. We'll have to find another time.

Your neighbors are having a very loud party:

Neighbor:	Don't worry. Everyone will leave in an hour.
Nonassertive Response:	Well, OK, as long as it's not longer than an hour.
Aggressive Response:	What right do you think you have to disturb the whole neighborhood? I'll show you! I'm calling the police.
Assertive Response:	You are disturbing the whole neighborhood. You have to keep the noise down. Otherwise I have no choice but to call the police.

PERFECTING ASSERTIVENESS

Understanding What It Means to Be Assertive

The first step in perfecting assertiveness is understanding the nature of an assertive response. When you are assertive, you stand up for your rights in an honest and forth-right manner, while still showing respect for the other person. In the examples of assertive, nonassertive, and aggressive responses given here, you can see that when you are assertive you don't let others take advantage of you, but you also acknowledge their needs and desires.

Three Useful Skills

Three skills that help improve assertiveness are owning your feelings, being empathic, and being tactful.

Owning your feelings.   Owning your feelings means letting others know how you feel about what they are doing. Avoid accusing others by saying things like: "You are inconsiderate." "You are pushy." "You're a slob." Instead, communicate how their actions make you feel: "I'm sorry, but I have other plans." "I'm sorry, but I can't oblige you." "It would make me happy if you would take better care of yourself." Owning your feelings will do much to increase your self-respect and the respect others have for you.

Being empathic.   Empathy is powerful medicine for enhancing cordial relationships. Other people will be much more ready to accept your expression of your desires if you are willing to acknowledge theirs. This does not mean that you have to *accept* what others want. You can disagree with others and still give them the courtesy of letting them know you understand how they feel.

Being tactful.   When you own your feelings and respond with empathy, you are much more likely to come across as tactful rather than rude. Nobody likes the feeling of being pushed around. If others are pushing you, instead of pushing back, stand firm and respond in a way that will win their respect.

Preferred and Disliked Influence Tactics

Here are some influence tactics that people find acceptable (Falbo, 1977):

Bargain: Reciprocating favors and making two-way exchanges
Compromise: Willingness to give up some wishes for the sake of agreement
Reason: Being reasonable and rational
Expertise: Relying on knowledge and experience

These influence tactics are disliked:

Threat: Making threats if you don't get your way
Deceit: Using false information, flattery, and lies
Ignore: Doing things your own way while ignoring the other person's needs
Evade: Getting your own way secretly without the other person's knowledge

People don't like others who try to influence them with threats, deceit, ignoring, or evasion. Perfecting assertiveness means being tactful and practicing the skills for negotiation outlined later in this chapter.

Accepting Your Rights and Responsibilities

People often get confused about the difference between being selfish and asserting their rights. Aggression is selfish because it is geared toward getting your needs met without regard for others. Assertiveness implies that you are willing to be flexible and to negotiate. However, it also implies that you have a bottom line and are committed to looking out for yourself. It is hardly selfish to express your beliefs, communicate your feelings, and stand up for your values. People who accuse you of being inconsiderate or selfish when you do this are acting aggressively and trying to make you feel guilty. When others accuse you of being inconsiderate and selfish, it is tempting to give in to nonassertiveness. But this is a cop-out. When you are nonassertive, you are forsaking your commitment to take responsibility for your life. As assertive people, we have to be willing to stand up to others' attempts to manipulate us. We have to bear up to their criticisms and rejections. As long as you know you are acting in a fair and mature manner, you have your self-respect. If others choose to be childish and aggressive, that is their problem.

Assertiveness Training Groups

Assertiveness is becoming more recognized as an effective skill for interacting with others. Many books have been written on the topic, and groups have been formed throughout the United States to help people perfect their assertiveness skills. These groups include the following experiences (Eisler & Frederiksen, 1980; Lange & Jakubowski, 1976):

1. A description and rationale for assertive behaviors to be learned.
2. A demonstration of assertive behaviors through modeling.
3. A chance to practice assertive behaviors in role-play situations.
4. An opportunity to receive suggestions and support from other group members as the assertive behaviors are practiced in real life.

Assertiveness training groups give participants the opportunity to practice the coping skills outlined in this book in an atmosphere of mutual support.

Coping Skill 10: Perfecting Assertiveness Skills

NEGOTIATING

To avoid suffering needless anger, you have to recognize that interpersonal relations are founded on negotiation. In some cases you can get your way by bullying others and overpowering them. If you always insist on getting your way, you will eventually pay a price. You may often win, but you will be lonely and isolated. Conversely, if you make it a habit to always be passive and give in to the wishes of others, you can avoid the efforts of negotiation but will end up feeling resentful. The best solution is to be a good negotiator. Here are some tips to help you improve your negotiating skills (Bazerman, 1986).

The Virtue of Compromise

Children are taught from a young age that they can't have everything they want. Ironically, we seem to forget this lesson when we grow up. Compromising is a skill that involves understanding your needs as well as the needs of others. You don't have to accept or agree with someone's desires, but you do need to let the person know that you have understood what they want.

Compromise is also an attitude wherein you don't look at interpersonal relations as win or lose situations. You have to be flexible enough to give the other person satisfaction. For both people to get something they want, each person may have to give something to the other.

Be Level-Headed

When you are negotiating, strong feelings are likely to come out. Recognize and accept these feelings and try to keep on an even keel. Here are several things you can do to prevent emotions from escalating to an unproductive level:

1. Avoid making rigid demands. Rigid demands rope you into a situation where any compromise seems like a loss.

2. Do not look at negotiations as a competition where one person wins and the other loses.
3. Use self-relaxation to stay in control of your feelings.
4. Make the atmosphere cordial by showing empathy.
5. Be assertive, and avoid nonassertive or aggressive responses.

Be a Coper

Copers know how to be assertive, flexible, and empathic. The outcome of a negotiation is weighed not only in terms of what you get but also in terms of how you conduct yourself. Circumstances sometimes dictate that you have to give more than you wish. However, if you do this out of choice and with tact, you can take pride in your ability to act in a mature and responsible manner.

Coping Skill 11: Being a Good Negotiator

APPRECIATING THE POWER OF FORGIVING

A valuable lesson many people learn as they are growing up is to appreciate the power of forgiving. When you forgive someone for mistreating you, you don't necessarily absolve that person from responsibility (Flanigan, 1992). Forgiving also does not mean that you forget the wrongdoing. But when you forgive, you release yourself from the burden of carrying your anger and free yourself up to get on with your life. The power of forgiveness lies in the possibility it offers for you to take the "upper hand" in a conflict. Because you forgive from a position of strength and self-confidence, the act of forgiveness enhances your self-efficacy and control in an unpleasant situation. Forgiveness follows the philosophy that we teach children: It is the stronger person who knows when not to fight back.

Coping Skill 12: Appreciating the Power of Forgiving

A BRIEF SUMMARY

Let me take a moment now to summarize the main points in this chapter about coping with anger. Anger is a natural response to frustration and mistreatment, and we are all destined to face occasions for anger throughout our lives. The first question to ask yourself when you are angry is whether you are making a realistic primary appraisal. Some life events give us good cause for feeling angry. Others are not worth getting angry about, and you have to question seriously whether you are making unreasonable demands on life that are causing needless anger. When your primary appraisal tells you that your anger is justified, your secondary appraisal determines what you are going to do about it. Sometimes it is in your best interest to express your anger. On other occasions, you may decide that although you are justifiably angry you will be better off controlling your anger with self-relaxation, stress inoculation, blowing off steam, and confronting the problem with assertiveness and negotiation. It is important to see yourself as a coper who knows how to work out strategies for relating with other people that, in the long run, will be in your best interest.

LIST OF SKILLS FOR COPING WITH ANGER

- *Coping Skill 1:* Being Emotionally Creative
- *Coping Skill 2:* Testing the Rationality of Your Primary Appraisals
- *Coping Skill 3:* Using Self-Relaxation to Maintain Control When You Are Frustrated and Mistreated
- *Coping Skill 4:* Using Stress Inoculation to Coach Yourself Through Anger-Provoking Life Events
- *Coping Skill 5:* Recognizing That Blowing Off Steam Is a Two-Stage Process
- *Coping Skill 6:* Believing in Yourself as a Coper
- *Coping Skill 7:* Taking Responsibility to Overcome Nonassertiveness
- *Coping Skill 8:* Understanding the Limits of Aggression
- *Coping Skill 9:* Appreciating the Benefits of Being Assertive
- *Coping Skill 10:* Perfecting Assertiveness Skills
- *Coping Skill 11:* Being a Good Negotiator
- *Coping Skill 12:* Appreciating the Power of Forgiving

SUGGESTIONS FOR FURTHER READING

Ellis, A. (1987). *Anger—How to live with and without it.* Secaucus, NJ: Citadel Press.

Flanigan, B. (1992). *Forgiving the unforgivable: Overcoming the bitter legacy of intimate wounds.* New York: Macmillan.

Lange, A. J., & Jakubowski, P. (1976). *Responsible assertive behavior.* Champaign, IL: Research Press.

McKay, M., Rogers, P. D., & McKay, J. (1989). *When anger hurts: Quieting the storm within.* Oakland, CA: New Harbinger.

Novaco, R. W. (1975). *Anger control.* Lexington, MA: D. C. Heath.

Stearns, C. Z., & Stearns, P. N. (1986). *Anger: The struggle for emotional control in American history.* Chicago: University of Chicago Press.

Coping with Conflicts in Close Relationships

You experience conflicts with people close to you when they do something you dislike or refuse to do something you like. Although this may be obvious, you now know enough to realize that your primary appraisals have a lot to do with what you choose to like and dislike. In this chapter I will teach you how to cope with conflicts in close relationships by reevaluating and modifying your appraisals. By increasing your flexibility and broadening your options, you can gain a greater sense of effectiveness.

STYLES OF LOVE AND ATTACHMENT

A good place to begin our exploration of close relationships is by understanding the differences in people's styles of love and attachment. Understanding love and attachment styles will help you decide what you want in your relationships.

Styles of Love

Close relationships have three active ingredients: *commitment, intimacy,* and *passion* (Sternberg, 1986; Sternberg & Grajeck, 1984). The presence or absence of these components determines the nature of the relationship (see Table 9.1):

Liking requires intimacy, but not commitment or passion.

Infatuation is "love at first sight." There is passion, but the relationship never develops to the depth of commitment and intimacy.

Empty love is commitment without intimacy and passion. It occurs in stagnant relationships where couples stay together out of inertia or because they don't believe in divorce.

Romantic love is a combination of intimacy and passion. It is a "heavy affair" without commitment.

TABLE 9.1   Three ingredients in close relationships

	Ingredients		
Type of Relationship	**Commitment**	**Intimacy**	**Passion**
Liking		X	
Infatuation			X
Empty love	X		
Romantic love		X	X
Fatuous love	X		X
Companionate love	X	X	
Consummate love	X	X	X

SOURCE: From "A Triangular Theory of Love," by R. J. Sternberg, 1986, *Psychological Review*, 93, 119–135. Copyright 1986 by the American Psychological Association. Adapted with permission.

> *Fatuous love* is "Hollywood" love. The man and woman fall madly in love and get married without really knowing each other.
> *Companionate love* is intimacy with commitment but not passion. It is a long-term friendship. It is platonic love or a close marriage lacking in sex.
> *Consummate love* is an ideal relationship that includes passion, commitment, and intimacy.

The kinds of love outlined in Table 9.1 suggest two important conclusions. On one hand, we must recognize that it is difficult, if not impossible, to maintain a long-term relationship at the level of consummate love. All relationships have their normal ups and downs. On the other hand, we must also realize that we have standards about what is acceptable and unacceptable in a long-term relationship. When you find yourself in a relationship that is not satisfactory, it is time to make a move. One option is to work with your partner to bring the ingredients that are missing into the relationship. A second option is to end the relationship.

Attachment Styles

When forming close relationships, people generally adopt one of three attachment styles: secure, avoidant, or anxious/ambivalent (N. L. Collins & Read, 1990; Feeney & Noller, 1990; Hazan & Shaver, 1987).

A *secure* attachment style is characterized by the following attitudes:

> I find it relatively easy to get close to others.
> I am comfortable depending on others.
> I am comfortable when others depend on me.
> I don't often worry about being abandoned or about someone getting too close to me.

People with a secure attachment style have feelings of happiness, friendship, and trust in their close relationships. They have high self-esteem and feel that others like them and care for them. A secure attachment style is related to the desire to appreciate, care for, and sacrifice oneself for significant others. People with a secure attachment style are comfortable with trust, closeness, and dependency because they expect others to respond with acceptance, closeness, and support (Baldwin, Fehr, Keedian, Seidel, & Thompson, 1993).

An *avoidant* attachment style is characterized by the following attitudes:

I am somewhat uncomfortable being close to others.
I find it difficult to trust people.
I am nervous when anyone gets too close.
I don't enjoy being dependent on others.

People with an avoidant attachment style tend to keep to themselves, and they "hold back" from getting too involved in relationships. They view trust, closeness, and dependency as risky because they expect others to hurt and reject them (Baldwin et al., 1993). An avoidant attachment style is associated with a lack of passion and love for significant others.

An *anxious/ambivalent* attachment style is characterized by the following attitudes:

I find that others are reluctant to get as close as I would like.
I often worry that my partner doesn't really love me.
I want to merge completely with another person, and this desire sometimes scares people away.
I am worried about getting too close to someone and then being abandoned.

People with an anxious/ambivalent attachment style tend to be insecure and jealous in their close relationships. They approach relationships with an attitude of wanting to be close, but they are preoccupied with the fear of rejection.

It is perhaps not surprising that people with a secure attachment style are more satisfied with their close relationships and feel a greater sense of trust, commitment, and pleasure with others (Fuller & Fincham, 1995; Simpson, 1990). An avoidant attachment style helps protect people from feeling too bad when relationships are terminated, but people who relate with this style pay the price of not enjoying their relationships very much while they last.

The love and attachment styles people desire in close relationships depend on their cultural background and individual preferences (Dion & Dion, 1993). This discussion was intended to provide some options and possibilities. Again, you have standards about what kinds of attachments are acceptable and unacceptable in your interpersonal relationships. When your attachments with significant others do not meet your expectations, you need to decide what to do about it.

Coping Skill 1: Deciding What You Want in a Relationship

RELATIONSHIP SATISFACTION

Another way to understand close relationships is by looking at how satisfied people are with a particular relationship. Satisfaction in close relationships can be measured with the Relationship Assessment Scale (Hendrick, 1988). Respondents are asked to rate the following questions on a scale ranging from 1 (not at all) to 5 (very much):

It is well worth taking the time and effort to make the best of your personal relationships.

1. How well does your partner meet your needs?
2. In general, how satisfied are you with your relationship?
3. How good is your relationship compared to most?
4. How often do you wish you hadn't gotten into this relationship?
5. To what extent has your relationship met your original expectations?
6. How much do you love your partner?
7. How many problems are there in your relationship?

People who give high ratings to items 1, 2, 3, 5, and 6 and low ratings to items 4 and 7 are most satisfied with their relationships. An average score of 4 to 5 indicates relatively high satisfaction with a relationship, and an average score of 3 or below suggests a relatively low amount of satisfaction with a relationship.

Coping Skill 2: Assessing Your Satisfaction

TAKING ACTIVE RESPONSIBILITY

When you have interpersonal conflicts, you must take active responsibility for finding a solution. In Chapter 1 you learned about the danger of avoiding problems because they usually catch up with you in the long run. This lesson is reinforced in a study of how people cope with marital conflicts (Menaghan, 1982). A community survey indicated that people generally use one of four different kinds of strategies for dealing with conflicts in their marriage: negotiation, optimistic comparisons, ignoring, and resignation.

Negotiation: Sitting down and talking things out. Working out a fair compromise.

Optimistic comparisons: Appreciating the marriage in comparison with others. Viewing the marriage as improving over time.

Ignoring: Telling yourself that conflicts don't matter. Underestimating how much the difficulties really bother you.

Resignation: Keeping dissatisfactions to yourself. Not communicating directly with your partner.

The participants were studied for a period of four years to learn how these different coping styles influenced their marriage. Not surprisingly, ignoring and resignation were not effective in resolving marital conflicts. Couples who reacted to conflicts with ignoring and resignation suffered the greatest distress and were rarely able to solve their problems. Other coping strategies that are associated with relationship dissatisfaction are acting out one's emotions, disengaging and withdrawing, and resorting to alcohol and drugs (Ptacek & Dodge, 1995).

In contrast, the active skills of negotiation and optimistic comparison were both useful for resolving marital conflicts. Negotiation requires skill, patience, and cooperation from the other person. Optimistic comparison is an appraisal you can make for yourself to gain a more objective perspective about your relationships with close others.

A good way to take active responsibility in a relationship is to understand the value of empathy. Three kinds of empathy are important in promoting feelings of closeness in a relationship: *perspective taking, empathic concern,* and *compassion* (Davis & Oathout, 1987). Perspective taking means taking the time to see the issues from your partner's perspective. Empathic concern is a genuine caring about how your partner is feeling. Compassion means putting yourself in your partner's shoes and experiencing the same feelings and emotions he or she is experiencing. When both partners in a relationship take active responsibility for demonstrating these kinds of empathy, their happiness and satisfaction are likely to increase.

Coping Skill 3: Taking Active Responsibility

EVALUATING EXPECTATIONS

Realistic and Unrealistic Expectations

Conflicts usually begin when the other person does something negative or neglects to do something positive. Your reaction is colored by your expectations about what you can reasonably ask for (see Figure 9.1). This is a good place to do some serious reality testing and to seek objective feedback. One group of researchers constructed a questionnaire that measures realistic and unrealistic expectations in close relationships (Eidelson & Epstein, 1982). Check whether you agree or disagree with the following statements.

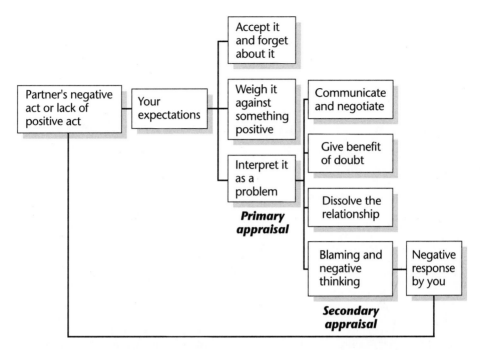

FIGURE 9.1   Appraising and coping with conflicts in close relationships

	Strongly agree	Agree	Disagree	Strongly disagree
1. It is destructive when people in close relationships have differences and disagreements.	____	____	____	____
2. My partner should always be aware of how I feel.	____	____	____	____
3. My partner is never going to change.	____	____	____	____
4. My partner should always satisfy me sexually.	____	____	____	____
5. My partner does not have the same needs I do.	____	____	____	____

If you think carefully about these beliefs, you will realize that they sound good but are not very realistic. Marriage partners who hold such unrealistic beliefs have difficulty accepting their spouse's "imperfect" behaviors, and they respond negatively with hostility and rejection (Bradbury & Fincham, 1993). It is not surprising that unrealistic expectations will result in less satisfying marriages than expectations that are more true to life, such as the following (Bradbury & Fincham, 1988):

Disagreements do occur in close relationships.

My partner cannot be a mind reader.

My partner can change if I am willing to negotiate.

Sex is almost always an issue to be worked on in close relationships.

People often have similar needs in a relationship.

Attributions for Desirable and Undesirable Behaviors

Closely related to realistic and unrealistic expectations is the question of how people in close relationships explain each other's desirable and undesirable behaviors. Men and women in close relationships were asked to describe their major conflicts (Harvey, Wells, & Alvarez, 1978; Orvis, Kelley, & Butler, 1976). Two interesting results emerged, showing that we are less objective about conflicts with close others than we might believe. First, men and women tended to justify their own negative acts in relationships as reflecting "good intentions" or as caused by events beyond their control. For example, they explained their aggressive and irresponsible actions as a reaction to something their partner had done. In a similar manner, they claimed their criticisms and demands were a sign of concern and helpfulness. Failure to share feelings and show affection were blamed on external demands and pressures. When explaining the causes of their partner's behaviors, people's perceptions were very different. Men and women felt that negative acts by their partners were intentional and reflected a lack of commitment and caring. In short, both men and women found it easy to forgive their own negative actions and difficult to forgive their partner's negative actions.

A second important finding was that men's and women's perceptions about their partners' wishes and desires were not always accurate. For example, sexual relations were seen as a more important source of conflict by men than by women. However, men falsely assumed that their partners felt the same way about sex as they did. Women made a similar error by underestimating men's views of the importance of sexual incompatibility. Women falsely assumed that their partners felt the same about sexual issues as they did. Conflicts related to financial problems and time spent on work and education were rated as more important by women than by men. Women overestimated men's ratings of importance on these issues, assuming that men felt the same way they felt. Men underestimated women's ratings of importance on these issues, assuming that women's feelings were similar to theirs.

There are two fairly strong predictors of marital satisfaction and marital stability (Karney & Bradbury, 1995):

1. The ability of husbands and wives to initiate and reciprocate positive behaviors toward each other.
2. The ability of husbands and wives to restrain from initiating negative behaviors and to avoid responding negatively to each other's undesirable behaviors.

Husbands and wives are most likely to engage in positive behaviors and to avoid negative behaviors when they share mutual trust and give each other the benefit of the doubt. Couples experiencing marital dissatisfaction cite these kinds of undesirable behaviors: being critical, being distant, not helping out with chores, not giving support

(Fincham & Bradbury, 1992, 1993). They often give these explanations for such behavior:

> "My spouse's behavior was due to his/her personality."
> "My spouse's behavior is not likely to change."
> "My spouse's behavior reflects a basic problem in our marriage."
> "My spouse behaved in this way for selfish reasons."
> "My spouse deserves to be blamed for his/her behavior."

Couples who have a harmonious marriage are able to make these more adaptive attributions for each other's undesirable behaviors:

> "My spouse's behavior was influenced by the situation."
> "My spouse does not always act this way."
> "My spouse's behavior is not a reflection of our total relationship."
> "My spouse's behavior was not desirable, but I know he/she cares about me."
> "I can forgive my spouse for this behavior."

It is not surprising that maladaptive explanations for a spouse's undesirable behaviors result in marital distress (Bradbury & Fincham, 1992; G. E. Miller & Bradbury, 1995). If you interpret the behaviors of a significant other as reflecting undesirable personality characteristics and negative intentions, you are likely to respond with either hostility or avoidance. Neither of these behaviors is conducive to the kind of patience and cooperation required for you and your significant other to work together to find compromises or solutions to your problems.

Coping Skill 4: Reevaluating Expectations

DESIRED AREAS OF CHANGE

Another way to analyze your expectations in close relationships is by looking at what things you would like your partner to change. To clarify this aspect of relationships, researchers developed the Areas of Change Questionnaire, which measures how much people want their partners to change in areas ranging from sex and affection, finances and household matters, friends and relatives, to work and child rearing (Margolin, Talovic, & Weinstein, 1983). When husbands and wives who were getting along fairly well (nondistressed couples) took this questionnaire, they agreed on most areas of desired change, except for sex (see Table 9.2). Husbands ranked improved sexual relations as the most important change they wanted from their wives. Wives wanted many changes from their husbands ahead of sex (13th on their list of desired changes). Not surprisingly, compared with nondistressed couples, distressed couples expressed far more desire for their partners to change. More than half of the distressed couples surveyed wanted their partners to make changes in communicating emotions clearly, not arguing as much, starting conversations, showing appreciation, sexual relationships, and spending close time together. One interesting aspect of the Areas of Change Questionnaire is that it is both objective and subjective. The areas of change

TABLE 9.2   Desired areas of change in nondistressed couples

Husbands	Wives
Improved sexual relations	Express his emotions clearly
Express her emotions clearly	Start interesting conversations with me
Accept praise	Show appreciation for things I do well
Start interesting conversations with me	Spend time keeping the house clean
Show appreciation for things I do well	Help in planning our free time
Leave me time to myself	Go out with me
Spend time keeping the house clean	Help with housework when asked
Not letting work interfere with relationship	Accomplish his responsibilities promptly

SOURCE: From "Areas of Change Questionnaire: A Practical Approach to Marital Assessment," by G. Margolin, S. Talovic, and C. D. Weinstein, 1983, *Journal of Consulting and Clinical Psychology, 51,* 920–931. Copyright 1983 by the American Psychological Association. Adapted with permission.

we wish from people close to us are real to the extent that they reflect our true desires. Our desired changes are also subjective because they are based on our perceptions about what is going on in the relationship. You can do a lot to reduce misunderstandings by being sensitive to changes you desire from others as well as changes others desire from you.

Coping Skill 5: Being Sensitive to Desired Areas of Change

PRIMARY APPRAISAL

When you make a primary appraisal about a negative act (or the lack of a positive act) by someone close, you are asking whether this is something you can accept. For instance: "X did something negative or neglected to do something positive. Can I live with it? Or is it unacceptable and therefore a problem?"

Practicing Tolerance

You can save yourself a lot of grief by accepting the fact that neither you nor those close to you are perfect. Some things are just not worth getting upset about. If you think about it, it's obvious that your relationships with others will be greatly enhanced if you can practice tolerance. Things that bug you and hurt your feelings are a burden. When you can say, "OK, I can accept it and forget about it," you gain a feeling of self-efficacy and control. By being tolerant, you are saying, "I am flexible enough to get along without everything I want."

The value of tolerance was demonstrated in a study comparing reactions of distressed and nondistressed couples to positive and negative behaviors by their spouses (Jacobson, Follette, & McDonald, 1982). Not surprisingly, distressed couples were more likely than nondistressed couples to be upset and bothered when a spouse did something negative. Interestingly, distressed couples were also more pleased when a spouse did something positive. This study demonstrates that distressed husbands and wives are on edge because they take each other's actions too seriously. They are so pre-occupied with getting immediate gratification from their partners that they can't flow with the ups and downs that are normal in a close relationship. In contrast, nondis-tressed husbands and wives are more comfortable with each other because they have learned to place each other's positive and negative behaviors into the perspective of a long-term relationship. They flow more easily with the inevitable ups and downs that occur in a marriage.

Coping Skill 6: Practicing Tolerance

Balancing the Negatives and Positives

Another way to live with the imperfections of close others is by balancing their nega-tive and positive actions. Even though people close to you are not perfect, they usu-ally do more things you like than dislike. Reminding yourself of their good deeds will often help you accept their not-so-good deeds. Of course, this would be easier to do if we were all perfect and completely objective. Research has shown, however, that human beings are rarely objective, especially when judging the actions of others. Our perceptions of someone's behaviors are very naturally affected by our expectations, needs, and values (Baron & Byrne, 1987, chap. 3).

A good example of people's subjectivity in reading each other's actions is shown in a study where men and women in close relationships talked together about their conflicts (Gaelick, Bodenhausen, & Wyer, 1985). The couples consented to have the conversations videotaped. The videotapes were later analyzed by researchers who carefully coded each couple's communication patterns. One important finding was that men and women were much more sensitive to each other's negative messages than they were to each other's positive messages. In other words, both men and women were quick to reciprocate their partners' hostility. It was much more difficult for them to return their partners' expressions of love.

There are three possible reasons couples have a hard time reciprocating expres-sions of love. First, people often do not communicate feelings of love very clearly. Second, people generally have a tendency to be more "on the lookout" for hostility than for love. Finally, when individuals do recognize expressions of love, it is some-times difficult for them to open up and communicate love in return. Balancing the positives and negatives requires an awareness of how those close to us are expressing their positive feelings.

Balancing the negatives and positives also means that you must give others credit for their attempts to do nice things for you. People have a tendency to react very per-sonally to negative actions by those close to them but often take their positive actions for granted. As you learned earlier in this chapter, distressed couples have a particular problem giving fair weight to each other's positives and negatives. Distressed couples blame their partners' negative behaviors on unacceptable motives and bad intentions. Nondistressed couples have learned to give each other the benefit of the doubt. Nondistressed couples are also able to give their partners credit and appreciation for positive actions. Because distressed couples don't recognize the good intentions behind their partners' positive behaviors, they aren't able to fully appreciate these positives in the relationship (Jacobson, McDonald, Follette, & Berley, 1985).

Coping Skill 7: Balancing the Negatives and Positives

Deciding There Is a Problem

Practicing tolerance and balancing the negatives and positives does not imply that you have no right to decide what is acceptable and unacceptable in a close relationship. This discussion is intended to help you become more objective. It is in your best interest to reevaluate your expectations and to place other people's negative and positive actions and words into their proper perspective. It is also in your best interest to be aware of your needs and to acknowledge your bottom line—what you can and cannot live with in a close relationship. You have every right to decide which positives you want from others and which negatives you are not willing to tolerate.

Coping Skill 8: Acknowledging Your Right to Determine Your Needs in a Relationship

OVERCOMING JEALOUSY

Check how often you have these feelings or reactions toward your current romantic partner.

	Never	Rarely	Sometimes	Often
1. I suspect he/she is attracted to someone else.	___	___	___	___
2. I am worried that someone else is trying to seduce him/her.	___	___	___	___
3. I suspect he/she is secretly seeing someone else.	___	___	___	___
4. I think that others may be romantically interested in him/her.	___	___	___	___
5. I question my partner about his/her whereabouts.	___	___	___	___

	Never	Rarely	Sometimes	Often
6. I join in whenever I see him/her talking to a potential rival.	_____	_____	_____	_____
7. I call unexpectedly, just to see if he/she is home.	_____	_____	_____	_____
8. I question him/her about previous or present romantic relationships.	_____	_____	_____	_____

Now check how the following events make you feel.

	Very pleased	Pleased	Upset	Very upset
9. He/she is flirting with someone.	_____	_____	_____	_____
10. He/she smiles in a very friendly manner at a potential rival.	_____	_____	_____	_____
11. He/she comments on how good-looking someone else is.	_____	_____	_____	_____
12. Someone else is trying to spend time alone with him/her.	_____	_____	_____	_____

These experiences are adapted from the Multidimensional Jealousy Scale (Pfeiffer & Wong, 1989). *Cognitive jealousy* is measured by items 1 through 4, *behavioral jealousy* is measured by items 5 through 8, and *emotional jealousy* is measured by items 9 through 12. Emotional and behavioral jealousy are related to feelings of unhappiness, and cognitive jealousy can be the root of considerable anxiety.

Jealousy can have a negative impact on your life if you allow it to get the best of you. By gaining a clearer understanding of this complex emotion, you will be able to cope with jealousy-provoking situations in a more effective manner. The first thing to recognize is that you do not have an inborn need to be jealous. While people in some cultures are fiercely jealous, jealousy is unknown in other cultures (Mead, 1986). Jealousy is inevitably related to the desire to control someone else who is important to us (Davis, 1986). When you are jealous, you are dependent on another person and also insecure (Berscheid & Fei, 1986). It is as if you demand a guarantee that this person will always be available to please you. Obviously, this isn't very realistic. Looking back at Figure 2.2 in Chapter 2, you can see that a jealousy-provoking situation is a life event. What kinds of appraisals are likely to result in feelings of jealousy? Probably demands such as:

"I demand that X be available whenever I need him/her."
"X isn't treating me right unless he/she caters to my needs."

"X is a bad person because he/she is not giving me what I want."
"X owes it to me to treat me the way I desire."

These kinds of beliefs put you in a no-win situation because they are unrealistic and bound to make you feel miserable (Ellis, 1987b). Margaret Mead (1986) explains the experience of jealousy in the following way: "It is a negative, miserable state of feeling, having its origin in a sense of insecurity and inferiority" (p. 121). Jealousy is generally viewed as a destructive emotion stemming from negative feelings about yourself (Fitness & Fletcher, 1993).

You can use your powers of rational thinking to talk yourself through jealousy-provoking situations by saying things such as:

"I truly desire X's affection, but I know it is not in my power to demand things I don't own."
"Sometimes I get what I want from X, and sometimes I don't. I have to balance the positives and the negatives."
"The more I demand things from others, the more I set myself up for frustration. I have to rely on my own resources to get my needs met."
"It's a pain and a disappointment when others don't give me what I want, but it is a fact of life I must learn to accept."

Surveys of how people cope with jealousy have obtained the following results. A community survey in New Zealand found that women tended to cope with jealousy by confronting their partners, expressing distress with tearful or angry recriminations, and attempting to make themselves more interesting and attractive (Mullen & Martin, 1994). Men were more likely than women to cope with jealousy by ignoring the problem and hoping it would go away. Men and women did not differ in their use of the following coping responses: demanding commitment from their partners, contemplating ending the relationship, or confiding in family or friends. Jealousy caused the greatest problems for younger people in their teens and twenties. Older people, and people who had a greater number of previous relationships, were less troubled by jealousy. Jealousy was also less of a problem for people with high self-esteem.

People responding to a U.S. survey were asked how they coped when they experienced jealousy at school or work, in their family, and in friendships and romantic relationships (Salovey & Rodin, 1988). The most successful copers were men and women who took an attitude of self-reliance. Instead of upsetting themselves or the people about whom they felt jealous, they got busy with other activities in their lives. Successful copers appraised jealousy as an inconvenient hassle. They used the following coping skills to acknowledge their jealousy and to keep it from throwing their lives off track:

- Constructively dealing with anger
- Not feeling sorry for themselves
- Not ruminating about the unfairness of the situation
- Avoiding blaming other people
- Keeping up their own self-esteem

- Staying busy with meaningful activities
- Forcing themselves to let go

Many of the coping strategies outlined in Chapter 3 are useful for coping with jealousy. Let's review them now.

Support systems: Use your support people to lean on for caring when the person you *really* want it from is unwilling or unavailable.

Problem solving: Use your problem-solving skills to identify realistic strategies for obtaining love and nurturing. Remember that you can't demand love and nurturing from a particular person.

Self-relaxation: Use your self-relaxation skills to tone down feelings of insecurity, frustration, and anger.

Maintain internal control: Remind yourself that your worth is based on your personal accomplishments and resources and isn't controlled by another person.

Exercise: Exercise is a good method for distracting yourself from your unhappy feelings and doing something good for yourself.

Sense of humor: Don't take yourself too seriously. Learn to laugh at your propensity for making yourself miserable

Reward yourself for accomplishments: Don't put yourself down for feeling jealous. Give yourself credit for owning your jealousy and for taking responsibility to overcome it.

Coping Skill 9: Overcoming Jealousy

COPING WITH AN UNSATISFACTORY RELATIONSHIP

If you have reevaluated your expectations and balanced the negatives and positives and are still not satisfied with a relationship, it is time to make a secondary appraisal, to say: "My relationship with X has a problem. What am I going to do about it?" I will discuss some options you may wish to consider.

Taking Positive Action

When a relationship is threatened, both partners must decide together whether they are willing to give what it takes to pull it back together. If you are both motivated to improve the relationship, professional therapists and counselors can be very helpful.

Something partners can do on their own is an exercise called *caring days* developed by Richard Stuart (1980), which stimulates constructive actions and positive feelings. The partners make a list of 20 positive actions they would like from each other. The following rules must be followed:

1. The actions must be *positive*. Each person asks the partner to do things the person likes. No one is allowed to ask the partner to stop doing things the person dislikes.
2. The actions must be specific. For example, rather than asking the partner to be more affectionate say, "Hug me three times a day," "In the evening, ask me how my day went." "Help with the dishes."
3. The actions must be small behaviors that can be done every day.
4. The actions should not be things the partner is touchy about or that have been the subject of recent conflict.

When the lists are completed, the partners sign a contract agreeing that they both promise to do at least five of the acts on each list every day. Both partners make a daily log on which they record each other's positive actions. This log helps them jointly monitor their progress and reinforces them for their efforts.

COMMUNICATING AND NEGOTIATING

Another option you have when someone close to you behaves in an unacceptable way is to communicate your dissatisfaction and negotiate a solution. This is where your assertiveness skills (see Chapter 8) can be very useful. Remember that assertiveness means being honest, straightforward, and nonaggressive. To help you appreciate the value of communication and negotiation, let's look first at some less effective methods of getting your needs met by close others.

People in close relationships identified six tactics they most often employ to influence their romantic partners (Buss, Gomes, Higgins, & Lauterbach, 1987):

Charm: "I compliment my partner so he/she will do it." "I try to be loving and romantic when I ask for things." "I act charming so he/she will do it."

Silent treatment: "I ignore my partner until he/she does what I want." "I don't respond to my partner until he/she does what I want." "I am silent until my partner does what I want."

Coercion: "I demand that my partner do what I want." "I yell at my partner until he/she does what I want." "I threaten my partner until he/she does what I want."

Logical arguments: "I give my partner reasons why he/she should do what I want." "I ask my partner why he/she doesn't do what I want." "I explain why I want him/her to do what I want."

Passive-aggression: "I pout until he/she does what I want." "I sulk until he/she does what I want." "I am difficult to get along with until he/she does what I want."

Self-downing: "I put myself down so he/she will do what I want." "I act inadequate so he/she will do what I want." "I act humble so he/she will do what I want."

The striking thing about these influence tactics is that *none* of them is very adaptive. Couples who engaged in these tactics rated themselves and were rated by people who interviewed them as dissimilar, mismatched, and not likely to stay together. It is instructive that the people sampled in this study did not report much use of communication and negotiation.

Researchers studying communication styles that cause particular problems between husbands and wives found the following three patterns (N. Epstein, Pretzer, & Fleming, 1987):

1. *Critical and defensive:* Refuses to acknowledge mistakes, refuses to accept criticism, dogmatic and rigid about opinions, inappropriately blames spouse, fails to give compliments.
2. *Withdrawn and submissive:* Talks too little, fails to express opinions, is too compliant, fails to express emotions, talks too slowly and quietly.
3. *Dominant and controlling:* Talks too much, asks too many questions, interrupts when spouse is talking, changes topics during discussions, talks too loudly.

Although all three of these styles end up blocking communication, the one related to the highest level of marital distress was being critical and defensive.

Now that you are familiar with problematic communication styles, let's consider some suggestions for communicating more effectively (Stuart, 1980).

Learning to Listen

Carl Rogers is generally acknowledged as having pointed out that we are often so preoccupied with our own thoughts and feelings that we don't really listen to what others are trying to tell us. Consider the following exchange:

Person A: How was your vacation?

Person B: It was great!

Person A: My vacation was good, too. We went to Hawaii and . . .

It is clear that Person A would rather talk about himself than listen to what person B has to say. Now compare the above conversation with this one:

Person A: How was your vacation?

Person B: It was great!

Person A: That sounds exciting. Tell me about it.

Here person A is actually listening to person B. Person A is being responsive (see Chapter 6) and is expressing a personal interest. You can practice listening skills with another person by agreeing to communicate in the following manner. Let's say your partner makes a statement. Before you respond, you have to repeat the meaning of this statement. Your partner then has a chance to acknowledge that you heard the statement accurately or to correct you. After showing your partner that you really understood the statement, it is your turn to talk. Your partner then repeats the meaning of your statement and receives feedback from you. For example:

Person A: I'm disappointed because you rarely show me affection.

Person B: You are insecure. You want more from me.

Person A: That's not what I said. Try again.

Person B: You want more affection.

Person A: You didn't say anything about my feelings.

Person B: You want more affection. You're being grouchy.

Person A: No, I'm disappointed because I want more affection from you.

Person B: You're disappointed. You want me to give you more affection.

Person A: Right.

Although it would be cumbersome to carry on all conversations in this manner, you can see how helpful this exercise can be for teaching us to listen to each other.

Owning Your Feelings

Compare the following statements:

A: You never do anything around the house.

B: I want your help with the housecleaning.

A: You never tell me you love me.

B: Once in a while I want you to tell me you love me.

A: Do you want to go to the movies?

B: I would like to go to the movies.

A: Your selfishness and inconsiderateness makes me angry.

B: I am angry because you didn't tell me you would be home late.

In the A statements the speaker is being indirect, and it is not clear what he or she really wants. In the B statements the speaker is owning feelings and saying exactly what he or she wants. When you own your feelings, you say, "I feel _____ when you do _____." Owning statements are *I* statements. *You* statements, such as, "*You* make me feel _____" or "*You* are _____" are nonimmediate and avoid responsibility.

A survey of married couples found that respondents were more likely to react in a negative and antagonistic manner if their spouses communicated feelings of dissatisfaction in an accusatory manner by making the following kinds of statements (Kubany, Bauer, Muraoka, Richard, & Read, 1995):

"You are making me unhappy."
"You disappointed me."
"You're making me furious."
"You're annoying me."

Respondents reported that they were more likely to be sympathetic and conciliatory if their spouses communicated feelings of dissatisfaction in an assertive manner by making the following kinds of statements:

"I am unhappy."
"I'm disappointed."
"I'm furious."
"I'm getting annoyed."

Five Rules for Constructive Communication

The following rules for constructive communication will help you make the most of your efforts to be clear and straightforward with others.

Rule 1: Own communications by using the word *I*.

Rule 2: Don't make generalizations about the other person's character: "You are inconsiderate." "You are lazy." Instead, focus on specific actions: "I want you to come home on time." "I want you to help with the housework."

Rule 3: Avoid making things absolute with words like *always* and *never*: "You are always messy." "You never help." Instead, try to create a positive attitude: "Sometimes you're neat. I wish you would be neat more often." "I appreciate it when you help, and it would mean a lot to me if you would help more often."

Rule 4: Use good timing. Try to respond to the person's actions right after they happen. If you miss the opportunity to respond immediately, wait until an appropriate time to give positive and negative feedback.

Rule 5: Be constructive. When you tell the other person about something you dislike, also tell her or him what you like.

Good communication skills are among the most important predictors of marital satisfaction (Gottman, 1979; Markman, 1981). Researchers have demonstrated that when married persons are trained to engage in constructive communication, blood pressure goes down and marital satisfaction increases (Ewart, Taylor, Kraemer, & Agras, 1984; Hahlweg & Markman, 1988; Markman, Floyd, Stanley, & Storaasli, 1988). It is advantageous for couples to learn and practice effective communication skills early in their relationship as a preventive measure rather than waiting to improve their communication skills after problems have developed (Markman, Floyd, Stanley, & Lewis, 1986; Markman & Hahlweg, 1993; Markman, Renick, Floyd, Stanley, & Clements, 1993).

Negotiating a Contract

Earlier in this chapter you learned about tactics people in close relationships use to influence each other. What was missing in each of those tactics was honest communication and the willingness to negotiate. An interesting perspective on the process of negotiation is apparent in this study of conflict resolution between college roommates (Sillars, 1981). Students reported that they used one of three general conflict-resolution strategies:

1. *Avoidance:* Avoiding the person, not talking about the problem, hinting but not coming out and stating feelings, joking about the problem, denying there is a problem, changing the subject.
2. *Influence:* Making demands, faulting the other person, being hostile, making threats, asking the other person to change.
3. *Communication:* Saying clearly what is bothering you, asking about the other person's feelings, accepting responsibility, suggesting ideas to solve the problem.

Interestingly, the strategy used most often was avoidance (57%). Influence was used 11% of the time, and communication was used 32% of the time. Students were more likely to communicate with their roommates when they accepted responsibility for helping to resolve conflicts in the relationship. Students who blamed their roommates for causing the conflict were more likely to engage in influence and avoidance.

It should be clear by this time that constructive negotiation requires us to take responsibility for helping resolve conflicts we have with close others. In addition, if you want your partner to make changes, it makes sense that you should offer to make changes in return. Negotiation between people in close relationships should be in the spirit of a two-winner approach. This can be accomplished by making a contract that has three columns: My Gain, Your Gain, Our Gain. It is a good idea for both partners to sign this contract to affirm their commitment to carry out the agreement. Negotiation must be a cooperative venture in which each person is willing to give a bit for the sake of the relationship. In this way, even though we end up giving, we are giving for a good cause, and we gain something in return. Negotiations between people in close relationships do not involve one person taking an inflexible position and waiting for the other person to give in. Negotiation between close people is cooperative because both partners accept the following facts of life: "We can't have everything our way." "It is impossible to find a perfect partner."

Coping Skill 10: Communicating and Negotiating

GIVING THE BENEFIT OF THE DOUBT

One coping skill that is useful in all close relationships is the ability to forgive your partner for doing things you don't like. It is easier to forgive others when you can give them the benefit of the doubt. For instance, you can say to yourself: "What my partner did (or didn't do) causes a problem for me. However, I know that my partner has good intentions and many positive sides. So, even though I'm not happy about it, I can forgive and give my partner the benefit of the doubt."

The value of giving the benefit of the doubt was demonstrated in four studies comparing the reactions of distressed and nondistressed couples to positive and negative actions by their partners (Fincham, Beach, & Baucom, 1987; Fincham & O'Leary, 1983; Holtzworth-Munroe & Jacobson, 1985; Thompson & Kelley, 1981). Because nondistressed couples gave their partners credit for positive acts, they found it easier to live with each other's negative acts. Distressed couples were preoccupied with the negatives. They spent a lot of time focusing on dissatisfactions about their partners and had difficulty appreciating their partners' redeeming qualities. This research demonstrates that people in happy relationships know how to give credit for positives contributed by their partners.

Coping Skill 11: Giving the Benefit of the Doubt

BLAMING AND NEGATIVE THINKING

All of the responses for coping with unsatisfactory relationships described so far involve taking a positive action-oriented approach. The final option, blaming and negative thinking, is not recommended because it is destructive. Blaming and negative thinking is worth discussing, however, because it is always tempting to avoid responsibility by blaming your partner for relationship problems. Researchers have shown that distressed couples engage in blaming and negative thinking far more often than do nondistressed couples (Fincham, 1985; Fincham, Beach, & Baucom, 1987; Fincham, Beach, & Nelson, 1987; Kyle & Falbo, 1985). People in unhappy relationships feel that their partners are more responsible for relationship problems than they are. They view their partners' negative behaviors as resulting from selfishness, an uncaring attitude, and lack of commitment. People who are unhappy with a relationship tend to say the following kinds of things to themselves:

> "My partner wouldn't act this way if he/she really cared about me."
> "I refuse to be responsible unless my partner does something nice for me."
> "I'm going to get even and make my partner suffer for not treating me right."

People in happy relationships are able to put their feelings into perspective:

> "If I want my partner to respond differently, I have to take the initiative."
> "I don't always like it, but I know things will work out best if I'm flexible enough to show my partner some affection."
> "I want to tell my partner I'm angry, but it won't help our relationship to make him/her suffer."

Blaming and negative thinking inevitably lead us to act in a negative way toward our partners. Unless your partner can use some of the coping skills described in this chapter, her or his response is likely to be negative or a refusal to engage in a positive act. You will be caught in a vicious cycle in which negative behaviors, feelings, and thoughts outweigh your ability to make adaptive appraisals (Bradbury & Fincham, 1987; Fincham & Bradbury, 1988).

Coping Skill 12: Avoiding the Temptation to Engage in Blaming and Negative Thinking

ENDING THE RELATIONSHIP

Three things generally lead people to dissolve a relationship: dissimilarity, boredom, and negative feelings (Baron & Byrne, 1987, chap. 6).

Dissimilarity: You realize that you and the other person have little in common. There are too many differences in values, interests, and goals for a sustained relationship.

Boredom: The relationship becomes stagnant. You are not growing together or moving with each other in a purposeful direction.

Negative feelings: The negatives outweigh the positives. There is too much criticizing, complaining, and nagging and too little love, support, and affection.

When a relationship is threatened and you and your partner are not motivated to make improvements, it is time to consider going your separate ways. At this point, you must take control of your life and assume responsibility for your actions.

BEING WILLING TO WORK

Good relationships don't come easy; they require continuous effort. George Levinger put it very clearly when he said: "What counts in making a happy marriage (or any other satisfactory relationship) is not so much how compatible you are, but how you deal with incompatibility" (in Goleman, 1985, p. 19).

Dealing with conflicts in close relationships requires your commitment to practice coping skills *consistently*.

Coping Skill 13: Being Willing to Work

LIST OF SKILLS FOR COPING
WITH CONFLICTS IN CLOSE RELATIONSHIPS

- *Coping Skill 1:*   Deciding What You Want in a Relationship
- *Coping Skill 2:*   Assessing Your Satisfaction
- *Coping Skill 3:*   Taking Active Responsibility
- *Coping Skill 4:*   Reevaluating Expectations
- *Coping Skill 5:*   Being Sensitive to Desired Areas of Change
- *Coping Skill 6:*   Practicing Tolerance
- *Coping Skill 7:*   Balancing the Negatives and Positives
- *Coping Skill 8:*   Acknowledging Your Right to Determine Your Needs in a Relationship
- *Coping Skill 9:*   Overcoming Jealousy
- *Coping Skill 10:* Communicating and Negotiating
- *Coping Skill 11:* Giving the Benefit of the Doubt
- *Coping Skill 12:* Avoiding the Temptation to Engage in Blaming and Negative Thinking
- *Coping Skill 13:* Being Willing to Work

SUGGESTIONS FOR FURTHER READING

Beck, A. T. (1988). *Love is never enough.* New York: Harper & Row.

Ellis, A. (1975). *How to live with a "neurotic"* (rev. ed.). New York: Crown.

Ellis, A., & Harper, R. A. (1961). *A guide to successful marriage.* North Hollywood, CA: Wilshire Books.

Gottman, J. (1994). *Why marriages succeed or fail.* New York: Simon & Schuster.

Lazarus, A. A. (1985). *Marital myths: Two dozen mistaken beliefs that can ruin a marriage (or make a bad one worse).* San Ramon, CA: Impact Publishers.

Markman, H. J., Stanley, S., & Blumberg, S. L. (1993). *Fighting for your marriage: Positive steps for preventing divorce and preserving a lasting love.* San Francisco: Jossey-Bass.

Rogers, C. R. (1972). *Becoming partners: Marriage and its alternatives.* New York: Dell.

10

Coping with Loss

Loss is an inevitable part of life. Loss encompasses a number of events, ranging from dissolved relationships and separation to death. Different kinds of losses mean different things to different people. However, some things about going through a loss are common for all of us. In this chapter I will focus on the processes that make loss a human experience. It is helpful to understand these processes and to recognize that loss is a part of life that touches everyone, everywhere. Learning about loss as a human experience can help you gain peace of mind over the losses in your life. Because this chapter is only an introduction to a deep issue, it cannot provide solutions for all problems. People whose lives are seriously disrupted by a loss will find it beneficial to take advantage of organized groups and professional support.*

APPRAISING A LOSS

Our first reaction to a loss is to make a primary appraisal. Because losses are usually traumatic and often unexpected, a primary appraisal is almost automatic. In Chapter 2 you learned that primary appraisals can help free us from life events that are not worth getting upset about. Because most losses are upsetting, it is desirable to accept them as real problems and to go through the appropriate grieving process. When you deny the importance of a loss, you cheat yourself out of an important experience of mourning and reconciliation.

After accepting a loss as a problem worthy of grief, what kinds of secondary appraisals can you make? Coping successfully with a loss does not mean fixing it or turning it around. In an adaptive secondary appraisal you tell yourself that you have *grief work* to do (Lindeman, 1944). Grieving is an active process. You will be affected

---

*Most cities have clearinghouses with lists of support groups. You can also call your local hospital or community mental health center for lists of support groups. Support groups are usually listed each week in a local newspaper.

by various feelings, and you need to take time to accomplish certain tasks. Now let's look at the experiences and tasks of grief work.

Coping Skill 1: Accepting a Loss as Worthy of Grief Work

THE EXPERIENCE OF MOURNING

Even though the experience of mourning a loss is not pleasant, it is a part of life that is shared by everyone. The experience of mourning a loss affects your feelings, your body, your thoughts, and your behavior (Worden, 1982).

Feelings

Depending on the loss, people experience a number of different feelings (Vickio, Cavanaugh, & Attig, 1990):

Sadness: You may feel empty, dejected, and depressed, and possibly like crying unexpectedly. It is often necessary to allow yourself to feel the pain of a loss before moving on to the stage of acceptance and reconciliation.

Anger: You may feel frustrated at the unfairness of the loss and at the fact that you can't control it. Avoid turning this anger against yourself and realize that, although you can't control the loss, you do have control of your grief work.

Guilt: You may feel guilty because you weren't "perfect" and because you couldn't prevent the loss. Recognize that we are all fallible human beings living in an unpredictable world.

Anxiety: You may wonder, "Can I survive this loss?" You have come face-to-face with your vulnerability and your mortality. Use the coping skills in Chapter 3 to boost your feelings of self-efficacy.

Loneliness: This is an empty feeling that is a combination of sadness and anxiety. Review the information in Chapter 6 to find ways to deal with your loneliness.

Fatigue: You may feel tired and worn out. This is a normal reaction to stress and should not be seen as a deficiency or sign of weakness.

Shock: You may feel shock if the loss is sudden or unexpected. Shock, disbelief, and numbness comprise the first stage of grief work.

Relief: It is important to recognize some losses as a mixed blessing that combines sadness and relief. There is no need to feel guilty about having both of these feelings.

Physical Reactions

The feelings experienced after a loss usually affect us physically. If you anticipate these sensations, they won't feel as strange or scary when they happen: hollowness in the stomach, tightness in the chest, tightness in the throat, oversensitivity to noise, shortness of breath, weakness of muscles, dry mouth, or lack of energy.

Thoughts

You may have a number of thoughts after undergoing a loss, and you may be surprised to learn how often these thoughts are experienced by others. These thoughts can include:

Disbelief: Disbelief occurs during the first stage of grief work. It is hard at first to accept the reality of the loss.

Confusion: You may feel confused and find it difficult to keep your mind on one topic. Give yourself a break and don't expect your performance to be up to its normal level.

Preoccupation: Your thinking may be almost completely focused on the loss and on wishes and desires to return to the past. Preoccupation is common during the second stage of grief work.

Imagination: You may imagine what things were like before the loss and pretend you are back in the past or that the person you have lost is still here. This kind of thinking is part of the second stage of grief work.

Behaviors

The experience of loss can affect a number of daily behaviors. If you can anticipate these behavioral changes, they won't appear frightening or abnormal:

Sleeping: It is common after experiencing a loss to have trouble sleeping.

Eating: Eating patterns are often affected. Some people eat more. Others find eating difficult.

Social withdrawal: It may be useful at first to spend time alone with your thoughts and feelings. Later in the grief work you will be ready to push yourself into resuming social activities.

Dreaming: It is common to dream about the lost person.

Activity: You will probably experience a change in activity. You may feel listless and apathetic, or you may feel restless and have difficulty remaining still. Acknowledge this change in activity as a normal part of grief.

Crying: Crying is a normal reaction to a loss. If crying in front of others is uncomfortable, schedule time alone when you can give in to the need to express grief.

Coping Skill 2: Being Open to the Experience of Mourning

STAGES OF GRIEF WORK

Experts who have studied loss and grief have outlined a series of stages that people work through as they attempt to reach a point of reconciliation after experiencing a loss (Rando, 1984; Worden, 1982). The amount of time required to complete these stages of grief work and the degree to which grief is finally resolved is an individual matter (Stroebe & Stroebe, 1991; Wortman & Silver, 1987, 1989). Find the pace and style of working through grief that is best suited to your needs. The stages of grief are:

Shock, disbelief, numbness: You feel stunned. It is difficult to accept the loss, and you are tempted to deny that it really happened. Your immediate concern is to block out painful feelings.

Yearning and searching: You ask, "Why did it happen to me?" You may feel anger at your inability to reverse the loss. You may cling to unrealistic expectations that things will end up as before.

Despair and disorganization: You feel depressed about the reality of the loss and see no hope that things will ever get better.

Acceptance and reorganization: Finally, you give up false hopes and accept the loss as a reality. As a result of this acceptance, you begin to make plans and push yourself to get on with your life.

New identity: You adapt to your life as different from the way it was and recognize how you have grown as a result of your grief work.

It is useful to view the stages of grief work as tasks that you must take the responsibility to solve. This way of looking at grief work reinforces your feelings of internal control and self-efficacy. It is not desirable to interpret stages of grief as phases that *happen* to you. This will cause you to feel passive and dependent, and it undermines your identity as a problem solver.

***Coping Skill 3: Recognizing the Stages
of Grief Work as Tasks for Which You Are Responsible***

TASKS OF GRIEF WORK

Now that you have an understanding of the mourning and grief work following a loss, let's look at the tasks for which you are responsible. These four tasks must be accomplished when doing grief work after a loss (Worden, 1982).

Task 1. Accepting the reality of the loss. You must face the fact that the loss is real and that you can't return to the past. This is a painful and difficult thing to do, and it takes time. You can make it easier for yourself by looking forward to the freedom and relief you will feel when you are finally able to let go. When working on task 1, avoid getting caught in two undesirable places. First, don't insulate yourself by downplaying or denying the importance of the loss. Being alive in this world means allowing yourself the experience of mourning. Second, set a date when you will be completely ready to let go of objects, plans, and desires that reinforce a false hope that the loss can be reversed.

Task 2. Experiencing pain and grief. Open yourself up to the mourning experiences described earlier. It is sometimes difficult to accomplish this task because people around you may be uncomfortable with your need to take time for feeling pain and sadness. This is a period when you need to find a good balance between being alone and taking advantage of support systems.

Task 3. Adjusting to a new life.   Our lives are different following a loss. There is no way to get around this. Your life is made up of chapters, and you never know when one chapter will end and a new one will begin. Accept the fact that life is a challenge that requires you to learn new skills and to adapt to new experiences.

Task 4. Getting on with life.   When you get to task 4, you are ready to accept the fact that it is time to get on with your life. This does not mean that your loss is forgotten. Your past experiences, both good and bad, are what help you to mature. Getting on with your life doesn't mean forsaking people or events in your past. It simply means that you are ready to begin a new chapter.

Coping Skill 4: Taking Time to
Accomplish the Four Tasks of Grief Work

INTEGRATING THE LOSS INTO YOUR LIFE EXPERIENCE

When you experience a loss, one of the first questions is "Why?" Because we want to believe we live in a predictable and meaningful world (Janoff-Bulman, 1989), we ask "Why did it happen?" Your success in coping with a loss has a lot to do with finding an acceptable meaning. This is not always easy because many losses are sudden and unexpected. Some people have religious beliefs to help them find explanations for the loss (McIntosh, Silver, & Wortman, 1993). Others have accepted the unpredictability of loss and grief, as well as the unpredictability of joy and happiness, as facts of life with which they must learn to live. People often suffer more when they get caught up in trying to "undo" a loss by thinking about all the things they could have or should have done differently. In some cases, a loss might have been prevented if the person in grief had acted differently. In many cases, there is nothing the person in grief could have done to prevent the loss. However, no matter what the person could or could not have done to prevent the loss, the loss did occur, and it cannot be reversed. Dwelling on "what might have been" is rarely helpful and usually causes the person in grief to suffer even more.

A survey of college students who had recently lost a parent found that their faith in the meaningfulness of the world was reduced (Schwartzberg & Janoff-Bulman, 1991). Even more dramatic was the fact that only half of the students could find a satisfactory answer for their parents' deaths. This study teaches us two important lessons. First, a crucial part of coping with loss is finding a way to integrate this loss into your overall life experience. Second, no matter how young you are, you need to prepare yourself for the inevitability of experiencing losses in your life.

People who had lost loved ones in auto accidents, or whose infants had died from sudden infant death syndrome, were interviewed about how they coped with these losses (C. G. Davis, Lehman, Wortman, Silver, & Thompson, 1995). On the whole, people suffered more from these losses if they spent a lot of time thinking about what they might have done differently. Focusing on the "what ifs" after suffering a loss provides a sense of gaining control over what happened. Unfortunately, because the loss is irreversible, the sense of control gained by rethinking your actions is an illusion. The negative effects of getting caught up in trying to "undo" a loss with obsessive thinking are made even worse when compounded with feelings of guilt. The way to get out of this trap is to develop an attitude of acceptance for events you cannot change (Persons, 1995). In fact, parents who were not preoccupied with finding a meaning for their infants' deaths generally suffered less distress than parents who were still looking for an explanation (Downey, Silver, & Wortman, 1990). Acceptance is not always easy, and it requires both courage and maturity. Perhaps you can gain inspiration by remembering Reinhold Niebuhr's Serenity Prayer (see Chapter 5; Bartlett, 1982): "God, give us grace to accept with serenity the things that cannot be changed, courage to change the things which should be changed, and the wisdom to distinguish the one from the other."

Coping Skill 5: Integrating the Loss into Your Life Experience

CONTROLLING OBSESSIVE THINKING

In Chapter 5 you learned that a useful skill for coping with depression is to control obsessive thinking by keeping busy. The same principle is true for coping with loss. During periods of grief, it is important to stop yourself from spending too much time ruminating about your unhappy feelings. A survey of people who had recently lost a family member found that almost everyone ruminated about their loss to some degree (Nolen-Hoeksema, Parker, & Larson, 1994). They got caught up in saying the following kinds of things to themselves:

"Why did it have to happen?"
"I'll never get over this."
"Why is it so hard for me?"
"I might flunk out of school or lose my job."
"I just can't seem to pull myself together."

The kinds of feelings expressed in these statements are understandable, and it is not surprising that people would have them after losing a loved one. However, when people who had suffered a loss dwelled on these kinds of thoughts and could not distract themselves by keeping busy, their suffering was intensified. The suggestions for keeping busy presented in Chapter 5 are very applicable for people who have suffered a loss. Another way to reduce the temptation to ruminate is by enlisting support people to provide a distraction. It is not particularly helpful for support people to encourage the person in grief to talk about his or her depressed feelings. This only encourages the bereaved person to ruminate more. In addition, listening to ruminating thoughts puts quite a strain on the support people. Support people can be most helpful by providing sympathy and understanding and by encouraging the bereaved person in a low-key and nonjudgmental manner to continue with her or his life.

Coping Skill 6: Controlling Obsessive Thinking

UNRESOLVED GRIEF

There are many reasons people find it difficult to complete grief work after suffering a loss. First, it is tempting to avoid the pain and hard work that grief work requires. In addition, we are often reluctant to let go of someone who has departed. However, people with unresolved grief often suffer in the long run because they have unfinished business that needs to be taken care of before they can get on with their lives. Some symptoms of unresolved grief include (Rando, 1984):

- Overactivity without a sense of loss
- Development of a psychosomatic or medical illness
- Alteration in relationships with friends and relatives
- Hostility against people associated with the loss
- Social withdrawal
- Depression, tension, agitation, insomnia
- Poor self-care habits
- A feeling that the loss occurred very recently even though it happened years ago
- Guilt and self-reproach

There are six forms of unresolved grief (Rando, 1984):

Absent grief: Feelings of grief and mourning are totally absent. It is as if the loss had never occurred. The person is either in a state of shock or in complete denial.

Inhibited grief: It is possible for the person to mourn certain aspects of the loss in bits and pieces. However, the mourner is always guarded and never succeeds in completing all the stages of grief work.

Delayed grief: Grief work is delayed for an extended period of time. Another loss or stressful event in the person's life triggers a delayed grief reaction many years after the loss occurred. At this point, the person can either complete the grief work or avoid it once more and allow it to remain unresolved.

Conflicted grief: This is an uneven response where certain emotions take over a person's life to the point where grief work is never completed. For example, a person may channel all of her or his energy into anger or guilt. The anger and guilt become part of the person's life because they have not been placed in their proper perspective.

Chronic grief: The person freely experiences the loss but never begins grief work. The mourning and grief continue indefinitely to the point where the person may develop pathological reactions such as depression, panic, and total withdrawal.

Unanticipated grief: This reaction may occur when a loss is catastrophic and completely unexpected. The traumatic reaction is so severe that it is difficult for the person to begin the task of grief work. A person in this situation needs support. With enough time and encouragement, the grief work will get started.

Abbreviated grief is a shortened form of grief work. It is sometimes mistaken for unresolved grief because it takes place more quickly than many grief reactions. Abbreviated grief often occurs when a person has had time to get prepared for the loss. Much of the grief work has already been accomplished before the loss occurs.

DISENFRANCHISED GRIEF

Disenfranchised grief is grief experienced by people who suffer a loss that is not or cannot be openly acknowledged, publicly mourned, or socially supported (Doka, 1989). Some examples of disenfranchised grief include the following:

Death of a gay lover: Gay people may find it difficult to mourn the death of a lover when they are unaccepted by their own families or by the family of their lover. The situation is even more difficult if the lover has died from AIDS because of the fear and stigma associated with this disease.

Death of a divorced spouse: The death of a divorced spouse is accompanied by many conflicted feelings, often including unresolved anger and hurt, fond memories and love, and lack of reconciliation with the spouse's family. These circumstances can prevent a satisfactory experience of resolving feelings surrounding the spouse's death.

Death of an unborn baby: Often, we are not prepared to mourn the death of an unborn baby. If the death occurs in a hospital, there is little support from busy nurses and doctors. In addition, friends and family might not identify with the baby as an actual person who requires a formal farewell. If the mother had mixed feelings about having the baby in the first place, she must resolve conflicted feelings of guilt and sadness.

Children who suffer loss: Children are often prevented from resolving losses by being isolated from the rituals appropriate to their culture. Adults may have good intentions in "protecting" children from sadness and grief. However, because losses are unavoidable, it is more helpful to teach children how to deal with them in the first place.

It is important to understand that loss is part of your life experience. Use whatever rituals are meaningful to you to find reconciliation. When coping with disenfranchised grief, support groups can be very helpful.

Coping Skill 7: Appreciating the Necessity for Attending to Unresolved and Disenfranchised Grief

THREE FACTORS
INFLUENCING THE SUCCESS OF GRIEF WORK

Three factors influencing the success of grief work are the nature of the relationship with the person who is lost, the suddenness of the loss, and the strength of your support system (Wortman & Silver, 1987).

1. *The nature of the relationship:* It is more difficult to recover from losing a person when your relationship with that person was ambivalent. Ambivalent relationships are those in which issues of commitment and trust are not resolved. There is "unfinished business" in the relationship causing feelings of hurt, anger, hostility, and guilt. When the person departs, these feelings are often intensified. It is also difficult to recover from losing a person on whom you were very dependent. You may feel a strong desire to "hang on" and experience a sense of helplessness because that person fulfilled so many of your needs.

2. *The suddenness of the loss:* It is easier to recover from a loss if you have time to prepare for it. When a loss is expected, a lot of grief work can be accomplished before it occurs. Unexpected losses are traumatic because they remind us of the unpredictable nature of this world.

3. *Support systems:* A good support system does much to help in the recovery from loss. As you learned in Chapter 3, a support system can provide nurturance and bolster your sense of self-worth, trust, and life-direction.

FINDING A MEANING FOR DEATH

It is much easier to cope with death when it has some kind of meaning. Some cultures are *death accepting* (Rando, 1984), viewing death as an inevitable and natural part of the life cycle. Death and dying are integrated into the daily patterns of living. Other cultures are *death defying*, believing in an afterlife and having rituals for preparing people for a new life after they depart from this earth. Still other cultures are *death denying*. In these cultures there is a refusal to confront the reality and inevitability of death. It is probably fair to say that people from death-denying cultures are most vulnerable to unresolved grief about death because they have no answer for death's meaning (Becker, 1973; Schoenberg, 1980). Two important books, *Facing Death* (R. Kavanaugh, 1974) and *On Death and Dying* (Kübler-Ross, 1969), have pointed out the importance of coming to terms with death. Indeed, once you accept the inevitability of death, it is possible to appreciate some of its benefits, such as (Koestenbaum, 1976):

- Death helps us savor life.
- Death provides an opposite by which to judge being alive.
- Death gives meaning to courage and integrity, allowing us to express our convictions effectively.
- Death provides us with the strength to make major decisions.
- Death reveals the importance of intimacy in our lives.

- Death helps us ascribe meaning to our lives retroactively, which is especially useful for older people.
- Death shows us the importance of ego-transcending achievements.
- Death allows us to see our achievements as having significance.

Whether you rely on your culture, your religion, or your personal philosophy, it is important to make death a meaningful part of your life experience.

Coping Skill 8: Finding a Meaning for Death

A PERSONAL PROGRAM FOR GRIEF WORK

In this section I will outline a personal program for grief work (D. J. Kavanagh, 1990). As with all personal programs, the steps must be individualized to suit your own needs. You can work through the following steps with an individual therapist, in groups, or with other kinds of support persons.

Appreciating that Grief Work Is a Ritual

When you experience a loss, your challenge is to find meaning in this loss, to reconcile yourself to its reality, and to move on with your life. Reaching a reasonable sense of closure on a loss is often accomplished through a ritual (Imber-Black, 1991). Most cultures have some kind of ceremony to mark the passing of someone who has died or departed (McGoldrick et al., 1991). In some cultures these ceremonies are sad and mournful. In other cultures they are lively times of remembrance and celebration. The point is that you need to do *something* to mark the occasion of your loss so you can integrate it into your life experience.

Recognizing Your Skills

In times of crisis, one of the first things you should do is take inventory of your strengths and skills. Say to yourself, "How can I best use my strengths and skills in this situation?" Also, consider what additional skills might be useful for you to develop to turn this crisis into a constructive life experience.

Confronting Your Loss

Losses often result in unpleasant emotional reactions. However, it is not in your best interest to deal with grief by using avoidance (see Chapter 1). The way through unpleasant feelings is through *exposure* (Callahan & Burnette, 1989; Kavanagh, 1990; Mawson, Marks, Ramm, & Stern, 1981). Confront your emotions by feeling them. People in grief are advised to *encounter* the objects, places, and other cues that remind them of the person who left them. Depending on your preferences, you can do this slowly and gradually (guided exposure) or all at once (flooding). It is helpful to confront your loss with support and reassurance from others.

Finding Meaningful Activities

Getting busy is a useful skill for distracting yourself from depressive ruminations. Putting your energy into meaningful activities also provides you with an opportunity for getting over the life disruptions brought about by a loss. Some examples of negative outcomes following a loss include (Lehman et al., 1993):

- A disruption of goals
- Withdrawal from others
- A pessimistic attitude toward life
- Lack of interest in the future
- Loss of religious faith

Meaningful activities after a loss can help distract you from life disruptions and reestablish a sense of hope and purpose in life.

Using Constructive Thinking

When you are working through a loss, use the skills outlined in Chapter 3 for talking yourself through challenges. Also, use the skills for healthy thinking that were described in Chapter 2.

Enlisting Support People

When doing grief work, it is highly advisable to develop and utilize support systems (see Chapter 3).

Controlling Drug and Alcohol Use

Some people are prone to drug and alcohol abuse during times of grief and sadness. Encourage (or force) yourself to substitute more healthy coping responses of self-relaxation and exercise (see Chapter 3).

Coping Skill 9: Working Through a Personal Program for Grief Work

GETTING THROUGH A SEPARATION OR DIVORCE

Almost everyone is touched by divorce, either personally or through close relations and friends. Divorce is an unpleasant experience, and it forces people to make significant adjustments in their lives. The *psychological adjustments* required during a divorce include: coping with loneliness, finding new meaning in life, coping with anger, coping with guilt and low self-esteem, and seeking new sources of love and nurturance. The *tactical adjustments* required by divorce include: finding a new living situation, gaining financial stability, and managing the responsibilities of a single parent.

Given the number of major adjustments required by a divorce, it is no wonder that divorce is such a stressful experience.

Four Stages of a Divorce Experience

People typically go through four stages from the beginning to the end of a divorce (Kressel, 1986):

1. *Predecision period:* This is the time in a marriage when partners begin to feel dissatisfaction. They know things are not right. The relationship becomes tense. Couples may fight, or they may withdraw from each other. Perhaps they will seek counseling. It becomes clear that the marriage is in trouble and that constructive steps must be taken.

2. *Decision period:* During this phase, couples decide whether or not to work through counseling to save their marriage or to call it quits and get a divorce. This is a difficult period because no decision is foolproof and all decisions are painful and require significant effort and adjustment. There is a feeling of relief once a decision has been made. There is also anxiety about an uncertain future.

3. *Negotiation:* Negotiations are usually conducted with the aid of therapists, mediators, and lawyers. A couple undertaking counseling to save their marriage makes a contract outlining the conditions of their therapeutic work. Couples who have decided on divorce must achieve an equitable division of financial and child-rearing responsibilities.

4. *Reconciliation:* Reconciliation after a divorce is finalized is difficult. Feelings of guilt, loneliness, and anger place significant barriers between the individuals. Each partner must learn to cope with these feelings well enough to get on with his or her life and to carry on with the financial and child-rearing settlement in a smooth and tactful manner.

The Mourning Process

Mourning a divorce means mourning a loss. It is necessary to go through this mourning process to reach a state of reconciliation.

Using Good Coping Skills

People who are best prepared to cope with a separation or divorce share the following characteristics (Brehm, 1987): They have an independent source of income; they know how to carry out the daily tasks of living (cooking, paying bills, car and household maintenance, and so forth); they have a social support system independent of their partner; they know how to enjoy being alone; and they are flexible enough to adapt to new situations.

A good place to begin this discussion of strategies for coping with separation and divorce is with the problem-solving skills outlined in Chapter 3. First, make a list of the challenges facing you so you can work out the best possible course of action. Some of these challenges may be:

Evaluating your satisfaction with the relationship
Deciding on active steps you can take to confront the problem
Recognizing and dealing with feelings of sadness, grief, loneliness, and anger

Working out a plan to support yourself financially
Learning how to live independently
Finding ways to receive emotional support and nurturance
Maintaining self-esteem and feelings of competence
Finding meaningful activities that will help you get on with your life

Use your problem-solving skills to find a good course of action, and consider the additional coping skills discussed in Chapter 3 as well. Practice the skills of rational thinking and self-efficacy described in Chapter 2. Other chapters in this book provide suggestions about how to cope with specific feelings brought forth by divorce, such as loneliness, failure, anxiety, depression, and anger.

LEARNING HOW TO LET GO

One of the most difficult tasks to accomplish when you lose someone is to let that person go. In this section I will discuss a number of suggestions about how to let go and get on with your life after someone has left you.

Accepting the Fact That You Can't Own Others

When you lose someone special, you get angry and frustrated because it doesn't seem fair. After all, nobody asked you if it was all right for that person to be taken out of your life. It is often difficult to accept the fact that relationships are a benefit of life and not a right. Giving up the desire to own people who are close to you is not easy because we truly wish we could dictate the outcome of our relationships. However, when you relinquish your demand for ownership, you will be released from a tremendous burden. It is hard enough in life to manage tasks for which you are responsible. Don't put yourself in the no-win situation of demanding power over events that are not yours to control.

Getting Unhooked from the Addiction

Love relationships have been described as addictions because we often derive a majority of our gratification from one person (Wanderer & Cabot, 1978). When that person leaves, we are at a loss because we have put all our eggs in one basket. How can all those good things be replaced when that particular person is gone? Here are two steps to follow:

1. *Be philosophical.* Remember, the gratification you received was a *benefit* of life, not a right. Try not to demand instant gratification of all your desires. There is no law that says you should have nurturance, caring, and sex whenever you want them. This is a harsh fact, but your primary appraisal of a loss will be more objective if you can put your wants, demands, and expectations into perspective.

2. *Replace the missing nurturance.* Use your support systems; trade hugs and kind words with people you know. Begin new relationships. Keep in mind, though, that contracting for nurturance is not guaranteed to make you feel better instantly. It isn't

easy to replace a person after you've gotten used to his or her style and way of doing things. The important thing is to see yourself as a person who understands that overcoming an addiction is hard work. You know you can survive without immediate gratification.

Thinking Rationally

The experience of loss often triggers unrealistic and irrational thoughts. You may feel that the loss was unfair. If you demand control over everything that happens to you, you may feel anger, frustration, and jealousy. You may tell yourself that life is no longer worth living. This is the time to review the information on Albert Ellis's rational-emotive therapy discussed in Chapter 2. Analyze the emotions you are choosing to experience as a result of your demands and expectations. If you decide that some of them are not in your best interest, you can get your thinking under control with the following techniques.

Thought stopping.   Wear a rubber band on your wrist, and whenever you start thinking unrealistic, irrational, or maladaptive thoughts, snap the rubber band and tell yourself, "Stop!" Here are some typical irrational things we say to ourselves after a loss:

"I will be alone forever."
"My life is worthless now."
"I'm too old to start again."
"It's not fair."
"If only I had done things differently."

The goal of thought stopping is to catch yourself when you start thinking in ways that are sure to bring you down. Learn to substitute the following more realistic and rational thoughts:

"I now feel alone, and I don't like it."
"I'm not enjoying my life right now."
"My life is going to be different now. Loss is not fun, but it is part of life."
"I can't control the lives of others."

As you can see, the rational thoughts you want to think after thought stopping are not intended to make everything bright and rosy. It would be ridiculous to tell yourself after a loss that everything is fine. The purpose of thinking rationally is to use your emotional energy to experience legitimately unhappy feelings. That is, don't compound your misery by making demands of life that have no bearing in reality.

Stimulus control.   If you feel that you simply must take time for irrational thoughts during your grief work, use the technique of *stimulus control*. Find a particular spot and use it only for irrational thinking. Then schedule specific times each day when you go to this location and think irrational thoughts. Your assignment is to concentrate on demands and expectations that make you miserable. However, you are allowed to think these thoughts only during your scheduled time in your designated spot. During the rest of the day, you are bound to strict thought stopping.

Taking a balanced view.   People have a tendency to aggrandize someone they've lost. You may focus on all the good things you miss about the person while forgetting that she or he also had faults. It is touching to remember the best about those close to us. However, you have to be careful not to exaggerate your misery by convincing yourself that this person was so perfect and absolutely wonderful that you can't survive the loss. A good suggestion is to make a "crime sheet" on which you list the person's faults (Wanderer & Cabot, 1978). You need to understand that although you legitimately miss this person, your life is still worth living.

Saying Your Final Good-Bye

Here is a good method for saying your final good-bye (Wanderer & Cabot, 1978). Collect all the letters, photos, and other articles associated with the person you lost. While working through the first stages of grief, people often hide these items because it is too painful to have them in sight. Later, when you are ready to accept the loss and get on with your life, get these materials out for a final farewell. This day is called your "implosion day" because these articles are bound to stir up strong feelings. You are at a stage in your grief work where you are ready to handle feelings of legitimate sadness because you have successfully put to rest your unrealistic demands and expectations. When your implosion day is over, keep these articles or dispose of them as you see fit. You will always remember the person you lost, but it is time to begin a new life chapter.

Coping Skill 10: Learning How to Let Go

RECOGNIZING YOUR INDIVIDUALITY

Mourning a loss is a personal experience, and it is important to recognize the need to cope with losses in your own way. The stages and tasks of grief work outlined earlier in this chapter provide a framework to help you understand your personal reactions in times of loss. However, experiences in coping with loss depend on your individuality (Stroebe & Stroebe, 1991). To appreciate this point, let's look at three myths of coping with loss and put them in perspective (Wortman & Silver, 1987, 1989):

> *Myth 1:* Distress and depression are inevitable.
> *Myth 2:* People must all go through the same stages to cope with a loss.
> *Myth 3:* Losses can be completely resolved.

Distress and Depression Are Not Inevitable

Although it is certainly common to react to losses with feelings of distress and depression, these reactions are not inevitable. It is possible to face some losses calmly and to maintain positive feelings about yourself and your life. Remember that failure to experience distress and depression in times of loss does not necessarily indicate something is wrong with you. In addition, you don't always have to experience distress and depression before you can cope with a loss in a satisfactory manner.

People Cope with Losses in Their Own Ways

The different stages of grief work outlined here are useful because they offer *possibilities* for people who are coping with grief. However, people inevitably cope with loss in their own ways. It is important to recognize and appreciate this individuality. It is a disservice to hold people who are coping with grief to a "time table" of stages they must necessarily go through. Many people suffering from losses have been harmed by others who became impatient with them because they were not working through their grief in the "proper way" (Wortman, Carnelley, Lehman, Davis, & Exline, 1995). Coping with loss is a creative process through which people in grief (with nonjudgmental support from others) work out a way to incorporate the loss into their lives.

Some Losses Are Never Completely Resolved

It is a mistake to assume that you can resolve all of your losses completely. It is important to reconcile loss well enough to get on with your life, but our losses may still touch us from time to time. It is not uncommon to have dreams, memories, and associations that bring feelings of sadness years after a loss has occurred. These relapses into the past should not be seen as signs of weakness. To a large degree, mourning a loss means learning to integrate your complex feelings into a life full of challenges and learning experiences.

Coping Skill 11: Recognizing Your Individuality

HOW TO OFFER SUPPORT

Understanding how to offer support allows us to be helpful to others who have suffered a loss. It will also bring us more in touch with our needs from others in times of loss. The following suggestions for offering support come from researchers who interviewed people after they suffered a stressful loss (Lehman, Ellard, & Wortman, 1986):

> *Helpful responses:* Expressing genuine caring and concern, allowing the griever to express feelings, being available when needed, and offering the opportunity for activities
>
> *Unhelpful responses:* Offering advice, encouraging a positive outlook, interfering in the griever's life, and downplaying the griever's loss

Respondents said they derived the greatest comfort from others who were good listeners and who allowed them to express their feelings. It was also helpful to have support people who communicated genuine caring and were available to be leaned on when needed. Grieving respondents also found comfort in spending time with others who had suffered similar kinds of losses.

Responses that were not appreciated included statements that downplayed the griever's sense of loss. People who offered advice or encouragement to look at the brighter side of life often did more harm than good. Respondents said that they needed time to work things out for themselves. They valued concern and support but resented those who tried to push them to act in ways that denied their feelings.

Why do people trivialize each other's distress (Lazarus, 1984b)? Mainly because it is a burden when those close to us are suffering. We'd prefer that they pull themselves together rather than relying on us for support. The problem with trivializing distress is that it promotes a false expectation that just a little positive thinking will make everything better. It is true that developing self-efficacy and feelings of internal control are valuable coping skills. However, this does not mean that people should deny their suffering. The negative effects of trivializing human distress will come up again in Chapter 13 when we look at helpful and unhelpful responses given to cancer patients. The point is that we value support from others in our efforts to cope with our losses and grief. But above all, we expect people to take us seriously.

Coping Skill 12: Understanding How to Offer Support

OBTAINING SUPPORT

People suffering a loss face an ironic challenge when it comes to obtaining support. On one hand, we are expected to display grief after a loss. On the other hand, other people are uncomfortable with expressions of grief. Therefore, although people in grief want to lean on others for support, they also have to provide reassurance that they won't lean on any particular person too much. It is necessary for people in grief to communicate to potential support people: "Yes, I am hurting, and I could use your support. But I'm also coping, and I won't fall apart" (Silver, Wortman, & Crofton, 1990). We can only hope that this message will serve as a self-fulfilling prophecy.

Coping Skill 13: Understanding How to Obtain Support

LIST OF SKILLS FOR COPING WITH LOSS

- *Coping Skill 1:* Accepting a Loss as Worthy of Grief Work
- *Coping Skill 2:* Being Open to the Experience of Mourning
- *Coping Skill 3:* Recognizing the Stages of Grief Work as Tasks for Which You Are Responsible
- *Coping Skill 4:* Taking Time to Accomplish the Four Tasks of Grief Work
- *Coping Skill 5:* Integrating the Loss into Your Life Experience
- *Coping Skill 6:* Controlling Obsessive Thinking

- *Coping Skill 7:* Appreciating the Necessity for Attending to Unresolved and Disenfranchised Grief
- *Coping Skill 8:* Finding a Meaning for Death
- *Coping Skill 9:* Working Through a Personal Program for Grief Work
- *Coping Skill 10:* Learning How to Let Go
- *Coping Skill 11:* Recognizing Your Individuality
- *Coping Skill 12:* Understanding How to Offer Support
- *Coping Skill 13:* Understanding How to Obtain Support

SUGGESTIONS FOR FURTHER READING

Becker, E. (1973). *The denial of death.* New York: Free Press.

Freeman, L. (1978). *The sorrow and the fury: Overcoming hurt and loss from childhood to old age.* Englewood Cliffs, NJ: Prentice-Hall.

Kavanaugh, R. (1974). *Facing death.* Baltimore: Penguin.

Koestenbaum, P. (1976). *Is there an answer to death?* Englewood Cliffs, NJ: Prentice-Hall.

Kushner, H. S. (1983). *When bad things happen to good people.* New York: Avon.

Rose, N. J., & Olson, J. M. (Eds.). (1995). *What might have been: The social psychology of counterfactual thinking.* Mahwah, NJ: Erlbaum.

Schneider, J. (1984). *Stress, loss, and grief: Understanding their origins and growth potential.* Baltimore: University Park Press.

Tatelbaum, J. (1980). *The courage to grieve.* New York: Lippincott & Crowell.

Walsh, F., & McGoldrick, M. (Eds.). (1991). *Living beyond loss: Death in the family.* New York: Norton.

11

Coping with Aging

It's a good bet that younger readers will approach this chapter with disinterest, thinking "it has nothing to do with me." For some, aging is of little concern because they cannot fathom ever getting old. For others, the topic of aging is depressing. Let me clarify two facts: (1) you will get old, and (2) aging is not necessarily depressing. Even if you feel this chapter has nothing to do with you, it will still help you better understand your parents, your grandparents, and other elders with whom you come in contact.

Aging is a life event that affects everyone. People from all cultures throughout history have had to come to terms with the reality of aging and the inevitability of death. A primary appraisal of aging tells us that it is an experience that we may not always like but one that we must accept. Given this fact, we want our secondary appraisal to result in coping responses that will help make the most of the aging experience.

In this chapter I focus on skills for maintaining self-esteem and self-efficacy during old age. These skills are especially relevant for societies such as ours, where elderly people often suffer stigma and lack of support.

WHY PSYCHOLOGISTS STUDY AGING

Aging presents challenges and adjustments for all people, so it stands to reason that we would want to understand as much about this process as possible. Interestingly, it has been only within the last 20 years that psychologists have developed gerontology into a major research topic. Psychologists have devoted attention to the study of aging because of a growing consciousness about the lack of preparation for growing old in much of U.S. society. Another reason for the development of this research area is the fact that the elderly population in the United States (and the world) is steadily increasing. In 1900, only 4% of Americans were over 65 years of age, but in 1970, 10% were over 65. By the year 2000, it is estimated that 13% of all Americans will be over age

65, and this percentage is expected to increase to 20% by the year 2030 (H. G. Cox, 1988).

Because elderly people are beginning to comprise a larger proportion of the population, they are gaining the power and influence to ensure better treatment from society.

TWO CHALLENGES OF AGING

Aging brings two major challenges. The first is physical, a result of the inevitable decline that occurs as our bodies get older. The second challenge is psychological, and it results from the need to rise above the stigma of old age and to maintain a sense of self-esteem, mastery, and competence. I will discuss both of these challenges in this chapter.

Physical Challenges in Aging

Common medical problems experienced by elderly people include (Libow, 1977):

Arthritis: This is a common ailment with no medical cure.

Bones: Aging bones weaken and break more easily. (See a physician for a recommended diet and exercise.)

Bowels: Constipation and changes in regularity are common in later life. (See a physician for a recommended diet, including fruits and other fibrous foods.)

Breast: Breast cancer is a concern for women. (Regular self-examination should be performed.)

Eyes: Cataracts are common but are usually treatable. Farsightedness is experienced by most people.

Heart: Arteriosclerosis, heart attacks, heart failure, and other problems are likely. (It is important at a young age to follow good health care practices such as not smoking, a proper diet, and regular exercise.)

Mobility: There is a detriment in mobility and increased difficulty with walking.

Prostate: Prostate problems are common in older men. (Have regular physical checkups.)

Stroke: This is the most common reason for elderly people to be placed in nursing homes. (See a physician for preventive health practices.)

Although most elderly people experience some of these problems, large differences exist between people in how rapidly they age.

A survey of elderly people found that they experienced the following physical challenges (H. G. Cox, Sekhon, & Norman, 1978): getting up and down stairs, 40% of the respondents; washing and bathing, 20%; housecleaning, 30%; doing the laundry, 30%; using the telephone, 35%; dressing, 15%; and cooking, 19%. These experiences of physical decline are not pleasant, but elderly people cope with them by realizing that they are doing as well or better than most people of their age (Heidrich & Ryff, 1993a, 1993b).

Although elderly people experience problems with aging, it is worth pointing out that these difficulties are not as bad as younger people believe. A poll by Louis Harris and Associates (1975) compared younger and older Americans' opinions about how much elderly people suffer from problems such as fear of crime, adequate housing and clothing, medical care, and social support. It was interesting to find that younger people's estimates of how much elderly people suffer from these problems were far greater than the elderly people's actual reports. Also worth noting is that in a national survey, people in the 65–85 age bracket rated themselves as being happier than people in any other age group (C. H. Russell, 1989). In the same survey, elderly people said they were less troubled by loneliness and finances than middle-aged and younger people. Elderly people were also generally satisfied with their current state of health. More than 80% of the elderly people surveyed agreed with the following statements (Harris & Associates, 1981):

1. As I look back on my life, I am fairly well satisfied.
2. Compared with other people my age, I make a good appearance.
3. I've gotten pretty much what I expected out of life.

We seem to fear old age and anticipate that it will be worse than it actually is.

While surveys of elderly people indicate that they often view their lives in a positive manner, the fears and negative perceptions many of us have about growing older can result in a negative self-fulfilling prophecy. If you *expect* aging to be negative and painful, it will surely turn out that way. If you *expect* that elderly people are slow, forgetful, and incompetent, you will most likely start acting this way as you grow older. The goal of this chapter is to enhance your options as you grow older. You are not destined to be "over the hill" and in a state of hopeless decline if you remain flexible and realize that aging has constructive possibilities (Langer et al., 1988; Piper & Langer, 1987).

Coping Skill 1: Making Aging a Positive Self-Fulfilling Experience

THE JOY OF COMPETENCE

It is a refreshing experience to observe children at play. Children love exploring and testing things to learn how they work. They are persistently curious and don't easily give up if their first attempts at creating something are not successful. The sight of children interacting with their world is a poignant example of what Robert W. White (1959) described as the *motivation for competence*. White called attention to people's natural desire to have an effect on their environment, to make things happen, and to achieve "joy in being a cause."

As children grow into adulthood, many of the tasks and skills they practiced and rehearsed when they were younger become automatic. For example, once you have learned to ride a bicycle, to dress yourself, or to eat by yourself, you can do these activities without thinking much about them. We go through many of our daily routines with little mental effort. This is quite a change from childhood when we had to consciously attend to everything we did. For adults living in a complex world, there is a real advantage in the automatic performance of routine activities because it reserves brain power for mastering new challenges in life. It is the opportunity to master these challenges that satisfies the need for competence and promotes feelings of self-efficacy.

Throughout adulthood, most people are able to experience a satisfactory degree of influence on their lives and on the world around them through work, family, hobbies, and social activities. When people grow older and reach retirement age, a number of things happen that undermine their opportunities to be competent. First, there is the stigma of old age. Elderly people in U.S. society are often stereotyped as being forgetful and less able to do things. A second life change faced by elderly people is retirement, which deprives them of the means for achieving competence they have used all of their lives. Elderly people are also commonly relieved of the gratification they once received from being the head of their family. These life changes can be detrimental because they take away major opportunities for being socially competent. Elderly people need to maintain personal relationships where their input is valued, otherwise they are likely to become isolated and develop styles of interacting that are seen as odd or idiosyncratic (Hansson, 1989).

A third factor undermining competence in old age is the decrement that occurs in physical ability and in hearing and vision. Because of stigmas and stereotypes, forced retirement, and physical decline, elderly people are often deprived of goals and challenges for achieving feelings of competence and self-efficacy. In many cases, the lives of senior citizens revolve around overlearned, automatic activities that were mastered years ago. While the overlearning of activities served a useful purpose in the past, it is now a detriment because it instills false feelings of incompetence. There is little joy when one's life is made up only of routines.

THE STIGMA OF OLD AGE

In many societies elderly people are held in high esteem. They are respected as family leaders and acknowledged for their wisdom. This is not the case in much of U.S. society. Senior citizens are portrayed in movies and television as foolish, humorous, and forgetful (Greenberg, Korzenny, & Atkin, 1979). Children learn to make fun of the elderly and to see them in a negative light. As we grow older (and we *will* grow older), we need to devote our energies toward maintaining our dignity and pride. In working toward this goal, we can offer our services to organizations such as the Gray Panthers, which was founded to combat discrimination against the elderly.*

Coping Skill 2: Maintaining Dignity and Pride

A challenging stigma associated with old age is the use of aging as a metaphor for ill health and general decline (Newquist, 1985). When people take this kind of

*The Gray Panthers, 3635 Chestnut Street, Philadelphia, PA 19104. Write and ask about a chapter in your area.

attitude toward aging, they are vulnerable to a negative self-fulfilling prophecy. If you perceive your life as going downhill as you get older, your belief may very well become a reality. You will probably become so preoccupied with your aches and pains that you will wake up every morning with stress and anxiety about the fact that your life is no longer worthwhile. People around you will pick up on the messages you are sending and will start treating you as if you have nothing more to offer. In addition to resisting the metaphor of aging as "decline," it is also worth thinking about what to call people who are older. The term *old person* has so many negative connotations that we need a different word to identify people who have been around for a long time (Perdue & Gurtman, 1990). The term *senior citizen* may be suitable. In some cultures the term *elder* is used to convey respect for senior members of society.

Another problem resulting from the stigma of old age is that elderly people are often reluctant to seek medical attention for legitimate ailments, fearing that they won't be taken seriously. Family members and friends respond to complaining elderly people by urging them to take it easy and discouraging them from doing things for themselves. However, this is the time when it is most important for the elderly to use their assertiveness skills (see Chapter 8). It is true that we will all suffer various physical detriments as we get older. Some tips about how to master the physical challenges that come with aging are given later in this chapter. However, it is also true that taking a pessimistic view of aging is not in our best interest. Use the ideas in this chapter to develop coping skills so that aging will be a positive rather than a negative self-fulfilling experience.

BEING FUTURE-ORIENTED

After years of using aging as a metaphor for decline, it shouldn't surprise you to learn that many elderly people find it difficult to be oriented toward the future. One research study found that a large proportion of elderly people were future-oriented to the extent that they looked forward to events related to their families (Reker & Wong, 1985). However, less than 10% of these people had any plans or expectations related to their own personal development. This is unfortunate. It is true that young people have a greater variety of experiences, changes, and accomplishments to look forward to than elderly people do (Ryff, 1991). However, old age is not a time to give up on ourselves. There are always skills to be learned and challenges to be mastered.

Coping Skill 3: Being Future-Oriented

AGING AS A LIFE TASK

One way to remain future-oriented as we grow older is to view aging as a life task (Cantor, Norem, Niedenthal, Langston, & Brower, 1987). The value of this outlook is that it keeps us aware of goals to accomplish. Erik Erikson (1963) outlined the stages of growth and development. In this chapter the relevant stages are those of middle age and later life:

Middle age: The life task of middle age (ages 35 through 60) is *generativity versus stagnation.* Most people have accomplished the challenges of completing their education, raising families, and settling on their careers. The challenge during these years is to maintain a sense of usefulness and productivity. Involve yourself in activities, hobbies, and personal relationships that offer a sense of satisfaction and accomplishment.

Later life: The life task of later life (age 60 and older) is *integrity versus despair.* We want to look back on our life and feel it was worthwhile. We must reconcile our satisfactions with our regrets and resolve the following issues (Peck, 1968): (1) We must realize that our worth does not depend on our job history or on how much money we made but rather on our quality as a human being; (2) we must balance loss of physical strength and lowered resistance to illness against satisfying memories and meaningful interpersonal relationships; (3) we must come to terms with our mortality by caring for others.

As you can see, the best way to get through the stages of middle age and later life is to prepare for them ahead of time. You can begin by reviewing your life now. Are you satisfied with what you are doing? If not, it is time to consider new directions.

A number of specific tasks that must be accomplished during later life are: (1) preparing a will, (2) making plans for our death and funeral, (3) completing "unfinished business" with people close to us, and (4) discussing with loved ones how we would like to be remembered. These are tasks we often avoid because they remind us of our mortality. However, facing and accomplishing them provides a sense of competence and self-efficacy.

Coping Skill 4: Completing Your Life Tasks

The Importance of Continuity

It should be clear by now that old age is not the time to withdraw or to disengage yourself from the lifestyle you have learned to prefer (Dreyer, 1986). Try to maintain your times of activity, times of relaxation, and time spent alone at comfortable levels. Old age should not come as a shock where your whole sense of self is disrupted.

One common method for maintaining a feeling of continuity throughout life is the *life review* (Kamptner, 1989). We all have memories, and often photographs, diaries, and other mementos, to preserve the meaningfulness of our lives. A life review can be done individually or in groups (Weiss, 1995a, 1995b). The goal of the life review is to put together your life experiences to arrive at an integrated picture of yourself (Butler, 1963). It is important, especially in old age, to appreciate your identity as a person with values, attitudes, and experiences that have developed over the course of your life history (Erikson, Erikson, & Kivnick, 1986).

Coping Skill 5: Recognizing the Importance of Continuity

FORGETFULNESS AS A BUM RAP

How do we explain why a young person forgets something very simple? We usually assume the person is preoccupied or, at worst, careless. But what if an elderly person makes the same mistake? We may very likely attribute it to senility. Elderly people get a bum rap because they are stigmatized for making many of the same errors we all make every day.

Research studies indicate that although elderly people are sometimes slower on mental tasks, they are able to compensate with thoughtfulness and experience (Cox, 1988, pp. 97–100; Meer, 1986). Many studies of memory and performance placed elderly people at a disadvantage by comparing them with college students who are in top form for performing on mental tasks. Other studies unfairly compared elderly people with younger people who had the benefit of more education. But elderly people do very well on tasks requiring immediate memory and memory for things that happened in the past. They sometimes have difficulty remembering a list of things if something happens to distract them between the time they learn the list and the time they are tested. However, even when they don't remember the list exactly, they can recall its meaning. For example, college students may do better than elderly people in reciting the exact words of a poem they have memorized. Elderly people, however, will do just as well in describing the poem's message. One fair conclusion from research on memory and problem solving is that young people do better than elderly people in cramming and coming up with quick responses. When elderly people are given the opportunity to take their time and use the knowledge they have gained throughout their lives, their performance shows little decline.

Coping Skill 6: Appreciating the Value of Thoughtfulness and Experience

EXERCISING YOUR MIND

Although the brain is not made of muscle that atrophies from disuse, you can suffer psychologically if you lose the opportunity to think creatively, solve problems, and experience the pleasure of being competent. This loss is not uncommon among the elderly and has been the focus of a research program undertaken by Ellen Langer (Langer, 1979, 1981). Langer worked with residents of nursing homes, who are in the peculiar position of being well cared for physically while often suffering mentally and psychologically. Residents in many nursing homes lead routine and regimented lives. All of their physical needs are met. They don't have to think about housekeeping and preparing meals. Unfortunately, many of them live in an environment with institutional furniture, uninspiring room decorations, and minimal stimulation. We are all aware of the value of providing young children with stimulating environments that offer the opportunity for mastering sounds and colors and learning how to put things together. We certainly don't desire to live a life where we can't control what is going on around us. Why does society give up on elderly people and force them into a routine existence? Where is the "joy in being a cause" in most nursing home environments?

Langer and her associates (Langer, Rodin, Beck, Weinmen, & Spitzer, 1979) conducted an illuminating series of studies. They gave nursing home residents an opportunity to exercise their minds. Elderly people in one study had four visits by a young person who engaged them in personal conversations. The elderly residents were encouraged by their visitors to think of new ideas and to remember things from one visit to the next. This experience had a remarkable effect. Four stimulating conversations were enough to make these elderly people happier and more alert, sociable, and active. The four stimulating conversations also resulted in significant improvements on tests of memory.

In a second study, elderly people were provided with the opportunity to work on some challenging puzzles (Avorn & Langer, 1982). The elderly residents in one group were offered a lot of help with the puzzles. Those in a second group were encouraged but were left to solve the puzzles on their own. It shouldn't be a surprise that participants in the second group did better. In addition to solving the puzzles more accurately, they experienced a significant increase in self-confidence. If you think about it, you can understand why the performance of the elderly people in the first group actually got worse. Isn't it more fun to figure things out for yourself?

A third study demonstrated the technique of attending to daily chores and decisions (Perlmuter & Langer, 1983). This might not sound very exciting to people with challenging and demanding lives. However, it can serve a good purpose for those who are restricted to routine lives. Even restricted people can recognize their ability to choose what they will wear, what they will eat or drink, and what they will read or watch on TV. By attending to daily choices, elderly people can reaffirm their ability to exercise control over their lives.

Coping Skill 7: Exercising Your Mind

THE POWER OF COMPETENCE AND SELF-RELIANCE

Exercising Competence in Your Living Situation

Let's return to the point about how elderly people are deprived of self-efficacy when their lives become routine and they no longer have challenges to master. Ellen Langer and Judith Rodin demonstrated how this false sense of incompetence can be overcome (Langer & Rodin, 1976; Rodin & Langer, 1977). They provided nursing home residents with an opportunity to experience competence. The residents were encouraged to exercise control by voicing their ideas for changes in the nursing home, deciding on their room decorations, and planning their free-time activities. The residents were also given a personal house plant to care for.

These opportunities for exercising competence might not seem very great. However, compared with the institutionalized life the residents had been living, they made a big difference. Compared with nursing home residents of equal age and health, residents who exercised this small amount of competence felt significantly more control over their lives. They were happier, more alert, and more sociable. Not only did the opportunity to exercise competence help these elderly people psycholog-

Successful aging requires that you keep active in body and mind.

ically, it also helped them physically. Nursing home residents who exercised competence lived longer. The fact that having some control over their lives helped these
people live longer is remarkable. However, you won't find it surprising once you have
considered the studies on helplessness described in Chapter 15 (see also Shupe,
1985).

In another study, opportunities for exercising competence in residential care facilities for elderly people were measured to see if they were related to the well-being of
the people living in these environments (Timko & Moos, 1989). Six measures were
derived to identify ways residents might be able to exercise competence:

Policy choice is the extent to which the facility provides options from which residents can select patterns of daily living. (Is there a curfew? Are residents
allowed to drink a glass of wine or beer?)

Resident control is the extent to which residents have a voice in running the facility. (Is there a residents' council? Are residents involved in deciding what
kinds of new activities or programs will occur?)

Policy clarity refers to the clarity of facility policies. (Is there a handbook for residents? Is there an orientation session?)

Independence is the degree to which self-sufficiency is supported and encouraged.
(Are residents learning to do more things on their own? Are the residents
encouraged to make their own decisions?)

Resident influence is the extent to which residents believe they can influence the
rules and policies of the facility. (Do residents have any say in making the
rules? Can residents change things here if they really try?)

Organization is the extent to which residents know what to expect in their day-to-day lives. (Is this place very well organized? Is there a sense of stability and predictability?)

A number of questions were addressed in this study. First, it was determined that elderly people living in apartments had more opportunities to control their lives than elderly people living in residential care facilities. Elderly people living in nursing homes had the least amount of control over their lives. A second finding was that all six ways of exercising competence described above were related to elderly people's well-being. Elderly people who had the greatest opportunities to exercise competence (regardless of where they lived) were more active, more independent, and more satisfied with their lives. A third finding was that elderly people whose physical functioning was limited required special efforts to help them find ways to exercise competence in their lives.

There is a growing recognition of the importance of designing homes for the elderly that facilitate the experience of competence (Moos & Lemke, 1994). Homes for the elderly can benefit their residents by encouraging the following practices (Teitelman & Priddy, 1988):

1. Promoting choice and predictability among residents
2. Promoting feelings of control and responsibility among residents
3. Encouraging residents to learn and practice effective communication skills
4. Eliminating dependency-engendering stereotypes among staff

Maintaining Self-Reliance in Old Age

The value of taking a self-reliant approach toward life begins in childhood and continues throughout old age. It is not always easy to maintain a coping attitude toward life, and everyone experiences times when they feel like giving up. When you have a setback, try not to be too hard on yourself, but remember that it's up to you to pull yourself up and start using your coping skills again.

Old age presents particular challenges for senior citizens who suffer physical impairments that reduce the amount of control they have over their lives. It is not surprising that elderly people whose lives have been compromised by strokes, arthritis, diabetes, and other ailments experience a loss of self-efficacy and well-being and often suffer significant psychological distress (Reich & Zautra, 1991). It is crucial for elderly people to find avenues for exercising self-reliance even when they are impaired. Social support systems can be very helpful. Immediately after a personal loss or impairment, social support people can be most helpful by offering nurturance, assistance, and someone to "lean on." As time goes on, it becomes more helpful for social support systems to encourage independence, self-reliance, and self-efficacy (Zautra, Reich, & Newsom, 1995). It is also beneficial for elderly people who are coping with impairment to bring daily pleasures into their lives (Zautra, Reich, & Guarnaccia, 1990). These pleasures don't have to be large. What is most valuable is making each day meaningful with small positive experiences.

Classes and training groups for teaching self-reliance skills can be very helpful. Participants in these classes make an inventory of their daily lives in which they find examples of positive and negative events that are within their control and that are beyond their control (Zautra et al., 1995). Participants learn strategies for exercising more control where it is possible and for coping more effectively when control is not possible. The purpose of these training groups is to help participants develop the following kinds of self-reliance:

1. *Control over positive outcomes* is exemplified by the attitude that "I can do just about anything I really set my mind to" and "What happens to me in the future mostly depends on me."
2. *Positive event efficacy* is the perceived ability to create or to bring about positive events in one's life. This is expressed in the attitude "I know how to have a good time" and "I can create positive experiences in my life."
3. *Coping efficacy* is satisfaction with past coping efforts and confidence in coping with future stressors. ("I have handled my problems pretty well." "I am confident about my ability to find solutions to life challenges in the future.")
4. *Mastery over negative life events* is the attitude that "I can solve most of my problems" and "I don't have to be pushed around in life."

Elderly people, including those who are physically impaired, who participate in training groups experience a significant increase in self-efficacy and self-reliance and in their overall well-being and mental health. Even though the things elderly people are able to control may be limited, it is a great benefit to "know that you can do it" (Zautra & Wrabetz, 1991).

The message from the research studies outlined in this section is loud and clear. Human beings thrive when they exercise competence and deteriorate when their opportunities for experiencing self-efficacy are lost. It is important for us to always have activities in our lives that we can control.

Coping Skill 8: Finding Opportunities for Exercising Competence and Self-Reliance

ADJUSTING TO OLD AGE

Elderly people view the following factors as defining good adjustment (Ryff, 1989b):

- Being oriented toward others
- Accepting change
- Continuing one's personal growth
- Enjoying life
- Maintaining a sense of humor

Poor adjustment was defined by elderly people in the following way:

- Being cranky and complaining
- Being self-centered
- Withdrawing and having no interests

- Not being able to accept change
- Being self-critical and insecure

As far as personality traits go, elderly people are happier and have a greater sense of well-being if they have developed a reasonable level of extraversion, agreeableness, and conscientiousness (see Chapter 1; Costa, Metter, & McCrae, 1994). As with younger and middle-aged adults, neuroticism is associated with poor adjustment in old age.

In the remainder of this chapter I will focus on suggestions about how to adjust to old age. The following factors have been correlated with successful adjustment to aging (Clark & Anderson, 1967; Cox, 1988, p. 109):

- A feeling of self-sufficiency and autonomy
- A good support system
- A reasonable amount of physical comfort
- A sufficiently stimulating lifestyle
- Sufficient mobility to engage in satisfying activities
- A sense of meaning and purpose in life

Some Useful Goals and Activities

An interview study with elderly people identified the following factors associated with successful aging: entertainment and diversions, socializing, and productive activities (Clark & Anderson, 1967). Elderly people with low morale complained of feeling dependent, lonely, and bored. The skill of developing support systems and good interpersonal relationships is discussed later in this chapter. Here are some other skills that can make aging a good experience (Reker, 1985):

Stress control: Practice the self-relaxation skills described in Chapter 3. It is important to always take time to find inner peace and tranquility.

Self-responsibility: Take as much responsibility for your own needs as possible. But remember that it is OK to ask for help when you need it. You are still in control of your life when you take the initiative to ask for things you need (Zevon, Karuza, & Brickman, 1982).

Nutrition: Make an effort to plan a diet that is both healthy and enjoyable.

Physical fitness: It is never too late to obtain benefits from an exercise program (deVries, 1983). However, it is important to consult a physician about the most suitable methods for maintaining physical fitness. Six factors influence the likelihood that older people will engage in physical activity (Courneya, 1995): (1) believing that physical activity is good for your health; (2) feeling confident that you can overcome barriers to activity, such as laziness, bad weather, lack of time, or unavailability of exercise facilities; (3) a feeling of social pressure from others; (4) a positive attitude about engaging in physical activity; (5) a feeling of confidence that you can motivate yourself to engage in physical activity; and (6) the intention and resolve to do it.

Enjoy the process as well as the product: Our culture is product-oriented. People are valued for their speed in producing things. We are often so preoccupied with the outcome of work that we forget to take pleasure in the creative process. As you grow older, you may not be able to work as quickly, or even as accurately, as you once did. However, you can still experience pleasure in doing things (Langer et al., 1988; Piper & Langer, 1987).

Appreciating life experiences: Many researchers have pointed out the value of taking time to review your life experiences. This does not imply living in the past and neglecting your orientation toward the future. The point of this exercise is to appreciate the lessons you have learned and the things you have accomplished. A good way to put your life into perspective is by sharing your autobiography. You can write it, narrate it on tape, or discuss it with others. An important reason for reviewing your life experiences is to remind yourself that you have many dimensions. Avoid getting trapped in the role of an old person who has nothing to offer.

THE VALUE OF INDIVIDUALITY

Researchers have demonstrated quite clearly how people lose their individuality when they are lumped into groups and categories (Hamilton, 1979; Hamilton & Rose, 1980). We stereotype people who are different from us according to race, religion, nationality, and any other characteristic we can think of. Even though we know that *we* are individuals, we tend to see people from other groups as identical. This stereotyping also occurs with the elderly. Instead of looking at senior citizens as individuals, we often think of them as having similar characteristics. The challenge for elderly people, then, is to assert their individuality. But this is not easy because our society also resists nonconformists. Just look at the struggles experienced by people from racial and religious minorities who have attempted to maintain their identity over the course of history. Women have also faced resistance in gaining their rights and overcoming the negative stereotypes they suffer in U.S. society. Our society sees the model elderly person as docile, nondemanding, and invisible.

It is ironic that one method for asserting individuality in old age is to think unconventional thoughts. Unfortunately, while unconventional thinking is useful for making life interesting and exercising the mind, it can also be viewed as abnormal and a sign of senility. Langer and her colleagues make a convincing argument that one way to fight the boredom of old age is to think creatively and invent new ideas (Langer, Beck, Janoff-Bulman, & Timko, 1984). They found that elderly people who were labeled as "senile" (but who were actually in good health) were more creative problem solvers than elderly people of comparable age and health who were not labeled as senile. On top of this, the "senile" people who exercised their minds with creative and unusual ideas lived longer.

Have you ever felt like acting out as a way of expressing yourself? As members of an outgroup in our society, elderly people must make the choice between conforming and losing their individuality or asserting themselves and facing some inevitable disapproval.

Coping Skill 9: Asserting Your Individuality

SOME USEFUL SUGGESTIONS ABOUT AGING

A good way to conclude this chapter is by considering some suggestions about aging provided by B. F. Skinner and Margaret Vaughan (1983) in their book, *Enjoy Old Age*. These suggestions can be divided into two sections. The first group of suggestions focuses on ways to master the physical detriments that occur as we grow older. The second group concerns methods for maximizing our relationships with other people.

When considering the following suggestions about aging, notice the distinction between *primary control* and *secondary control* (Rothbaum, Weisz, & Snyder, 1982). Primary control involves shaping or changing your physical and social environment. Secondary control is accomplished by adapting or accommodating yourself to the physical and social environment. It has been pointed out several times in this book that adaptive coping requires us to make the distinction between things we can and cannot control. Because people often have less primary control over their lives as they grow older, it is important for them to appreciate the possibilities of secondary control. Exerting secondary control is far different from becoming helpless and giving up. It is a worthy challenge to use your creativity and problem-solving skills to master the limitations imposed by old age (Schulz, Heckhausen, & Locher, 1991).

Mastering Physical Limitations

It is hard to think of any way to view the physical detriments accompanying old age in a positive light. Unfortunately, our primary appraisal of physical decline tells us that it is inevitable. We have to face physical limitations with a secondary appraisal that offers some good avenues for coping. Skinner and Vaughan provide a list of practical suggestions. For example, when your vision gets weaker, compensate by making sure you have good eyeglasses and comfortable lighting. A magnifying glass can help with small print, and a small flashlight is useful in restaurants and other places with low lighting. Libraries have books with large print, and many books and magazines are available on recordings. Many helpful devices are available for enhancing hearing.

Changes can also make the home environment more comfortable (Simon, 1987). Find household utensils and kitchen items that are manageable. Look for clocks that are not difficult to read and telephones that are easy to dial. Make sure stairs and doorway thresholds are well marked and lighted. Good shoes and a walking stick will help you get around with greater ease, and a comfortable chair can be a real pleasure.

The point of these suggestions is to get across the concept of mastery and competence. Elderly people are often embarrassed to wear hearing aids or to be seen using a cane. Instead, they sit at home and suffer. Successful coping results from facing physical detriments with a problem-solving attitude. Think about tools you can use and changes you can make in your environment to master your physical limitations.

Coping Skill 10: Mastering Physical Limitations

Maximizing Personal Relationships

An important factor related to the life satisfaction of elderly people is a sense of connection with other people (Heidrich & Ryff, 1993a). Some examples of social connection are expressed in the following attitudes:

1. After retirement, I find myself still interested in many things that have to do with my former job or career.
2. I find I have as many responsibilities now as I did when I was middle-aged.
3. Even when your children are gone, you still have an important role as a parent.
4. I find I have many fulfilling roles in life now.
5. I get a lot of positive benefits from associating with groups of older people.
6. As I get older, I continue to be involved with social and community groups.
7. As a senior citizen, I can still contribute to society.

Most communities have groups and activities that provide opportunities for elderly people to develop personal relationships with one another. When it comes to maximizing personal relationships with those who are younger, the elderly face a challenge because people of different ages don't always have things in common. You are probably very aware of the generation gap between teenagers and parents. There is also a generation gap separating elderly people from those who are younger. How can this gap be overcome? One way for elderly people to approach this challenge is by considering what they want from their relations with younger people. Two needs that many elderly people share are to exercise control and to communicate affection.

When it comes to exercising control in personal relationships, elderly people are often at a disadvantage. Most young people want to be independent, and they can be impatient and nonreceptive to an older person's suggestions and advice. Probably the worst way for elderly people to exercise control in their relationships with younger people is by nagging and becoming "backseat drivers." It is more fruitful to take a problem-solving approach. A better way to relate with a younger person is by recognizing that person's need for independence and exercising self-control over the urge to give advice. The challenge is to communicate your knowledge and experience in a manner that the young person can accept. This is not always easy but will certainly keep you thinking and exercising your mind. Real mastery comes not from nagging and fussing but from allowing young people a sense of independence. If you present yourself as someone with knowledge and experience, younger people will seek your advice when they are ready.

Two suggestions can be given for bridging generation gaps when communicating affection. First, learn about the interests of people who are important to you. Skinner and Vaughan recommend Jonathan Swift's resolution not to bore younger people by telling the same stories over and over. Elderly people must realize that although their roots and growth experiences are in the past, younger people are primarily oriented toward the future. When relating with younger people, it is often necessary to tune in to their perspective.

A second suggestion for communicating affection with younger people is to help them understand you better. Young people don't know what it is like to be an elderly person. If, for example, you have trouble with your eyesight or hearing, it is helpful to let others know how to communicate with you. It is usually best to let your needs be known. If you try to hide the fact that you have trouble following conversations or being mobile, you will suffer in the long run. This doesn't mean that you should complain about every ache and pain. The challenge will be to exert competence and teach others the things they need to know so your interactions can be mutually gratifying.

Coping Skill 11: Maximizing Personal Relationships

A CONCLUDING THOUGHT

By employing good coping skills, you can face the challenge of aging with humor, dignity, tranquility, and satisfaction. Rather than looking at old age with an attitude of helplessness, maintain a life philosophy of being a coper (see Chapter 15). In this spirit, Dylan Thomas exhorts:

Do not go gentle into that good night,
Old age should burn and rave at close of day;
Rage, rage against the dying of the light. *

LIST OF SKILLS FOR COPING WITH AGING

- *Coping Skill 1:* Making Aging a Positive Self-Fulfilling Experience
- *Coping Skill 2:* Maintaining Dignity and Pride
- *Coping Skill 3:* Being Future-Oriented
- *Coping Skill 4:* Completing Your Life Tasks
- *Coping Skill 5:* Recognizing the Importance of Continuity
- *Coping Skill 6:* Appreciating the Value of Thoughtfulness and Experience
- *Coping Skill 7:* Exercising Your Mind
- *Coping Skill 8:* Finding Opportunities for Exercising Competence and Self-Reliance
- *Coping Skill 9:* Asserting Your Individuality
- *Coping Skill 10:* Mastering Physical Limitations
- *Coping Skill 11:* Maximizing Personal Relationships

*Dylan Thomas, *Poems of Dylan Thomas.* Copyright 1952 by Dylan Thomas. Reprinted by permission of New Directions Publishing Corporation.

SUGGESTIONS FOR FURTHER READING

Belsky, J. K. (1990). *The psychology of aging: Theory, research, and interventions* (2nd ed.). Pacific Grove, CA: Brooks/Cole.

Butler, R. N. (1975). *Why survive? Being old in America.* New York: Harper & Row.

Erikson, J. M., Erikson, E. H., & Kivnick, H. (1986). *Vital involvement in old age.* New York: Norton.

Fries, J. F., & Crapo, L. M. (1981). *Vitality and aging.* New York: W. H. Freeman.

Kimmel, D. C. (1974). *Adulthood and aging.* New York: Wiley.

Russell, C. H. (1989). *Good news about aging.* New York: Wiley.

Skinner, B. F., & Vaughan, M. E. (1983). *Enjoy old age.* New York: Norton.

Ward, R. A. (1984). *The aging experience.* New York: Harper & Row.

Weiss, J. C. (1988). *The "feeling great" wellness program for older adults.* Binghamtom, NY: Haworth Press.

12

Coping with Pain

Pain is a private experience. We can't sense other people's pain, and we cannot communicate to others exactly how our pain feels to us. This is what makes pain such a fascinating topic. Although everyone feels pain, each of us reacts in our own individual manner.

In this chapter I will discuss two kinds of pain: acute and chronic. *Acute pain* is pain of relatively short duration. When you hit your head, cut yourself, or suffer some other kind of injury, you experience pain that you know will eventually go away. The same is true for dental work, surgery, and childbirth. Although the pain from these experiences can be severe, it has a limited duration. Coping with acute pain involves finding ways to bear up and "hang in there" until it is over. *Chronic pain* is pain with which people have to live. Back problems, arthritis, and certain injuries result in pain that is either almost always present or that can flare up at any moment. Coping with chronic pain requires that you learn to live a meaningful and satisfying life despite the constant burden of pain.

INFLUENCES ON PAIN

Cultural Influences

The subjectivity of pain is apparent in studies of people's reactions to pain in various cultures (Zborowski, 1969). In some cultures, people are very open to expressions of pain and see nothing wrong with grimacing and moaning when experiencing pain. An example of this attitude is found in the following statement: "Sometimes it hurts so bad that you just have to yell and scream, or moan, or let it out in some way. It's a release. It makes you feel better." In other cultures, people are more stoic and are encouraged to keep their pain to themselves. An example of this attitude is: "I don't yell or scream or fuss about it. That won't help. I just keep it to myself and live with it. Sometimes you just have to be tough and not act like a baby."

Motivational Influences

The subjectivity of pain is also demonstrated in studies of people's motivations for tolerating pain. Volunteers in one research study were exposed to pain from a pressure cuff placed around the upper arm (Lambert, Libman, & Posner, 1960). The cuff was designed with hard rubber projections that could be pressed into the arm with increasing force until the volunteers asked for the pain to be terminated. These volunteers were willing to tolerate more pain when they were motivated to make a good showing for the sake of the particular religious group with which they were affiliated. Participants in another study were exposed to electric shocks under one of two different conditions (Zimbardo, Cohen, Weisenberg, Dworkin, & Firestone, 1969). Participants in one group felt they were taking the shocks out of free choice. Participants in a second group felt pressured by the researchers to take the shocks. Which people were willing to tolerate the greatest shocks? You can probably figure out that the participants who felt they were taking the shocks out of free choice demonstrated less pain than the participants who felt pressured to take the shocks. When forced to put up with pain, people often have no qualms about complaining. However, if you feel you have in some way chosen to accept pain, you have some incentive to increase your tolerance before complaining.

Imagine a football player who intercepts a pass during the last seconds of a championship game. He runs down the field, and three players tackle him just before he is able to make a touchdown. His leg is broken; his team loses. Now imagine a football player who intercepts a pass during the last seconds of the game, runs down the field, and is tackled by three players just as he crosses the line for a touchdown. His leg is broken; his team wins. Both players have exactly the same injury. Which one suffers most from the pain?

MEASURING PAIN

The subjectivity of pain is further underscored by the fact that the only way to measure pain is by recording what people say or by observing how they act. There is no instrument for obtaining a purely objective and standard measure of pain. Pain is usually measured using one or more of these three methods: rating scales, pain behaviors, and daily activity. An understanding of these methods will help you better appreciate how pain is experienced.

Pain Rating Scales

The simplest way to measure pain is to have people rate their pain on a scale of 0 to 10 or 1 to 100. The higher the rating, the greater the pain. However, if different researchers use different scales, it is difficult to compare their results. For this reason, researchers and therapists have developed standardized pain rating scales. One commonly used pain rating scale is the McGill Pain Questionnaire, developed by Ronald Melzack (1975). The McGill Pain Questionnaire has people rate their pain on two kinds of scales. The first scale is called Present Pain Intensity. For example, people rate the degree of pain they are presently experiencing on a scale of 0 to 5: no pain is 0, mild pain is 1, discomforting pain is 2, distressing pain is 3, horrible pain is 4, and excruciating pain is 5. The second scale of the McGill Pain Questionnaire is the Pain Rating Index. This scale measures three dimensions of pain: sensory aspects, affective aspects, and evaluative aspects. Here is a shortened version of the Pain Rating Index:

Sensory Aspects of Pain

Throbbing	_____	Jumping	_____
Pounding	_____	Flashing	_____
Pinching	_____	Shooting	_____
Gnawing	_____	Tugging	_____
Crushing	_____	Wrenching	_____
Dull	_____	Tender	_____
Aching	_____	Splitting	_____
Radiating	_____	Numb	_____
Penetrating	_____	Tearing	_____
Squeezing	_____	Hot	_____
Cold	_____	Burning	_____
Pricking	_____	Stabbing	_____

Affective Aspects of Pain

Fearful	_____	Punishing	_____
Frightful	_____	Grueling	_____
Terrifying	_____	Cruel	_____
Vicious	_____	Killing	_____
Sickening	_____	Exhausting	_____

Evaluative Aspects of Pain

Annoying	_____	Dreadful	_____
Miserable	_____	Unbearable	_____

People are given a list of words and check the ones that describe their pain. Their score is determined by the number of words checked. Because the three Pain Rating Index scales overlap to some degree, it is possible to combine them into a total score representing the total number of words checked on all three scales (Turk, Rudy, & Salovey, 1985).

Another scale for assessing emotional responses to pain is the Pain Discomfort Scale (Jensen, Karoly, & Harris, 1991). Respondents rate the following statements on a 5-point scale (0 = this is very untrue for me; 4 = this is very true for me):

1. I am scared about the pain I feel.
2. The pain I experience is unbearable.
3. The pain I feel is torturing me.
4. My pain does not stop me from enjoying life.

5. I have learned to tolerate the pain I feel.
6. I feel helpless about my pain.
7. My pain is a minor annoyance to me.
8. When I feel pain, I am hurting, but I am not distressed.
9. I never let the pain in my body affect my outlook on life.
10. When I am in pain, I become almost a different person.

People who have the most emotional distress and depression about their pain tend to agree with statements 1, 2, 3, 6, and 10 and to disagree with statements, 4, 5, 7, 8, and 9.

Pain Behaviors

Pain behaviors let us know that someone is in pain. You can see pain in people's facial expressions, in their body language, and in their vocal expressions. Pain behaviors have been measured in a systematic way by making videotapes of people as they go through various exercises, such as walking, picking up an object on the floor, side bends, toe touching, sit-ups, and leg raises. The videotapes are then scored on pain behaviors such as these:

Guarded movement: Slow, cautious movement or jerky movement
Bracing: Bracing oneself on the floor, walls, or furniture or leaning on objects to move around
Position shifts: Wiggling or moving body to find "comfortable spot"
Partial movement: Limited range of motion or not making a complete movement
Grimacing: Grimacing facial expressions or biting lip, gritting teeth
Limitation statements: Statements related to doubts about ability to complete exercise; or about pain, fatigue, stiffness, numbness; or about hesitation, fear, or unwillingness to attempt exercise
Sounds: Grunts, moans, or other pain-related sounds

Pain behaviors are scored on how often they occur in a specific period of time, and a total pain behavior score is derived by adding up a person's total on each of the pain behaviors (Follick, Ahern, & Aberger, 1985; Keefe & Block, 1982; Kleinke & Spangler, 1988b).

Daily Activity

Measures of daily activity are particularly relevant for people who suffer from chronic pain that interferes with their life functioning. The theory behind measures of daily activity is that although people may *feel* pain they still need to keep busy and get on with their lives. Daily activity is measured by having people keep a log of what they are doing during each hour of the day. Are they lying down, sitting, standing, or engaging in some kind of movement? The distinction is often made between "up-time," when the person is engaging in some kind of activity, and "down-time," when the person is lying down or in bed (Follick, Ahern, & Laser-Wolston, 1984; Fordyce et al., 1984).

COPING WITH ACUTE PAIN

When people suffer from acute pain, they want to find strategies for holding their own and bearing up until the worst of it is over. Researchers have discovered a number of useful skills for coping with acute pain. Most research studies on coping with pain actually put volunteers through a painful experience. In some studies, volunteers were taught to use various coping skills, and the researchers determined which worked best. In other studies, volunteers were asked to employ their own methods for coping with the pain, and the researchers identified the kinds of people who were most successful. Several techniques were used to induce pain (Edens & Gil, 1995). One method was the pressure cuff described earlier. Electric shock and a heavy weight on the finger have also been used as pain stimuli. The most common method of manipulating pain was to have the volunteers put a hand in ice water and keep it there for as long as they could. Pain tolerance was measured by the number of minutes the volunteers could keep their hand in the cold water. In some studies the volunteers also rated the degree of their pain on a pain rating scale.

The researchers discovered eight useful skills for coping with pain: taking a coping attitude, practicing self-relaxation, finding a distraction, using creative imagery, using ice, talking yourself through the pain, maintaining a sense of humor, and keeping realistic expectations. Let's learn how each of these coping skills works (Turk, Meichenbaum, & Genest, 1983).

Taking a Coping Attitude

What is the difference between people who are good and not so good at coping with pain? You have already seen how people's willingness to tolerate pain is affected by their motivation and culture. It is sometimes amazing what people can do when they *want* to. This is what a coping attitude is all about. It is an attitude of wanting to take control of your life, to bolster your feelings of self-efficacy, and to follow a problem-solving orientation when faced with challenges such as pain (Bandura, O'Leary, Taylor, Gauthier, & Gossard, 1987; Litt, 1988).

People who are good at tolerating pain are referred to by researchers as *copers*. These people find ways to distract themselves from the painful feelings. Copers take this kind of attitude when undergoing pain: "This really hurts. Let's see, what can I do to bear up to this pain? I have to distract myself . . . to think about other things. Relax. Think about something pleasant. Don't focus on the pain. Put my mind someplace else. I'll be able to tolerate the pain better this way."

People who are not good at tolerating pain are called *catastrophizers*. They lose control to their painful feelings. They focus on how much it hurts and convince themselves that they can't stand it and that there is nothing they can do to increase their tolerance. Catastrophizers take the following kinds of attitudes when undergoing pain (Sullivan, Bishop, & Pivik, 1995):

They *ruminate* by saying: "I want the pain to go away." "I can't keep it out of my mind." "I keep thinking about how much it hurts."

They *magnify* their suffering by saying: "Something serious may happen." "The pain may get worse." "This pain reminds me of other painful experiences."

They feel *helpless* and say things like: "I can't go on." "It's terrible, and it's never going to get any better." "I can't stand it anymore."

There is no easy way to know why some people grow up to be copers while others grow up to be catastrophizers. However, understanding the difference between coping and catastrophizing can help all of us learn how to take a coping attitude (Spanos, Brown, Jones, & Horner, 1981; Spanos, Radtke-Bodorik, Ferguson, & Jones, 1979; Spanos, Stam, & Brazil, 1981; Stam & Spanos, 1980).

Coping Skill 1: Taking a Coping Attitude

Practicing Self-Relaxation

In a study comparing the effectiveness of several pain coping skills, self-relaxation was found to be most helpful for most people (Hackett & Horan, 1980). Self-relaxation is also a preferred treatment modality for people with chronic pain (Kleinke, 1987). This is because self-relaxation is relatively easy to learn, and its benefits are felt soon after it is put to use. When you are in pain, it is a simple matter to remind yourself to take a deep breath and begin using your relaxation skills. The more you practice the self-relaxation procedure outlined in Chapter 3, the better you will do. Of course, self-relaxation does not necessarily make the pain disappear. However, it can help you bear up and tolerate it better.

Coping Skill 2: Using Self-Relaxation

Finding a Distraction

In addition to calming you down, self-relaxation increases your coping capacity by taking your attention away from the pain, anxiety, anger, or whatever is bothering you. You can gain even more control over your attention by learning how to use techniques of distraction. That is, you can take your attention away from the pain by focusing your mind on other things. What you think about is not as important as forcing yourself to ignore the painful sensations. Researchers have tested the effects of distractions by exposing research participants to pain while they engaged in various activities such as solving problems, counting backward, looking at slides, listening to music, and thinking pleasant thoughts. Results of these studies showed that distraction generally helped people tolerate greater amounts of pain (McCaul & Malott, 1984).

Distractions that require a lot of involvement are usually better than minimal distractions because the former are more likely to keep your attention off the pain. Distractions that involve pleasant thoughts, such as thinking fond memories or making exciting plans, have the benefit of putting you in a positive mood. Distractions seem to work best for pain that is moderate but not too severe. When pain sensations are very strong, it is hard to find distractions that will outweigh the pain. When the pain is too strong to ignore, continue self-relaxation and use some of the techniques of creative imagery described in the next section.

Distraction is a skill that requires practice. First of all, you have to ignore the painful sensations. Second, you must think of ways to keep your mind focused on other things. Some people find it easiest to distract themselves by having someone else keep them occupied or by attending to things that are going on around them. Others seek distraction by occupying their minds with thoughts and images. One way to keep your mind occupied is to engage in repetitive acts such as counting or repeating words and phrases. Another strategy is to let your thoughts wander to whatever images, memories, and fantasies come to mind. The point is that you need to actively work at and practice distraction as a coping skill (Farthing, Venturino, & Brown, 1984).

Coping Skill 3: Using Distraction

Using Creative Imagery

Techniques of creative imagery were devised by psychologists to help people use their mental power to greater advantage. Creative imagery can be of value when you are coping with pain that is too severe to ignore with distraction. The idea behind creative imagery is to "flow with the pain." You can't fight it, and you can't get rid of it. So, for as long as it lasts, you have to find a way to incorporate it into your life. How can you do this? Here are some techniques that have been found effective in experimental research (Barber, Spanos, & Chaves, 1974; Chaves & Barber, 1974; Hackett & Horan, 1980; Singer, 1974; Spanos, Horton, & Chaves, 1975; Worthington & Shumate, 1981).

Disassociating.   Imagine that the place that hurts is no longer a part of your body. If the pain is in your arm, visualize your arm as separate from the rest of your body. Your arm is detached and floating through the sky. If the pain is in your head, imagine working the pain out of your head, through your arms, and out the tips of your fingers. Or imagine undergoing surgery where the "infected" pain-ridden part of your brain is removed. When you use disassociation, the pain still exists, but it becomes a smaller factor in your overall being.

Fantasizing.   You can change the meaning of pain by fantasizing that you are suffering for a good cause. Imagine that you are a soldier, athlete, or other kind of hero. Your pain is a small price to pay for a major effort you have accomplished. You can also picture yourself as a superhuman being who has a very high tolerance for pain.

Imagining numbness.   Imagine that the part of your body that hurts is slowly becoming numb. You can feel the sensation of numbness starting in your extremities and slowly spreading to the place where you are feeling pain. As the feelings of numbness build, concentrate on them more and more. Eventually it will be difficult to distinguish between what is pain and what is numbness. You can enhance the feelings of numbness by imagining that novocaine has been injected into the painful area and that its effects are slowly spreading.

Focusing on sensations.   You can't escape the sensations of pain, but you can focus on them and study what they are about. If you are having dental work, consider the pain as an indication that the dentist is repairing and removing the damaged, "rotten" parts of your teeth. The pain is a sign that good work is being done. If you have a headache, imagine the pain as being caused by bands of steel around your head that you can slowly loosen as you relax. Focus on the pain as a message that your body is functioning properly. A good healthy body should feel pain under appropriate circumstances. An unhealthy, "dead" body does not feel pain. Pay attention to the pain as an interesting and unique sensation. Is it steady or intermittent? Is it throbbing or pulsating? Does it feel hot or cold? How could you describe the pain to others? How many different words can you think of that indicate exactly how it feels?

People differ widely in how much they use imagery in their lives. Some people will find that the techniques for using creative imagery make perfect sense. To others, the same techniques might seem strange and perhaps even bizarre.

There are two important points to be made about such differences between people. First, each of you have to devise a strategy for coping with pain that works best for you. Coping with pain is an individual matter that is based on your particular personality, preferences, and strengths. A second point to consider is that new skills and ways of looking at the world can be learned. As you adapt these pain coping skills to fit your personality, remember that you can also benefit by remaining flexible and investing the time and effort to practice and master new techniques.

Coping Skill 4: Using Creative Imagery

Using Ice

One effective method for taking the edge off many types of pain is to apply ice. Using an ice pack or even rubbing the painful area with an ice cube can provide a pleasant numbing sensation. Most athletes regularly use ice to control swelling and to soothe their aches and pains. The advantage of ice is that it helps to relieve pain without the harmful side effects of medication (Melzack, Jeans, Stratford, & Monks, 1980).

Coping Skill 5: Using Ice

Talking Yourself Through the Pain

All three phases of talking yourself through challenges that were outlined in Chapter 3 are useful for coping with pain. Coach yourself as you prepare for pain, confront pain, and reflect back on your performance. Learn how to make the following kinds of statements to yourself:

"This is painful, but I can use my coping skills to handle it."

"It hurts, but I know I will survive."

"One step at a time. I won't let the pain get the best of me."

"Relax. Think about how to cope with this pain."

"Let me run through my list of coping skills and find the best ones for this situation."

"My coping skills might not get rid of the pain, but they will make it more tolerable."

Talking yourself through pain can serve as a useful distraction, can bolster your feelings of self-efficacy, and can keep you on track as you pull together your resources to live through the painful experience.

Coping Skill 6: Talking Yourself Through the Pain

Maintaining a Sense of Humor

I recently underwent a painful medical procedure and was struck by the fact that the doctor kidded and joked with me as he pricked and probed. Apparently, my doctor was aware of research that found that people were willing to tolerate greater pain if their sense of humor was enlivened with humor—such as listening to tapes of comedians like Lily Tomlin and Bill Cosby (Cogan, Cogan, Waltz, & McCue, 1987). Laughter helps increase tolerance for pain in two ways. First, laughter is a good distraction. Second, laughter puts you in a positive frame of mind so the impact of the pain is not so great.

Coping Skill 7: Maintaining a Sense of Humor

Keeping Realistic Expectations

A final skill for coping with acute pain is to keep realistic expectations. Pain is a signal that your body is functioning properly and is warning you that you are hurt. Pain is unpleasant, but it is not an awful, terrible sensation that you can't bear. An interesting finding has come out of the pain research studies that is important to remember. Research participants often learned to use pain coping skills to increase their ability to bear up to and tolerate pain. However, these same people usually reported that the pain still hurt. Coping skills do not make pain magically disappear. The coping skills described here are meant to bolster your feelings of self-efficacy and internal control and to help you become a coper. They should help you tolerate pain more effectively, and with some luck, they will make the pain less distressing (Hackett & Horan, 1980; Scott & Barber, 1977).

Coping Skill 8: Keeping Realistic Expectations

CHRONIC PAIN

Because chronic pain is likely to stay with a person for most of his or her life, it requires skills for coping with pain as well as skills for coping with life disruption. When it comes to coping with chronic pain, all of the skills described for coping with acute pain are useful. People with chronic pain will find it helpful to learn and practice these skills every day. Coping with life disruption requires an understanding of chronic pain and the psychological effects it has on people who are destined to spend much of their lives in pain.

The Prevalence of Chronic Pain

To get an idea of the prevalence of chronic pain, we can look at a community survey that was conducted in Canada in 1984 (Crook, Rideout, & Browne, 1984). This survey found that 15% of female and 12% of male adults were suffering from a chronic pain problem. The most common pain complaints were back problems and headaches. People with chronic pain spent an average of 12 days in the hospital per year, and they reported that pain interfered with their work and with their general health. People suffering from chronic pain had cut down on their daily activities, and they saw few options besides medication for pain relief.

The annual cost of chronic pain in the United States has been estimated at over $100 billion. This figure includes $45 billion for the costs of health care and $55 billion in employment losses. There are 40 million Americans with chronic headaches, 18 million Americans with chronic back pain, and almost 100 million more Americans suffer from some kind of chronic pain. People with chronic pain may have hundreds of hospital visits a year, numerous surgical procedures, and health care bills of up to $100,000 a year (Bonica & Black, 1974; *U.S. News & World Report*, 1987).

The Experience of Chronic Pain

People suffering from chronic pain must learn to cope not only with the daily experience of pain but also with the life disruption caused by their chronic pain problem. Chronic pain challenges people to come to terms with the fact that they must learn to live with their pain and pull themselves out of feelings of sadness and depression. Chronic pain also impinges on interpersonal relationships and requires special adjustments for pain sufferers and the people close to them.

Coming to terms with chronic pain.   One of the most difficult challenges for people with chronic pain is to accept the fact that they must learn to live a satisfying and productive life in spite of their pain. It is tempting to get caught up in the hope of finding a magic cure or a miracle drug that will alleviate the pain forever. Although the ability to fantasize and daydream can be healthy, people with chronic pain face the danger of putting their lives on hold while they wait for a cure.

Coping Skill 9: Coming to Terms with Chronic Pain

Dealing with sadness, depression, and anger. Being faced with chronic pain is a good reason for feeling depressed. Chronic pain inevitably requires that you give up activities that have been rewarding and meaningful. People with chronic pain must work through the grieving process described in Chapter 10. Chronic pain sufferers can make the mistake of closing themselves off emotionally and denying feelings of sadness, depression, and anger that are normal reactions to a major life disruption. You can't learn to live with these feelings until you accept them as real (Blumer & Heilbronn, 1982; Hendler, 1984; Kleinke, 1991).

Coping Skill 10: Dealing with Sadness, Depression, and Anger

Adjustments in interpersonal relationships. Chronic pain inevitably impinges on interpersonal relationships. Some chronic pain sufferers want to be tough and not ask for help and understanding from others. By keeping their suffering to themselves, they avoid the discomfort that comes from asking for favors. However, this kind of reaction also causes them to feel isolated and misunderstood. Other chronic pain sufferers get caught up in the role of being a "patient." They receive sympathy and attention but face the danger of taking on an attitude of helplessness and becoming a burden on others. People with chronic pain must learn to communicate that although they desire care and nurturance they are willing to hold up their end of a relationship to the best of their ability.

Coping Skill 11: Making Adjustments in Interpersonal Relationships

Coping Strategies Used by Chronic Pain Patients

A survey was taken of coping strategies used by people with chronic pain before they began a treatment program in a multidisciplinary pain clinic (Kleinke, 1992). The coping strategies could be grouped into four categories: self-management, helplessness, medical remedies, and social support. Let's look at each of these strategies:

> *Self-management:* Think about other things, do something I enjoy (hobbies, etcetera), try consciously to relax, increase my concentration on work or household activities, go for a walk.
>
> *Helplessness:* Think about how awful it is, feel bad because I have to suffer, focus on how much it really hurts, feel I can't stand it any longer, do nothing because nothing really helps.
>
> *Medical remedies:* Use a heating pad or ice, elevate the painful area or use a pillow for support, lie down or go to bed, apply pain-reducing ointment, take pain-relieving medications.
>
> *Social support:* Talk to friends, family, spouse; ask for help and support from others; try to be around other people; let others know I am in pain.

At the time of admission to the pain clinic, the most effective pain coping strategies were self-management and social support. The least effective coping strategies were helplessness and medical remedies. Patients who endorsed social support as a coping strategy were the most successful in learning to tolerate their pain during the course of the treatment program. While working in the pain treatment program, participants learned how to use the pain coping strategies described in this chapter. By the time they completed the pain program, their pain ratings and pain behaviors had significantly decreased (Kleinke & Spangler, 1988a, 1988b).

Other researchers have also found that chronic pain patients adjust most successfully when they take an *active approach* (staying busy, ignoring and distracting themselves from the pain) rather than a *passive approach* (depending too much on others, overuse of pain-relieving medication, giving up meaningful activities, not communicating their feelings) toward their pain problem (Brown & Nicassio, 1987; Brown, Nicassio, & Wallston, 1989).

Adaptive and Maladaptive Pain Coping Strategies

Research studies with chronic pain patients have identified several adaptive and maladaptive pain coping strategies (Brown & Nicassio, 1987; Brown, Nicassio, & Wallston, 1989; Keefe & Dolan, 1986; Keefe et al., 1987; Kleinke, 1992; Rosenstiel & Keefe, 1983; Turner & Clancy, 1986; Turner, Clancy, & Vitaliano, 1987).

Adaptive pain coping strategies.   Self-management and social support were the most useful pain coping strategies. Patients who endorsed self-management and social support as pain coping strategies were better adjusted on a number of measures. They were less hopeless and lonely, reported fewer physical problems, were more active, more positive toward themselves, and less likely to say they suffered as a result of their pain. Endorsement of self-management and social support was also associated with scores indicating better adjustment on the Minnesota Multiphasic Personality Inventory (MMPI) (Kleinke, 1994).

Maladaptive pain coping strategies.   Helplessness and medical remedies were not adaptive as pain coping strategies. Patients who endorsed helplessness and medical remedies as pain coping strategies were less well-adjusted on measures of loneliness, had more complaints of physical problems, and were less well-adjusted on MMPI scores (Kleinke, 1994). They were less active, more negative toward themselves, and reported greater suffering from their pain.

Two other maladaptive pain coping strategies are catastrophizing and engaging in cognitive distortions (Keefe, Brown, Wallston, & Caldwell, 1989; T. W. Smith, Peck, Milano, & Ward, 1988; T. W. Smith, Peck, & Ward, 1990). It is also not adaptive to take a pessimistic attitude toward life.

Catastrophizing is characterized by focusing on the following kinds of thoughts:

"My pain is terrible and will never get better."
"My pain is awful, and it overwhelms me."

"I feel my life isn't worth living."

"I feel like I can't stand it anymore."

It is understandable that people suffering from chronic pain would have these kinds of feelings. However, they need to force themselves not to ruminate about their misfortunes.

Cognitive distortions are characterized by irrational or illogical thinking (see Chapter 2). People suffer more from chronic pain when they engage in the following kinds of cognitive distortions:

> A man spends 2 hours on housework despite his pain and then puts himself down for not doing a very good job.
>
> A woman finishes all of her work competently and leaves work an hour early to do some therapy for her pain. She tells herself, "My boss is sure to think I am a flake."

Another kind of cognitive distortion is allowing chronic pain to get the best of you by viewing it as alien, mysterious, and caused by some fault of your own (D. A. Williams & Keefe, 1991). Admittedly, it is difficult to look at chronic pain as a friend. However, the more familiar you become with your adversaries (such as chronic pain), and the more you understand them and how they operate, the less fear you will have about how much they can harm you.

Pessimism and neuroticism.   A life attitude characterized by pessimism and neuroticism (see Chapter 1) is not helpful for people with chronic pain (Affleck, Tennen, Urrows, & Higgins, 1992; Long & Sangster, 1993). Pessimism and neuroticism are associated with passivity, helplessness, and self-blame. To cope successfully with chronic pain, it is necessary to develop a coping attitude toward life characterized by hope, optimism, and self-reliance (see Chapter 15).

Coping with Rheumatoid Arthritis

Another way to understand the process of coping with chronic pain is by looking at research focused on a specific and well-known chronic pain problem—rheumatoid arthritis. Rheumatoid arthritis (RA) is a chronic illness that affects more than 8 million people in the United States (Lambert & Lambert, 1987). It involves painful inflammation of the joints that flares up in an unpredictable manner. When it gets extreme, arthritis can result in disfigurement of the joints and in loss of functional ability. More than half of RA patients suffer significant work disability within 5 years of disease onset (Yelin, Meenan, Nevitt, & Epstein, 1980). The debilitating effects of arthritis result in depression and decreased well-being and life satisfaction. There is no cure for RA, and medical treatments for the pain are often only marginal and temporary. For this reason, developing good coping skills is essential for people who suffer from this illness.

Some effective and ineffective coping skills.   Among the most effective skills for coping with RA that have been identified in research studies are *information* *seeking* and *cognitive restructuring* (Manne & Zautra, 1989; Revenson & Felton, 1989; Zautra & Manne, 1992):

> *Information seeking* involves learning about rheumatoid arthritis and understanding its process and prognosis so that it is not fearful and mysterious.
>
> *Cognitive restructuring* includes efforts to look at the illness in an adaptive manner by accepting it as a challenge and appreciating the fact that many people are suffering more from it than you are.

Among the least effective coping responses to RA are *self-blame, emotional expression,* and *wish-fulfilling fantasy*:

> *Self-blame* involves blaming yourself or looking for other sources of blame for the illness.
>
> *Emotional expression* consists of expressing your emotional strain by acting out depression or anger in interpersonal relationships.
>
> *Wish-fulfilling fantasy* is a passive response in which you just hope the illness will go away.

The Value of Social Support

Social support is helpful for chronic pain sufferers because it is encouraging to know that there are people who care (Jamison & Virts, 1990). For people who have chronic pain but are in generally good health, it is helpful to have support people who give encouragement for self-reliance and independence. Chronic pain sufferers in poor health benefit more from support that offers someone to lean on for assistance with life responsibilities. Not surprisingly, critical remarks from significant others are detrimental to a pain sufferer's well-being (Manne & Zautra, 1989; Reich & Zautra, 1995a, 1995b).

Some Conclusions About Coping with Chronic Pain

The purpose of learning and practicing effective pain coping strategies is to increase your sense of competence and self-efficacy (see Chapter 2). People who suffer from chronic pain are more likely to engage in active pain coping strategies when they are confident in their abilities to do so (Altmaier, Russell, Kao, Lehmann, & Weinstein, 1993; Dolce, 1987; Jensen, Turner, & Romano, 1991; Kores, Murphy, Rosenthal, Elias, & North, 1990; C. A. Smith, Dobbins, & Wallston, 1991). To obtain this confidence, chronic pain sufferers must accomplish the following goals:

1. They must learn how to use effective pain coping skills. This requires making a commitment to set up and follow a rigorous schedule for practicing these skills.
2. They must set realistic goals so they don't get discouraged when their pain coping skills are not 100% effective.
3. They must take pride in their efforts and give themselves credit for maintaining control over their lives.

The pain coping strategies outlined in this chapter are helpful for people with chronic pain. However, it is true that people whose chronic pain is very severe might experience less benefit from pain coping strategies compared with people who are suffering from chronic pain that is moderate or low (Jensen & Karoly, 1991). People with severe chronic pain need an extra boost of encouragement to stick with a pain management program and not give up and settle for a passive existence.

THE PROMISE OF PAIN TREATMENT CLINICS

In recognition of the debilitating effects of chronic pain, more than 1,000 pain treatment clinics have been set up throughout the United States. Many of these clinics are affiliated with hospitals and universities and incorporate teaching and research in their programs. Other clinics are operated by well-intentioned but less qualified therapists who are responding to an increasing market for treatment of chronic pain. People intending to seek the services of pain treatment programs are advised to choose clinics that have been nationally certified (Block, 1982; Follick, Ahern, Attanasio, & Riley, 1985; W. E. Fordyce, 1976; Kerns, Turk, & Holzman, 1983; Roy, 1984; Turk, Holzman, & Kerns, 1986).

Goals of Pain Treatment Clinics

A pain treatment clinic is designed to help people who have chronic pain for which there is no medical cure. The clinics are geared toward teaching people skills they can use to live meaningful and satisfying lives that will outweigh their experience of chronic pain. That is, the participants in pain clinics are taught pain coping skills that will help them live more effectively with their pain but that in most cases will not make their pain disappear. The goal of pain treatment clinics is not to cure chronic pain (which unfortunately is not possible) but rather to help people suffering from chronic pain make a clear commitment to get on with their lives (W. E. Fordyce, 1988). The clinics have programs designed to help chronic pain sufferers accomplish these challenges: come to terms with chronic pain; deal with sadness, depression, and anger; and make adjustments in interpersonal relationships.

An Overview of the Pain Treatment Clinic

Pain treatment clinics offer both inpatient and outpatient programs. People participating in inpatient programs come to live in the pain clinic, which is usually a separate unit of a hospital. The pain treatment program lasts from 3 to 4 weeks. Participants live in a "community" where they are responsible for taking care of their rooms, making their beds, and doing various chores. They are more like students than patients because they are not in the program to be "treated" or "cured" but rather to learn useful coping skills. Participants in the outpatient programs attend classes several times a week and are taught skills that they practice daily at home.

The Pain Treatment Program

The pain treatment clinic is based on a *multidisciplinary* model that takes into account all of the facets of chronic pain (Novy, Nelson, Francis, & Turk, 1995):

- *Emotional experiences* of sadness, depression, and anger
- *Activities and behaviors* that are limited by chronic pain as well as the kinds of pain behaviors (limping, grimacing, vocal expressions) that chronic pain provokes
- *Cognitive activities* related to how people with chronic pain think about and talk themselves through their pain
- *Sensory and physical sensations* resulting from the pain

Participants in pain clinics work with professionals ranging from medical doctors, nurses, physical therapists, and social workers to clinical psychologists. Medical doctors make sure that all possible avenues of medical diagnosis have been covered, and they attend to any medical needs participants may have while they are in the program. Nurses work individually with the participants on all phases of their treatment programs. Physical therapists teach the participants to understand their physical strengths and limitations. They provide an individualized treatment plan outlining exercises that the participants agree to practice every day. Social workers meet with the participants and their families to work out a plan that will help them live harmoniously in spite of the chronic pain problem. Clinical psychologists provide classes to teach the skills for coping with pain described earlier in this chapter. They also conduct group meetings where participants can share their experiences and gain insight into effective ways for finding life satisfaction. Participants in pain treatment clinics also benefit from each other. They find a good source of support in their community living arrangement and often arrange to keep in touch after the pain treatment program is completed. Evaluation studies have shown that multidisciplinary pain clinics based on the above model are successful in helping the majority of chronic pain patients lead more productive lives (W. E. Fordyce, Brockway, Bergman, & Spengler, 1986; Kleinke & Spangler, 1988a; McArthur, Cohen, Gottlieb, Naliboff, & Schandler, 1987a, 1987b).

PRIMARY AND SECONDARY APPRAISAL OF PAIN

A good way to conclude this chapter is by relating this discussion of pain and pain coping skills to the processes of primary and secondary appraisal.

Primary Appraisal of Pain

It stands to reason that your primary appraisal of pain will be negative. It is not very often that people enjoy the experience of pain. However, when you make a primary appraisal of pain, ask yourself whether it is in your best interest to view the pain as horrible, unbearable, and catastrophic or as unpleasant, inconvenient, and undesirable but one of life's many challenges with which you can live. Don't deny your feelings of anger, fear, and depression because they are normal reactions to pain. But when you recognize these feelings, it is useful to follow the suggestions for rational thinking in Chapter 2.

Secondary Appraisal of Pain

In this chapter you learned a number of coping skills to apply when making a secondary appraisal of pain and considering what you can do about it. When confronted with pain, go through your list of coping skills and find the ones that will be most useful. Use the kind of problem-solving approach described in Chapter 3. By mastering your pain coping skills, you will strengthen your feelings of self-efficacy and be better prepared to live with your next pain experience.

LIST OF SKILLS FOR COPING WITH PAIN

- *Coping Skill 1:* Taking a Coping Attitude
- *Coping Skill 2:* Using Self-Relaxation
- *Coping Skill 3:* Using Distraction
- *Coping Skill 4:* Using Creative Imagery
- *Coping Skill 5:* Using Ice
- *Coping Skill 6:* Talking Yourself Through the Pain
- *Coping Skill 7:* Maintaining a Sense of Humor
- *Coping Skill 8:* Keeping Realistic Expectations
- *Coping Skill 9:* Coming to Terms with Chronic Pain
- *Coping Skill 10:* Dealing with Sadness, Depression, and Anger
- *Coping Skill 11:* Making Adjustments in Interpersonal Relationships

SUGGESTIONS FOR FURTHER READING

Caudill, M. A. (1995). *Managing pain before it manages you.* New York: Guilford.
Hanson, R. W., & Gerber, K. E. (1993). *Coping with chronic pain: A guide to patient self-management.* New York: Guilford.
Hendler, N., & Fenton, J. A. (1986). *How to cope with chronic pain.* Cockeysville, MD: Liberty.
Melzack, R., & Wall, P. D. (1982). *The challenge of pain.* New York: Basic Books.
Smoller, B., & Schulman, B. (1982). *Pain control: The Bethesda Program.* Garden City, NY: Doubleday.

Coping with Illness and Maintaining Health

The remaining chapters of this book are different from Chapters 4 through 12 in that they don't contain specific lists of coping skills. These chapters take a more personal approach, examining particular experiences of people who have been confronted with difficult life experiences. In addition to reading about the personal experiences of copers, you will also gain further knowledge of the conclusions reached from research on a number of important topics.

The focus of this chapter is on maintaining health. I will discuss health problems that affect many people and outline suggestions for coping with them. In addition, you will learn about the advantages of primary prevention and the value of developing a hardy, low-stress personality. Chapter 14 is devoted to people's experiences with traumatic events. Chapter 15 summarizes the theme of this book by discussing coping as a lifestyle.

MAINTAINING HEALTH

In recent years there has been a growing attempt by health professionals to teach people how to decrease their risk of illness. Engaging in health-maintaining behaviors is called *primary prevention* (Caplan, 1964). Primary prevention makes good sense because it is obviously to our advantage to avoid illness and to maintain health by taking care of ourselves.

Although very few people disagree with the concept of primary prevention, consider the following negative health practices: cigarette smoking, alcohol and drug abuse, poor diet, insufficient exercise, and failure to wear seat belts. This list only touches the surface of ways in which people place themselves in jeopardy. Recognition of the value of teaching good health practices has resulted in development of the fields of behavioral medicine and health psychology (Krantz, Grunberg, & Baum, 1985; Pomerleau & Rodin, 1986; Rodin & Salovey, 1989; S. E. Taylor, 1987,

1994). *Behavioral medicine* is defined as "the broad interdisciplinary field of scientific investigation, education, and practice which concerns itself with health, illness, and related physiological dysfunction" (Gatchel & Baum, 1983, p. 10). A good way to find out about current research in the field is by consulting the *Journal of Behavioral Medicine. Health psychology* refers to the particular contributions to behavioral medicine made by psychologists. These activities may be in the areas of rehabilitation, neuropsychology, and health maintenance and promotion (Johnstone et al., 1995). A primary journal in this field is *Health Psychology.*

A major goal of psychologists is to promote preventive health practices by emphasizing "individual responsibility in the application of behavioral and biomedical science knowledge and techniques for the maintenance of health and the prevention of illness and dysfunction by a variety of self-initiated individual or shared activities" (Matarazzo, 1980, p. 813). This definition suggests that we are each responsible for taking care of our health by using coping skills found to be effective by scientific research. These skills will be discussed in the following sections of this chapter.

Controlling Your Health

Check whether you agree or disagree with the following statements:

	Strongly agree	Agree	Disagree	Strongly disagree
1. If I take care of myself, I can avoid illness.	___	___	___	___
2. Good health is largely a matter of good fortune.	___	___	___	___
3. Whenever I get sick, it is because of something I've done or not done.	___	___	___	___
4. No matter what I do, if I am going to get sick I will get sick.	___	___	___	___
5. People's ill health results from their own carelessness.	___	___	___	___
6. Most people do not realize the extent to which their illnesses are controlled by accidental happenings.	___	___	___	___
7. I am directly responsible for my health.	___	___	___	___
8. People who never get sick are just plain lucky.	___	___	___	___

These statements come from the Health Locus of Control Scale (Wallston, Wallston, Kaplan, & Maides, 1976). People who agree with statements 1, 3, 5, and 7 tend to have an internal locus of control regarding their health. They take responsibility for their health by seeking information about and engaging in good health practices. People who agree with statements 2, 4, 6, and 8 tend to have an external locus of control regarding their health. They don't recognize the value of preventive health, and they underestimate their responsibility for maintaining good health. You will feel more satisfied and secure about your health if you have a sense of self-efficacy characterized by the following kinds of attitudes (Marshall, 1991):

> "I am generally able to take care of a health problem through my own efforts."
> "When I have a health problem, I am usually able to cope with it on my own."
> "If I become sick, I have the power to make myself well again."

It is a major challenge in our society to encourage people to become actively involved in taking care of their health (Kaplan, 1991). People who engage in good daily health care practices report fewer problems with physical illness and psychological distress (Nowack, 1989). It has also been shown that individuals who developed a conscientious attitude during childhood live longer (Friedman et al., 1993). I hope this chapter will reinforce your feelings of internal control over your health.

The Challenge of Taking Responsibility

What percentage of people do you think would agree with this statement: "I want to take better care of my health"? Almost everybody. OK. Here are 12 things each of us can do right now to control our health (Matarazzo, 1984):

1. Get 7 to 8 hours of sleep daily.
2. Eat breakfast every day.
3. Get your weight to a normal level.
4. Don't smoke.
5. Use alcohol moderately or not at all.
6. Get regular physical activity.
7. Wear seat belts.
8. Don't drive at excessive speeds.
9. Learn good diets and follow them.
10. If you are a woman, learn how to do regular breast exams.
11. If you are a man, learn how to do regular prostate exams.
12. Find a physician with whom you can communicate.

Following these recommendations will increase your life expectancy. Yet how many people who read this book will change their lifestyles? Very few. This shows how challenging the fields of behavioral medicine and health psychology can be. It is easy to agree that you should take control over your health. But how do you get yourself to do it?

STRESS

Much has been written about how stress can negatively affect physical and emotional health. Hundreds of research studies have been conducted to learn how people adapt when they are faced with stressful life events such as these (Holmes & Rahe, 1967; Maddi, Bartone, & Puccetti, 1987):

Death of a loved one	Change in financial status
Divorce	Personal injury or illness
Marital separation	Injury or illness in family
Marriage	Starting school
Loss of job	Marriage of son or daughter
Pregnancy	Abortion
Sexual difficulties	Marital infidelity
Change of job	Assaulted or robbed
Change of residence	Involved in lawsuit
Loss of significant friendship	Gain of a new family member
Violation of law	Involved in accident

You can test your current life stress by checking off which life events are currently happening to you. The major conclusion of these research studies is that stressful events can be detrimental. People who are experiencing a number of stressful life events at one time are at particularly high risk. However, the negative effects of life changes depend on the person who is experiencing them and on her or his primary and secondary appraisals and coping skills. An awareness of stressful life events can help place difficult times in your life in perspective. You are not doomed to suffer ill effects from stressful events if you master the coping skills discussed in this book.

If you are undergoing stressful events, give yourself a break and don't expect everything you do to be perfect. Your first coping skill during stressful life events is to just "hang in there." After you have a chance to appraise the situation, you can decide which coping skills are most appropriate (Holmes & Masuda, 1974; Kessler, Price, & Wortman, 1985; Krantz, Grunberg, & Baum, 1985; Maddi, Bartone, & Puccetti, 1987).

Developing a Low-Stress Personality

It was suggested in Chapter 3 that if human beings inhabit the earth long enough they may develop a natural relaxation response instead of the fight-or-flight response that seems to characterize our reaction to challenges at the present time. Given the competitive nature of our present world, along with its noise, traffic jams, and pollution, a fight-or-flight response is not particularly adaptive. However, many people utilize this style of coping without thinking much about it. Although they often get what they want in the short run, they pay an emotional and physical price in the long run. The kind of fight-or-flight response I have been talking about is referred to by psychologists as a *Type* A behavior pattern. For example, how closely do the following questions describe your lifestyle?

1. Does your job carry a heavy responsibility?
2. Do you drive yourself harder than most others to accomplish things?
3. Do you play games to win?
4. Does it make you restless to watch someone else taking too long with a job?
5. Do you eat rapidly?
6. Do you get frustrated and angry when waiting in lines?
7. Are you under a lot more pressure than most people?

These questions are adapted from an interview used to assess people who fit the Type A pattern (Rosenman, 1978).Type A people can be characterized by the following traits:

Time urgency: Type A people are in a hurry. They feel as if they never have enough time to accomplish everything being demanded of them.

Competitiveness: Type A people are habitually competitive. They are so worried about preserving their image of being worthy and "successful" that they don't have time to relax and have fun.

Hostility: Type A people's sense of time urgency causes them to feel angry when they are delayed or when others get in their way. Their competitiveness prevents close personal relationships because they are on guard against anyone who might try to get ahead of them.

Need for control: Type A people have an inordinate need to control events in their lives, including the behavior of people around them.

The emotional and physical price paid by Type A people is high. They are less likely to have satisfactory personal relationships. They are also more susceptible to heart disease, and they have a higher risk of death (Gatchel & Baum, 1983; Matarazzo, 1984). One reason Type A people suffer so much from life stress is that they have difficulty accepting what they can and cannot control (Glass, 1977; Wright et al., 1990). You have been advised throughout this book that some life events are best "controlled" by your willingness to let them take their course. Type A people burn themselves out because their primary appraisals tell them that virtually *everything* is threatening, and their secondary appraisals don't accurately discriminate between life events they can and cannot change. Type A people also disadvantage themselves because they engage in the kinds of cognitive distortions discussed in Chapter 2 (Westra & Kuiper, 1992). On top of this, the hostile attitude of Type A people predisposes them toward more interpersonal stress (T. W. Smith, 1992).

The lesson you can learn from Type A people is that it is good to slow down and take life a little easier. Here is some useful advice (Gatchel & Baum, 1983, p. 212):

- Be calm and attentive when relating to others.
- Speak slowly in a low, mellow tone.
- Don't interrupt when others are talking.
- Don't get angry when someone disagrees with you.
- Keep your body relaxed.
- Breathe slowly.
- Smile.

Developing an Attitude of Hardiness

People who adapt best to stressful life events are those who have developed an attitude of *hardiness* (Kobasa, 1979; Kobasa, Maddi, & Kahn, 1982; Kobasa, Maddi, Puccetti, & Zola, 1985). Developing a hardy attitude involves building a sense of commitment, control, and challenge.

Commitment means taking an active role in your life. When you are committed, your life has a purpose. You are not a passive bystander. You assume responsibility for making your life meaningful.

Control refers to an internal locus of control on the Health Locus of Control Scale previously described. Control is achieved by developing your internal control (Chapter 3) and self-efficacy (Chapter 2). Control is the opposite of helplessness (see Chapter 15). Control occurs when you take charge, make adaptive primary and secondary appraisals, and implement good coping skills.

Challenge is realized by appreciating the benefits of growth and change. This requires you to be flexible. New experiences are often stressful, and it is tempting to seek stability to maintain your sense of security. Being open to change can be difficult at first, but it will make you stronger in the long run.

People with an attitude of hardiness take a problem-solving attitude toward life and make effective use of social support systems (P. G. Williams, Wiebe, & Smith, 1992). Hardy people generally do not rely on self-blame, wishful thinking, or avoidance as strategies for coping with problems. Hardiness is the opposite of the neurotic personality style described in Chapter 1.

Using Support Systems

The skills for building a support system that were described in Chapter 3 can be beneficial to your physical and emotional well-being. A good support system can help moderate the effects of stressful life events. Support from others also provides encouragement and relieves depression during rehabilitation and adaptation to illness and injury (Holahan, Moos, Holahan, & Brennan, 1995). Of course, the use of support systems is an individual matter. Some people are very open about sharing their stresses and derive benefit from a broad support system. Others prefer to keep their troubles to themselves and to rely on a very small support system. It is important to recognize that it is not healthy to isolate yourself during times of stress. It is in your best interest to build the kind of support system that works best for you (Cohen & Syme, 1985; Kessler, Price, & Wortman, 1985; Pomerleau & Rodin, 1986; Reis, Wheeler, Nezlek, Kernis, & Spiegel, 1985; Wallston, Alagna, DeVillis, & DeVillis, 1983).

COPING WITH NOISE, CROWDING, AND POLLUTION

Noise, crowding, and pollution represent stresses caused by human technological development. Are these stresses detrimental to our health? The best way to answer this question is to look at each of them separately.

Noise

During the past 10 years, noise levels have steadily increased in the United States (Suter, 1991). There is growing concern about the detrimental effects of noise on people's well-being, and attempts to regulate noise are being made by government agencies (Staples, 1996).

One of the most comprehensive studies of the effects of noise on health and psychological functioning was the Los Angeles Noise Project (Cohen, Evans, Stokols, & Krantz, 1986). The purpose of this study was to learn how the noise from Los Angeles International Airport affected children who attended schools in the direct vicinity of the airport. These children, who were exposed to high levels of aircraft noise approximately every 2.5 minutes, were compared with children of comparable ages and backgrounds who attended schools in other areas of the city. On the average, the children exposed to the high levels of noise had higher blood pressure and poorer performance on learning tasks requiring attention and memory. This research and other studies cited by its authors leave little doubt that constant exposure to noise can be detrimental. One of the most disturbing things about noise pollution is that it is usually unpredictable and beyond our control. We are distressed not only from the distraction caused by the noise but also by the frustration of not being able to stop it.

Crowding

Crowding disturbs us most when it interferes with what we are trying to do. Most of us have been in situations, such as parties and social gatherings, where being crowded was not a problem. However, when close proximity with others hampers our daily activities, crowding can be disturbing. In psychiatric hospitals and prisons, where close proximity intensifies other maladaptive behaviors, crowding has been implicated with higher than average rates of illness, emotional problems, suicide, and death (V. C. Cox, Paulus, & McCain, 1984; Paulus, McCain, & Cox, 1978).

Andrew Baum and his colleagues examined the reactions of college students who found themselves living in crowded dormitories (Baum, Aiello, & Calesnick, 1978; Baum, Fisher, & Solomon, 1981; Baum & Gatchel, 1981; Rodin & Baum, 1978). One of the most disturbing experiences for students living in crowded environments was their reduced feeling of personal control. Students who were living in crowded rooms found it troublesome to have such limited privacy. Those in dormitories with long corridors had little choice over their social contacts and were not able to develop a sense of community. As a result of the loss of personal control resulting from their crowded living conditions, the students tended to become withdrawn. They were dissatisfied with their living situations, and they had difficulty cooperating and being friendly with others. To assist students living in dormitories with long corridors, Baum and Davis (1980) persuaded the university to remodel the space into two suites of rooms separated by a lounge. This change in living space had a very positive effect on the morale and social interactions of the students.

Although the students suffering from crowding in the above study were assisted by the researchers, there are many occasions where we can cope with crowding by helping ourselves. Here are some suggestions (Kleinke, 1986b, chap. 6).

It is worthwhile to learn and practice skills that will help you cope with the environmental stresses in your life.

Set priorities: If being in a crowded situation interferes with your concentration, focus on specific goals. By setting priorities, you can protect yourself from feeling overwhelmed.

Think adaptively: It helps to talk yourself through stressful situations (see Chapter 3), and crowding can sometimes be stressful. A good example of adaptive thinking is found in a study where research participants were sent into crowded stores to fill a shopping list as quickly as they could (Langer & Saegert, 1977). Participants were much more successful when they were taught how to coach themselves through the challenge of getting their task done in spite of the crowd.

Take action: Do something to enhance your sense of control over an uncomfortable situation. Sometimes you can modify the physical setting. If this is not possible, maintain a sense of competence by maintaining your composure and engaging others in a polite and assertive manner.

Pollution

The first thing that must be acknowledged about pollution is its direct threat to our physical health:

> The health effects of air pollution include respiratory infection, irritation, and disease. Photochemical oxidants (smog) produce irritation and respiratory discomfort at ambient levels. Some upper respiratory impairment has also been noted. . . . Ambient

ranges of sulfur dioxide irritate upper respiratory passages, reduce mucosal clearance activity, and reduce pulmonary function. Sulfur dioxide has also been associated with upper respiratory infections, bronchitis, and asthma. Oxides of nitrogen reduce pulmonary function and resistance to some diseases, inflame bronchial passages, and interfere with hemoglobin peroxidation. Some respiratory illnesses may be associated with nitrogen oxides as well. Carbon monoxide has been associated with cardiovascular disease, reduced birth weights, and in cases of acute exposure, with headaches, dizziness, and nausea. Research on various particulates including toxic metals like lead and mercury have revealed various human impacts including pulmonary lesions, carcinoma, mesothelial tissue damage, and pulmonary cancer for mercury; gastrointestinal disturbances, anemia, retardation, and impaired neural functioning for lead; thyroid disturbances, and cancer from asbestos. (S. Cohen et al., 1986, pp. 129–130)

This is bad enough. When these health risks are compounded by the stress resulting from the knowledge that you are being poisoned and that there is little you can do about it, you begin to appreciate the devastating impact of human-caused pollution.

Some Conclusions

One problem that noise, crowding, and pollution have in common is the threat they pose to our sense of personal control. When the ability to control our lives becomes too limited, we suffer from the kinds of helplessness discussed in Chapter 15. What can you do to cope? When it is possible to alter the conditions causing noise, crowding, and pollution, do so. Although you can be effective and constructive in working toward environmental reform, don't intensify your stress with unrealistic expectations and unfocused anger. It is also important to remember that even though the world is often difficult to change, you can always manage your own reactions. These coping skills, which were described in Chapter 3, should help you cope successfully with environmental stresses:

> *Support systems* can encourage you to improve your environment.
> *Problem solving* can help you identify ways to improve your environment and strategies for making this happen.
> *Self-relaxation* is good for controlling your bodily arousal when faced with environmental stress.
> *Internal control* can help you prevent feelings of helplessness.
> *Talking yourself through the challenge* can help you maintain your composure when faced with environmental stress.

COPING WITH HOSPITALIZATION

Being hospitalized is stressful for most people. Hospitals instill a fear of the unknown, a loss of control over our lives, and a genuine concern about our well-being. It is difficult to cope because, even though you want to maintain a sense of self-efficacy, you are often in a situation that makes you feel helpless. Shelley Taylor (1979) has described three coping styles commonly used by hospital patients, all of which have disadvantages:

Depersonalization: These patients cope by "tuning out" and turning off their emotions. Because of this, they are often treated as nonpersons and end up feeling anxious and depressed.

Helplessness: These patients cope by being passive and compliant. They wait for the hospital staff to tell them what to do. They don't complain and don't ask questions. However, they are often neglected and end up feeling helpless and depressed.

Reactance: These patients cope by aggressively standing up for themselves. They ask questions, demand attention, and complain when their needs are not satisfied. Patients who respond with reactance often end up alienating the hospital staff, who then treat them in a condescending manner. As a result, the patients suffer frustration and anger.

When confined in a hospital, the challenge is to find the proper balance between being assertive, getting proper treatment, and maintaining good relations with the hospital staff, who are typically busy, tired, and feeling overworked. This is no small task, considering that your social supports are often not with you and that you are suffering a good deal of stress and worry yourself. However, you can help yourself with rational thinking, self-relaxation, humor, assertiveness, and talking yourself through the challenge (see Chapter 3).

COPING WITH INVASIVE MEDICAL PROCEDURES

As a result of a growing interest in coping and health, researchers have investigated the kinds of responses that people find useful for coping with invasive medical procedures such as blood donations, hemodialysis, dental work, and heart surgery. The following suggestions can be derived from these studies.

1. It is helpful if patients are provided with some sense of participation or control during the medical procedure. For example, allowing you to choose which arm you prefer to offer for blood donations helps you to be more relaxed about having blood withdrawn (Mills & Krantz, 1979). Even though your opportunity for control might be minimal, it still provides the experience of working with the medical staff rather than being a passive "object" that is being operated upon.

2. When undergoing a medical procedure over which you have limited control, it helps to distance yourself, focus your attention elsewhere, and even to pretend it isn't happening (Christensen, Benotsch, Lawton, & Wiebe, 1995; Kaloupek & Stoupakis, 1985; Kaloupek, White, & Wong, 1984; Miller, Roussi, Caputo, & Kruus, 1995).

3. When a medical procedure offers an opportunity for control (such as controlling your diet or monitoring your fluid intake), a more active problem-solving coping response can be beneficial (Christensen et al., 1995). In other words, when you can, get involved in your medical treatment.

4. It helps to maintain a sense of optimism (see Chapter 15). An optimistic attitude keeps you from dwelling on negative feelings and ruminating about fears that are either unrealistic or beyond your control (Scheier et al., 1989). An optimistic attitude

also encourages you to pull yourself through a medical procedure by enhancing your overall sense of well-being.

5. Other useful skills for coping with medical procedures include self-relaxation and self-efficacy (Litt, Nye, & Shafer, 1995). It can be helpful to practice going through the medical procedure in your mind while using self-relaxation to maintain your confidence that you can do it.

PREPARING FOR SURGERY

It is becoming more common for people to go through some kind of training or preparation before they have surgery. Many physicians have videotapes and pamphlets describing surgical procedures. Patients are often encouraged to visit the hospital before the surgery so it won't seem like such a strange and scary place.

There has been a great deal of interest in learning how patients can best prepare themselves for surgery. Research studies on this topic have generated a number of useful strategies.

Providing Information

It is beneficial for people to be prepared for surgery by gaining information about what will be done to them and what sensations, discomforts, and inconveniences they will experience (K. O. Anderson & Masur, 1983; S. M. Miller, Combs, & Stoddard, 1989; Taylor & Clark, 1986). Two principles related to providing information about surgery are: (1) people take comfort in having the opportunity to understand and prepare for what will happen to them, and (2) it is best to fit the type of information provided to the needs and desires of surgery patients. Some people prefer to be informed about specific details of the surgical procedure. Others feel more comfortable with a general explanation of what to expect without the "gory" details.

Using Your Coping Skills

Some of the coping skills described in Chapter 3 are particularly helpful for getting through surgery. Self-relaxation is a very useful coping skill, especially when you view your self-relaxation skills as a way of exerting self-efficacy in a stressful situation (Gattuso, Litt, & Fitzgerald, 1992). Humor and social support systems can be very beneficial. You can also maintain a sense of internal control by talking yourself through the challenge. A moderate amount of anxiety before surgery is OK. If you completely denied your concerns, you might not take the time to inform and prepare yourself properly. But by practicing good coping skills, you can tone down the really high levels of fear that are detrimental (Janis, 1958). Talking with others who have successfully coped with similar surgical procedures can also be helpful. Children (and presumably adults) benefit greatly when they have the opportunity to watch a film showing someone like them modeling good coping skills through all stages of the surgery experience (Melamed, 1984). One thing you don't want to do when facing surgery is to engage in the kinds of catastrophizing responses described in Chapter 12 (Jacobsen & Butler, 1996).

A good example of using coping skills to get through surgery can be found in a study of hospital patients who were about to undergo surgery (Langer, Janis, & Wolfer, 1975). The patients were trained to cope with their impending surgery by making adaptive primary and secondary appraisals. Although the surgery was inconvenient, they knew it would be beneficial in the long run. They were taught how they could maintain a feeling of control over their hospitalization by enjoying the attention they would receive from the hospital staff and visitors and by using the time to take stock of their lives and enjoy a vacation from outside pressures. The patients also practiced using the pain control strategies outlined in Chapter 12. As a result of their training in the use of coping skills, these patients recovered from their surgery more quickly than other patients undergoing the same surgical procedures. They were less anxious, more relaxed, and felt less need for pain-relieving medication.

Another example of the principles of coping with surgery is seen in childbirth. Although there are various approaches toward preparing women for childbirth, they all address the following goals:

- Reducing anxiety by providing accurate expectations
- Enhancing feelings of self-efficacy by teaching self-management skills
- Teaching self-relaxation
- Teaching women and their partners to use distraction
- Teaching controlled breathing (which enhances self-relaxation and distraction)
- Encouraging social support before, during, and after childbirth

Using these coping skills has been shown to help women control their anxiety and pain and go through childbirth with a more positive experience (Leventhal, Leventhal, Shacham, & Easterling, 1989; Wideman & Singer, 1984).

COPING WITH HEADACHES

Surveys have indicated that 15% of men and 25% of women experience regular debilitating headaches (Holroyd, 1986). Headaches are responsible for millions of dollars in lost work and for a sizable proportion of visits to doctors' offices. A large industry is supported by the market for headache remedies. The two most common kinds of headaches are *migraine headaches* and *tension headaches*.

Migraine Headaches

Migraine headaches are characterized by an intense throbbing and pounding pain that is felt in the forehead or temple, or around the ears or eyes. Migraines usually start on one side of the head and are often associated with nausea. There are often visual disturbances such as flashing lights and blurred sight. A migraine attack typically lasts from 1 to 2 days. Migraine headaches are thought to result from an irregular flow of blood in the brain, often preceded by a constriction of arteries and a reduced blood supply, followed by dilation of arteries with inflammation, swelling, and pain.

Tension Headaches

Tension headaches are characterized by a sensation of tightness, pressure, or constriction. They feel as if a vise or band of steel has been tightened around the head. Tension headaches can last for days, weeks, and even months. They are generally thought to result from muscle tension, although some researchers believe that changes in blood flow are also responsible.

Treating Headaches

People with severe and recurrent headaches are advised to take the following steps in seeking treatment:

1. Consult with a physician to rule out neurological complications and temporomandibular joint dysfunction, which is related to improper functioning of the jawbone.
2. Assess your diet, particularly in the case of migraine headaches. Caffeine and alcohol can be especially problematic.
3. Assess current life stressors that may be precipitating the headaches.
4. Assess moods of anger and depression, which may both precipitate and result from headache suffering.
5. Become educated about headaches to instill a sense of self-efficacy and internal control.
6. Avoid misuse of medication.
7. Master self-relaxation.

Research studies have indicated that self-relaxation can be beneficial for both migraine and tension headaches. Biofeedback training is useful in some cases because it helps headache sufferers focus on the most crucial areas of their bodies (Adams, Feuerstein, & Fowler, 1980; Andrasik, Blanchard, Neff, & Rodichok, 1984; Blanchard, Andrasik, Neff, et al., 1982, 1983). It is also therapeutic for headache sufferers to look at their lifestyles. How do you handle interpersonal conflict? Are your appraisals of life challenges reasonable? Have you fallen into the Type A behavior pattern discussed earlier? Although it is not always possible to expect a complete cure, the steps outlined here have provided relief for many headache sufferers.

COPING WITH CANCER

Cancer is a stressful life event that affects one out of three individuals and nearly three out of four families in the United States (American Cancer Society, 1985). Due to its pervasiveness and the uncertainty of its causes and prognosis, cancer is one of the most serious and long-lasting stresses facing many people. One way to help alleviate your fears of cancer is to gain as clear a picture as possible of your risk of contracting cancer. People, in general, overestimate their risk of cancer (Kreuter & Strecher, 1995). When this excessive fear of cancer is combined with a high monitoring style (see Chapter 1) of ultrasensitivity to "serious" symptoms, it can result in significant psychological distress (Schwartz, Lerman, Miller, Daly, & Masny, 1995). The best way to cope with the threat of cancer is to get as clear a picture as possible of your risk. Depending on your level of risk, your physician can advise you about precautionary steps to take. Committing yourself to a preventive plan will help you refrain from engaging in unnecessary worries and ruminations.

You can learn a good deal about coping by recognizing the resiliency and willpower of those who have been forced to cope with cancer. To this end, Shelley Taylor and her colleagues conducted extensive interviews to learn how people cope with cancer and to identify effective styles of coping (S. E. Taylor, 1983; S. E. Taylor, Lichtman, & Wood, 1984; Wood, Taylor, & Lichtman, 1985). Participants in one series of studies were women with breast cancer and their family members. The patients ranged in age from 29 to 78 years. Almost all of them had undergone surgery, and the prognosis of their illness ranged from very good to poor. The coping skills employed by these patients to adjust to their experience of having cancer fell into three major categories: searching for meaning, maintaining self-efficacy, and building self-esteem.

Searching for Meaning

Human beings have a need to find meaning in their lives and to feel they have some understanding about why things are the way they are. Finding meaning in your life is a coping skill because it helps you understand why you exist. A sense of meaning provides a reason for enjoying good times and tolerating bad times. The cancer patients did two things to reaffirm their sense of meaning. First, they searched for an explanation of why their cancer occurred. Some patients felt that their cancer was due to stress. Others believed it was caused by diet or carcinogens. Another group of patients attributed their cancer to heredity. Although the causes of cancer are not completely understood by medical science, these patients had the need to find a reason for their cancer. The particular kind of explanation adopted did not seem to make a great difference. What was important was finding an explanation that gave personal meaning to the cancer experience.

Maintaining Self-Efficacy

Many of the patients coped with their cancer by maintaining their feelings of self-efficacy. Two-thirds of the cancer victims believed they had at least some control over their cancer. This is interesting because, in strict medical terms, the patients' chances of affecting the outcome or recurrence of their cancer was very limited. However, believing that they continued to have power to take charge of their lives, both physically and psychologically, was a valuable coping skill. The cancer victims maintained their self-efficacy in a number of ways. Many of them resolved to live with a positive attitude, and they refused to take on an identity of helplessness and passivity. They also exercised their self-efficacy by keeping busy. They practiced self-relaxation, involved themselves in exercise programs, and added more healthy foods to their diets. Another activity that helped patients maintain a sense of control over their lives was seeking information and knowledge about cancer. They acquired books and pamphlets and attended groups with the goal of actively confronting the major life event of cancer that was threatening them.

A valuable coping skill for people with chronic illness is maintaining a sense of control over their lives (S. E. Taylor, Helgeson, Reed, & Skokan, 1991). Even people with serious illnesses who require significant medical intervention have a greater sense of well-being if they can find (or believe in) some aspects of their illness over which they can exert control. Information seeking is another useful skill for coping with chronic illness because it reinforces the feeling that you are taking control over your life and doing something instead of passively waiting for things to get better (Felton & Revenson, 1984).

Building Self-Esteem

The cancer patients attempted to fight against feelings of depression and despair by engaging in thoughts and activities that would bolster their self-esteem. One strategy used by many patients was to compare themselves with those who were less fortunate. For example, an older woman compared herself with women who were younger. "The people I really feel sorry for are these young gals. To lose a breast when you're so young must be awful. I'm 73; what do I need a breast for?" (S. E. Taylor, 1983, p. 1166). A young married woman compared herself with women who were single. "If I hadn't been married, I think this thing would have really gotten to me. I can't imagine dating or whatever knowing you have this thing and not knowing how to tell the man about it" (S. E. Taylor, 1983, p. 1166). The ability to boost your self-esteem and life appreciation by recognizing those who are less fortunate is a universal coping skill (Perloff, 1987; Wood et al., 1985).

The cancer patients also bolstered their self-esteem by recognizing their bout with cancer as a valuable life experience. Many of the patients gained the impetus to make the changes in their jobs, living situations, and personal relationships they had been putting off. Other patients took the opportunity to travel, to read new books, and to treat themselves to enjoyable activities. These patients who attempted to build their self-esteem in the face of their serious illness said to themselves, in one way or another, "Life has presented me with a difficult challenge. What can I do to make the most of it?"

Using Support Systems

People with chronic illness benefit from the use of support systems (see Chapter 3). Cancer patients reach out for support from the medical profession, from their friends and families, and from organized support groups. Interviews with cancer patients indicate that using support systems as a coping skill is an individual matter (Taylor, Falke,

TABLE 13.1   Helpful and unhelpful actions reported by cancer patients

Support People	Helpful Actions	Unhelpful Actions
Spouse	Physical presence (just being there)	Critical of patient's response to cancer
	Expressing concern, empathy, and affection	Minimizing impact of cancer on patient
	Calmly accepting patient's cancer	Expressing too much worry and pessimism
Family	Expressing concern, empathy, and affection	Minimizing impact of cancer on patient
	Physical presence (just being there)	Critical of patient's response to cancer
	Providing practical assistance	Expressing little concern, empathy, or affection
Friends	Expressing concern, empathy, and affection	Avoiding social contact with patient
	Providing practical assistance	Expressing too much worry and pessimism
	Calmly accepting patient's cancer	Minimizing impact of cancer on patient
Nurses	Expressing concern, empathy, and affection	Providing technically incompetent medical care
	Providing practical assistance	Minimizing impact of cancer on patient
	Being pleasant and kind	Expressing little concern, empathy, or affection
Physicians	Providing useful information or advice	Providing insufficient information
	Expressing optimism about prognosis and patient's ability to cope	Expressing little concern, empathy, or affection
	Providing technically competent medical care	Providing technically incompetent medical care

SOURCE: From "Victim's Perceptions of Social Support: What Is Helpful from Whom?" by G. A. Dakof and S. E. Taylor, 1990, *Journal of Personality and Social Psychology, 58,* 80–89. Copyright 1990 by the American Psychological Association.

Shoptaw, & Lichtman, 1986). Some patients benefit from having many support people. Others limit their support people to just a few. Some patients prefer individual support people. Others prefer groups. It does not appear that everyone suffering a severe illness should necessarily join a support group. However, the ability to seek support according to your individual preferences and needs is a useful coping skill.

Another way to understand the value of support people is by gaining a sense of how people can help. Dakof and Taylor (1990) asked cancer patients what kinds of actions were helpful and unhelpful from the following people: spouse and family, friends, physicians, and nurses (see Table 13.1). It is interesting to see that the most helpful actions from loved ones included expressing concern, empathy, and affection and accepting the patient's cancer. Good care and useful information and advice were valued from physicians and nurses. Also instructive is the fact that people's attempts to minimize the patient's illness were viewed as unhelpful. As you learned in Chapter 10, it is rather thankless when others trivialize your distress (Lazarus, 1984b).

In addition to the helpful actions listed in Table 13.1, people suffering from cancer and other stressful life events find comfort in hearing about people who successfully coped with similar stresses (Buunk, Collins, Taylor, VanYperen, & Dakof, 1990; S. E. Taylor, Aspinwall, Giuliano, Dakof, & Reardon, 1993). Knowing that others have been able to bear up to similar trauma can give you a sense of hope that you can do it, too.

Some Useful Coping Strategies

Now that you have an overview of the process of coping with cancer, let's turn to the results from studies that investigated the usefulness of specific strategies for coping with cancer (C. S. Carver et al., 1993; Dunkel-Schetter, Feinstein, Taylor, & Falke, 1992; Feifel, Strack, & Nagy, 1987; Stanton & Snider, 1993). These studies were designed to take a careful look at the relation between the personal adjustment, life satisfaction, and well-being of cancer patients and their use of coping strategies.

Adaptive coping responses. The following coping responses were adaptive and helped the cancer patients to function more effectively:

  Positive reframing: Trying to see the positive side of the experience with cancer; learning something from the battle with this illness
  Acceptance: Learning to live with the cancer; accepting the cancer as a reality
  Social support: Talking to other people to learn and to express feelings; obtaining advice and support
  Positive change: Changing or growing as a person in a good way; rediscovering what is important in life
  Maintaining objectivity: Treating the cancer as a challenge; not dwelling on the cancer and continuing on with one's life
  Active involvement: Being actively involved in decisions regarding treatment; regularly asking the doctor for advice about how to best manage the illness

It is most beneficial to use these adaptive coping skills flexibly rather than to apply only one or two of them to all situations (Collins, Taylor, & Skokan, 1990).

Maladaptive coping responses. The following coping responses were not helpful for the cancer patients:

  Denial: Refusing to accept the reality of the cancer; pretending that the cancer does not exist
  Helplessness: Giving up; losing interest in taking care of oneself
  Cognitive escape: Hoping for a miracle; resigning oneself to fate; not talking about it with others

Behavioral escape: Eating, drinking, or using drugs; avoiding responsibilities and interpersonal interactions

Overall, it is apparent that the most useful coping responses for cancer patients involve maintaining control and mastery over their lives and holding on to the feelings of hope and optimism that are described in Chapter 15 (Thompson, Sobolew-Shubin, Galbraith, Schwankovsky, & Cruzen, 1993). Even though it might not be possible to control the disease and the medical interventions for cancer, it is still possible to take charge of your emotional and behavioral reactions by using good problem-solving strategies.

Support Programs for Cancer Patients

People suffering from cancer (and other illnesses) can benefit from support programs that are designed to help the patients learn and practice useful coping skills (Fawzy, Fawzy, Arndt, & Pasnau, 1995; Gordon et al., 1980; Meyer & Mark, 1995). These programs provide the following kinds of experiences:

1. Education about the illness and possible medical treatments, including prognosis and side effects. Patients are also taught how to manage their physical health with exercise, diet, self-relaxation, and other methods of self-care.
2. Counseling sessions in which patients can share their feelings and discuss options for improving their lives.
3. Social services to help patients obtain home care and other assistance they need for daily living.
4. Training in the use of adaptive coping strategies.

COPING WITH AIDS

AIDS is one of the world's major health problems. Some 1.5 million Americans are infected with the HIV virus. In 1992, 250,000 Americans had been diagnosed with AIDS, and 112,000 had died from the disease (Centers for Disease Control, 1992). AIDS is the second leading cause of death among American men ages 24 to 45 and is the sixth most common cause of death among women in this age group (Kelly & Murphy, 1992). The number of people infected with HIV is steadily increasing, and there is no sign that this pattern will change in the foreseeable future.

Two factors make AIDS particularly devastating and challenging. First, because there is presently no cure, its victims face death. Second, AIDS is a communicable disease that could be confined if people practiced preventive behaviors. In the United States, the majority of AIDS victims are homosexual and bisexual people and intravenous drug users. However, AIDS also afflicts heterosexuals, and the number of AIDS cases contracted through heterosexual sex is growing (Batchelor, 1988; Herek & Glunt, 1988). Everyone is vulnerable to this disease, and it is important that we all work together to reduce its impact.

The Importance of Prevention

Because AIDS is a communicable disease, it can be confined with primary prevention. But how can people be convinced to practice protected sex and (if addicted to drugs) to use sterilized needles? Education is the first step. A number of school districts have developed good AIDS education programs for adolescents (Brooks-Gunn, Boyer, & Hein, 1988; Flora & Thoresen, 1988). It is also important to get at factors controlling people's behaviors, such as group norms and personal responsibility (DesJarlais & Friedman, 1988; Fisher, 1988; Morin, 1988). Health care programs promoting education, group support, and personal efficacy have successfully influenced people to engage in AIDS prevention behavior (Stall, Coates, & Hoff, 1988).

The Burden of AIDS Victims

AIDS victims bear a terrible burden. As well as facing death, they suffer stigma and blame. They are given less respect than people suffering from other serious illnesses (Herek & Glunt, 1988; B. Weiner, Perry, & Magnusson, 1988). Why is this so? One reason is that because AIDS is a communicable disease it is easier to blame AIDS victims for being irresponsible. Second, AIDS is often associated with stigmatized people in our society. Another reason for blaming AIDS victims is to rationalize our own fears. By "blaming the victim" we can externalize this devastating disease and pretend it can't happen to us (Kleinke, 1986b, chap. 4; Ryan, 1971; Walster, 1966).

In addition to stigma, AIDS forces catastrophic changes in a person's life. AIDS victims frequently lose their jobs and face eviction from their living situation. They are often denied police and health care services, and they suffer prejudice from insurance companies. They experience physical symptoms such as weakness, diarrhea, unintended weight loss, and chills as well as impairments in their thinking and memory (Chesney & Folkman, 1994). It is no wonder that AIDS victims feel like "walking time bombs existing in limbo" (Tross & Hirsch, 1988).

Some Useful Coping Strategies

Surveys of people with HIV infection have identified their use of the following responses for coping with their disease (Fleishman & Fogel, 1994; Folkman, Chesney, Pollack, & Coates, 1993):

Avoidance Coping

> "I push it out of my mind."
> "I go on as if nothing happened."
> "I avoid being with people."

Positive Coping

> "I make plans for the future."
> "I look on the bright side."
> "I try to learn more about AIDS."

Seeking Social Support

"I ask friends or relatives for advice."
"I express my feelings to others."
"I seek understanding from friends."

In general, the HIV infected respondents were less depressed and better adjusted when they used positive coping and more depressed and less well-adjusted when they relied on avoidance coping. Seeking social support was helpful when the support given to the HIV infected respondents was matched to their individual needs and preferences.

Three coping styles associated with particularly high levels of anxiety and depression in HIV infected people are *self-blame* (focusing so much on blaming yourself for the illness that there is little energy left for constructive action), *emotional expression* (using expressions of anger or humor to cloud the question of what to do about your predicament), and *wish-fulfilling fantasy* (passively hoping that the disease will take care of itself) (Commerford, Gular, Orr, Reznikoff, & O'Dowd, 1994).

A coping style that is particularly helpful for HIV infected people is *optimism* (see Chapter 15; S. E. Taylor et al., 1992). Optimism is associated with better adjustment to the stresses of having HIV infection and with greater efforts toward positive health care. People at risk for HIV infection are also more likely to follow preventive health behaviors when they have good social support systems and when they are committed to taking responsibility for their behaviors (Folkman, Chesney, Pollack, & Phillips, 1992; Van der Velde & Van der Pligt, 1991). People with HIV infection who take a fatalistic attitude toward their lives and who avoid confronting their feelings are less well-adjusted, and they are not conscientious about their health care.

In addition to optimism, a valuable coping style for people with AIDS or HIV infection is maintaining a sense of control over their illness (S. E. Taylor et al., 1991). Gay men with AIDS were better adjusted when they took the attitude that they were working in a partnership with their physicians to control their disease (Reed, Taylor, & Kemeny, 1993). These men did not accept the thought that they had to "give up" control of their lives to the medical establishment. Their sense of well-being was reinforced by the belief that they had the responsibility and competence to manage the daily challenges of their illness.

Psychotherapy for AIDS Victims

Because HIV infected individuals experience such a high degree of distress, support groups and psychotherapy are often helpful (Kelly & Murphy, 1992; McKusick, 1988). Some useful coping skills that can be taught in therapeutic settings include the strategies for managing anxiety, depression, and loss that are discussed in this book. Research indicates that AIDS victims adapt better to their illness, and live longer, when they take an active role in coping with their illness (Reed, Kemeny, Taylor, Wang, & Visscher, 1994). Therapeutic programs designed to help AIDS victims cope with their disease typically include the following interventions (Chesney & Folkman, 1994):

Exercise training to help clients improve their physical fitness, overall health, and psychological well-being.

Appraisal training to help clients make adaptive appraisals (see Chapter 2). Making adaptive appraisals increases the likelihood of matching appropriate coping skills to a particular challenge or problem.

Coping training to help clients learn and practice positive coping skills, such as problem solving, self-relaxation, and humor.

Social support training to help clients obtain the social support that suits their needs.

Self-efficacy training to help clients maintain an attitude of active involvement and mastery.

People with AIDS need to be encouraged not to take a fatalistic attitude toward their illness by telling themselves to "prepare for the worst" and to accept their disease as a fate over which they have no control. Although the disease of AIDS is a reality, the lives of those with this disease are open to possibilities and challenges.

The Stresses of Caregiving

Taking care of a person with AIDS involves all the stresses of watching someone dying before your eyes. However, there are some factors related to caring for an individual with AIDS that make the experience particularly difficult (Folkman, Chesney, & Christopher-Richards, 1994). First, caregivers of AIDS victims are often their partners, who are men in their 20s, 30s, and 40s. This is a young age to be caring for a dying person with whom you have had an intimate relationship. Being a caregiver at such a young age also interferes with the caregiver's job, education, and career development. A second burden faced by caregivers of AIDS victims is that the caregivers often have little or no support from their families because of the stigma attached to being associated with a person who has AIDS. A third area of adjustment for men who are caring for AIDS victims is that most role models for caregiving are women. Male caregivers must develop their caregiving skills on their own. A fourth burden faced by caregivers of AIDS victims is that many of these caregivers are HIV positive themselves. While watching a loved one die, they are forced to come to terms with their own mortality.

Caregivers of AIDS victims can benefit from support groups that are focused on helping them make this stressful time into a meaningful life experience (Folkman & Stein, 1996). Training programs that can teach caregivers of AIDS victims essential medical and nursing skills are also very helpful for enhancing the caregiver's sense of efficacy and competence (Folkman, Chesney, Cooke, Boccellari, & Collette, 1994).

BALANCING SELF-EFFICACY AND ACCEPTANCE

A good way to sum up this discussion of skills for coping with chronic illness is by appreciating the need to balance the benefits of self-efficacy against the reality of accepting things you can't control. On one hand, you don't want to blame yourself for illness and avoid responsibility by passively wishing that things would get better. On the other hand, you must be realistic about what you can and cannot change. Devote your energy to activities that will give meaning to your life and help you feel good about yourself. Avoid beating your head against the wall and being preoccupied with symptoms of chronic illness that are part of life and out of your control (Folkman, 1984; Folkman, Lazarus, Gruen, & DeLongis, 1986; Manne & Sandler, 1984).

A CONCLUDING THOUGHT

A major theme of this chapter is that many life events can affect your health and well-being (Adler & Matthews, 1994). Some of these you can control, and others you can't control. Life events beyond your control require that you develop good coping skills to maintain feelings of competence, hope, and self-efficacy. Health care practices that you can freely choose for extending your life pose a special challenge. Learn how to encourage people not to place their health and safety in jeopardy, and learn to become more reliable in taking care of yourself and those you love.

SUGGESTIONS FOR FURTHER READING

DeLoach, C., & Greer, B. G. (1981). *Adjustment to severe physical disability: A metamorphosis.* New York: McGraw-Hill.

Friedman, H. S. (1991). *The self-healing personality.* New York: Henry Holt.

Holroyd, K. A., & Creer, T. L. (Eds). (1986). *Self-management of chronic disease.* New York: Academic Press.

Levitt, P. M., & Guralnick, E. S. (1985). *You can make it back: Coping with serious illness.* New York: Facts on File Publications.

Peterson, C., & Bossio, L. M. (1991). *Health and optimism.* New York: Free Press.

Taylor, S. E. (1994). *Health psychology* (3rd ed.). New York: McGraw-Hill.

14

Coping with Injury and Trauma

There are many examples in life of people who have borne up to traumas, tragedies, accidents, and disasters. Stories about individuals who maintained their will to survive such difficult challenges are an inspiration to us all. Because the purpose of this book is to teach coping skills derived from research on large groups of people, I have not recounted personal anecdotes about human fortitude and heroism. However, much can be learned from people who have gone through traumatic events, and some examples of such coping experiences are explored in this chapter. The challenges of injury and trauma are good topics for discussion because they are commonly experienced and because people's coping responses to these life events have been studied in scientific research.

COPING WITH INJURY

The fortitude shown by people who have been disabled in accidents is inspiring. When we see disabled people exercising their willpower to make their lives meaningful and productive, we often wonder, "Where do they find the strength?" Let's begin by looking at some of the difficulties and challenges faced by victims of serious injury.

Suffering a severe injury is a devastating experience. In many cases, the individual loses the ability to lead a normal life. This loss requires the person to go through the stages of grief work described in Chapter 10. Injury victims are vulnerable to hopelessness and depression (see Chapter 5). They suffer stigma because others are uncomfortable with their disabilities. They are at high risk for drug abuse because they are often given addictive pain-relieving medication. Coping with all of this is a tremendous challenge.

Two major needs of injury victims are social support and an opportunity to build self-esteem. Successful adjustment requires virtually all of the coping skills outlined in Chapter 3.

Researchers have attempted to understand how injury victims cope by interviewing victims of serious accidents who were destined to spend the rest of their lives with major disabilities (Bulman & Wortman, 1977; Elliott, Witty, Herrick, & Hoffman, 1991; R. G. Frank et al., 1987; Schulz & Decker, 1985).

The first challenge for these accident victims was to find a meaningful answer to the question, "Why me?" Some victims found the answer in God's will. Others felt that their injuries were a calculated risk for engaging in a dangerous but pleasurable activity. Other victims understood their injuries to be the result of a natural risk of living in a dangerous and unpredictable world. It didn't matter so much what kind of answer was found to the "why me" question as long as the answer was meaningful and satisfying. Victims who suffered most were those who desired, but could not find, a meaningful reason for the accident.

A second challenge for accident victims was to maintain a sense of self-efficacy and control over their lives. The accident victims were less depressed and impaired if they had good problem-solving skills and could find many different options for getting on with their lives. This is difficult because it requires the ability to motivate yourself and to find a balance between independence and asking for help when it is needed. It is not adaptive to fault others, and it is important not to feel helpless and sink into depression. These accident victims were able to adapt by acknowledging their choice of engaging in the behavior that resulted in the accident. They also worked hard to maintain control over their lives by involving themselves in rehabilitation and meaningful activities once the reality of their disability was accepted.

A third challenge for accident victims was to find a good support system. Having a good support system was one of the most useful coping skills for providing victims with a positive sense of well-being.

COPING WITH DISASTERS

The development of health psychology and behavioral medicine has stimulated a growing interest in how people are affected by disasters and how they cope with their traumatic experiences. It is not surprising to learn that disasters have a negative impact, resulting in depression, anxiety, bodily symptoms, alcohol and drug abuse, and symptoms of post-traumatic stress disorder, which will be described later in this chapter (Rubonis & Bickman, 1991; Steinglass & Gerrity, 1990). However, some people are able to cope with disasters more effectively than others. To find out why this is so, let's look at the kinds of coping responses that are more or less effective for bearing up to the traumatic experience of disasters. I will discuss the outcome of research on three different kinds of disasters that occurred in the United States: Buffalo Creek, Three Mile Island, and the 1989 San Francisco earthquake. The first two disasters had an added dimension that made them particularly detrimental—they were caused by human beings and were therefore potentially avoidable.

Buffalo Creek

The Buffalo Creek disaster occurred in 1972 as a result of corporate negligence. For some time, a mining company had dumped coal waste into a mountain stream in

West Virginia, causing an artificial dam to form that was incapable of holding back the mass of water building up behind it. After several days of rain, the dam gave way, which caused a devastating flood that wiped out entire communities as it roared down the valley. The Buffalo Creek disaster had a traumatic impact on survivors that they will carry with them for the rest of their lives. Interviews with survivors indicated that they were suffering from the following psychological and emotional problems (Lifton & Olson, 1976).

Death imprint and death anxiety: Two years after the disaster, survivors were still vividly reliving the devastating experience of destruction and death. For some, it was as if the flood had just happened yesterday. Many survivors reported having anxiety attacks whenever it rained. Terrifying dreams were also common. Psychiatric symptoms of depression, obsessive fear, and changes in character and lifestyle were common (Titchener & Kapp, 1976).

Death guilt: Survivors had a need to ask themselves why they survived while others died. They also ruminated about their inability to save their loved ones. They had trouble accepting the fact that they were helpless bystanders to human-caused death and destruction.

Psychic numbing: One common defensive reaction to disasters is psychic numbing. The trauma is so painful that the anxiety, sadness, guilt, and anger are denied. This is a useful coping response in the short run because it offers immediate respite (it's like going into shock). However, remaining numb and emotionally withdrawn causes problems in the long run by preventing people from living full and meaningful lives.

Unfocused rage: Because the disaster was caused by human negligence, it is understandable that the victims would feel rage. Unfortunately, it was difficult to get satisfaction and obtain justice. Those who died could not be returned, and the people responsible were anonymous members of a powerful corporation.

Difficulty in finding a meaning: As you will see in the discussion of the Three Mile Island disaster, human-caused disasters are particularly difficult to accept because they have no meaning. Natural disasters can be accepted as an uncontrollable act of nature. Human-caused disasters, in contrast, remind us of our vulnerability to uncontrolled technology. The Buffalo Creek victims were also in the discomforting position of being dependent on a mining company for their employment—for their food and housing—yet this mining company had betrayed them.

Five factors related to the Buffalo Creek disaster made it particularly difficult for its victims to cope in a successful manner (Lifton & Olson, 1976). Understanding these factors gives us some insight into the human reaction to traumas:

1. The disaster was sudden. There was no idea that it could happen. It caused complete terror.
2. The disaster was caused by irresponsibility and lack of consideration by fellow human beings.

3. It was difficult for the survivors to put the disaster behind them. The same coal company responsible for the disaster was still in business, and the destruction caused by the flood would be visible for years to come.
4. The victims lived in an isolated community, and they had little political power. They saw no opportunity to reform the powerful coal company that controlled their lives, and they did not have the resources to move away.
5. The destruction was total. Small hamlets were completely destroyed. Those who died were known to everyone. There was a feeling of total loss and breakdown of the community structure. Because everyone was a victim, it was difficult to find social support.

Later in this chapter you will see why the Buffalo Creek survivors were vulnerable to post-traumatic stress disorder. It is a tragedy that these people were trapped in such a difficult situation. I hope we can learn from their experience.

Three Mile Island

In 1979 an accident at the Three Mile Island nuclear plant in Pennsylvania exposed people living nearby to a dangerous level of radiation. A series of studies conducted after this accident focused on three interesting and important questions.

How did the victims suffer?   The psychological effects of the accident were studied by comparing people living within 5 miles of the damaged nuclear plant with comparable groups of people living within 5 miles of either an undamaged nuclear plant or a coal-fired power station. The reason for choosing these comparison groups was to control for whatever stress may naturally result from living near a power plant. Although victims of the Three Mile Island disaster were similar to the other groups in age, education, and income, they suffered significantly more physical and psychological stress. Several years after the nuclear accident, victims of the Three Mile Island disaster were still more depressed and psychologically disturbed than comparable people living near undamaged power plants. The Three Mile Island victims also continued to suffer higher levels of physiological stress (Baum, Gatchel, & Schaeffer, 1983; D. L. Collins, Baum, & Singer, 1983; Davidson & Baum, 1986).

How did the victims cope?   Although the stress suffered by victims of the Three Mile Island disaster was severe, some victims coped more successfully than others. People who stood up best to the disaster employed the following coping skills (Baum, 1988; Baum, Fleming, & Singer, 1983):

1. They engaged in emotion-focused coping (see Chapter 1). They dealt with their emotions by talking themselves through the disaster (see Chapter 3) and appraising it in a way that protected them from feeling overwhelmed.
2. They focused their energies on things they could change, such as their feelings of personal responsibility about taking care of themselves and planning their future.
3. They did not insist on changing things beyond their control, and they did not waste much energy blaming others.
4. They used social support systems (see Chapter 3).

What did we learn?   One important conclusion coming out of the Three Mile Island studies is that disasters caused by human error often result in more long-lasting stress than disasters caused by nature. Why is this so? We know that natural disasters are beyond our control. When a natural disaster strikes, there is nobody to blame. Technological disasters are more stressful because they remind us of our fallibilities. The technologies we create to fulfill the needs of our society can backfire and cause hardship and suffering. Human-caused disasters remind us of our precarious control over our own creations. Technological disasters also tend to result in longer lasting stress because they often don't have a clear beginning or end. Most natural disasters strike swiftly and then are over. In contrast, our technology poses a constant, nagging threat. We live under the shadows of nuclear plants, toxic waste dumps, and hazardous industries that may wreak havoc at any time (Baum, 1988).

1989 Loma Prieta Earthquake

The 1989 Loma Prieta earthquake was the largest earthquake in the San Francisco Bay Area since 1906, measuring 7.1 on the Richter scale. This earthquake resulted in collapsed highway bridges, fires, destroyed homes and businesses, and 62 deaths. Although there have been even more devastating earthquakes in modern times, there were no psychologists available to study their impact. When the 1989 earthquake occurred, researchers were prepared to assess how its traumatic effects were moderated by people's propensity to ruminate on depressive thoughts (Nolen-Hoeksema & Morrow, 1991). The same negative effects from rumination described in Chapter 5 were found for earthquake survivors. Earthquake survivors were more depressed after their frightening experience if they ruminated about it by dwelling on the following kinds of thoughts:

"I keep thinking about the people who were killed."
"The terror I felt during the shaking keeps going through my mind."
"I can't stop reliving the experience and thinking about how bad it was."

Preparing for Disasters

A study of university students in Los Angeles found that the majority of these students "coped" with the possibility of a major earthquake by downplaying the likelihood that a damaging earthquake would occur and simply not thinking about it (Lehman & Taylor, 1987). Interestingly, the students living in housing that was more vulnerable to earthquake damage paid less attention to the possibility of an earthquake than did students living in housing that was less vulnerable to earthquake damage. Denying the probability and lethality of impending disasters works in the short run to reduce tension, anxiety, and stress. The problem with this coping style is that although people are protecting themselves emotionally they are neglecting to make preparations that could save them in the event that the disaster occurred.

   People are more likely to take active steps to prepare for disasters, or to exert pressure to make their living conditions safer, if they feel they have some control over events that might harm them (Rochford & Blocker, 1991). There is a greater likelihood that people will get involved in actions to protect their community if they take a *problem-focused* orientation (see Chapter 1) that involves being active, assessing the options, problem solving, and expressing opinions (Bachrach & Zautra, 1985). A problem-focused orientation is associated with an attitude of self-efficacy that reinforces the belief that we can positively influence our lives. People are less likely to get involved in community actions to prevent disasters when they adopt an *emotion-focused* response characterized by passivity, not thinking about potential disasters, not expressing opinions, and hoping that a disaster won't happen.

It is true that some potential disasters are easier to predict or control than are others. However, the harm from any disaster could be reduced if we took appropriate precautions. The challenge is finding a constructive way to (1) avoid the temptation to deny the possibility of a disaster, (2) take active steps to make our living situation as safe as possible, and (3) view the work we are doing to protect ourselves as a rational coping skill rather than as an indication of panic, fear, or impending doom.

COPING WITH RAPE

Being raped is a traumatic experience that often has long-lasting negative consequences. Rape victims commonly suffer from anxiety, sexual dissatisfaction, depression, and family problems (Atkeson, Calhoun, Resick, & Ellis, 1982; E. M. Ellis, Atkeson, & Calhoun, 1981; Feldman-Summers, Gordon, & Meagher, 1979; Kilpatrick, Resick, & Veronen, 1981). Because rape is a serious crime in the United States, it is important for everyone to participate in programs designed to reduce the incidence of rape. It is also useful to understand how victims manage to cope when they have been raped.

Some Facts About Rape

Rape is defined as "a sexual invasion of the body by force, an incursion into the private, personal inner space without consent—in short an internal assault from one of several avenues and by one of several methods that constitutes a deliberate violation of emotional, physical, and rational integrity and is a hostile, degrading act of violence" (Brownmiller, 1975, p. 376).

Rape must be understood in light of the following facts (Gilliland & James, 1988):

1. *Rape is not sex:* Rape is about power, dominance, and violence.
2. *Rape is an uninvited act:* Rape victims are violated against their will.
3. *Rape may happen to anyone:* Although we may stigmatize rape victims, the fact is that we are all vulnerable.
4. *Rapists come from every segment of society:* We might like to believe that rapists come from the lower strata of society. However, the truth is that anyone is capable of committing rape.
5. *Many sexual assaults go unreported:* Rape is a far greater problem than we realize because many sexual assaults are never reported.

6. *Most perpetrators of sexual assault are men:* Men between the ages of 18 and 35 are the perpetrators in 99% of all sexual assaults in the United States.

Rape victims can be assisted in their recovery with good coping skills and strong support systems. Victims of violent crime can benefit from professional help, especially if they seek services promptly and stick with them until they are on the road to recovery (Norris, Kaniasty, & Scheer, 1990).

How Women Cope with Rape

Researchers have studied skills for coping with rape by interviewing women rape victims about their experiences and their attempts to adjust and get on with their lives. Women rape victims report that they cope by employing these strategies (Burgess & Holstrom, 1979):

- Seek reasons for why the rape occurred
- Minimize the impact of the rape by telling themselves that it was not really so terrifying
- Suppress their reactions to the rape by refusing to think about it
- Keep busy and engage in activities
- Use self-relaxation and meditation to reduce stress
- Withdraw from other people
- Use drugs and alcohol

It is apparent that some of these methods of coping with rape are more adaptive than others. To learn more about the effectiveness of various coping skills, a group of researchers interviewed women rape victims and correlated their choice of coping styles with three measures of personal adjustment (C. B. Meyer & Taylor, 1986): depression, anxiety, and sexual satisfaction. Among the least effective coping responses were withdrawing from others and staying isolated. Suppressing one's feelings and minimizing the impact of the rape didn't seem to hurt, but it also did not help. Use of drugs and alcohol was not measured in this study, but it is likely that this is not an effective coping strategy—especially in the long run.

Among the most effective coping responses were techniques that involved some form of stress reduction, such as self-relaxation, physical activity, and rational thinking. Using support systems that suit one's needs is also an effective coping strategy.

The researchers were particularly interested in learning how the rape victims explained the traumatic experience to themselves. How is it possible to give meaning to a crime such as this? The most reasonable explanation for crimes such as rape appears to be that we live in an imperfect world. Accepting the fact that the world is sometimes a bad place doesn't necessarily make us feel better, but it keeps us from falling into depression and putting ourselves down. But remember that because we accept the world as imperfect doesn't mean that we might not want to take an active role in making it better.

Explanations for rape that were not adaptive were those related to self-blame (Frazier, 1991). Women who suffered most from depression, anxiety, and sexual dissatisfaction said the following kinds of things to themselves:

"I should have been more cautious."
"I am too trusting."
"I was raped because I made some kind of mistake."
"I can't take care of myself."
"Maybe I deserved it."
"It was my fault."

These kinds of self-downing statements are similar to those described in Chapter 5 for people who are depressed. They are also similar to statements made by people who are poor at coping with failure (see Chapter 4). It is clearly not adaptive to find meaning in the experience of being a crime victim by blaming yourself. Given this fact, it might surprise you to learn that at least half of the women rape victims do just that. They take personal responsibility for the fact that someone raped them. Why is this so? Much of this self-blame results from the fact that people like to believe that they live in a fair and just world. To believe in this kind of world, it is necessary to convince yourself that victims must somehow deserve their plight. Women rape victims also blame themselves because our society has a history of sexism that excuses men for sexual misconduct and encourages women to accept their misfortunes.

The Attitudes Toward Rape Victims Scale

Check how much you agree or disagree with the following items from the Attitudes Toward Rape Victims Scale (Ward, 1988).

	Strongly agree	Agree	Disagree	Strongly disagree
1. A raped woman is a less desirable woman.	____	____	____	____
2. Most women secretly desire to be raped.	____	____	____	____
3. A healthy woman can successfully resist a rape if she really tries.	____	____	____	____
4. Sexually experienced women are not really damaged by rape.	____	____	____	____
5. A woman should blame herself for rape.	____	____	____	____
6. In most cases when a woman was raped, she deserved it.	____	____	____	____
7. Accusations of rape by bar girls, dance hostesses, and prostitutes should be viewed with suspicion.	____	____	____	____

	Strongly agree	Agree	Disagree	Strongly disagree
8. Women provoke rape by their appearance and behavior.	_____	_____	_____	_____

A survey of the Attitudes Toward Rape Victims Scale found that neither men nor women agreed with the above statements (Ward, 1988). However, men were not offended by these statements nearly as much as were women. Other studies have also found that men are more inclined than women to hold women responsible for being raped and to excuse a rapist for his criminal behavior (Kleinke & Meyer, 1990; Kleinke, Wallis, & Stalder, 1992).

Raising Your Consciousness

Research on rape is valuable because it raises our consciousness about rape victims. We can appreciate the importance of helping rape victims maintain their sense of worthiness and self-esteem after suffering a traumatic crime.

Helping Rape Victims

The following five experiences are useful for people who have experienced rape or other kinds of assault (Foa, Hearst-Ikeda, & Perry, 1995).

1. Educating yourself about the kinds of reactions (such as flashbacks, nightmares, toublesome thoughts, anxiety, self-blame) experienced by assault victims.
2. Learning and practicing self-relaxation.
3. Reliving the trauma in a safe and supportive setting.
4. Confronting situations that are safe but that have been avoided.
5. Learning to minimize self-blame and to talk to yourself in a positive manner.

COPING IN CONCENTRATION CAMPS

It is almost impossible to conceive of coping with the horrors imposed on human beings in the Nazi concentration camps. Yet prisoners in these camps did cope, and some lived to tell about it. A very profound personal account of coping in a Nazi concentration camp is offered by Viktor Frankl (1967) in his book *Man's Search for Meaning*. In this section you will learn about the strategies used by concentration camp prisoners to maintain their self-esteem and will to live. Attention is also paid to the psychological and emotional strains suffered by concentration camp survivors and the ways they are coping with them. This section is followed by one on post-traumatic stress disorder, which is relevant to all of the traumas discussed in this chapter.

Seven major coping responses were used by prisoners during their internment in Nazi concentration camps: differential focus on the good, survival for some purpose, psychological distancing, mastery, will to live, hope, and social support (Dimsdale, 1974; Schmolling, 1984).

Differential focus on the good: In spite of the horrible events occurring, some prisoners attempted to focus their attention on whatever good they could find, such as finding a small carrot in the field or seeing a sunset.

Survival for some purpose: The will to survive is a strong source of motivation. It was a remarkable strength shown by prisoners who were determined to live, if for no other reason than to bear witness to the world about what happened.

Psychological distancing: Prisoners distanced themselves in a number of ways from the experiences suffered in the camps:

1. *Intellectualizing:* Bruno Bettelheim (1943) described how he coped with being interned in a Nazi prison by taking the role of an observer who would study this situation and write about it.
2. *Religious conviction:* Religious convictions were a source of strength because they made the suffering less personal and in some cases provided hope of some kind of existence after death.
3. *Time focus:* It was possible to distance oneself from the magnitude of the horror by living 1 day, 1 hour, or even 1 minute at a time.
4. *Humor:* In the hardest of times, prisoners still maintained their capacity to salve their pain with humor.

Mastery: The theme of mastery and self-efficacy has appeared throughout this book. It is important to always find something you can do to demonstrate your competence. Although the lives of prisoners were extremely limited, there were still opportunities to use their minds and to devote their energies toward helping others and maintaining a sense of worthiness and self-esteem.

Will to live: You will understand this concept more fully after reading the examples of helplessness in Chapter 15. Human beings have a powerful source of strength when they refuse to give up and are determined to survive.

Hope: In Chapter 15 you will also learn about the power of hope: "Where there is life, there is hope." It often doesn't matter how realistic the hope is so long as it is held and nurtured.

Religion: Many prisoners derived strength from their religion. They found ways to practice their religious beliefs and often endured punishment to maintain their faith.

Social support: Social support was a major source of strength for prisoners, whether it came from groups or individual friendships. Sometimes the social support was nurturing and sometimes it was confrontational. Many times survival depended on the fact that prisoners were not willing to allow each other to give up and die.

Due to the extreme harshness, horror, and cruelty suffered by prisoners, it is not surprising that many became totally overwhelmed and gave up. A poignant example of helplessness exhibited by these victims is described in Chapter 15. Also not surprising is that those who were lucky enough to survive are still carrying scars of this terrible experience. Researchers have identified a number of stresses suffered by Nazi concentration camp survivors (Ehrlich, 1988; Marmar & Horowitz, 1988). These include difficulty concentrating, nervousness and irritability, sleep disturbances and flashbacks, survivor guilt, feelings of isolation, and loss of identity.

Researchers have also identified coping skills used by the survivors who have been most successful in adjusting to their concentration camp experience (Ehrlich, 1988; Kahana, Harel, & Kahana, 1988). These adaptive coping skills include the following:

Seeking support people with whom they can share the Holocaust experiences (having a spouse who was also a concentration camp survivor was particularly helpful)

Devoting physical and emotional energy to care for other people

Using problem-focused coping (see Chapter 1) as a way of taking active steps to maintain self-esteem and a sense of competence and efficacy

Having meaningful employment or other gratifying life activities

Being future-oriented

Useful therapy for Holocaust survivors includes social support, family counseling, and grief work (Ehrlich, 1988).

COPING WITH POST-TRAUMATIC STRESS DISORDER (PTSD)

The Experience of PTSD

Post-traumatic stress disorder (PTSD) has become familiar to many people since the Vietnam War. Individuals who suffer PTSD were exposed to a traumatic event that continues to interfere with their lives. They usually experience the following symptoms (Gilliland & James, 1988):

1. Reexperience the trauma through flashbacks, recurrent intrusive thoughts or dreams, or the sudden notion that the traumatic event is happening right now
2. Withdrawal, numbing of feelings, detachment from others
3. Strong desire for love and support conflicting with outbursts of anger
4. Hyperalertness, problems sleeping, guilt, memory impairment, trouble concentrating, avoidance of activities that arouse recollection of the traumatic event

Studies of World War II veterans found that soldiers who were exposed to heavy combat believe this experience has helped them to value their lives and to learn how to cope with adversity. However, many of these soldiers suffered long-lasting emotional and psychological problems, including nightmares, flashbacks, anxiety, bad memories, depression, and guilt (Elder & Clipp, 1988, 1989). The Vietnam War was even more debilitating. It has been estimated that 33 to 60% of Vietnam combat veterans suffer from PTSD (Brende & Parson, 1985, p. 1). This is not surprising when you consider the following kinds of trauma to which Vietnam veterans were exposed (Gilliland & James, 1988):

Hypervigilance: Soldiers had long tours of duty where they were in constant danger. They never knew from one moment to the next when they might be attacked, injured, or killed.

Lack of goals: Because the war dragged on, there was rarely a feeling of accomplishment. No territory was ever "won." The only measure of victory was a "body count" (MacPherson, 1984).

Victim/victimizer role: This was a guerrilla war where civilians were friends as well as enemies. Soldiers were thrown into the role of being both victims and victimizers.

Lack of debriefing: A soldier could be sweating for his life in the jungle one day and a couple of days later be sitting on his porch at home (MacPherson, 1984). This was a war in which soldiers were motivated to survive their tour of duty and get home alive. For this reason, survivors often felt guilty about those who died or were injured. They were happy to go home but felt bad about leaving their comrades behind.

Antiwar sentiment: The impact of antiwar sentiment on returning veterans was devastating. These men had suffered and risked their lives, many returning with disabling injuries. However, they were not regarded as heroes and were often treated with disdain. Many soldiers had extreme difficulty starting a new life after returning from the war.

Given the stresses soldiers suffered in the Vietnam War, it is understandable that many of them have experienced physical and psychological impairment (Kaylor, King, & King, 1987).

Although PTSD has received greater recognition since the Vietnam War, it is not new. The fact that people can suffer long-lasting psychological disturbance after trauma has been known for hundreds of years (Trimble, 1985). All of the traumas discussed in this chapter can be severe enough to result in PTSD. The following ten factors influence the onset and course of PTSD (Wilson, Smith, & Johnson, 1985):

1. *Degree of life-threat:* Traumatic events threatening one's life are likely to be most debilitating and to invoke the kind of death imprint described in the discussion of the Buffalo Creek disaster.

2. *Loss of significant others:* Bereavement is associated with prolonged stress responses. The death of significant others is a source of grief, guilt, rage, and depression.

3. *Suddenness of onset:* Traumas that occur without warning are particularly likely to instill a feeling of helplessness and loss of external control.

4. *Duration of trauma:* It is most difficult to adjust to traumas that are prolonged and that continue for a long time.

5. *Displacement from one's community:* It is particularly detrimental to be exposed to traumatic events that occur away from one's community or that result in community disintegration. Traumatic events are times when we desperately need the love and belongingness that come from our support systems.

6. *Potential for recurrence:* Traumatic events that are unpredictable, that might recur, and that cause distrust and hypervigilance are particularly disturbing.

7. *Exposure to death, dying, and destruction:* Exposure to death, dying, and destruction heightens intrusive imagery, psychic numbing, isolation, and grief.

8. *Degree of moral conflict*: It is bad enough to experience traumatic events that have some reason or justification. It is even more difficult to adjust to traumatic events that threaten one's personal values and instill a moral conflict.
9. *Personal role*: In some situations, people are placed in a role where they must react and cope with destruction. This is difficult. In other situations, people are obliged not only to react but also to perpetrate destruction. This is even more difficult.
10. *Natural versus human trauma*: It is usually easier to accept and cope with natural disasters than disasters caused by one's fellow human beings.

Therapy for PTSD

What kinds of therapy are helpful for people suffering with PTSD? The following six processes appear to help people cope more effectively (Epstein, 1991; Schwarz & Prout, 1991).

1. *Developing a trusting relationship with a therapist or support group*: PTSD victims suffer from emotions ranging from shame, guilt, and depression to anger and rage. They need to feel safe before these feelings can be recognized, accepted, and explored.
2. *Educating the individual about the stress recovery process*: It is reassuring to understand how symptoms of PTSD can result from trauma. Education helps to make PTSD less scary and mysterious and encourages victims to view themselves as copers rather than as weak and inadequate people.
3. *Learning and practicing stress management techniques*: Coping skills such as those discussed in Chapter 3 are useful for stress management, as are the skills of rational thinking and self-efficacy outlined in Chapter 2.
4. *Reexperiencing and desensitizing oneself from trauma*: This is a powerful but often effective process involving the methods of desensitization, flooding, and thought-stopping described in Chapter 7 (Cooper & Clum, 1989; Keane, Fairbank, Caddell, & Zimering, 1989; Keane, Fairbank, Caddell, Zimering, & Bender, 1985). With the support of trained professionals, people suffering from PTSD vividly relive the traumatic experience until they are in control of the experience rather than suffering by having the experience control them.
5. *Engaging in meaningful activities*: Meaningful activities provide an opportunity to experience the positive side of the world and to appreciate oneself as an interesting, caring, and competent person.
6. *Reconciling oneself to the traumatic experience*: As you will learn in the next section, we all have the need to find meaning in life and to believe in ourselves as worthwhile people. With professional guidance, victims can find a way to integrate the trauma they suffered into their total life experience.

SOME COMMON EXPERIENCES

Although the traumas and injuries described in this chapter are very different, people coping with them share several common experiences. When confronted with a traumatic experience or injury, our feelings about the "goodness of life" are threatened. We are forced to reconcile our suffering with our desire to maintain the following beliefs (Janoff-Bulman & Thomas, 1988): "The world is basically a good place. Life is meaningful. I am a worthwhile person." Much of this chapter is about how people who have suffered injury and trauma go about doing this. Three things people commonly experience when trying to regain their faith in the above beliefs are searching for meaning, recurrent thoughts, and self-blame (Janoff-Bulman & Thomas, 1988; Tait & Silver, 1989).

Searching for Meaning

Check whether you agree or disagree with the following statements:

	Agree	Disagree
1. People get what they are entitled to have.	___	___
2. A person's efforts are noticed and rewarded.	___	___
3. People earn the rewards and punishments they get.	___	___
4. People who meet with misfortune have brought it on themselves.	___	___
5. People get what they deserve.	___	___
6. Rewards and punishments are fairly given.	___	___
7. The world is a fair place.	___	___

These statements come from the Global Belief in a Just World Scale (Lipkus, 1991). People who believe in a just world are more likely than those who don't to agree with the above statements. There is value in believing the world is good and in not allowing yourself to become too jaded or cynical about life. Having faith in the world will help you to make the best of your life and to work with others to make the world a better place. However, to protect yourself from becoming disillusioned, you must accept the fact that not everything in life is fair (Lerner, 1980). Tragedies and traumas can happen to anyone. It is important to find a satisfactory answer for these negative events without blaming yourself or others for things that can't be controlled. The challenge is to reconcile your desire to live in a just world with life's unfairness. This is not always easy to do, but it is a necessary first step to getting on with your life. Part of the solution is to develop the kind of coping attitude toward life discussed in Chapter 15.

Recurrent Thoughts

It is common for people who have suffered major tragedies and even minor setbacks to keep thinking about them (Tait & Silver, 1989). These ruminations sometimes continue to occur for years and even for a lifetime. It is hard to get the negative experience out of mind. We think about it over and over and relive the negative emotions hundreds and even thousands of times.

There are three things to bear in mind regarding ruminations about negative events. First, recurrent thoughts are experienced by almost everyone. Recurrent thoughts serve a useful purpose because we need time to put things into perspective. You can't ignore a setback, injury, or trauma and pretend that it didn't happen. You must accept its reality and find a way to assimilate it into your life. Second, it is helpful to discuss your thoughts and feelings with a support person. If your feelings are complex and will require some time to sort out, you may benefit from working with a professional therapist. Third, you can prevent recurrent thoughts from getting the best of you by keeping busy and focusing on meaningful activities.

Self-Blame

Before you blame yourself for an illness or injury, remember that self-blame is a common human experience. If you blame yourself, you are no different from most other people. Self-blame can even serve a useful purpose if it motivates you to take responsibility for your actions. Self-responsibility will reinforce your feelings of being a competent and worthwhile person. However, self-blame can be destructive if you use it to undermine your character. It is important to recognize the distinction between accepting a mistake in your behavior and doubting your value as a person (Kiecolt-Glaser & Williams, 1987; Nielson & MacDonald, 1988; Solomon, Regier, & Burke, 1989).

THE POWER OF SELF-EXPRESSION

A coping skill that works well for many people who have suffered from trauma is to express this experience in some meaningful way. The value of self-expression as a coping skill was demonstrated in a study comparing three groups of people (Pennebaker & Susman, 1988). One group of people had never experienced a serious trauma (death of a family member or close friend, divorce or separation, sexual trauma, violence). A second group of people had experienced a serious trauma but had never talked to anyone about it. A third group of people had experienced a serious trauma and had confided their feelings to others. It might not be surprising to learn that people who had never experienced a serious trauma had a history of fewer illnesses than those who had experienced a trauma. However, it is quite interesting to know that those who experienced a trauma and shared this experience with others had fewer illnesses than did those who had experienced a trauma and kept it to themselves. In another study, surviving spouses of people who had died traumatic deaths (car accidents, suicide) were asked whether they had talked about this experience with other people after it had happened (Pennebaker & O'Heeron, 1984). Results of this study were similar: People who had talked about their spouse's death had fewer health problems than those who had not.

The opposite of expressing your experiences is *self-concealment*, which can be defined as "a predisposition to actively conceal from others personal information that one perceives as distressing or negative" (Larson & Chastain, 1990, p. 440). The Self-Concealment Scale includes the following kinds of items.

1. I have an important secret that I haven't shared with anyone.
2. My secrets are too embarrassing to share with others.

3. I have negative thoughts about myself that I never share with anyone.
4. There are lots of things about me that I keep to myself.

People who have undergone traumatic experiences are more likely to suffer from anxiety, depression, and bodily symptoms if their scores on the Self-Concealment Scale are high.

The studies just summarized indicate that people who don't talk to others about traumas tend to ruminate about their experiences and never have an opportunity to resolve these experiences and reach closure. These studies also suggest that making an active effort to express traumatic experiences can be a useful coping skill. This theory was tested in a series of studies (Pennebaker, 1989). Participants in these studies volunteered to write or talk about "the most upsetting or traumatic experience of their entire life." This assignment was very emotional for participants, and it was crucial that the experimenters offered informed consent.

> I should warn you that many people find this study quite upsetting. Many people cry during the study and feel somewhat sad or depressed during and after it. (Pennebaker, 1989, p. 215)

In addition, the experimenters made a particular effort to establish rapport with each participant. Confidentiality was guaranteed, and the experimenters carefully monitored each participant throughout the study. After completing their self-expression assignment, participants were debriefed by experimenters who had clinical training. Counseling was readily available for participants who felt the need for it. The kinds of experiences expressed in these studies included deaths, divorce and separation, family conflicts, illnesses, and (for participants who were college students) stresses associated with college. It is worth noting that most participants stated that they found the experience "valuable and meaningful" and that 98% of them said they would be willing to do it again (Pennebaker, 1989, p. 218). The value of the self-expression experience was expressed by the following kinds of statements:

> "It made me think things out and really realize what my problem is."
> "It helped me look at myself from the outside."
> "It was a chance to sort out my thoughts."

Results of these studies were dramatic. It was not unusual for participants to feel more depressed and anxious after disclosing their traumatic experiences. However, the long-term effects of this disclosure were beneficial. Compared with a matched group of participants who did not engage in the self-expression process, the self-disclosing participants had fewer health complaints, fewer stressful physiological responses, and a more healthy immune function (Pennebaker, Colder, & Sharp, 1990; Pennebaker, Hughes, & O'Heeron, 1987; Pennebaker, Kiecolt-Glaser, & Glaser, 1988).

Expressing your traumatic experiences can be painful, but in the long run it is a useful coping strategy. Self-expression helps you become aware of unfinished business that you have put out of awareness but that continues to take an emotional and physical toll. Through the process of self-expression (verbally, or through art, music, or writing), you can assimilate, come to terms with, and reconcile the "demons" in your life.

WHAT YOU CAN LEARN FROM COPERS

The previous chapters of this book focused on coping skills researchers have found to be effective for different kinds of challenging events. This chapter took a more personal approach by looking at the experiences of those who have lived through life crises. People who are good copers have learned how to use effective coping skills. They have also developed a self-identity as survivors. This theme will be continued in Chapter 15 as you learn about the life philosophy of being a coper. When you are through reading this book, you should have a good understanding of how to combine these aspects of being a good coper in a way that best matches your personal style.

SUGGESTIONS FOR FURTHER READING

Benedict, H. (1985). *Recovery: How to survive sexual assault—For women, men, teenagers, their friends and families.* Garden City, NY: Doubleday.

Frankl, V. E. (1967). *Man's search for meaning: An introduction to logotherapy.* Boston: Beacon Press.

Gil, E. (1984). *Outgrowing the pain.* Palo Alto, CA: Consulting Psychologists Press.

Grossman, R., & Sutherland, J. (1983). *Surviving sexual assault.* New York: Congdon & Weed.

Lerner, M. J. (1980). *The belief in a just world: A fundamental delusion.* New York: Plenum.

Pennebaker, J. W. (1990). *Opening up: The healing power of confiding in others.* New York: Morrow.

Viorst, J. (1986). *Necessary losses.* New York: Simon & Schuster.

Wilson, J. P., Harel, Z., & Kahana, B. (Eds.). (1988). *Human adaptation to extreme stress: From the Holocaust to Vietnam.* New York: Plenum.

15

Coping as
a Life Philosophy

As you read this book, you became familiar with terms such as *self-efficacy, competence,* and *mastery.* All of these terms support a life philosophy of believing in yourself as a coper. When faced with a life challenge, copers believe that although the experience might not be pleasant they can use their problem-solving skills to seek the best possible outcome. Copers refuse to be passive and helpless. They look for ways to take active control over their lives.

In this chapter I will focus on coping as a life philosophy. But first, let's look at the opposite extreme of coping—helplessness. An insight into the phenomenon of helplessness provides a different perspective on self-efficacy, competence, and mastery and a deeper appreciation of what it means to be a coper.

HELPLESSNESS

Helplessness occurs when people give up and allow external circumstances to take over their lives. Students would be helpless if their grades were determined randomly and had nothing to do with their performance. Infants would be helpless if their cries for nurturance were always ignored. Sick and elderly people are helpless when they are given no opportunity to do things for themselves. It should be clear to you by now that these kinds of helplessness often result in passivity and depression.

There is also another kind of helplessness—*learned helplessness.* This term was first used by Martin Seligman (1975) to describe conditions where we believe we are helpless or have learned to feel helpless when we really are not. Women in U.S. society have traditionally been taught to feel helpless about their mechanical and physical skills. Men have traditionally been taught to feel helpless about homemaking and nurturing young children. In severe cases of helplessness, people give up complete control over their lives and die. It is important to emphasize that these cases of helplessness are *learned.* They result from complete acceptance of a belief that you are doomed and there is nothing you can do about it. Consider the following examples of

helplessness described by anthropologists who studied people who believed they were
destined to death by certain life events:

> A Brazilian Indian condemned and sentenced by a so-called medicine man is help-
> less against his own emotional response to this pronouncement—and dies within
> hours. In Africa a young Negro unknowingly eats the inviolably banned wild hen. On
> discovery of his "crime," he trembles, is overcome by fear, and dies within 24 hours.

> In New Zealand a Maori woman eats fruit that she only later learns has come from a
> tabooed place. Her chief has been profaned. By noon of the next day she is dead.

> In Australia a witch doctor points a bone at a man. Believing that nothing can save
> him, the man rapidly sinks in spirits and prepares to die. He is saved only at the last
> moment when the witch doctor is forced to remove the curse.

> The man who discovers that he is being boned by an enemy is, indeed, a pitiable
> sight. He stands aghast with his eyes staring at the treacherous pointer, and with his
> hands lifted to ward off the lethal medium, which he imagines is pouring into his
> body. His cheeks blanch, and his eyes become glassy, and the expression of his face
> becomes horribly distorted. He attempts to shriek but usually the sound chokes in his
> throat, and all that one might see is froth at his mouth. His body begins to tremble
> and his muscles twitch involuntarily. He sways backward and falls to the ground, and
> after a short time appears to be in a swoon. He finally composes himself, goes to his
> hut and there frets to death. (Basedow, 1925; Cannon, 1942, 1957, p. 184; Richter,
> 1957, p. 191)

Bruno Bettelheim (1960) has described how he coped with being a prisoner in a
Nazi concentration camp by telling himself that he was a scientist who was going to
study this terrible event. By looking at his experience in this way, Bettelheim was able
to maintain a sense of self-efficacy. Many other prisoners felt completely helpless and
gave up control over their lives:

> Prisoners who came to believe the repeated statements of the guards—that there was
> no hope for them, that they would never leave the camp except as a corpse—who
> came to feel that their environment was one over which they could exercise no influ-
> ence whatsoever, these prisoners were in a literal sense, walking corpses. In the camps
> they were called "Moslems" (*Muselmänner*) because of what was erroneously viewed
> as a fatalistic surrender to the environment, as Mohammedans are supposed to
> blandly accept their fate. But these people had not, like real Mohammedans, made
> an act of decision and submitted to fate out of free will. On the contrary, they were
> people that were so deprived of affect, self-esteem, and every form of stimulation, so
> totally exhausted, both physically and emotionally, that they had given the environ-
> ment total power over them. (Bettelheim, 1960, pp. 151–152)·

Martin Seligman (1975) recounts a story told to him about a tough marine cor-
poral who was a prisoner in a North Vietnamese POW camp. The North Vietnamese
had a practice of releasing Americans from the POW camps from time to time if they
had proven themselves as "model prisoners." This marine survived the brutal conditions of the POW camp by holding on to the hope that if he worked hard and coop-
erated he would win such a release. He submitted to forced labor and carried loads of
rocks on his back barefoot without complaining. He gratefully ate his daily ration of
vermin-infested rice and dutifully followed his captors' orders. His faith that hard work

and stoicism would result in freedom kept him alive. After several years in the POW camp, this marine faced the harsh truth that the North Vietnamese had no intention of letting him go. His attempt to gain freedom by being a model prisoner was wasted. He became depressed, stopped eating, and refused to get out of bed. His fellow prisoners tried to help him by giving him care and nurturance. When that didn't work, they attempted to pull him out of his depression by using physical force. It became clear that he had lost all sense of control over his life, and within a few weeks he was dead.

These examples of helplessness are extreme, but they relate to the theme of this book because they demonstrate the importance to finding ways to maintain a sense of mastery and self-efficacy in our lives. It is true that people who are prisoners or who are afflicted with a terminal illness have little power over matters of life and death. However, as copers, these people can seek other ways to exercise self-efficacy by using their minds, thoughts, dreams, and hopes. The purpose of learning the coping skills described in this book is to develop tools to fall back on when things get tough. When faced with difficult life challenges, you can use your problem-solving skills to sort out your goals and decide which coping skills will help you hold your own and make the best out of this experience.

SELF-PRESERVATION

Human beings have a remarkable capacity for adapting to difficult situations. In Chapters 13 and 14 you saw how people survived tragedies, disasters, and threats to their health. They did this by finding ways to overcome feelings of helplessness. People who are survivors have learned how to use coping skills, and they have developed a life philosophy oriented toward self-preservation. Self-preservation is the opposite of helplessness. It involves approaching life in ways that bolster feelings of self-efficacy, mastery, and control. In the remainder of this chapter I will discuss the research on self-preservation and show you how it can be employed as a coping skill.

COPING WITH VICTIMIZATION

Shelley Taylor and her colleagues studied responses of people who were victims of negative life events and arrived at a number of conclusions that have important implications for self-preservation as a coping strategy (Taylor & Brown, 1988; Taylor, Wood, & Lichtman, 1983). For the most part, people don't want to feel like victims. Taking on the role of a victim means focusing on suffering and reminding yourself of your inability to prevent the cause of your victimization. People who have suffered harm are generally inclined to protect themselves by interpreting their victimization in a manner that will maintain their self-esteem. Here are several strategies for doing this.

Compare Yourself with Less-Fortunate Others

Like the cancer patients described in Chapter 13, some victims maintain their identity as effective people by comparing themselves with others who are less fortunate. No matter how bad the situation, there is always someone who is worse off. It is tempting to view your suffering as unique and more terrible than anybody else's, but this kind of thinking is likely to make you feel like a victim who is passive and depressed.

See the Positive Side

Victims often overcome helplessness by feeling thankful that things are not worse. It is ironic to think of a victim as being thankful. Yet seeing the positive side—that is, that your suffering is not as bad as it could have been—helps maintain optimism and hope.

Use Victimization as a Learning Experience

Another way some victims overcome helplessness is by appreciating what they learned as a result of their negative experience. Traumatic events give you an opportunity to discover new sides of yourself, to reevaluate your life priorities, and to interact with others in a mutually supportive manner. It is unfortunate that it sometimes takes a catastrophic event to force people to take an honest look at themselves. However, it is a tribute to the human capacity for self-preservation that people are able to gain new meanings even from terrible experiences.

Find Strength in Being a Survivor

It is easier to cope with being a victim when you find strength in being a survivor. It boosts your self-esteem to recognize that you are handling the situation better than others.

Self-Preservation as a Way of Looking at Life

Copers have learned how to look at life in ways that enhance their feelings of self-preservation. Looking at life as a coper means finding the right balance between realism and optimism in how you view yourself, your control over your environment, and your future (Taylor & Brown, 1988).

Strive for a Balanced View

You have learned from reading this book that being a good coper means not being too hard on yourself. When there is a choice between focusing on your faults or appreciating your virtues, it is usually more adaptive to appreciate your virtues. Research studies have shown that people are better adjusted and more satisfied with their lives when they see themselves as "better than average" (Kleinke & Miller, 1998; Taylor, 1989; Taylor & Brown, 1988). Appreciating your virtues doesn't mean that you should be grandiose and blind to your shortcomings. It means taking a balanced view of your strengths and weaknesses—don't bring yourself down by focusing on your imperfections.

Control Your View of the Environment

There are some events in your life that you realistically cannot control, and it would be foolish to believe otherwise. However, even when faced with uncontrollable events, there is always some way of exercising mastery. Although you may not be able to change the life event, you can always control how you think and react. Copers overcome helplessness by not insisting on controlling things they can't. When faced with difficult challenges, they use their problem-solving skills to identify some piece or aspect of this life event where they can take charge and feel competent.

Look to the Future

Copers are future-oriented. Negative experiences in the past cannot be undone, but there is always hope for better times in the future. The future provides an opportunity to use your learning experiences and coping skills to improve in relation to past mistakes and to experience satisfaction. Looking forward to the future inspires hope and optimism about new opportunities for exercising mastery and competence.

COPING AS A SELF-FULFILLING PROPHECY

Viewing yourself as a coper is a self-fulfilling prophecy. When you expect yourself to use good coping skills, you are more likely to do so. Check whether you agree or disagree with the following statements:

	Strongly agree	Agree	Disagree	Strongly disagree
1. In uncertain times, I usually expect the best.	___	___	___	___
2. I always look on the bright side of things.	___	___	___	___
3. I'm always optimistic about the future.	___	___	___	___
4. I'm a believer in the idea that "every cloud has a silver lining."	___	___	___	___
5. If something can go wrong for me, it will.	___	___	___	___
6. I hardly ever expect things to go my way.	___	___	___	___
7. Things never work out the way I want them to.	___	___	___	___
8. I rarely count on good things happening to me.	___	___	___	___

These statements come from the Life Orientation Test, which measures people's positive expectancies and feelings of optimism (Scheier & Carver, 1985). Optimists agree with statements 1 through 4 and disagree with statements 5 through 8. Research indicates that optimists make use of adaptive coping skills such as problem solving and building support systems (see Chapter 3). Optimists are less likely to use avoidant coping strategies. Optimists also focus on achieving their goals in the face of hindrances and distractions. Because their energies are devoted to developing self-efficacy, optimists have positive expectations about the future. As a result of their more effective coping skills, they suffer less from life stresses and have fewer physical and psychological complaints than pessimists (Aspinwall & Taylor, 1992; Reker & Wong, 1985; Scheier & Carver, 1985, 1992; Scheier, Weintraub, & Carver, 1986).

In contrast to optimists, pessimists cope less adaptively by focusing on negative feelings, withdrawing, and avoiding. The kind of negative thinking engaged in by pessimists causes a number of potential problems (Goodhart, 1985). For example:

- Negative thinking interferes with selection of effective coping strategies.
- Negative thinking lowers self-esteem.
- Negative thinking reinforces feelings of vulnerability.
- Negative thinking causes increased stress.

Another way to understand the difference between optimists and pessimists is by looking at how they view their lives in terms of three dimensions that were discussed in Chapter 5: stability, globality, and internality.

Stability versus instability: An attitude of stability means that you think that things in your life are predetermined and that there is not much you can do about them. An attitude of instability means that you believe events in your life can change. Things won't always be the way they are now.

Globality versus specificity: Globality describes the attitude that a single experience can affect your entire life. Specificity means putting things into perspective. When you believe in specificity, you realize you will have good and bad experiences throughout your life and that you don't have to be overwhelmed by any of them.

Internality versus externality: This lifestyle was explained in Chapter 3. An attitude of internality encourages you to take responsibility for getting what you need out of life. An attitude of externality places you in a more passive role because you give the world more control over your destiny.

Researchers have found that people who view the world with a generally pessimistic outlook are characterized by attitudes of stability, globality, and externality. These people often have poorer health than those who are more optimistic with attitudes of instability, specificity, and internality (Peterson, 1988; Peterson & Seligman, 1987). It has also been found that men who expressed attitudes of stability, globality, and externality in college had poorer physical health 20 to 40 years later than did men whose attitudes in college were oriented toward instability, specificity, and internality (Peterson, Seligman, & Vaillant, 1988). This finding is important because it suggests that attitudes of pessimism and optimism can have a direct influence on physical health.

Viewing yourself as a coper provides a boost to your self-esteem. Self-esteem is a durable source of strength because you carry it around with you. You can use your feelings of self-worth and competence to cope with life challenges even when other avenues of support are not available (Hobfoll & Leiberman, 1987).

THE POWER OF HOPE

Most of us are reminded of the harsh realities of life on a daily basis. We need to maintain a sense of reality to cope with the hassles that confront us. However, it also helps to nurture an attitude of hope—a belief that somehow you can make things turn out OK. Check how much you agree or disagree with the following statements:

	Strongly agree	Agree	Disagree	Strongly disagree
1. I can think of many ways to get out of a jam.	_____	_____	_____	_____
2. Even when others get discouraged, I know I can find a way to solve the problem.	_____	_____	_____	_____
3. There are lots of ways around my problem.	_____	_____	_____	_____
4. I can think of many ways to get things in life that are important to me.	_____	_____	_____	_____
5. I've been pretty successful in my life.	_____	_____	_____	_____
6. My past experiences have prepared me well for the future.	_____	_____	_____	_____
7. I meet the goals I set for myself.	_____	_____	_____	_____
8. I energetically pursue my goals.	_____	_____	_____	_____

These statements come from the Hope Scale (Snyder, 1989; Snyder, Irving, & Anderson, 1991). The Hope Scale is a good predictor of physical and mental health because it assesses two qualities that are essential for getting needs met. Statements 1 through 4 measure flexibility in finding *pathways* for getting what we want. Statements 5 through 8 measure how positive we are about our ability to *attain* our goals. Good copers take responsibility to pursue their goals actively, and they are open to finding the best coping strategies.

TAKING APPROPRIATE RESPONSIBILITY

Taking appropriate responsibility means taking charge of things you can control in your life without suffering needless stress and self-blame for life events beyond your control. Table 15.1 outlines four models applying to life events where you are either responsible or not responsible for (1) the cause of the problem and (2) the solution for the problem (Brickman et al., 1982).

Moral Model

In the moral model, you are responsible for a problem's cause and solution. Some examples of problems fitting the moral model are:

- Doing poorly on a test because you didn't study hard enough
- Someone being angry because you behaved badly
- Failing to engage in good health practices
- Failing to make constructive plans for the future

In the moral model it is up to you to assert yourself and make an active effort to do what is in your best interest. Follow the moral model when it is appropriate for you to take care of yourself.

Enlightenment Model

The enlightenment model holds you responsible for a problem's cause but not for its solution. Some examples of the enlightenment model are:

- Using your support systems
- Finding support in organized religion
- Participating in individual or group therapy

The enlightenment model applies to problems you might have caused but that are best solved with the help of others. Some examples of these problems include alcohol and drug abuse and eating disorders. Follow the enlightenment model when you realize it is not in your best interest to isolate yourself and that you can benefit from the help of others.

Compensatory Model

The compensatory model applies to problems that you didn't cause but that you must solve. Some examples of the compensatory model are:

- Rehabilitating yourself after an injury or illness
- Pursuing an education
- Bargaining, negotiating, and being assertive
- Coping with catastrophes and disasters
- Learning new skills

The compensatory model encourages you to take an active role in solving problems without blaming yourself for their cause.

TABLE 15.1   Four models of responsibility

Responsibility for Problem	Responsibility for Solution	
	High	Low
High	Moral model	Enlightenment model
Low	Compensatory model	Medical model

SOURCE: From "Models of Helping and Coping" by P. Brickman, V. C. Rabinowitz, J. Karuza, D. Coates, E. Cohn, and L. Kidder, 1982, *American Psychologist*, 37, 368–384. Copyright 1982 by the American Psychological Association. Adapted with permission.

Medical Model

The medical model is relevant for problems you didn't cause and that you can't solve. This model is called the medical model because it applies primarily to illnesses and injuries where you must depend on trained professionals for assistance. You are following the medical model when you pay an expert for a consultation or to provide services you can't do yourself. The medical model encourages you to rely on others for assistance without feeling weak or guilty because you can't solve the problem on your own.

These four models of responsibility are valuable because they can help you sort out the best strategies for dealing with problems in your life. You can see how rigidly following only one or two of these models can result in needless guilt and self-blame (for example, by leaning inappropriately on others) or loneliness and alienation (for example, by trying to solve everything by yourself).

BEING A WELL-ROUNDED PERSON

It is easier to be a good coper when you are well-rounded. Being a well-rounded person means having a multidimensional identity, being flexible, and taking an interest in others.

Having a Multidimensional Identity

Having a multidimensional identity is a valuable coping skill (Linville, 1987). People who have a one-sided view of themselves are very limited. They don't have a broad foundation of personal resources to fall back on when facing difficult challenges. For example, an athlete who bases his full identity on being a jock will find it difficult to maintain a sense of personal effectiveness when his athletic career is over. A businessperson who puts her entire life into her position will feel at a loss when she reaches the top and has no more competitive challenges. People who put the bulk of their self-value in raising children lose their sense of purpose when their children grow up and leave home to pursue their own lives. And lovers who derive all of their self-esteem from a single person feel empty and worthless when the love relationship ends.

Good copers have a life philosophy of developing their personal identity along many dimensions. It is important to learn how to gain a sense of self-fulfillment in more than one area of life. Pursue life activities that will give you many interests. That way, if one part of your life is challenged, you will have other dimensions of self-identity to rely on for feelings of self-esteem, mastery, and competence.

Being Flexible

Good copers have learned how to be flexible in their thinking and in their actions.

Thinking flexibly.   In Chapter 11, I urged you to be flexible in your perceptions about what it means to grow old and to avoid the self-fulfilling prophecy that aging means going downhill. This advice about thinking flexibly applies to more than aging. When you find yourself in a situation that is not in your best interest, it doesn't have to be that way. Of course, refusing to accept roles that are expected of you and getting out of harmful relationships requires pain and effort. You must sometimes decide whether it is worth suffering in the short run for the sake of being satisfied with yourself in the long run. Being a flexible thinker means you are at least willing to consider this choice. To live your life with a sense of competence and self-esteem is often difficult, but it is a *possibility*.

Acting flexibly.   To be flexible with your actions, you must have a large arsenal of coping skills and know how to use them appropriately in challenging situations (Paulhus & Martin, 1988). For example, when faced with a challenge, a variety of responses are at your disposal. Think about the ways you have already mastered in relating to people: being assertive, nurturant, or sympathetic; being a leader; being a follower; being a talker; being a listener; expressing anger; expressing consideration; bargaining; and compromising. You also know how to use the coping skills discussed in this book. Being competent in all of these ways of facing life challenges and relating to people provides a feeling of self-confidence. It is reassuring to have more than one option when confronted with a problem to solve.

You know you can skillfully match your coping strategies and interpersonal skills to the situation—and you are not afraid to use them. You are not restricted by responding to all challenges in the same manner.

Taking an Interest in Others

When you spend a lot of time thinking and worrying about yourself, you can become severely limited. Too much self-focus can cause you to avoid valuable experiences because you are preoccupied with guarding your self-esteem. However, when you devote time and energy to others, you are less apt to ruminate about your own problems. You may find yourself taking a more active role in life and, as a result, become a healthier and happier person (Crandall, 1980, 1984; Crandall & Putnam, 1980).

Choosing Healthy Friendships

Everyone is familiar with the admonition that people are judged by their choice of friends. However, the benefits that can be gained by associating with good role models are often overlooked. When you are in jeopardy, it is much more uplifting to have friends who are examples of adaptive rather than maladaptive ways of coping. Being a well-rounded person means taking control over your life by associating with people whose lifestyles have a positive impact (Taylor & Lobel, 1989).

THE BENEFITS OF CONSTRUCTIVE THINKING

In the previous section, you were advised of the value of approaching life challenges with a flexible orientation toward your appraisals and options. It is also beneficial to be flexible in the way you think about life. Seymour Epstein and his colleagues have defined the concept of *constructive thinking* by outlining thinking styles that contribute to and detract from our ability to view and respond to the world in a flexible manner (S. Epstein, 1992a; S. Epstein & Meier, 1989).

Adaptive Thinking Styles

Two adaptive thinking styles are *behavioral coping* and *emotional coping*. Behavioral coping is characterized by the following kinds of thinking styles:

- I am the kind of person who takes action rather than just thinks or complains about a situation.
- I look at challenges not as something to fear but as an opportunity to test myself and learn.
- I try to make an all-out effort in most things I do.
- When faced with upcoming unpleasant events, I usually carefully think through how I will deal with them.

When you engage in behavioral coping, you focus on taking effective action and maintaining an optimistic and hopeful attitude toward life. Behavioral coping is associated with the ability to focus on the future and not to dwell on negative experiences in the past.

Some examples of emotional coping are found in the following kinds of thinking styles:

- I don't let little things bother me.
- I can tolerate failure.
- I don't worry about things I can do nothing about.
- When unpleasant things happen to me, I don't dwell on them.

Emotional coping involves controlling your negative thinking so you don't ruminate on unpleasant thoughts (see Chapter 5).

Maladaptive Thinking Styles

Three maladaptive thinking styles are *categorical thinking, superstitious thinking,* and *negative thinking.*

Categorical thinking is illustrated in the following kinds of thinking styles:

- I tend to classify people as either for me or against me.
- If people treat me badly, I feel that I should treat them the same way.

- There are two possible answers to every question, a right one and a wrong one.
- I find it hard to change my mind once I have made a decision.

Categorical thinking is rigid and judgmental. It restricts your options because it focuses you on limited possibilities.

Superstitious thinking is characterized by the following kinds of thinking styles:

- I have found that talking about successes that I am looking forward to can keep them from happening.
- When something good happens to me, I believe it is likely to be balanced by something bad.
- I have at least one good luck charm.
- I believe in good and bad omens.

Superstitious thinking is associated with feelings of helplessness. You have a sense of not being able to control your destiny unless it can be done with magic and rituals.

Negative thinking is characterized by the following kinds of thinking styles:

- When things go wrong, I can't help thinking about how bad things are.
- When I am faced with a new situation, I tend to think the worst possible outcome will happen.
- I get so distressed when I notice that I am doing poorly in something that it makes me do worse.
- I tend to dwell more on unpleasant than pleasant incidents from the past.

Negative thinking is a way of overemphasizing how bad things are. Negative thinking is related to taking a "gloom and doom" attitude toward life and allowing feelings of anxiety and depression to interfere with daily tasks.

To be a constructive thinker, focus your energies on using adaptive thinking styles and minimizing the use of maladaptive thinking styles. Constructive thinkers have a greater sense of well-being, and they experience more satisfying lives (S. Epstein & Meier, 1989; S. Epstein & Katz, 1992). Constructive thinking is related to satisfaction with your work and your interpersonal relationships. Constructive thinkers are more satisfied with their physical and emotional health.

Constructive thinking is beneficial because it is associated with a flexible orientation toward life challenges. Constructive thinkers experience less stress because they don't ruminate on their faults and weaknesses. Because they take a problem-solving attitude, they don't become overwhelmed with stressful events. Approaching life challenges with constructive thinking results in fewer stress-related problems, such as headaches, stomachaches, and food, alcohol, and drug abuse. Because constructive thinkers are able to control their negative thinking, they cope better with anxiety and depression (Katz & Epstein, 1991). Another skill associated with constructive thinking is the ability to avoid engaging in unfavorable generalizations about yourself (S. Epstein, 1992b). For example, people who use maladaptive thinking styles place a large burden on themselves by reacting to negative experiences in the following ways:

- When someone puts me down, I can't let it rest.
- If I do poorly on a test, I feel like a total failure.
- When someone I like rejects me, I feel like a worthless person.

■ When something bad happens, I feel that more bad things are sure to follow.

In contrast, people who engage in constructive thinking give themselves a break with the following kinds of reactions to negative experiences:

■ When someone puts me down, I process it and then get on with my life.
■ If I do poorly on a test, I realize it is only a single test and not a sign of my overall competence.
■ When someone rejects me, I think about the many people in my life who like me.
■ When something bad happens, I believe it is likely to be balanced by something good.

People who react to negative experiences by being hard on themselves take a defensive attitude toward life. They are so preoccupied with avoiding pain that they don't have the time or the energy left to seek and experience pleasure. The value of constructive thinking is that it helps you put things in perspective. Take time to enjoy life's pleasures rather than spending all your energies thinking about and trying to avoid life's pains.

CONSTRUCTIVE THINKING AS SOCIAL INTELLIGENCE

Constructive thinking is not related to the kinds of skills measured on IQ tests. However, constructive thinking is related to your competence in facing life challenges in an intelligent manner. The key to this kind of "social intelligence" is flexibility (Cantor & Harlow, 1992; Cantor & Kihlstrom, 1987). Be flexible when you make primary and secondary appraisals. You will solve your life challenges more effectively if ou develop a flexible manner of perceiving yourself, your capabilities, and your options.

Making Flexible Primary Appraisals

You have been reminded many times in this book to be flexible in your primary appraisals. Don't avoid or deny life events that require your attention. But don't make the worst out of things and put stress on yourself that will do more harm than good.

Making Flexible Secondary Appraisals

When making secondary appraisals, it is in your best interest to take a problem-solving approach with an attitude of mastery and self-efficacy. If your primary appraisal tells you that a life event is a problem, use your creativity to respond in the best possible manner. If you only have one or two coping skills at your disposal, you are likely to get stuck by applying "solutions" that don't work. Paul Watzlawick (1983, 1988) points out the trouble people have when they are unable to respond to life challenges with flexibility. Because they have no other options, they simply apply "more of the same" solution that is already not working. It is like trying to fix everything with a hammer. Although this may seem obvious, we have all had experiences where we stubbornly applied an ineffective solution to a problem because we could not "see" more suitable alternatives.

Developing a Flexible Self-Identity

Developing a flexible self-identity is related to the process of becoming a well-rounded person. People have problems when they apply a single personality style to all situations. For example:

> Sometimes it is adaptive to be aggressive, but not *always*.
> Sometimes it is adaptive to be passive, but not *always*.
> Sometimes it is adaptive to trust people, but not *always*.
> Sometimes it is adaptive to "kiss things off" and have a good time, but not *always*.
> Sometimes it is adaptive to be suspicious of others, but not *always*.
> Sometimes it is adaptive to rigidly apply yourself to your work, but not *always*.

Instead of developing a fixed concept of who you are, you can benefit by taking a more flexible approach and asking, "How can I develop a personal style that is flexible enough to adapt to many different kinds of situations?" Your self-concept does not have to be rigid or permanent. There are many "possible selves" you can incorporate into your self-identity (Markus & Nurius, 1986).

PERSONAL STRIVINGS

To thrive, people need to have goals and challenges. We are happier and more satisfied with life when we are *striving* than when we are stagnant (Emmons, 1986, 1995). In general, it is good to have a balance between personal strivings that are specific and personal strivings that are philosophical. Some examples of specific personal strivings are:

- Staying in shape
- Getting along with a particular person
- Keeping up with work
- Working on a particular project

Some examples of philosophical strivings are:

- Being more positive and optimistic
- Bringing happiness to other people
- Showing more interest in others
- Understanding personal feelings

Specific personal strivings are useful because they help you focus on concrete activities with which you can get involved on a daily basis. Philosophical strivings are useful because they direct you toward more complex challenges that you would not address if your strivings were exclusively specific (Emmons, 1992).

Strivings that are directed toward enriching your life are more beneficial than strivings that are directed toward avoiding negative experiences. For example, it is more adaptive to say "I want to develop cordial relationships" than to say "I want to avoid conflicts." Saying "I want to make my job more interesting" is more helpful than saying "I don't want to get in trouble at work." Personal strivings are also more meaningful if they come from your own ideas and desires and are not imposed on you by others. You will gain a greater sense of well-being from your goals if you are committed to them and if they are realistic (Brunstein, 1993).

Personal strivings that are most closely related to feelings of well-being are focused on enhancing interpersonal relationships, such as:

- Being a good friend
- Being available when others need support
- Being friendly and affectionate
- Being open and tactful during conflicts

Contributing to the world and to the growth and development of other people are also related to life satisfaction.

Having personal strivings in many areas of life is related to the process of developing a multidimensional identity. There is more life satisfaction in having a broad range of personal strivings than there is in restricting personal strivings to narrow goals, such as making money or being famous.

Although personal strivings are beneficial, they present two challenges. First of all, when you have personal strivings that are in conflict, you will experience dissatisfaction and distress until you can find reconciliation (Emmons & Colby, 1995; Emmons & King, 1988). Some examples of conflicted strivings are:

- The desire to be physically attractive versus the desire to be unaffected by other people's opinions about your looks
- The desire to be independent versus the desire to be loved and nurtured
- The desire to be sociable versus the desire to spend time alone
- The desire for success versus the desire for modesty
- The desire to throw yourself into a relationship versus the desire to protect yourself

One way to cope with conflicted strivings is by reminding yourself that you are multidimensional and can learn to adapt your responses and behaviors to different kinds of situations. When you are uncertain of how you are coming across, it is helpful to rely on feedback from people close to you.

A second challenge presented by personal strivings is coping with the regrets you experience from strivings that you are unable to achieve (Lecci, Okum, & Karoly, 1994). Many of the suggestions for coping with failure will be helpful here (see Chapter 4). In general, the attributions or appraisals you make for unfulfilled goals will influence your adjustment to them. Instead of ruminating on disappointments or blaming them on personal weakness, you need to say the following kinds of things to yourself:

"Because I have many goals in life, I know I can't reach them all."
"Living a full life means having regrets as well as accomplishments."
"I need to balance my regrets against my satisfactions."
"Life is not designed to have everything work out my way."

PUTTING HAPPINESS IN PERSPECTIVE

For most people, happiness is an overriding goal in life. People devote considerable energy toward seeking happiness and holding on to it whenever they find it. Given the significance of happiness as a human value, it makes sense to put your desire to be happy in perspective. The problem with seeking happiness as a life goal is that it is unpredictable and elusive. Thomas Szasz (1990) likens happiness to a wet bar of soap: The harder you grab for it, the more it slips out of your hands. When asked about happiness as a life goal, Szasz quoted Socrates, who said he'd rather be an unhappy philosopher than a happy cow.

Defining Happiness

People define happiness in two general ways (Baumeister, 1991b; Waterman, 1993). One way to define happiness is to equate it with intense pleasure. This is the kind of happiness that is unpredictable and elusive. Because states of happiness come to us on an intermittent schedule, they can be addictive (the harder you grab, the more it slips away). These are what Szasz (1990) calls the "bonuses of life." Although states of happiness may make life worth living, it is risky for people to devote their lives to grabbing for them. It can be argued (as a value judgment) that many people have squandered their lives by focusing their energies on achieving momentary highs rather than taking these highs as they came and devoting their talents to long-term accomplishments. A second definition of happiness is a general satisfaction with life. Given this definition, happiness can be called *subjective well-being* (Diener, 1984), and it is characterized by items such as those on the Satisfaction with Life Scale (Diener, Emmons, Larsen, & Griffin, 1985; Pavot & Diener, 1993):

1. In most ways, my life is close to my ideal.
2. The conditions of my life are excellent.
3. So far I have gotten the important things I want in life.
4. I am satisfied with life.
5. If I could live my life over, I would change almost nothing.

The notion of life satisfaction suggests that it is more fruitful to achieve happiness by seeking emotional stability and serenity than it is to live for the unpredictable peaks of excitement and suffer through the low points in between. Research studies have shown that overall happiness is correlated more with the *frequency* of small pleasures experienced rather than with the achievement of fewer but highly *intense* pleasures (Diener, Sandvik, & Pavot, 1989).

Most people lose sight of how much happiness is a result of their expectations and perceptions as well as of the demands they make of life. It is true that you usually feel better when good things are happening to you and that you feel worse when bad things are happening to you (Feist, Bodner, Jacobs, Miles, & Tan, 1995). However, the effect of good and bad experiences on your well-being is also tempered by how you cope with these experiences and incorporate them into your life. In other words, your sense of self can go a long way toward helping you maintain your feelings of well-being even when your life experiences are not always pleasant. It is a mistake to assume that happiness is caused by external events. Many people truly believe they would be happy "if only" something (external) would happen. They say, "I would be happy *if only* . . .

> I could find the right romantic partner."
> I could win the lottery or make lots of money."
> the project I'm working on would be successful."
> some problem in my life would go away."

A good example of the fallacy of deriving your happiness from external events is seen in a study of people who won their state lottery (Brickman, Coates, & Janoff-Bulman, 1978). These people, who received from $50,000 to $1 million, were naturally happy about their good fortune. However, this happiness was surprisingly short-lived. For one thing, the experience of winning so much money had the effect of making the other pleasures of life less valuable. The lottery winners soon forgot how to find pleasure in activities that used to bring them satisfaction. Because they were blessed with the external gift of a lottery prize, the only thing worth looking forward to was winning an even larger lottery in the future. As suggested earlier, living your life for elusive pleasures has its costs. First, people waste a lot of time putting their lives on hold waiting for their "lucky day" (which, of course, may never come). Second, although the pleasure of external events may be intense, it is short-lived and often undermines the gratification that can be achieved from smaller but more predictable enjoyments that come from inside (Diener, Colvin, Pavot, & Allman, 1991).

A Program for Increasing Happiness

You can enhance your feelings of well-being by engaging in the following activities (Fordyce, 1977, 1981, 1983; Ryff, 1989a):

1. Be active and keep busy.
2. Develop satisfying personal relationships.
3. Be productive at meaningful work.
4. Be better organized and plan things out.
5. Control negative thinking.
6. Maintain challenging but realistic expectations and aspirations.
7. Develop positive, optimistic thinking.
8. Enjoy the present.
9. Determine personal goals for the future.
10. Be interested in other people.
11. Find your own self-identity.
12. Find solutions for negative experiences and problems.
13. Value the concept of serenity.

In a series of studies, researchers have demonstrated that people who were taught to practice these fundamental tenets reported being more happy than did people in a control group who did not receive this training. It appears that people can increase their happiness by learning and practicing strategies that work best for them.

Some Conclusions About Happiness

The following conclusions can be reached from research on happiness:

1. Life events that bring joy and elation can be savored and appreciated as long as they don't undermine the value of everyday pleasures. However, it is better to devote your energies toward achieving a satisfying life than it is to get side-tracked seeking momentary gratifications.
2. A satisfying life comes from learning to increase your satisfactions as well as learning to cope with your dissatisfactions.
3. Everybody needs close relationships with other people and a good support system.
4. The healthiest route is to set goals that are reasonable and that will provide satisfaction over the course of your life.
5. Life satisfaction comes more from appreciating the process of working through a challenge (being mastery-oriented, see Chapter 4) than from achieving a particular outcome (being performance-oriented).

RAISING CHILDREN TO BE COPERS

One of the best ways to master new ideas, concepts, and skills is to teach them to someone else. You might find it useful to put together what you have learned in this book by considering what it takes to grow up as a person who knows how to cope with life challenges. A good place to start is by looking at coping from its opposite extreme. How could you raise a child to be incompetent and helpless? One way is by raising the child in a world where he or she has little or no opportunity to experience success. Although no one would want to do this, it is clear that many children grow up just this way. Children who are not prepared with the fundamentals they need for school fall behind and come to see themselves as "slow," "dumb," or "learning disabled." Children who grow up in poverty have little opportunity to experience mastery and competence except by engaging in activities that are antisocial or illegal.

After considering the above description and the lessons you have learned in this book, it should be easy to appreciate the value of providing children with opportunities for experiencing self-efficacy, competence, and mastery. Children need to explore, to try things out, and to learn that they can have an effect on their social and physical environment.

Another way to teach children to be helpless is by making things too easy for them. Human beings need challenges to master and obstacles to overcome. It is through this process that we learn how to set meaningful goals and to develop an ability to tolerate failure. Our fast-food, quick-fix society encourages helplessness by making life simple, shallow, and easy (Skinner, 1986). If we want entertainment, we flip on the TV or read magazines that don't require much thought or concentration. If we are hungry, we indulge in frozen dinners. It takes a concerted effort to maintain a sense of self-efficacy and competence by pursuing hobbies, interests, and activities that require self-discipline and practice. Being a competent person in our society means spending the time to develop a sense of self-sufficiency and individuality. Children need good role models to teach them how to grow into well-rounded adults.

Children become copers by learning how to use coping skills such as those described in this book. When faced with life challenges, children can be taught to take responsibility for finding the best solution. A problem-solving orientation is a healthy substitute for throwing tantrums or giving up.

THE BENEFITS OF BEING A COPER

Being a coper means making the effort to learn and practice the skills taught in this book. A coper faces challenges with perseverance. When you can't control difficult situations, work on your own strategies, thinking styles, and emotional reactions. A coping attitude toward life provides copers with a heightened sense of competence and self-efficacy, but it requires personal energy. Is it worth the effort?

The following conclusions about the benefits of being a coper were derived from a research review compiled by Albert Bandura (1989):

1. Copers set high goals because they know how to use problem-solving skills when things get tough.
2. Because copers have learned how to put self-doubts into perspective, they are able to stay focused on the challenges before them.
3. Copers find strength in visualizing their possibilities for success.
4. The skills mastered by copers give them confidence to persevere and not to settle for mediocre outcomes.
5. Copers are future-oriented. They know how to make long-term plans by delaying immediate gratifications.
6. Copers know how to reward themselves for success.
7. Because of their problem-solving attitude, copers are less troubled by physical and emotional stress.

A coping attitude is a philosophy that says life will not always be the way you want it to be but your coping skills can help you make the best of it. I encourage you to practice the coping skills you have learned from this book—it's never too soon to begin reaping the benefits of pursuing a coping lifestyle!

SUGGESTIONS FOR FURTHER READING

Ellis, A. (1971). *Growth through reasoning*. North Hollywood, CA: Wilshire Books.

Ellis, A., & Becker, I. (1982). *A guide to personal happiness*. North Hollywood, CA: Wilshire Books.

Lazarus, A. A., & Fay, A. (1975). *I can if I want to*. New York: Morrow.

Seligman, M. E. P. (1991). *Learned optimism*. New York: Knopf.

Snyder, C. R. (1994). *The psychology of hope: You can get there from here*. New York: Free Press.

Taylor, S. E. (1989). *Positive illusions: Creative self-deception and the healthy mind*. New York: Basic Books.

Watzlawick, P. (1983). *The situation is hopeless, but not serious: The pursuit of unhappiness*. New York: Norton.

Watzlawick, P. (1988). *Ultra-solutions*. New York: Norton.

REFERENCES

Abbey, A. (1982). Sex differences in attributions for friendly behavior: Do males misperceive females' friendliness? *Journal of Personality and Social Psychology, 42*, 830–838.

Abbey, A. (1987). Misperceptions of friendly behavior as sexual interest: A survey of naturally occurring incidents. *Psychology of Women Quarterly, 11*, 173–194.

Adams, H. E., Feuerstein, M., & Fowler, J. L. (1980). Migraine headache: Review of parameters, etiology, and intervention. *Psychological Bulletin, 87*, 217–237.

Adler, N., & Matthews, K. (1994). Health psychology: Why do some people get sick and some stay well? *Annual Review of Psychology, 45*, 229–259.

Affleck, G., Tennen, H., Urrows, S., & Higgins, P. (1992). Neuroticism and the pain-mood relation in rheumatoid arthritis: Insights from a prospective daily study. *Journal of Consulting and Clinical Psychology, 60*, 119–126.

Alden, L., & Cappe, R. (1986). Interpersonal process training for shy clients. In W. H. Jones, J. M. Cheek, & S. R. Briggs (Eds.), *Shyness: Perspectives on research and treatment* (pp. 343–355). New York: Plenum.

Altmaier, E. M., Russell, D. W., Kao, C. F., Lehmann, T. R., & Weinstein, J. N. (1993). Role of self-efficacy in rehabilitation outcome among chronic low back pain patients. *Journal of Counseling Psychology, 40*, 1–5.

Amabile, T. M. (1990). Within you, without you: The social psychology of creativity and beyond. In M. A. Runco & R. S. Albert (Eds.), *Theories of creativity* (pp. 61–91). Newbury Park, CA: Sage.

Amabile, T. M., Hill, K. G., Hennessey, B. A., & Tighe, E. M. (1994). The Work Preference Inventory: Assessing intrinsic and extrinsic motivational orientations. *Journal of Personality and Social Psychology, 66*, 950–967.

American Cancer Society. (1985). *Cancer facts and figures 1985*. New York: Author.

American Psychiatric Association. (1994). *Diagnostic and statistical manual of mental disorders* (4th ed.). Washington, DC: Author.

Amirkhan, J. H. (1990a). A factor analytically derived measure of coping: The Coping Strategy Indicator. *Journal of Personality and Social Psychology, 59*, 1066–1074.

Amirkhan, J. H. (1990b). Applying attribution theory to the study of stress and coping. In S. Graham & V. S. Folkes (Eds.), *Attribution theory: Applications to achievement, mental health, and interpersonal conflict* (pp. 79–102). Hillsdale, NJ: Erlbaum.

Amirkhan, J. H. (1994). Criterion validity of a coping measure. *Journal of Personality Assessment, 62*, 242–261.

Amirkhan, J. H., Risinger, R. T., & Swickert, R. J. (1995). Extraversion: A "hidden" personality factor in coping? *Journal of Personality, 63*, 189–212.

Andersen, S. M. (1990). The inevitability of future suffering: The role of depressive predictive certainty in depression. *Social Cognition, 8*, 203–228.

Andersen, S. M., & Williams, M. (1985). Cognitive/affective reaction in the improvement of self-esteem: When thoughts and feelings make a difference. *Journal of Personality and Social Psychology, 49*, 1086–1097.

Anderson, C. A. (1983). Motivational and performance deficits in interpersonal settings: The effect of attributional style. *Journal of Personality and Social Psychology, 45*, 1136–1147.

Anderson, C. A., & Arnoult, L. H. (1985). Attributional style and everyday problems in living: Depression, loneliness, and shyness. *Social Cognition, 3*, 16–35.

Anderson, C. A., Horowitz, L. M., & French, R. deS. (1983). Attributional style of lonely and depressed people. *Journal of Personality and Social Psychology, 45*, 127–136.

Anderson, K. O., & Masur, F. T. (1983). Psychological preparation for invasive medical dental procedures. *Journal of Behavioral Medicine, 6*, 1–40.

Andrasik, F., Blanchard, E. B., Neff, D. F., & Rodichok, L. D. (1984). Biofeedback and relaxation training for chronic headache: A controlled comparison of booster treatments and regular contacts for long-term maintenance. *Journal of Consulting and Clinical Psychology, 52*, 609–615.

Arkin, R. M., & Baumgardner, A. H. (1985). Self-handicapping. In J. H. Harvey & G. Weary (Eds.), *Attribution: Basic issues and applications* (pp. 169–202). New York: Academic Press.

Arkin, R. M., Lake, E. A., & Baumgardner, A. H. (1986). Shyness and self-presentation. In W. H. Jones, J. M. Cheek, & S. R. Briggs (Eds.), *Shyness: Perspectives on research and treatment* (pp. 189–203). New York: Plenum.

Asendorpf, J. (1987). Videotape reconstruction of emotions and cognitions related to shyness. *Journal of Personality and Social Psychology, 53*, 542–549.

Asendorpf, J. (1989). Shyness as a final common pathway for different kinds of inhibition. *Journal of Personality and Social Psychology, 57*, 481–492.

Aspinwall, L. G., & Taylor, S. E. (1992). Modeling cognitive adaptation: A longitudinal investigation of the impact of individual differences and coping in college adjustment and performance. *Journal of Personality and Social Psychology, 63*, 989–1003.

Atkeson, B., Calhoun, K., Resick, P., & Ellis, B. (1982). Victims of rape: Repeated assessment of depressive symptoms. *Journal of Consulting and Clinical Psychology, 50*, 96–102.

Atkinson, J. W. (1957). Motivational determinants of risk-taking behavior. *Psychological Review, 64*, 359–372.

Atkinson, J. W. (1964). *An introduction to motivation.* New York: Van Nostrand.

Atonovsky, A. (1979). *Health, stress, and coping.* San Francisco: Jossey-Bass.

Averill, J. R. (1979). Anger. In H. Howe & R. Dienstbier (Eds.), *Nebraska symposium on motivation* (Vol. 26, pp. 1–80). Lincoln: University of Nebraska Press.

Averill, J. R. (1983). Studies on anger and aggression: Implications for theories of emotion. *American Psychologist, 38*, 1145–1160.

Averill, J. R. (1993). Illusions of anger. In R. B. Felson & J. T. Tedeschi (Eds.), *Aggression and violence: Social interactionist perspectives* (pp. 171–192). Washington, DC: American Psychological Association.

Averill, J. R. (1994). Anger. In *Encyclopedia of human behavior* (Vol. 1, pp. 131–139). New York: Academic Press.

Averill, J. R., & Thomas-Knowles, C. (1991). Emotional creativity. In K. T. Strongman (Ed.), *International review of studies on emotion* (Vol. 1, pp. 269–299). London: Wiley.

Avison, W. R., & Turner, R. J. (1988). Stressful life events and depressive symptoms: Disaggregating the effects of acute stressors and chronic stressors. *Journal of Health and Social Behavior, 29*, 253–264.

Avorn, J., & Langer, E. J. (1982). Induced disability in nursing home patients: A controlled trial. *Journal of the American Geriatrics Society, 30*, 397–400.

Bachrach, K. M., & Zautra, A. J. (1985). Coping with a community stressor: The threat of a hazardous waste facility. *Journal of Health and Social Behavior, 26*, 127–141.

Bahrke, M. S., & Morgan, W. P. (1978). Anxiety reduction following exercise and meditation. *Cognitive Therapy and Research, 2*, 323–333.

Baldwin, M. W., Fehr, B., Keedian, E., Seidel, M., & Thompson, D. W. (1993). An exploration of the relational schemata underlying attachment styles: Self-report and lexical decision approaches. *Personality and Social Psychology Bulletin, 19,* 746–754.

Ball, S. G., Otto, M. W., Pollack, M. H., Uccello, R., & Rosenbaum, J. F. (1995). Differentiating social phobia and panic disorder: A test of core beliefs. *Cognitive Therapy and Research, 19,* 473–482.

Bandura, A. (1977). Self-efficacy: Toward a unifying theory of behavioral change. *Psychological Review, 84,* 191–215.

Bandura, A. (1982). Self-efficacy mechanism in human agency. *American Psychologist, 37,* 122–147.

Bandura, A. (1989). Human agency in social cognitive theory. *American Psychologist, 44,* 1175–1184.

Bandura, A., Adams, N. E., & Beyer, J. (1977). Cognitive processes mediating behavioral change. *Journal of Personality and Social Psychology, 35,* 125–139.

Bandura, A., O'Leary, A. O., Taylor, C. B., Gauthier, J., & Gossard, D. (1987). Perceived self-efficacy and pain control: Opiod and nonopiod mechanisms. *Journal of Personality and Social Psychology, 53,* 563–571.

Barber, T. X., Spanos, N. P., & Chaves, J. F. (1974). *Hypnotism, imagination, and human potentialities.* New York: Pergamon Press.

Barnett, P. A., & Gotlib, I. H. (1988). Psychosocial functioning and depression: Distinguishing among antecedents, concomitants, and consequences. *Psychological Bulletin, 104,* 97–126.

Baron, R. A., & Byrne, D. (1987). *Social psychology.* Boston: Allyn & Bacon.

Bartlett, J. (1982). *Familiar quotations.* Boston: Little, Brown.

Basedow, R. H. (1925). *The Australian aboriginal.* Adelaide, Australia.

Batchelor, W. F. (1988). AIDS 1988: The science and the limits of science. *American Psychologist, 43,* 853–858.

Baum, A. (1988, April). Disasters, natural & otherwise. *Psychology Today, 22,* 56–60.

Baum, A., Aiello, J., & Calesnick, L. (1978). Crowding and personal control: Social density and the development of learned helplessness. *Journal of Personality and Social Psychology, 36,* 1000–1011.

Baum, A., & Davis, G. (1980). Reducing the stress of high-density living: An architectural intervention. *Journal of Personality and Social Psychology, 38,* 471–481.

Baum, A., Fisher, J., & Solomon, S. (1981). Type of information, familiarity, and the reduction of crowding stress. *Journal of Personality and Social Psychology, 40,* 11–23.

Baum, A., Flemming, R., & Singer, J. E. (1983). Coping with victimization by technological disaster. *Journal of Social Issues, 39,* 119–140.

Baum, A., & Gatchel, R. J. (1981). Cognitive determinants of reaction to uncontrollable events: Development of reactance and learned helplessness. *Journal of Personality and Social Psychology, 40,* 1078–1089.

Baum, A., Gatchel, R. J., & Schaeffer, M. A. (1983). Emotional, behavioral, and physiological effects of chronic stress at Three Mile Island. *Journal of Consulting and Clinical Psychology, 51,* 565–572.

Baumeister, R. F. (1991a). *Escaping the self.* New York: Basic Books.

Baumeister, R. F. (1991b). *Meanings of life.* New York: Guilford.

Baumeister, R. F., Kahn, J., & Tice, D. M. (1990). Obesity as a self-handicapping strategy: Personality, selective attribution of problems, and weight loss. *Journal of Social Psychology, 130,* 121–123.

Baumeister, R. F., & Leary, M. R. (1995). The need to belong: Desire for interpersonal attachments as a fundamental human motivation. *Psychological Bulletin, 117,* 497–529.

Baumeister, R. F., & Scher, S. J. (1988). Self-defeating behavior patterns among normal individuals: Review and analysis of common self-destructive tendencies. *Psychological Bulletin, 104,* 3–22.

Baumeister, R. F., Stillwell, A., & Wotman, S. R. (1990). Victim and perpetrator accounts of interpersonal conflict: Autobiographical narratives about anger. *Journal of Personality and Social Psychology, 59,* 994–1005.

Baumgardner, A. H., Heppner, P. P., & Arkin, R. M. (1986). Role of causal attribution in personal problem solving. *Journal of Personality and Social Psychology, 50,* 636–643.

Baumgardner, A. H., Lake, E. A., & Arkin, R. M. (1985). Claiming mood as a self-handicap: The influence of spoiled and unspoiled public identities. *Personality and Social Psychology Bulletin, 11,* 349–357.

Bazerman, M. H. (1986, June). Why negotiations go wrong. *Psychology Today, 20,* 54–58.

Beck, A. T. (1972). *Depression: Causes and treatment.* Philadelphia: University of Pennsylvania Press. (Original work published 1967)

Beck, A. T. (1979). *Cognitive therapy and the emotional disorders.* New York: International Universities Press.

Beck, A. T., & Emery, G. (1990). *Anxiety disorders and phobias: A cognitive perspective.* New York: Basic Books.

Beck, A. T., Epstein, N., Brown, G., & Steer, R. A. (1988). An inventory for measuring clinical anxiety: Psychometric properties. *Journal of Consulting and Clinical Psychology, 56,* 893–897.

Beck, A. T., Freeman, A., & Associates. (1990). *Cognitive therapy of personality disorders.* New York: Guilford.

Beck, A. T., Rush, A. J., Shaw, B. F., & Emery, G. (1979). *Cognitive therapy of depression.* New York: Guilford.

Beck, A. T., Ward, C. H., Mendelson, M., Mock, J., & Erbaugh, J. (1961). An inventory for measuring depression. *Archives of General Psychiatry, 4,* 53–63.

Beck, A. T., Weissman, A., Lester, D., & Trexler, L. (1974). The measurement of pessimism: The hopelessness scale. *Journal of Consulting and Clinical Psychology, 42,* 861–865.

Becker, E. (1973). *The denial of death.* New York: Free Press.

Bednar, R. L., Wells, M. G., & Peterson, S. R. (1989). *Self-esteem: Paradoxes and implications in clinical theory and practice.* Washington, DC: American Psychological Association.

Bedrosian, R. C., & Beck, A. T. (1980). Principles of cognitive therapy. In M. J. Mahoney (Ed.), *Psychotherapy process: Current issues and future directions* (pp. 127–152). New York: Plenum.

Benson, H. (1976). *The relaxation response.* New York: Avon.

Ben-Zur, H., & Breznitz, S. (1991). What makes people angry: Dimensions of anger-evoking events. *Journal of Research in Personality, 25,* 1–22.

Berglas, S. (1990). Self-handicapping: Etiological and diagnostic considerations. In R. L. Higgins, C. R. Snyder, & S. Berglas (Eds.), *Self-handicapping: The paradox that isn't* (pp. 151–186). New York: Plenum.

Berglas, S., & Jones, E. E. (1978). Drug choice as a self-handicapping strategy in response to noncontingent success. *Journal of Personality and Social Psychology, 36,* 405–407.

Berscheid, E., & Fei, J. (1986). Romantic love and sexual jealousy. In G. Clanton & L. G. Smith (Eds.), *Jealousy* (pp. 101–109). Lanham, MD: University Press of America.

Bettelheim, B. (1943). Individual and mass behavior in extreme situations. *Journal of Abnormal and Social Psychology 38,* 417–452.

Bettelheim, B. (1960). *The informed heart—Autonomy in a mass age.* Glencoe, IL: Free Press.

Billings, A. G., Cronkite, R. C., & Moos, R. H. (1983). Social-environmental factors in unipolar depression: Comparisons of depressed patients and nondepressed controls. *Journal of Abnormal Psychology, 92,* 119–133.

Billings, A. G., & Moos, R. H. (1981). The role of coping responses and social resources in attenuating the stress of life events. *Journal of Behavioral Medicine, 4,* 139–157.

Billings, A. G., & Moos, R. H. (1982). Psychosocial theory and research on depression: An integrative framework and review. *Clinical Psychology Review, 2,* 213–237.

Billings, A. G., & Moos, R. H. (1984). Coping, stress, and social resources among adults with unipolar depression. *Journal of Personality and Social Psychology, 46,* 877–891.

Billings, A. G., & Moos, R. H. (1985). Life stressors and social resources affect posttreatment outcomes among depressed patients. *Journal of Abnormal Psychology, 94,* 140–153.

Blanchard, E. B., Andrasik, F., Neff, D. F., Arena, J. G., Ahles, T. A., Jurish, S. E., Pallmeyer, T. P., Saunders, N. L., Teders, S. J., Barron, K. D., & Rodichok, L. D. (1982). Biofeedback and relaxation training with three kinds of headache: Treatment effects and their prediction. *Journal of Consulting and Clinical Psychology, 50,* 562–575.

Blanchard, E. B., Andrasik, F., Neff, D. F., Saunders, N. L., Arena, J. G., Pallmeyer, T. P., Teders, S. J., & Jurish, S. E. (1983). Four process studies in the behavioral treatment of chronic headache. *Behavior Research and Therapy, 21,* 1–12.

Blankstein, K. R., Toner, B. B., & Flett, G. L. (1989). Test anxiety and the contents of consciousness: Thought-listing and endorsement measures. *Journal of Research in Personality, 23,* 269–286.

Blatt, S. J. (1995). The destructiveness of perfectionism. *American Psychologist, 50,* 1003–1020.

Blatt, S. J., Quinlan, D. M., Chevron, E. S., & McDonald, C. (1982). Dependency and self-criticism: Psychological dimensions of depression. *Journal of Consulting and Clinical Psychology, 50,* 113–124.

Block, A. R. (1982). Multidisciplinary treatment of chronic low back pain: A review. *Rehabilitation Psychology, 27,* 51–63.

Blumer, D., & Heilbronn, M. (1982). Chronic pain as a variant of depressive disease. *Journal of Nervous and Mental Disease, 170,* 381–406.

Bolger, N. (1990). Coping as a personality process: A prospective study. *Journal of Personality and Social Psychology, 59,* 525–537.

Bolger, N., DeLongis, A., Kessler, R. C., & Schilling, E. A. (1989). Effects of daily stress on negative mood. *Journal of Personality and Social Psychology, 57,* 808–818.

Bonica, J. J., & Black, R. G. (1974). The management of a pain clinic. In M. Swerdlow (Ed.), *Relief of intractable pain* (pp. 116–129). Amsterdam: Excerpta Medica.

Bornstein, R. F. (1993). *The dependent personality.* New York: Guilford.

Bornstein, R. F. (1995). Interpersonal dependency and physical illness: The mediating roles of stress and social support. *Journal of Social and Clinical Psychology, 14,* 225–243.

Bourne, E. J. (1995). *The anxiety & phobia workbook.* Oakland, CA: New Harbinger Publications.

Bradburn, N. (1969). *The structure of well-being.* Chicago: Aldine.

Bradbury, T. N., & Fincham, F. D. (1987). Affect and cognition in close relationships: Towards an integrative model. *Cognition and Emotion, 1,* 59–87.

Bradbury, T. N., & Fincham, F. D. (1988). Individual difference variables in close relationships: A contextual model of marriage as an integrative framework. *Journal of Personality and Social Psychology, 54,* 713–721.

Bradbury, T. N., & Fincham, F. D. (1992). Attributions and behavior in marital interaction. *Journal of Personality and Social Psychology, 63,* 613–628.

Bradbury, T. N., & Fincham, F. D. (1993). Assessing dysfunctional cognition in marriage: A reconsideration of the Relationship Belief Inventory. *Psychological Assessment, 5,* 92–101.

Braginsky, B., & Braginsky, D. (1967). Schizophrenic patients in the psychiatric interview: An experimental study of their effectiveness at manipulation. *Journal of Consulting Psychology, 31,* 546–551.

Braginsky, B., Braginsky, D., & Ring, K. (1969). *Methods of madness: The mental hospital as a last resort.* New York: Holt, Rinehart & Winston.

Braginsky, D., Grosse, M., & Ring, K. (1966). Controlling outcomes through impression management: An experimental study of the manipulative tactics of mental patients. *Journal of Consulting Psychology, 30,* 295–300.

Brantley, P. J., Dietz, L. S., McKnight, G. T., Jones, G. N., & Tulley, R. (1988). Convergence between the Daily Stress Inventory and endocrine measures of stress. *Journal of Consulting and Clinical Psychology, 56,* 549–551.

Brantley, P. J., Waggoner, C. D., Jones, G. N., & Rappaport, N. B. (1987). A daily stress inventory: Development, reliability, and validity. *Journal of Behavioral Medicine, 10,* 61–74.

Brehm, S. S. (1987). Coping after a relationship ends. In C. R. Snyder & C. E. Ford (Eds.), *Coping with negative life events* (pp. 191–212). New York: Plenum.

Brende, J. O., & Parson, E. R. (1985). *Vietnam veterans: The road to recovery.* New York: Plenum.

Brickman, P., Coates, D., & Janoff-Bulman, R. (1978). Lottery winners and accident victims: Is happiness relative? *Journal of Personality and Social Psychology, 36,* 917–927.

Brickman, P., & Hendricks, M. (1975). Expectancy for gradual or sudden improvement and reactions to success and failure. *Journal of Personality and Social Psychology, 32,* 893–900.

Brickman, P., Rabinowitz, V. C., Karuza, J., Coates, D., Cohn, E., & Kidder, L. (1982). Models of helping and coping. *American Psychologist, 37,* 368–384.

Brooks-Gunn, J., Boyer, C. B., & Hein, K. (1988). Preventing HIV infection and AIDS in children and adolescents: Behavioral research and intervention strategies. *American Psychologist, 43,* 958–964.

Brown, G. P., Hammen, C. L., Craske, M. G., & Wickens, T. D. (1995). Dimensions of dysfunctional attitudes as vulnerabilities to depressive symptoms. *Journal of Abnormal Psychology, 104,* 431–435.

Brown, J. D. (1991). Staying fit and staying well: Physical fitness as a moderator of life stress. *Journal of Personality and Social Psychology, 60,* 555–561.

Brown, J. D., & Siegel, J. M. (1988). Attributions for negative life events and depression: The role of perceived control. *Journal of Personality and Social Psychology, 54,* 316–322.

Brown, K. G., & Nicassio, P. M. (1987). Development of a questionnaire for the assessment of active and passive coping strategies in chronic pain patients. *Pain, 31,* 53–64.

Brown, K. G., Nicassio, P. M., & Wallston, K. A. (1989). Pain coping strategies and depression in rheumatoid arthritis. *Journal of Consulting and Clinical Psychology, 57,* 652–657.

Brown, R. A., & Lewinsohn, P. M. (1984). A psychoeducational approach to the treatment of depression: Comparison of group, individual, and minimal contact procedures. *Journal of Consulting and Clinical Psychology, 52,* 774–783.

Brownmiller, S. (1975). *Against our will: Men, women, and rape.* New York: Simon & Schuster.

Bruch, M. A., Gorsky, J. M., Collins, T. M., & Berger, P. A. (1989). Shyness and sociability reexamined: A multicomponent analysis. *Journal of Personality and Social Psychology, 57,* 904–915.

Bruch, M. A., & Pearl, L. (1995). Attributional style and symptoms of shyness in a heterosexual interaction. *Cognitive Therapy and Research, 19,* 91–107.

Bruhn, J. G., & Phillips, B. U. (1984). Measuring social support: A synthesis of current approaches. *Journal of Behavioral Medicine, 7,* 151–169.

Brunstein, J. (1993). Personal goals and subjective well-being: A longitudinal study. *Journal of Personality and Social Psychology, 65,* 1061–1070.

Bulman, R. J., & Wortman, C. B. (1977). Attributions of blame and coping in the "real world": Severe accident victims react to their lot. *Journal of Personality and Social Psychology, 35,* 351–363.

Burger, J. M. (1984). Desire for control, locus of control, and proneness to depression. *Journal of Personality, 52,* 71–89.

Burger, J. M. (1995). Individual differences in preference for solitude. *Journal of Research in Personality, 29,* 85–108.

Burgess, A., & Holstrom, L. (1979). *Rape crisis and recovery.* Bowie, MD: Brady.

Buss, D. M., Gomes, M., Higgins, D. S., & Lauterbach, K. (1987). Tactics of manipulation. *Journal of Personality and Social Psychology, 52,* 1219–1229.

Butler, R. N. (1963). The life review: An interpretation of reminiscence in the aged. *Psychiatry, Journal for the Study of Interpersonal Process, 26,* 65–67.

Buunk, B. P., Collins, R. L., Taylor, S. E., VanYperen, N., & Dakof, G. (1990). The affective consequences of social comparison: Either direction has its ups and downs. *Journal of Personality and Social Psychology, 59,* 1238–1249.

Callahan, E. J., & Burnette, M. M. (1989). Intervention for pathological grieving. *The Behavior Therapist, 12,* 153–157.

Cannon, W. B. (1929). *Bodily changes in pain, hunger, fear, and rage.* New York: Appleton.

Cannon, W. B. (1942). "Voodoo" death. *American Anthropologist, 44,* 169–181.

Cannon, W. B. (1957). "Voodoo" death. *Psychosomatic Medicine, 19,* 182–190.

Cantor, N., & Harlow, R. (1992). Social intelligence and personality: Flexible life task pursuit. In R. J. Sternberg & P. Ruzgis (Eds.), *Personality and intelligence.* Cambridge: Cambridge University Press.

Cantor, N., & Kihlstrom, J. F. (1987). *Personality and social intelligence.* Englewood Cliffs, NJ: Prentice-Hall.

Cantor, N., & Norem, J. K. (1989). Defensive pessimism and stress and coping. *Social Cognition, 7,* 92–112.

Cantor, N., Norem, J. K., Niedenthal, P. M., Langston, C. A., & Brower, A. M. (1987). Life tasks, self-concept ideals, and cognitive strategies in a life transition. *Journal of Personality and Social Psychology, 53,* 1178–1191.

Caplan, G. (1964). *Principles of preventive psychiatry.* New York: Basic Books.

Carver, C. S., Pozo, C., Harris, S. D., Noriega, V., Scheier, M. F., Robinson, D. S., Ketcham, A. S., Moffat, F. L., Jr., & Clark, K. C. (1993). How coping mediates the effect of optimism on distress: A study of women with early stage breast cancer. *Journal of Personality and Social Psychology, 65,* 375–390.

Carver, C. S., & Scheier, M. F. (1986). Analyzing shyness: A specific application of broader self-regulatory principles. In W. H. Jones, J. M. Cheek, & S. R. Briggs (Eds.), *Shyness: Perspectives on research and treatment* (pp. 173–185). New York: Plenum.

Carver, C. S., & Scheier, M. F. (1994). Situational coping and coping dispositions in a stressful transaction. *Journal of Personality and Social Psychology, 66,* 184–195.

Carver, C. S., Scheier, M. F., & Weintraub, J. K. (1989). Assessing coping strategies: A theoretically based approach. *Journal of Personality and Social Psychology, 56,* 267–283.

Catanzaro, S. J., & Greenwood, G. (1994). Expectancies for negative mood regulation, coping, and dysphoria among college students. *Journal of Counseling Psychology, 41*, 34–44.

Catanzaro, S. J., & Mearns, J. (1990). Measuring generalized expectancies for negative mood regulation: Initial scale development and implications. *Journal of Personality Assessment, 54*, 546–563.

Centers for Disease Control. (1992, May). *HIV/AIDS surveillance.* Atlanta: Department of Health and Human Services.

Chambless, D. L., & Gracely, E. J. (1989). Fear of fear and the anxiety disorders. *Cognitive Therapy and Research, 13*, 9–20.

Chapin, M., & Dyck, D. G. (1976). Persistence in children's reading behavior as a function of N length and attribution retraining. *Journal of Personality and Social Psychology, 35*, 511–515.

Chaves, J. F., & Barber, T. X. (1974). Cognitive strategies, experimenter modeling, and expectation in the attenuation of pain. *Journal of Abnormal Psychology, 83*, 356–363.

Cheek, J. M., & Buss, A. H. (1981). The influence of shyness on loneliness in a new situation. *Personality and Social Psychology Bulletin, 7*, 572–577.

Cheek, J. M., Melchior, L. A., & Carpentieri, A. M. (1986). Shyness and self-concept. In L. M. Hartman & K. R. Blankstein (Eds.), *Perception of self in emotional disorder and psychotherapy* (pp. 113–131). New York: Plenum.

Chesney, M. A., & Folkman, S. (1994). Psychological impact of HIV disease and implications for intervention. *Psychiatric Clinics of North America, 17*, 163–182.

Christensen, A. J., Benotsch, E. G., Lawton, W. J., & Wiebe, J. S. (1995). Coping with treatment-related stress: Effects on patient adherence in hemodialysis. *Journal of Consulting and Clinical Psychology, 63*, 454–459.

Christensen, L., & Duncan, K. (1995). Distinguishing depressed from nondepressed individuals using energy and psychosocial variables. *Journal of Consulting and Clinical Psychology, 63*, 495–498.

Chwalisz, K., Altmaier, E. M., & Russell, D. W. (1992). Casual attributions, self-efficacy cognitions, and coping with stress. *Journal of Social and Clinical Psychology, 11*, 377–400.

Clark, M., & Anderson, B. C. (1967). *Culture and aging.* Springfield, IL: Charles C. Thomas.

Clifford, P. A., Tan, S., & Gorsuch, R. L. (1991). Efficacy of a self-directed behavioral health change program: Weight, body composition, cardiovascular fitness, blood pressure, health risk, and psychosocial mediating variables. *Journal of Behavioral Medicine, 14*, 303–323.

Cobb, S. (1976). Social support as a moderator of life stress. *Psychosomatic Medicine, 38*, 300–314.

Cogan, R., Cogan, D., Waltz, W., & McCue, M. (1987). Effect of laughter and relaxation on discomfort thresholds. *Journal of Behavioral Medicine, 10*, 139–144.

Cohen, D. R., Sherrod, D. R., & Clark, M. S. (1986). Social skills and the stress-protective role of social support. *Journal of Personality and Social Psychology, 50*, 963–973.

Cohen, S. (1992). Stress, social support, and disorder. In H. O. F. Veiel & U. Baumann (Eds.), *The meaning and measurement of social support* (pp. 109–124). New York: Hemisphere.

Cohen, S., Evans, G. W., Stokols, D., & Krantz, D. S. (1986). *Behavior, health, and environmental stress.* New York: Plenum.

Cohen, S., & Hoberman, H. M. (1983). Positive events and social supports as buffers of life change stress. *Journal of Applied Social Psychology, 13*, 99–125.

Cohen, S., & McKay, G. (1984). Social support, stress, and the buffering hypothesis: A theoretical analysis. In A. Baum, J. E. Singer, & S. E. Taylor (Eds.), *Handbook of psychology and health, Vol. 4.* Hillsdale, NJ: Erlbaum.

Cohen, S., & Syme, L. (Eds.). (1985). *Social support and health.* New York: Academic Press.

Cohen, S., Tyrrell, D. A. J., & Smith, A. P. (1991). Psychological stress and susceptibility to the common cold. *New England Journal of Medicine, 325*, 606–612.

Cohen, S., Tyrrell, D. A. J., & Smith, A. P. (1993). Negative life events, perceived stress, negative affect, and susceptibility to the common cold. *Journal of Personality and Social Psychology, 64*, 131–140.

Cohen, S., & Williamson, G. (1991). Stress and infectious disease in humans. *Psychological Bulletin, 109*, 5–24.

Collins, D. L., Baum, A., & Singer, J. E. (1983). Coping with chronic stress at Three Mile Island: Psychological and biochemical evidence. *Health Psychology, 2*, 149–166.

Collins, K. W., Dansereau, D. F., Garland, J. C., Holley, C. D., & McDonald, B. A. (1981). Control of concentration during academic tasks. *Journal of Educational Psychology, 73*, 122–128.

Collins, N. L., & Read, S. J. (1990). Adult attachment, working models, and relationship quality in dating couples. *Journal of Personality and Social Psychology, 58,* 644–663.

Collins, R. L., Taylor, S. E., & Skokan, L. A. (1990). A better world or a shattered vision? Changes in life perspectives following victimization. *Social Cognition, 8,* 263–285.

Commerford, M. C., Gular, E., Orr, D. A., Reznikoff, M., & O'Dowd, M. A. (1994). Coping and psychological distress in women with HIV/AIDS. *Journal of Community Psychology, 22,* 224–230.

Conger, J. C., & Farrell, A. D. (1981). Behavioral components of heterosocial skills. *Behavior Therapy, 12,* 41–55.

Conn, M. K., & Peterson, C. (1989). Social support: Seek and ye shall find. *Journal of Social and Personal Relationships, 6,* 345–358.

Conti, R., Amabile, T. M., & Pollak, S. (1995). The positive impact of creative activity: Effects of creative task engagement and motivational focus on college students' learning. *Personality and Social Psychology Bulletin, 21,* 1107–1116.

Cooper, H., Okamura, L., & McNeil, P. (1995). Situation and personality correlates of psychological well-being: Social activity and personal control. *Journal of Research in Personality, 29,* 395–417.

Cooper, N. A., & Clum, G. A. (1989). Imaginal flooding as a supplementary treatment for PTSD in combat veterans. *Behavior Therapy, 20,* 381–391.

Costa, P. T., & McCrae, R. R. (1990). Personality disorders and the five-factor model of personality. *Journal of Personality Disorders, 4,* 362–371.

Costa, P. T., & McCrae, R. R. (1992). Normal personality assessment in clinical practice: The NEO Personality Inventory. *Psychological Assessment, 4,* 5–13.

Costa, P. T., Metter, E. J., & McCrae, R. R. (1994). Personality stability and its contribution to successful aging. *Journal of Geriatric Psychiatry, 27,* 41–59.

Courneya, K. S. (1995). Understanding readiness for regular physical activity in older individuals: An application of the theory of planned behavior. *Health Psychology, 14,* 80–87.

Cox, H. G. (1988). *Later life: The realities of aging.* Englewood Cliffs, NJ: Prentice-Hall.

Cox, H. G., Sekhon, G., & Norman, C. (1978). Social characteristics of the elderly in Indiana. In *Proceedings/Indiana Academy of the Social Sciences* (Vol. 13, pp. 186–197).

Cox, V. C., Paulus, P. B., & McCain, G. (1984). Prison crowding research. *American Psychologist, 39,* 1148–1160.

Coyne, J. C., Aldwin, C., & Lazarus, R. S. (1981). Depression and coping in stressful life events. *Journal of Abnormal Psychology, 90,* 439–447.

Coyne, J. C., & Gotlib, I. H. (1983). The role of cognition in depression: A critical appraisal. *Psychological Bulletin, 94,* 472–505.

Coyne, J. C., Kessler, R. C., Tal, M., Turnbull, J., Wortman, C. B., & Greden, J. F. (1987). Living with a depressed person. *Journal of Consulting and Clinical Psychology, 55,* 347–352.

Crandall, J. E. (1980). Adler's concept of social interest: Theory, measurement, and implications for adjustment. *Journal of Personality and Social Psychology, 39,* 481–495.

Crandall, J. E. (1984). Social interest as a moderator of life stress. *Journal of Personality and Social Psychology, 47,* 164–174.

Crandall, J. E., & Putnam, E. L. (1980). Social interest and psychological well-being. *Journal of Individual Psychology, 36,* 151–168.

Crews, D. J., & Landers, D. M. (1987). A meta-analytic review of aerobic fitness and reactivity to psychosocial stressors. *Medical Science and Sports Exercise, 19,* 114–120.

Crook, J., Rideout, E., & Browne, G. (1984). The prevalence of pain complaints in a general population. *Pain, 18,* 299–314.

Cunningham, M. (1989). Reactions to heterosexual opening lines: Female selectivity and male responsiveness. *Personality and Social Psychology Bulletin, 15,* 27–41.

Cutrona, C. E. (1986). Objective determinants of perceived social support. *Journal of Personality and Social Psychology, 50,* 349–355.

Czajkowski, S. M., Hindelang, R. D., Dembroski, T. M., Mayerson, S. E., Parks, E. B., & Hjolland, J. C. (1990). Aerobic fitness, psychological characteristics, and cardiovascular reactivity to stress. *Health Psychology, 9,* 676–692.

Dakof, G. A., & Taylor, S. E. (1990). Victim's perceptions of social support: What is helpful from whom? *Journal of Personality and Social Psychology, 58,* 80–89.

Davidson, L. M., & Baum, A. (1986). Chronic stress and posttraumatic stress disorders. *Journal of Consulting and Clinical Psychology, 54,* 303–308.

Davis, C. G., Lehman, D. R., Wortman, C. B., Silver, R. C., & Thompson, S. C. (1995). The undoing of traumatic life events. *Personality and Social Psychology Bulletin, 21,* 109–124.

Davis, D., & Holtgraves, T. (1984). Perceptions of unresponsive others: Attributions, attraction, understandability, and memory of their utterances. *Journal of Experimental Social Psychology, 20,* 383–408.

Davis, D., & Perkowitz, W. T. (1979). Consequences of responsiveness in dyadic interaction: Effects of probability of response and proportion of content-related responses on interpersonal attraction. *Journal of Personality and Social Psychology, 37,* 534–550.

Davis, K. (1986). Jealousy and sexual property. In G. Clanton & L. G. Smith (Eds.), *Jealousy* (pp. 129–134). Lanham, MD: University Press of America.

Davis, M. H., & Oathout, H. A. (1987). Maintenance of satisfaction in romantic relationships: Empathy and relational competence. *Journal of Personality and Social Psychology, 53,* 397–410.

Deci, E. L., & Ryan, R. (1985). *Intrinsic motivation and self-determination in human behavior.* New York: Plenum.

Deffenbacher, J. L. (1980). Worry and emotionality in test anxiety. In I. G. Sarason (Ed.), *Test anxiety: Theory, research, and applications* (pp. 111–128). Hillsdale, NJ: Erlbaum.

Deffenbacher, J. L., Demm, P. M., & Brandon, A. D. (1986). High general anger: Correlates and treatments. *Behaviour Research & Therapy, 24,* 481–489.

Deffenbacher, J. L., & Stark, R. S. (1992). Relaxation and cognitive-relaxation treatments of general anger. *Journal of Counseling Psychology, 39,* 158–167.

Deffenbacher, J. L., & Suinn, R. M. (1985). Concepts and treatment of the generalized anxiety syndrome. In L. M. Ascher & L. Michelson (Eds.), *International handbook of assessment and treatment of anxiety disorders.* New York: Guilford.

Deffenbacher, J. L., Thwaites, G. A., Wallace, T. L., & Oetting, E. R. (1994). Social skills and cognitive-relaxation approaches to general anger reduction. *Journal of Counseling psychology, 41,* 386–396.

Deffenbacher, J. L., Zwemer, W. A., Whisman, M. A., Hill, R. A., & Sloan, R. D. (1986). Irrational beliefs and anxiety. *Cognitive Therapy and Research, 10,* 281–292.

DeGree, C. E., & Snyder, C. R. (1985). Adler's psychology (of use) today: Personal history of traumatic life events as a self-handicapping strategy. *Journal of Personality and Social Psychology, 48,* 1512–1519.

DeLongis, A., Coyne, J. C., Dakof, G., Folkman, S., & Lazarus, R. S. (1982). Relationship of daily hassles, uplifts, and major life events to health status. *Health Psychology, 1,* 119–136.

DeLongis, A., Folkman, S., & Lazarus, R. S. (1988). The impact of daily stress on health and mood: Psychological and social resources as mediators. *Journal of Personality and Social Psychology, 54,* 86–495.

DePaulo, B. M., Dull, W. R., Greenberg, J. M., & Swain, G. W. (1989). Are shy people reluctant to ask for help? *Journal of Personality and Social Psychology, 56,* 834–844.

DesJarlais, D. C., & Friedman, S. R. (1988). The psychology of preventing AIDS among intravenous drug users: A social learning conceptualization. *American Psychologist, 43,* 865–870.

deVries, H. A. (1983). Physiology of exercise and aging. In D. S. Woodruff & J. E. Birren (Eds.), *Aging: Scientific perspectives and social issues* (2nd ed., pp. 285–304). Pacific Grove, CA: Brooks/Cole.

Diener, C. I., & Dweck, C. S. (1978). An analysis of learned helplessness: Continuous changes in performance, strategy, and achievement cognitions following failure. *Journal of Personality and Social Psychology, 36,* 451–462.

Diener, E. (1984). Subjective well-being. *Psychological Bulletin, 95,* 542–575.

Diener, E., Colvin, C. R., Pavot, W. G., & Allman, A. (1991). The psychic costs of intense positive affect. *Journal of Personality and Social Psychology, 61,* 492–503.

Diener, E., Emmons, R. A., Larsen, R. J., & Griffin, S. (1985). The Satisfaction with Life Scale. *Journal of Personality Assessment, 49,* 71–75.

Diener, E., Sandvik, E., & Pavot, W. (1989). Happiness is the frequency, not intensity, of positive versus negative affect. In F. Strack, M. Argyle, & N. Schwarz (Eds.), *The social psychology of subjective well-being* (pp. 119–139). New York: Pergamon.

Dimsdale, J. E. (1974). The coping behavior of Nazi concentration camp survivors. *American Journal of Psychiatry, 131,* 792–797.

Dion, K. K., & Dion, K. L. (1993). Individualistic and collectivistic perspectives on gender and the cultural context of love and intimacy. *Journal of Social Issues, 49,* 53–69.

Dohrenwend, B. S., & Dohrenwend, B. P. (Eds.). (1974). *Stressful life events: Their nature and effects.* New York: Wiley.

Doka, K. J. (Ed.). (1989). *Disenfranchised grief: Recognizing hidden sorrow.* Lexington, MA: Lexington Books.

Dolce, J. J. (1987). Self-efficacy and disability beliefs in behavioral treatment of pain. *Behavior Research and Therapy, 25,* 289–299.

Downey, G., Silver, R. C., & Wortman, C. B. (1990). Reconsidering the attribution-adjustment relation following a major negative event: Coping with the loss of a child. *Journal of Personality and Social Psychology, 59,* 925–940.

Doyne, E. J., Chambless, D. L., & Beutler, L. E. (1983). Aerobic exercise as a treatment for depression in women. *Behavior Therapy, 14,* 434–440.

Dreyer, P. H. (1986). Postretirement life satisfaction. In S. Spacapon & S. Oskamp (Eds.), *The social psychology of aging* (pp. 109–133). Newbury Park, CA: Sage.

Dunkel-Schetter, C., Feinstein, L. G., Taylor, S. E., & Falke, R. L. (1992). Patterns of coping with cancer. *Health Psychology, 11,* 79–87.

Dunkel-Schetter, C., Folkman, S., & Lazarus, R. S. (1987). Correlates of social support receipt. *Journal of Personality and Social Psychology, 53,* 71–80.

Dweck, C. S. (1975). The role of expectations and attributions in the alleviation of learned helplessness. *Journal of Personality and Social Psychology, 31,* 674–685.

Dweck, C. S. (1991). Self-theories and goals: Their role in motivation, personality, and development. In R. A. Dienstbier (Ed.), *Nebraska symposium on motivation* (pp. 200–235). Lincoln: University of Nebraska Press.

Dweck, C. S., & Bush, E. S. (1976). Sex differences in learned helplessness: I. Differential debilitation with peer and adult evaluators. *Developmental Psychology, 12,* 147–156.

Dweck, C. S., Chiu, C., & Hong, Y. (1995). Implicit theories and their role in judgments and reactions: A world from two perspectives. *Psychological Inquiry, 6,* 267–285.

Dweck, C. S., Davidson, W., Nelson, S., & Enna, B. (1978). Sex differences in learned helplessness: II. The contingencies of evaluative feedback in the classroom. III. An experimental analysis. *Developmental Psychology, 14,* 268–276.

Dweck, C. S., & Gilliard, D. (1975). Expectancy statements as determinants of reactions to failure: Sex differences in persistence and expectancy change. *Journal of Personality and Social Psychology, 32,* 1077–1084.

Dweck, C. S., Goetz, T. E., & Strauss, N. L. (1980). Sex differences in learned helplessness: IV. An experimental and naturalistic study of failure generalization and its mediators. *Journal of Personality and Social Psychology, 38,* 441–452.

Dweck, C. S., & Leggett, E. L. (1988). A social-cognitive approach to motivation and personality. *Psychological Review, 95,* 256–273.

Dweck, C. S., & Reppucci, N. D. (1973). Learned helplessness and reinforcement responsibility in children. *Journal of Personality and Social Psychology, 25,* 109–116.

D'Zurilla, T. J., & Nezu, A. M. (1982). Social problem solving in adults. In P. C. Kendall (Ed.), *Advances in cognitive-behavior research and therapy* (Vol. 1, pp. 202–274). New York: Academic Press.

D'Zurilla, T. J., & Nezu, A. M. (1990). Development and preliminary evaluation of the Social Problem-Solving Inventory. *Psychological Assessment, 2,* 156–163.

Eaves, G., & Rush, A. J. (1984). Cognitive patterns in symptomatic and remitted unipolar major depression. *Journal of Abnormal Psychology, 93,* 31–40.

Edens, J. L., & Gil, K. M. (1995). Experimental induction of pain: Utility in the study of clinical pain. *Behavior Therapy, 26,* 197–216.

Ehrlich, P. (1988). Treatment issues in the psychotherapy of Holocaust survivors. In J. P. Wilson, Z. Harel, & B. Kahana (Eds.), *Human adaptation to extreme stress: From the Holocaust to Vietnam* (pp. 285–303). New York: Plenum.

Eidelson, R. J., & Epstein, N. (1982). Cognition and relationship maladjustment: Development of a measure of dysfunctional relationship beliefs. *Journal of Consulting and Clinical Psychology, 50,* 715–720.

Eisler, R. M., & Frederiksen, L. W. (1980). *Perfecting social skills: A guide to interpersonal behavior*. New York: Plenum.

Elder, G. H., Jr., & Clipp, E. C. (1988). Combat experience, comradeship, and psychological health. In J. P. Wilson, Z. Harel, & B. Kahana (Eds.), *Human adaptation to extreme stress: From the Holocaust to Vietnam* (pp. 131–156). New York: Plenum.

Elder, G. H., Jr., & Clipp, E. C. (1989). Combat experience and emotional health: Impairment and resilience in later life. *Journal of Personality, 57*, 311–341.

Elliott, E. S., & Dweck, C. S. (1988). Goals: An approach to motivation and achievement. *Journal of Personality and Social Psychology, 54*, 5–12.

Elliott, T. R., Witty, T. E., Herrick, S., & Hoffman, J. T. (1991). Negotiating reality after physical loss: Hope, depression, and disability. *Journal of Personality and Social Psychology, 61*, 608–613.

Ellis, A. (1962). *Reason and emotion in psychotherapy*. New York: Lyle Stuart.

Ellis, A. (1985). *Overcoming resistance: Rational-emotive therapy with difficult clients*. New York: Springer.

Ellis, A. (1987a). A sadly neglected cognitive element in depression. *Cognitive Therapy and Research, 11*, 121–146.

Ellis, A. (1987b). The impossibility of achieving consistently good mental health. *American Psychologist, 42*, 364–375.

Ellis, A., & Harper, R. A. (1975). *A new guide to rational living*. Englewood Cliffs, NJ: Prentice-Hall.

Ellis, E. M., Atkeson, B. M., & Calhoun, K. S. (1981). An assessment of long-term reaction to rape. *Journal of Abnormal Psychology, 90*, 263–266.

Emmons, R. A. (1986). Personal strivings: An approach to personality and subjective well-being. *Journal of Personality and Social Psychology, 51*, 1058–1068.

Emmons, R. A. (1992). Abstract versus concrete goals: Personal striving level, physical illness, and psychological well-being. *Journal of Personality and Social Psychology, 62*, 292–300.

Emmons, R. A. (1995). Striving and feeling: Personal goals and subjective well-being. In P. M. Gollwitzer & J. A. Bargh (Eds.), *The psychology of action: Linking motivation and cognition to behavior* (pp. 313–337). New York: Guilford.

Emmons, R. A., & Colby, P. M. (1995). Emotional conflict and well-being: Relation to perceived availability, daily utilization, and observer reports of social support. *Journal of Personality and Social Psychology, 68*, 947–959.

Emmons, R. A., & King, L. A. (1988). Conflict among personal strivings: Immediate and long-term implications for psychological and physical well-being. *Journal of Personality and Social Psychology, 54*, 1040–1048.

Endler, N. S., Kantor, L., & Parker, J. D. A. (1994). State-trait coping, state-trait anxiety and academic performance. *Personality and Individual Differences, 16*, 663–670.

Endler, N. S., & Parker, J. D. A. (1990). Multidimensional assessment of coping: A critical evaluation. *Journal of Personality and Social Psychology, 58*, 844–854.

Endler, N. S., & Parker, J. D. A. (1994). Assessment of multidimensional coping: Task, emotion, and avoidance strategies. *Psychological Assessment, 6*, 50–60.

Epstein, N., Pretzer, J. L., & Fleming, B. (1987). The role of cognitive appraisal in self-reports of marital communication. *Behavior Therapy, 18*, 51–69.

Epstein, S. (1991). The self-concept, the traumatic neurosis, and the structure of personality. In D. Ozer, J. M. Healy, Jr., & A. J. Stewart (Eds.), *Perspectives in personality* (Vol. 3, Part A, pp. 63–91). London: Jessica Kingsley.

Epstein, S. (1992a). Constructive thinking and mental and physical well-being. In L. Montada, S. Filipp, & M. J. Lerner (Eds.), *Life crises and experiences of loss in adulthood* (pp. 385–409). Hillsdale, NJ: Erlbaum.

Epstein, S. (1992b). Coping ability, negative self-evaluation, and overgeneralization: Experiment and theory. *Journal of Personality and Social Psychology, 62*, 826–836.

Epstein, S., & Katz, L. (1992). Coping ability, stress, productive load, and symptoms. *Journal of Personality and Social Psychology, 62*, 813–825.

Epstein, S., & Meier, P. (1989). Constructive thinking: A broad coping variable with specific components. *Journal of Personality and Social Psychology, 57*, 332–350.

Erikson, E. H. (1963). *Childhood and society* (2nd ed.). New York: Norton.

Erikson, J. M., Erikson, E. H., & Kivnick, H. (1986). *Vital involvement in old age*. New York: Norton.

Ewart, C. K., Taylor, C. B., Kraemer, H. C., & Agras, W. S. (1984). Reducing blood pressure reactivity during interpersonal conflict: Effects of marital communication training. *Behavior Therapy, 15*, 473–484.

Falbo, T. (1977). Multidimensional scaling of power strategies. *Journal of Personality and Social Psychology, 35*, 537–547.

Farthing, G. W., Venturino, M., & Brown, S. W. (1984). Suggestion and distraction in the control of pain: Test of two hypotheses. *Journal of Abnormal Psychology, 93*, 266–276.

Fawzy, F. I., Fawzy, N. W., Arndt, L. A., & Pasnau, R. O. (1995). Critical review of psychosocial interventions in cancer care. *Archives of General Psychiatry, 52*, 100–113.

Feeney, J. A., & Noller, P. (1990). Attachment style as a predictor of adult romantic relationships. *Journal of Personality and Social Psychology, 58*, 281–291.

Feifel, H., Strack, S., & Nagy, V. T. (1987). Coping strategies and associated features of medically ill patients. *Psychosomatic Medicine, 49*, 616–625.

Feist, G. J., Bodner, T. E., Jacobs, J. F., Miles, M., & Tan, V. (1995). Integrating top-down and bottom-up structural models of subjective well-being: A longitudinal investigation. *Journal of Personality and Social Psychology, 68*, 138–150.

Feldman-Summers, S., Gordon, P. E., & Meagher, J. R. (1979). The impact of rape on sexual satisfaction. *Journal of Abnormal Psychology, 88*, 101–105.

Felton, B. J., & Revenson, T. A. (1984). Coping with chronic illness: A study of illness controllability and the influence of coping strategies on psychological adjustment. *Journal of Consulting and Clinical Psychology, 52*, 343–353.

Ferrari, J. R. (1991). Self-handicapping by procrastinators: Protecting self-esteem, social-esteem, or both? *Journal of Research in Personality, 25*, 245–261.

Ferrari, J. R. (1992). Procrastinators and perfect behavior: An exploratory factor analysis of self-presentation, self-awareness, and self-handicapping components. *Journal of Research in Personality, 26*, 75–84.

Fincham, F. D. (1985). Attribution processes in distressed and nondistressed couples: 2. Responsibility for marital problems. *Journal of Abnormal Psychology, 94*, 183–190.

Fincham, F. D., Beach, S. R., & Baucom, D. H. (1987). Attributional processes in distressed and nondistressed couples: 4. Self-partner attribution differences. *Journal of Personality and Social Psychology, 52*, 739–748.

Fincham, F. D., Beach, S. R., & Nelson, G. (1987). Attribution processes in distressed and nondistressed couples: 3. Causal and responsibility attributions for spouse behavior. *Cognitive Therapy and Research, 11*, 71–85.

Fincham, F. D., & Bradbury, T. N. (1988). The impact of attributions in marriage: Empirical and conceptual foundations. *British Journal of Clinical Psychology 27*, 77–90.

Fincham, F. D., & Bradbury, T. N. (1992). Assessing attributions in marriage: The Relationship Attribution Measure. *Journal of Personality and Social Psychology, 62*, 457–468.

Fincham, F. D., & Bradbury, T. N. (1993). Marital satisfaction, depression, and attributions: A longitudinal analysis. *Journal of Personality and Social Psychology, 64*, 442–452.

Fincham, F. D., & O'Leary, K. D. (1983). Causal inferences for spouse behavior in maritally distressed and nondistressed couples. *Journal of Social and Clinical Psychology, 1*, 42–57.

Fisher, J. D. (1988). Possible effects of reference group-based social influence on AIDS-risk behavior and AIDS prevention. *American Psychologist, 43*, 914–920.

Fitness, J., & Fletcher, G. J. O. (1993). Love, hate, anger, and jealousy in close relationships: A prototype and cognitive appraisal analysis. *Journal of Personality and Social Psychology, 65*, 942–958.

Flanigan, B. (1992). *Forgiving the unforgivable.* New York: Macmillan.

Fleishman, J. A., & Fogel, B. (1994). Coping and depressive symptoms among people with AIDS. *Health Psychology, 13*, 156–169.

Flora, J. A., & Thoresen, C. E. (1988). Reducing the risk of AIDS in adolescents. *American Psychologist, 43*, 965–970.

Foa, E. B., Hearst-Ikeda, D., & Perry, K. J. (1995). Evaluation of a brief cognitive-behavioral program for the prevention of chronic PTSD in recent assault victims. *Journal of Consulting and Clinical Psychology, 63*, 948–955.

Folkins, C. H., & Sime, W. E. (1981). Physical fitness training and mental health. *American Psychologist, 36*, 373–389.

Folkman, S. (1984). Personal control and stress and coping processes: A theoretical analysis. *Journal of Personality and Social Psychology, 46*, 839–852.

Folkman, S., Chesney, M. A., & Christopher-Richards, A. (1994). Stress and coping in caregiving partners of men with AIDS. *Psychiatric Clinics of North America, 17*, 35–53.

Folkman, S., Chesney, M. A., Cooke, M., Boccellari, A., & Collette, L. (1994). Caregiver burden in HIV-positive and HIV-negative partners of men with AIDS. *Journal of Consulting and Clinical Psychology, 62*, 746–756.

Folkman, S., Chesney, M. A., Pollack, L., & Coates, T. (1993). Stress, control, coping, and depressed mood in human immunodeficiency virus-positive and -negative gay men in San Francisco. *Journal of Nervous and Mental Disease, 181*, 409–416.

Folkman, S., Chesney, M. A., Pollack, L., & Phillips, C. (1992). Stress, coping, and high-risk sexual behavior. *Health Psychology, 11*, 218–222.

Folkman, S., & Lazarus, R. S. (1980). An analysis of coping in a middle-aged community sample. *Journal of Health and Social Behavior, 21*, 219–239.

Folkman, S., & Lazarus, R. S. (1988). Coping as a mediator of emotion. *Journal of Personality and Social Psychology, 46*, 839–852.

Folkman, S., Lazarus, R. S., Dunkel-Schetter, C., DeLongis, A., & Gruen, R. J. (1986). Dynamics of a stressful encounter: Cognitive appraisal, coping, and encounter outcomes. *Journal of Personality and Social Psychology, 50*, 992–1003.

Folkman, S., Lazarus, R. S., Gruen, R. J., & DeLongis, A. (1986). Appraisal, coping, health status, and psychological symptoms. *Journal of Personality and Social Psychology, 50*, 571–579.

Folkman, S., & Stein, N. L. (1996). A goal-process approach to analyzing narrative memories for AIDS related stressful events. In N. L. Stein, P. A. Ornstein, B. Tversky, & C. Brainerd (Eds.), *Memory for every day and emotional events*. Hillsdale, NJ: Erlbaum.

Follick, M. J., Ahern, D. K., & Aberger, E. W. (1985). Development of an audiovisual taxonomy of pain behavior: Reliability and discriminant validity. *Health Psychology, 4*, 555–568.

Follick, M. J., Ahern, D. K., Attanasio, V., & Riley, J. F. (1985). Chronic pain programs: Current aims, strategies, and needs. *Annals of Behavioral Medicine, 7*, 17–20.

Follick, M. J., Ahern, D. K., & Laser-Wolston, N. (1984). Evaluation of a daily activity diary for chronic pain patients. *Pain, 19*, 373–382.

Fontana, A. F., Klein, E. B., Lewis, E., & Levine, L. (1968). Presentation of self in mental illness. *Journal of Consulting and Clinical Psychology, 32*, 110–119.

Fordyce, M. W. (1977). Development of a program to increase personal happiness. *Journal of Counseling Psychology, 24*, 511–521.

Fordyce, M. W. (1981). *The psychology of happiness: Fourteen fundamentals*. Fort Myers, FL: Cypress Lake Media.

Fordyce, M. W. (1983). A program to increase happiness: Further studies. *Journal of Counseling Psychology, 30*, 483–498.

Fordyce, W. E. (1976). *Behavioral methods in chronic pain and illness*. St. Louis: C. V. Mosby.

Fordyce, W. E. (1988). Pain and suffering: A reappraisal. *American Psychologist, 43*, 276–283.

Fordyce, W. E., Brockway, J., Bergman, J. A., & Spengler, D. (1986). Acute back pain: A control-group comparison of behavioral vs. traditional management methods. *Journal of Behavioral Medicine, 9*, 127–140.

Fordyce, W. E., Lanske, D., Calsyn, D. A., Shelton, J. L., Stolov, W. C., & Rock, D. L. (1984). Pain measurement and pain behavior. *Pain, 18*, 53–69.

Frank, J. D. (1973). *Persuasion and healing* (rev. ed.). Baltimore: Johns Hopkins University Press.

Frank, R. G., Umlauf, R. L., Wonderlich, S. A., Askanazi, G. S., Buckelew, S. P., & Elliott, T. R. (1987). Differences in coping styles among persons with spinal cord injury: A cluster-analytic approach. *Journal of Consulting and Clinical Psychology, 45*, 206–215.

Frankel, A., & Prentice-Dunn, S. (1990). Loneliness and the processing of self-relevant information. *Journal of Social and Clinical Psychology, 9*, 303–315.

Frankl, V. E. (1967). *Man's search for meaning: An introduction to logotherapy*. Boston: Beacon Press.

Frankl, V. E. (1969). *The will to meaning: Foundations and applications of logotherapy*. New York: World.

Frazier, P. A. (1991). Self-blame as a mediator of postrape depressive symptoms. *Journal of Social and Clinical Psychology, 10*, 47–57.

Freemont, J., & Craighead, L. W. (1987). Aerobic exercise and cognitive therapy in the treatment of dysphoric moods. *Cognitive Therapy and Research, 11*, 241–251.

Friedman, H. S., Tucker, J. S., Tomlinson-Keasey, C., Schwartz, J. E., Wingard, D. L., & Criqui, M. H. (1993). Does childhood personality predict longevity? *Journal of Personality and Social Psychology, 65*, 176–185.

Frost, R. O., Marten, P., Lahart, C., & Rosenblate, R. (1990). The dimensions of perfectionism. *Cognitive Therapy and Research, 14*, 449–468.

Frost, R. O., Turcotte, T. A., Heimberg, R. G., Mattia, J. I., Holt, C. S., & Hope, D. A. (1995). Reactions to mistakes among subjects high and low in perfectionistic concern over mistakes. *Cognitive Therapy and Research, 19*, 195–205.

Fuchs, C. Z., & Rehm, L. P. (1977). A self-control behavior therapy program for depression. *Journal of Consulting and Clinical Psychology, 45*, 206–215.

Fuller, T. L., & Fincham, F. D. (1995). Attachment style in married couples: Relation to current marital functioning, stability over time, and method of assessment. *Personal Relationships, 2*, 17–34.

Gaelick, L., Bodenhausen, G. V., & Wyer, R. S., Jr. (1985). Emotional communication in close relationships. *Journal of Personality and Social Psychology, 49*, 1246–1265.

Garcia, S., Stinson, L., Ickes, W., Bissonnette, V., & Briggs, S. R. (1991). Shyness and physical attractiveness in mixed-sex dyads. *Journal of Personality and Social Psychology, 61*, 35–49.

Gatchel, R. J., & Baum, A. (1983). *An introduction to health psychology.* New York: Random House.

Gattuso, S. M., Litt, M. D., & Fitzgerald, T. E. (1992). Coping with gastrointestinal endoscopy: Self-efficacy enhancement and coping style. *Journal of Consulting and Clinical Psychology, 60*, 133–139.

Gelles, R. J. (1972). *The violent home.* Newbury Park, CA: Sage.

Gilliland, B. E., & James, R. K. (1988). *Crisis intervention strategies.* Pacific Grove, CA: Brooks/Cole.

Glass, C. R., & Shea, C. A. (1986). Cognitive therapy for shyness and social anxiety. In W. H. Jones, J. M. Cheeks, & S. R. Briggs (Eds.), *Shyness: Perspectives on research and treatment* (pp. 315–327). New York: Plenum.

Glass, D. C. (1977). *Behavior patterns, stress and coronary disease.* Hillsdale, NJ: Erlbaum.

Gold, J. A., Ryckman, R. M., & Mosley, N. R. (1984). Romantic mood induction and attraction to a dissimilar other: Is love blind? *Personality and Social Psychology Bulletin, 10*, 358–368.

Goldberg, L. R. (1993). The structure of phenotypic personality traits. *American Psychologist, 48*, 26–34.

Goldfried, M. R. (1971). Systematic desensitization as training in self-control. *Journal of Consulting and Clinical Psychology, 37*, 228–234.

Goldfried, M. R., & Davison, G. C. (1976). *Clinical behavior therapy.* New York: Holt, Rinehart & Winston.

Goldfried, M. R., Decenteceo, E., & Weinberg, L. (1974). Systematic rational restructuring as a self-control technique. *Behavior Therapy, 5*, 247–254.

Goldfried, M. R., Padawer, W., & Robins, C. (1984). Social anxiety and the semantic structure of heterosocial interactions. *Journal of Abnormal Psychology, 93*, 87–97.

Goleman, D. (1985, April 16). Marriage: Research reveals ingredients of happiness. *New York Times*, p. 19.

Goodhart, D. E. (1985). Some psychological effects associated with positive and negative thinking about stressful event outcomes: Was Pollyanna right? *Journal of Personality and Social Psychology, 48*, 216–232.

Gordon, W. A., Freidenbergs, I., Diller, L., Hibbard, M., Wolf, C., Levine, L., Lipkins, R., Ezrachi, O., & Lucido, D. (1980). Efficacy of psychosocial intervention with cancer patients. *Journal of Consulting and Clinical Psychology, 48*, 743–759.

Goswick, R. A., & Jones, W. H. (1981). Loneliness, self-concept, and adjustment. *Journal of Psychology, 107*, 237–240.

Gotlib, I. H., & Lee, C. M. (1989). The social functioning of depressed patients: A longitudinal assessment. *Journal of Social and Clinical Psychology, 8*, 223–237.

Gottman, J. G. (1979). *Empirical investigation of marriage.* New York: Academic Press.

Gough, H. G., & Thorne, A. (1986). Positive, negative, and balanced shyness. In W. H. Jones, J. M. Cheek, & S. R. Briggs (Eds.), *Shyness: Perspectives on research and treatment* (pp. 205–225). New York: Plenum.

Greenberg, B. S., Korzenny, F., & Atkin, C. K. (1979). The portrayal of the aging: Trends on current television. *Research on Aging, 1*, 319–334.

Greenwald, D. P. (1977). The behavioral assessment of differences in social skill and social anxiety in female college students. *Behavior Therapy, 8*, 925–937.

Greist, J. H., Jefferson, J. W., & Marks, I. M. (1986). *Anxiety and its treatment.* New York: Warner Books.

Haaga, D. A. F., Fine, J. A., Terrill, D. R., Stewart, B. L., & Beck, A. T. (1995). Social problem-solving deficits, dependency, and depressive symptoms. *Cognitive Therapy and Research, 19*, 147–158.

Hackett, G., & Horan, J. J. (1980). Stress inoculation for pain: What's really going on? *Journal of Counseling Psychology, 27*, 107–116.

Haemmerlie, F. M., & Montgomery, R. L. (1984). Purposefully biased interactions: Reducing hetero-social anxiety through self-perception theory. *Journal of Personality and Social Psychology, 47*, 900–908.

Hahlweg, K., & Markman, H. J. (1988). Effectiveness of behavioral marital therapy: Empirical status of behavioral techniques in preventing and alleviating marital distress. *Journal of Consulting and Clinical Psychology, 56*, 440–447.

Halgin, R. P., Weaver, D. D., Edell, W. S., & Spencer, P. G. (1987). Relation of depression and help-seeking history to attitudes toward seeking professional psychological help. *Journal of Counseling Psychology, 34*, 177–185.

Hamilton, D. L. (1979). A cognitive-attributional analysis of stereotyping. In L. Berkowitz (Ed.), *Advances in experimental social psychology* (Vol. 12, pp. 53–84). New York: Academic Press.

Hamilton, D. L., & Rose, T. L. (1980). Illusory correlation and the maintenance of stereotypic beliefs. *Journal of Personality and Social Psychology, 39*, 832–845.

Hammen, C. L., & Cochran, S. D. (1981). Cognitive correlates of life stress and depression in college students. *Journal of Abnormal Psychology, 90*, 23–27.

Hansson, R. O. (1989). Old age: Testing the parameters of social psychological assumptions. In S. Spacapan & S. Oskamp (Eds.), *The social psychology of aging* (pp. 25–51). Newbury Park, CA: Sage.

Hansson, R. O., & Jones, W. H. (1981). Loneliness, cooperation, and conformity among American undergraduates. *Journal of Social Psychology, 115*, 103–108.

Harris, L., & Associates. (1975). *The myth and reality of aging in America.* Washington, DC: National Council on Aging.

Harris, L., & Associates. (1981). *Aging in the eighties: America in transition.* Washington, DC: National Council on Aging.

Harris, M. B. (1992). Beliefs about how to reduce anger. *Psychological Reports, 70*, 203–210.

Harris, R. N., & Snyder, C. R. (1986). The role of uncertain self-esteem in self-handicapping. *Journal of Personality and Social Psychology, 51*, 451–458.

Harvey, J. H., Wells, G. L., & Alvarez, M. D. (1978). Attribution in the context of conflict and separation in close relationships. In J. H. Harvey, W. J. Ickes, & R. F. Kidd (Eds.), *New directions in attribution research* (Vol. 2, pp. 235–260). Hillsdale, NJ: Erlbaum.

Hazaleus, S. L., & Deffenbacher, J. L. (1986). Relaxation and cognitive treatments of anger. *Journal of Consulting and Clincal Psychology, 54*, 222–226.

Hazen, C., & Shaver, P. (1987). Romantic love conceptualized as an attachment process. *Journal of Personality and Social Psychology, 52*, 511–524.

Hedlund, S., & Rude, S. S. (1995). Evidence of latent depressive schemas in formerly depressed individuals. *Journal of Abnormal Psychology, 104*, 517–525.

Heiby, E. M. (1982). A self-reinforcement questionnaire. *Behavior Research and Therapy, 20*, 397–401.

Heiby, E. M. (1983a). Assessment of frequency of self-reinforcement. *Journal of Personality and Social Psychology, 44*, 1304–1307.

Heiby, E. M. (1983b). Toward the prediction of mood change. *Behavior Therapy, 14*, 110–115.

Heiby, E. M. (1986). Social versus self-control skills deficits in four cases of depression. *Behavior Therapy, 17*, 158–169.

Heiby, E. M., Ozaki, M., & Campos, P. E. (1984). The effects of training in self-reinforcement and reward: Implications for depression. *Behavior Therapy, 15*, 544–549.

Heidrich, S. M., & Ryff, C. D. (1993a). Physical and mental health in later life: The self-system as mediator. *Psychology and Aging, 8*, 327–338.

Heidrich, S. M., & Ryff, C. D. (1993b). The role of social comparisons processes in the psychological adaptation of elderly adults. *Journal of Gerontology, 48*, 127–136.

Heimberg, R. G., Keller, K. E., & Peca-Baker, T. (1986). Cognitive assessment of social-evaluative anxiety in the job interview. *Journal of Counseling Psychology, 33*, 190–195.

Heimberg, R. G., Vermilyea, J. A., Dodge, C. S., Becker, R. E., & Barlow, D. H. (1987). Attributional style, depression, and anxiety: An evaluation of the specificity of depressive attributions. *Cognitive Therapy and Research, 11*, 537–550.

Heitzman, C. A., & Kaplan, R. M. (1988). Assessment of methods for measuring social support. *Health Psychology, 7*, 75–109.

Heller, K., Swindle, R. W., & Dusenbury, L. (1986). Component social support processes: Comments and integration. *Journal of Consulting and Clinical Psychology, 54*, 466–470.

Hendler, N. (1984). Depression caused by chronic pain. *Journal of Clincal Psychiatry, 45*, 30–36.

Hendrick, S. S. (1988). A generic measure of relationship satisfaction. *Journal of Marriage and the Family, 50*, 93–98.

Henry, L. C. (Ed.). (1959). *Best quotations for all occasions.* New York: Fawcett.

Heppner, P. P., Cook, S. W., Wright, D. M., & Johnson, W. C., Jr. (1995). Progress in resolving problems: A problem-focused style of coping. *Journal of Counseling Psychology, 42*, 279–293.

Heppner, P. P., & Hillerbrand, E. T. (1991). Problem-solving training: Implications for remedial and preventive training. In C. R. Snyder & D. R. Forsyth (Eds.), *Handbook of social and clinical psychology* (pp. 681–698). New York: Pergamon.

Heppner, P. P., & Peterson, C. H. (1982). The development and implications of the Personal Problem-Solving Inventory. *Journal of Counseling Psychology, 29*, 66–75.

Herek, G. M., & Glunt, E. K. (1988). An epidemic of stigma: Public reactions to AIDS. *American Psychologist, 43*, 886–891.

Higgins, R. L., & Berglas, S. (1990). The maintenance and treatment of self-handicapping: From risk-taking to face-saving—and back. In R. L. Higgins, C. R. Snyder, & S. Berglas (Eds.), *Self-handicapping: The paradox that isn't* (pp. 187–238). New York: Plenum

Higgins, R. L., & Harris, R. N. (1988). Strategic "alcohol" use: Drinking to self-handicap. *Journal of Social and Clinical Psychology, 6*, 191–202.

Higgins, R. L., & Snyder, C. R. (1989). Excuses gone awry: An analysis of self-defeating excuses. In R. Curtis (Ed.), *Self-defeating behaviors: Experimental research, clinical impressions, and practical applications* (pp. 99–130). New York: Plenum.

Hirt, E. R., Deppe, R. K., & Gordon, L. J. (1991). Self-reported versus behavioral self-handicapping: Empirical evidence for a theoretical distinction. *Journal of Personality and Social Psychology, 61*, 981–991.

Hobfoll, S. E., & Leiberman, J. R. (1987). Personality and social resources in immediate and continued stress resistance among women. *Journal of Personality and Social Psychology, 52*, 18–26.

Hoffman, M. A., & Teglasi, H. (1982). The role of causal attributions in counseling shy subjects. *Journal of Counseling Psychology, 29*, 132–139.

Holahan, C. J., & Moos, R. H. (1987). Personal and contextual determinants of coping strategies. *Journal of Personality and Social Psychology, 52*, 946–955.

Holahan, C. J., Moos, R. H., Holahan, C. K., & Brennan, P. L. (1995). Social support, coping, and depressive symptoms in a late-middle-aged sample of patients reporting cardiac illness. *Health Psychology, 14*, 152–163.

Hollon, S. D., & Kendall, P. C. (1980). Cognitive self-statements in depression: Development of an automatic thoughts questionnaire. *Cognitive Therapy and Research, 4*, 383–395.

Holmes, T. H., & Masuda, M. (1974). Life change and illness susceptibility. In B. S. Dohrenwend & D. P. Dohrenwend (Eds.), *Stressful life events: Their nature and effects* (pp. 45–72). New York: Wiley.

Holmes, T. H., & Rahe, R. H. (1967). The Social Readjustment Rating Scale. *Journal of Psychosomatic Research, 11*, 213–218.

Holroyd, K. A. (1986). Recurrent headache. In K. A. Holroyd & T. L. Creer (Eds.), *Self-management of chronic disease* (pp. 373–413). New York: Academic Press.

Holtzworth-Munroe, A., & Jacobson, N. S. (1985). Causal attributions of married couples: When do they search for causes? What do they conclude when they do? *Journal of Personality and Social Psychology, 48*, 1398–1412.

Hunsley, J. (1987). Internal dialogue during academic examinations. *Cognitive Therapy and Research, 11*, 653–664.

Ickes, W., Robertson, E., Tooke, W., & Teng, G. (1986). Naturalistic social cognition: Methodology, assessment, and validation. *Journal of Personality and Social Psychology, 51*, 66–82.

Imber-Black, E. (1991). Rituals and the healing process. In F. Walsh & M. McGoldrick (Eds.), *Living beyond loss: Death in the family* (pp. 207–223). New York: Norton.

Ingram, R. E., & Wisnicki, K. S. (1988). Assessment of positive automatic thoughts. *Journal of Consulting and Clinical Psychology, 56*, 898–902.

Ishiyama, F. I. (1991). A Japanese reframing technique for brief social anxiety treatment: An exploratory study of cognitive and therapeutic effects of Morita therapy. *Journal of Cognitive Psychotherapy: An International Quarterly, 5*, 55–70.

Jacobsen, P. B., & Butler, R. W. (1996). Relation of cognitive coping and catastrophizing to acute pain and analgesic use following breast cancer surgery. *Journal of Behavioral Medicine, 19*, 17–29.

Jacobson, E. (1938). *Progressive relaxation.* Chicago: University of Chicago Press.

Jacobson, N. S., Follette, W. C., & McDonald, D. W. (1982). Reactivity to positive and negative behavior in distressed and nondistressed couples. *Journal of Consulting and Clinical Psychology, 50*, 706–714.

Jacobson, N. S., McDonald, D. W., Follette, W. C., & Berley, R. A. (1985). Attributional processes in distressed and nondistressed couples. *Cognitive Therapy and Research, 9*, 35–50.

Jamison, C., & Scogin, F. (1995). The outcome of cognitive bibliotherapy with depressed adults. *Journal of Consulting and Clinical Psychology, 63*, 644–650.

Jamison, R. N., & Virts, K. L. (1990). The influence of family support on chronic pain. *Behaviour Research & Therapy, 28*, 283–287.

Janis, I. L. (1958). *Psychological stress: Psychoanalytic and behavioral studies of surgical patients.* New York: Wiley.

Janoff-Bulman, R. (1989). Assumptive worlds and the stress of traumatic events: Applications of the schema construct. *Social Cognition, 7*, 113–136.

Janoff-Bulman, R., & Thomas, C. E. (1988). Toward an understanding of self-defeating responses following victimization. In R. C. Curtis (Ed.), *Self-defeating behaviors: Experimental research and practical implications* (pp. 215–234). New York: Plenum.

Jasnoski, M. L., Holmes, D. S., Solomon, S., & Aguiar, C. (1981). Exercise, changes in aerobic capacity, and changes in self-perceptions: An experimental investigation. *Journal of Research in Personality, 15*, 460–466.

Jensen, M. P., & Karoly, P. (1991). Control beliefs, coping efforts, and adjustment to chronic pain. *Journal of Consulting and Clinical Psychology, 59*, 431–438.

Jensen, M. P., Karoly, P., & Harris, P. (1991). Assessing the affective component of chronic pain: Development of the pain discomfort scale. *Journal of Psychosomatic Research, 35*, 149–154.

Jensen, M. P., Turner, J. A., & Romano, J. (1991). Self-efficacy and outcome expectancies: Relationship to chronic pain coping strategies and adjustment. *Pain, 44*, 263–269.

Johnstone, B., Frank, R. G., Belar, C., Berk, S., Bieliauskas, L. A., Bigler, E. D., Caplan, B., Elliott, T. R., Glueckauf, R. L., Kaplan, R. M., Kreutzer, J. S., Mateer, C. A., Patterson, D., Puente, A. E., Richards, J. S., Rosenthal, M., Sherer, M., Shewchuk, R., Siegel, L. J., & Sweet, J. J. (1995). Psychology in health care: Future directions. *Professional Psychology: Research and Practice, 26*, 341–365.

Jones, E. E., & Rhodewalt, F. (1982). *The Self-Handicapping Scale.* Princeton, NJ: Princeton University, Department of Psychology.

Jones, W. H. (1982). Loneliness and social behavior. In L. A. Peplau & D. Perlman (Eds.), *Loneliness: A sourcebook of current theory, research, and therapy* (pp. 238–252). New York: Wiley-Interscience.

Jones, W. H., Carpenter, B. N., & Quintana, D. (1985). Personality and interpersonal predictors of loneliness in two cultures. *Journal of Personality and Social Psychology, 48*, 1503–1511.

Jones, W. H., Hobbs, S. A., & Hockenbury, D. (1982). Loneliness and social skill deficits. *Journal of Personality and Social Psychology, 42*, 682–689.

Jones, W. H., Sansone, C., & Helm, B. (1983). Loneliness and interpersonal judgments. *Personality and Social Psychology Bulletin, 9*, 437–441.

Kahana, B., Harel, Z., & Kahana, E. (1988). Predictors of psychological well-being among survivors of the Holocaust. In J. P. Wilson, Z. Harel, & B. Kahana (Eds.), *Human adaptation to extreme stress: From the Holocaust to Vietnam* (pp. 171–192). New York: Plenum.

Kaloupek, D. G., & Stoupakis, T. (1985). Coping with a stressful medical procedure: Further investigation with volunteer blood donors. *Journal of Behavioral Medicine, 8*, 131–148.

Kaloupek, D. G., White, H., & Wong, M. (1984). Multiple assessment of coping strategies used by volunteer blood donors: Implications for preparatory training. *Journal of Behavioral Medicine, 7,* 35–60.

Kamptner, N. L. (1989). Personal possessions and their meanings in old age. In S. Spacapan & S. Oskamp (Eds.), *The social psychology of aging* (pp. 165–196). Newbury Park, CA: Sage.

Kanfer, R., & Zeiss, A. M. (1983). Depression, interpersonal standard setting, and judgments of self-efficacy. *Journal of Abnormal Psychology, 92,* 319–329.

Kanner, A. D., Coyne, J. C., Schaefer, C., & Lazarus, R. S. (1981). Comparison of two modes of stress measurement: Daily hassles and uplifts versus major life events. *Journal of Behavioral Medicine, 4,* 1–39.

Kaplan, H. B. (1970). Self-derogation and adjustment to recent life experiences. *Archives of General Psychiatry, 22,* 324–331.

Kaplan, H. B., Johnson, R. J., & Bailey, C. A. (1986). Self-rejection and the explanation of deviance: Refinement and elaboration of a latent structure. *Social Psychology Quarterly, 49,* 110–128.

Kaplan, H. B., Martin, S. S., & Johnson, R. J. (1986). Self-rejection and the explanation of deviance: Specification of the structure among latent constructs. *American Journal of Sociology, 92,* 384–411.

Kaplan, H. B., & Peck, B. M. (1992). Self-rejection, coping style, and mode of deviant response. *Social Science Quarterly, 73,* 903–919.

Kaplan, H. B., & Pokorny A. D. (1969). Self-derogation and psychosocial adjustment. *Journal of Nervous and Mental Disease, 149,* 421–434.

Kaplan, H. B., & Pokorny, A. D. (1976a). Self-derogation and suicide. I: Self-derogation as an antecedent of suicidal responses. *Social Science and Medicine, 10,* 113–118.

Kaplan, H. B., & Pokorny, A. D. (1976b). Self-derogation and suicide. II: Suicidal responses, self-derogation, and accidents. *Social Science and Medicine, 10,* 119–121.

Kaplan, R. M. (1991). Health-related quality of life in patient decision making. *Journal of Social Issues, 47,* 69–90.

Karney, B. R., & Bradbury, T. N. (1995). The longitudinal course of marital quality and stability: A review of theory, method, and research. *Psychological Bulletin, 118,* 3–34.

Katz, L., & Epstein, S. (1991). Constructive thinking and coping with laboratory-induced stress. *Journal of Personality and Social Psychology, 61,* 789–800.

Kavanagh, D. J. (1990). Towards a cognitive-behavioral intervention for adult grief reactions. *British Journal of Psychiatry, 157,* 373–383.

Kavanaugh, R. (1974). *Facing death.* Baltimore: Penguin.

Kaylor, J. A., King, D. W., & King, L. A. (1987). Psychological effects of military service in Vietnam: A meta-analysis. *Psychological Bulletin, 102,* 257–271.

Keane, T. M., Fairbank, J. A., Caddell, J. M., & Zimering, R. T. (1989). Implosive (flooding) therapy reduces symptoms of PTSD in Vietnam combat veterans. *Behavior Therapy, 20,* 245–260.

Keane, T. M., Fairbank, J. A., Caddell, J. M., Zimering, R. T., & Bender, M. E. (1985). A behavioral approach to assessing and treating post-traumatic stress disorder in Vietnam veterans. In C. R. Figley (Ed.), *Trauma and its wake* (pp. 257–294). New York: Brunner/Mazel.

Keefe, F. J., & Block, A. R. (1982). Development of an observation method for assessing pain behavior. *Behavior Therapy, 13,* 363–375.

Keefe, F. J., Brown, G. K., Wallston, K. A., & Caldwell, D. S. (1989). Coping with rheumatoid arthritis pain: Catastrophizing as a maladaptive strategy. *Pain, 37,* 51–56.

Keefe, F. J., Caldwell, D. S., Queen, K. T., Gil, K. M., Martinez, S., Crisson, J. E., Ogden, W., & Nunley, J. (1987). Pain coping strategies in osteoarthritis patients. *Journal of Consulting and Clinical Psychology, 55,* 208–212.

Keefe, F. J., & Dolan, E. (1986). Pain behavior and pain coping strategies in low back and myofascial pain dysfunction syndrome patients. *Pain, 24,* 49–56.

Keller, S., & Seraganian, P. (1984). Physical fitness level and autonomic reactivity to psychosocial stress. *Journal of Psychosomatic Research, 28,* 279–287.

Kelley, K., Byrne, D., Przbyla, D. P. J., Eberly, C., Eberly, B., Greendlinger, V., Wan, C. K., & Gorsky, J. (1985). Chronic self-destructiveness: Conceptualization, measurement, and initial validation of the construct. *Motivation and Emotion, 9,* 135–151.

Kelly, J. A., & Murphy, D. A. (1992). Psychological interventions with AIDS and HIV: Prevention and treatment. *Journal of Consulting and Clinical Psychology, 60,* 576–585.

Kendall, P. C. (1992). Healthy thinking. *Behavior Therapy, 23,* 1–11.

Kendzierski, D. (1990). Exercise self-schemata: Cognitive and behavioral correlates. *Health Psychology, 9,* 69–82.

Kerns, R. D., Turk, D., & Holzman, A. D. (1983). Psychological treatment for chronic pain: A selective review. *Clinical Psychology Review, 3,* 15–26.

Kessler, R. D., Price, R. H., & Wortman, C. B. (1985). Social factors in psychopathology: Stress, social support, and coping processes. In M. R. Rosenzweig & L. W. Porter (Eds.), *Annual review of psychology* (Vol. 39, pp. 531–572). Palo Alto, CA: Annual Reviews.

Kiecolt-Glaser, J. K., & Williams, D. A. (1987). Self-blame, compliance, and distress among burn patients. *Journal of Personality and Social Psychology, 53,* 187–193.

Kilpatrick, D. G., Resick, P. A., & Veronen, L. J. (1981). Effects of a rape experience. *Journal of Social Issues, 37,* 105–122.

King, A. C., Taylor, C. B., Haskell, W. L., & DeBusk, R. F. (1989). Influence of regular aerobic exercise on psychological health: A randomized, controlled trial of healthy middle-aged adults. *Health Psychology, 8,* 305–324.

Kirsch, I. (1986). Early research on self-efficacy: What we already know without knowing we knew. *Journal of Social and Clinical Psychology, 4,* 339–358.

Kirsch, I., Mearns, J., & Catanzaro, S. J. (1990). Mood-regulation expectancies as determinants of dysphoria in college students. *Journal of Counseling Psychology, 37,* 306–312.

Klein, D. C., Fencil-Morse, E., & Seligman, M. E. P. (1976). Learned helplessness, depression, and the attribution of failure. *Journal of Personality and Social Psychology, 33,* 508–510.

Klein, D. C., & Seligman, M. E. P. (1976). Reversal of performance deficits and perceptual deficits in learned helplessness and depression. *Journal of Abnormal Psychology, 85,* 11–26.

Kleinke, C. L. (1978). *Self-perception: The psychology of personal awareness.* New York: W. H. Freeman.

Kleinke, C. L. (1979). Effects of personal evaluations. In G. J. Chelune (Ed.), *Self-disclosure—Origins, patterns, and implications of openness in interpersonal relationships* (pp. 59–79). San Francisco: Jossey-Bass.

Kleinke, C. L. (1984a). Comparing depression coping strategies of schizophrenic men and depressed and nondepressed college students. *Journal of Clinical Psychology, 40,* 420–426.

Kleinke, C. L. (1984b). Two models for conceptualizing the attitude-behavior relationship. *Human Relations, 37,* 333–350.

Kleinke, C. L. (1986a). Gaze and eye contact: A research review. *Psychological Bulletin, 100,* 78–100.

Kleinke, C. L. (1986b). *Meeting and understanding people.* New York: W. H. Freeman.

Kleinke, C. L. (1987). Patients' preference for pain treatment modalities in a multidisciplinary pain clinic. *Rehabilitation Psychology, 32,* 113–120.

Kleinke, C. L. (1988). The depression coping questionnaire. *Journal of Clinical Psychology, 44,* 516–526.

Kleinke, C. L. (1991). How chronic pain patients cope with depression: Relation to treatment outcome in a multidisciplinary pain clinic. *Rehabilitation Psychology, 36,* 207–218.

Kleinke, C. L. (1992). How chronic pain patients cope with pain: Relation to treatment outcome in a multidisciplinary pain clinic. *Cognitive Therapy and Research, 16,* 669–685.

Kleinke, C. L. (1994). MMPI scales as predictors of pain-coping strategies preferred by patients with chronic pain. *Rehabilitation Psychology, 39,* 123–128.

Kleinke, C. L., & Dean, G. O. (1990). Evaluation of men and women receiving positive and negative responses with various acquaintance strategies. *Journal of Social Behavior and Personality, 5,* 369–377.

Kleinke, C. L., & Kahn, M. L. (1980). Perceptions of self-disclosure: Effects of sex and physical attractiveness. *Journal of Personality, 48,* 190–205.

Kleinke, C. L., Kahn, M. L., & Tully, T. B. (1979). First impressions of talking rates in opposite-sex and same-sex interactions. *Social Behavior and Personality, 7,* 81–91.

Kleinke, C. L., Meeker, F. B., & LaFong, C. (1974). Effects of gaze, touch, and use of name on evaluation of "engaged" couples. *Journal of Research in Personality, 7,* 368–373.

Kleinke, C. L., Meeker, F. B., & Staneski, R. A. (1986). Preference for opening lines: Comparing ratings by men and women. *Sex Roles, 15,* 585–600.

Kleinke, C. L., & Meyer, C. (1990). Evaluation of rape victim by men and women with high and low belief in a just world. *Psychology of Women Quarterly, 14,* 343–353.

Kleinke, C. L., & Miller, W. F. (1998). How comparing oneself favorably with others relates to well-being. *Journal of Social and Clinical Psychology.*

Kleinke, C. L., & Spangler, A. S., Jr. (1988a). Predicting treatment outcome of chronic back pain patients in a multidisciplinary pain clinic: Methodological issues and treatment implications. *Pain, 33,* 41–48.

Kleinke, C. L., & Spangler, A. S., Jr. (1988b). Psychometric analysis of the audiovisual taxonomy for assessing pain behavior in chronic back-pain patients. *Journal of Behavioral Medicine, 11,* 83–94.

Kleinke, C. L., Staneski, R. A., & Mason, J. K. (1982). Sex differences in coping with depression. *Sex Roles, 15,* 877–889.

Kleinke, C. L., Staneski, R. A., & Weaver, P. (1972). Evaluation of a person who uses another's name in ingratiating and noningratiating situations. *Journal of Experimental Social Psychology, 8,* 457–466.

Kleinke, C. L., Wallis, R., & Stalder, K. (1992). Evaluation of a rapist as a function of expressed intent and remorse. *Journal of Social Psychology, 132,* 525–537.

Kobasa, S. C. (1979). Stressful life events, personality, and health: An inquiry into hardiness. *Journal of Personality and Social Psychology, 37,* 1–11.

Kobasa, S. C., Maddi, S. R., & Kahn, S. (1982). Hardiness and health: A prospective study. *Journal of Personality and Social Psychology, 42,* 168–177.

Kobasa, S. C., Maddi, S. R., Puccetti, M. C., & Zola, M. A. (1985). Effectiveness of hardiness, exercise and social support as resources against illness. *Journal of Psychosomatic Research, 29,* 525–533.

Koestenbaum, P. (1976). *Is there an answer to death?* Englewood Cliffs, NJ: Prentice-Hall.

Kohn, P. M., Lafreniere, K., & Gurevich, M. (1991). Hassles, health, and personality. *Journal of Personality and Social Psychology, 61,* 478–482.

Konecni, V. J. (1984). Methodological issues in human aggression research. In R. M. Kaplan, V. J. Konecni, & R. W. Novaco (Eds.), *Aggression in children and youth.* The Hague, Netherlands: Nijhoff.

Kores, R. C., Murphy, W. D., Rosenthal, T. L., Elias, D. B., & North, W. C. (1990). Predicting outcome of chronic pain treatment via a modified self-efficacy scale. *Behavior Research and Therapy, 28,* 165–169.

Krantz, D. S., Grunberg, N. E., & Baum, A. (1985). Health psychology. In M. R. Rosenzweig & L. W. Porter (Eds.), *Annual review of psychology* (Vol. 39, pp. 349–383). Palo Alto, CA: Annual Reviews.

Kressel, K. (1986). Patterns of coping in divorce. In R. H. Moos (Ed.), *Coping with life crises: An integrated approach* (pp. 145–153). New York: Plenum.

Kreuter, M. W., & Strecher, V. J. (1995). Changing inaccurate perceptions of health risk: Results from a randomized trial. *Health Psychology, 14,* 56–63.

Kubany, E. S., Bauer, G. B., Muraoka, M. Y., Richard, D. C., & Read, P. (1995). Impact of labeled anger and blame in intimate relationships. *Journal of Social and Clinical Psychology, 14,* 53–60.

Kübler-Ross, E. (1969). *On death and dying.* New York: Macmillan.

Kupke, T. E., Calhoun, K. S., & Hobbs, S. A. (1979). Selection of heterosocial skills: II. Experimental validity. *Behavior Therapy, 10,* 336–346.

Kupke, T. E., & Hobbs, S. A. (1979). Selection of heterosocial skills: I. Criterion-related validity. *Behavior Therapy, 10,* 327–335.

Kyle, S. O., & Falbo, T. (1985). Relationships between marital stress and attributional preferences for own and spouse behavior. *Journal of Social and Clinical Psychology, 3,* 339–351.

L'Abate, L., & Milan, M. A. (Eds.). (1985). *Handbook of social skills training and research.* New York: Wiley.

Lakey, B., & Cassady, P. B. (1990). Cognitive processes in perceived social support. *Journal of Personality and Social Psychology, 59,* 337–343.

Lambert, C. E., & Lambert, V. A. (1987). Hardiness: Its development and relevance to nursing. *Image, 19,* 92–95.

Lambert, W. E., Libman, E., & Posner, E. G. (1960). The effect of increased salience of a membership group on pain tolerance. *Journal of Personality, 28,* 350–357.

Lange, A. J., & Jakubowski, P. (1976). *Responsible assertive behavior.* Champaign, IL: Research Press.

Langer, E. J. (1979). The illusion of incompetence. In L. C. Perlmuter & R. A. Monty (Eds.), *Choice and perceived control* (pp. 301–313). Hillsdale, NJ: Erlbaum.

Langer, E. J. (1981). Old age: An artifact? In S. Kiesler & J. McGaugh (Eds.), *Behavior: Biology and aging* (pp. 255–281). New York: Academic Press.

Langer, E. J., Beck, P., Janoff-Bulman, R., & Timko, C. (1984). An exploration of relationships among mindfulness, longevity, and senility. *Academic Psychology Bulletin, 6,* 211–226.

Langer, E. J., Chanowitz, B., Palmerino, M., Jacobs, S., Rhodes, M., & Taylor, P. (1988). Nonsequential development and aging. In C. N. Alexander & E. J. Langer (Eds.), *Higher stages of human development: Perspectives on adult growth* (pp. 114–136). New York: Oxford University Press.

Langer, E. J., Janis, I. L., & Wolfer, J. A. (1975). Reduction of psychological stress in surgical patients. *Journal of Experimental Social Psychology, 11,* 155–165.

Langer, E. J., & Rodin, J. (1976). The effects of choice and enhanced personal responsibility for the aged: A field experiment in an institutional setting. *Journal of Personality and Social Psychology, 34,* 191–198.

Langer, E. J., Rodin, J., Beck, P., Weinmen, C., & Spitzer, L. (1979). Environmental determinants of memory improvement in later adulthood. *Journal of Personality and Social Psychology, 37,* 2003–2013.

Langer, E. J., & Saegert, S. (1977). Crowding and cognitive control. *Journal of Personality and Social Psychology, 35,* 175–182.

Langston, C. A., & Cantor, N. (1989). Social anxiety and social constraint: When making friends is hard. *Journal of Personality and Social Psychology, 56,* 649–661.

Larson, D. G., & Chastain, R. L. (1990). Self-concealment: Conceptualization, measurement, and health implications. *Journal of Social and Clinical Psychology, 9,* 439–455.

Lazarus, R. S. (1984a). Puzzles in the study of daily hassles. *Journal of Behavioral Medicine, 7,* 375–389.

Lazarus, R. S. (1984b). The trivialization of distress. In B. L. Hammonds & C. J. Scheirer (Eds.), *Psychology and health* (pp. 125–144). Washington, DC: American Psychological Association.

Lazarus, R. S., & Folkman, S. (1984). *Stress, appraisal, and coping.* New York: Springer.

Leary, M. R. (1983). Social anxiousness: The construct and its measurement. *Journal of Personality Assessment, 47,* 66–75.

Leary, M. R., & Downs, D. L. (1995). Interpersonal functions of the self-esteem motive: The self-esteem system as a sociometer. In M. H. Kernis (Ed.), *Efficacy, agency, and self-esteem* (pp. 123–144). New York: Plenum.

Leary, M. R., Schreindorfer, L. S., & Haupt, A. L. (1995). The role of low self-esteem in emotional and behavioral problems: Why is low self-esteem dysfunctional? *Journal of Social and Clinical Psychology, 14,* 297–314.

Leary, M. R., Tambor, E. S., Terdal, S. K., & Downs, D. L. (1995). Self-esteem as an interpersonal monitor: The sociometer hypothesis. *Journal of Personality and Social Psychology, 68,* 518–530.

Leary, M. R., Tchividjian, L. R., & Kraxberger, B. E. (1994). Self-presentation can be hazardous to your health: Impression management and health risk. *Health Psychology, 13,* 461–470.

Lecci, L., Okum, M., & Karoly, P. (1994). Life regrets and current goals as predictors of psychological adjustment. *Journal of Personality and Social Psychology, 66,* 731–741.

Lefcourt, H. M. (1976). *Locus of control: Current trends in theory and research.* New York: Halstead.

Lefcourt, H. M., Davidson, K., Shepherd, R., Phillips, M., Prkachin, K., & Mills, D. (1995). Perspective-taking humor: Accounting for stress moderation. *Journal of Social and Clinical Psychology, 14,* 373–391.

Lefcourt, H. M., & Davidson-Katz, K. (1991a). Locus of control and health. In C. R. Snyder & D. R. Forsyth (Eds.), *Handbook of social and clinical psychology* (pp. 246–266). New York: Pergamon.

Lefcourt, H. M., & Davidson-Katz, K. (1991b). The role of humor and the self. In C. R. Snyder & D. R. Forsyth (Eds.), *Handbook of social and clinical psychology* (pp. 41–56). New York: Pergamon.

Lefcourt, H. M., Martin, R. A., Fick, C. M., & Saleh, W. E. (1985). Locus of control for affiliation and behavior in social interactions. *Journal of Personality and Social Psychology, 48,* 755–759.

Lehman, D. R., Davis, C. G., Delongis, A., Wortman, C. B., Bluck, S., Mandel, D. R., & Ellard, J. H. (1993). Positive and negative life changes following bereavement and their relations to adjustment. *Journal of Social and Clinical Psychology, 12,* 90–112.

Lehman, D. R., Ellard, J. H., & Wortman, C. B. (1986). Social support for the bereaved: Recipients' and providers' perspectives on what is helpful. *Journal of Consulting and Clinical Psychology, 54,* 438–446.

Lehman, D. R., & Taylor, S. E. (1987). Date with an earthquake: Coping with a probable, unpredictable disaster. *Personality and Social Psychology Bulletin, 13,* 546–555.

Lepore, S. J., Allen, K. A. M., & Evans, G. W. (1993). Social support lowers cardiovascular reactivity to an acute stressor. *Psychosomatic Medicine, 55,* 518–524.

Lerner, M. J. (1980). *The belief in a just world: A fundamental delusion.* New York: Plenum.

Leventhal, E. A., Leventhal, H., Shacham, S., & Easterling, D. V. (1989). Active coping reduces reports of pain from childbirth. *Journal of Consulting and Clinical Psychology, 57,* 365–371.

Lewinsohn, P. M. (1975). Engagement in pleasant activities and depression level. *Journal of Consulting and Clinical Psychology, 43,* 729–731.

Libow, L. (1977). Medical problems of older people. In A. Bosco & J. Porcino (Eds.), *What do we really know about aging*. Stony Brook, NY: State University of New York at Stony Brook.

Lifton, R. J., & Olson, E. (1976). The human meaning of total disaster: The Buffalo Creek experience. *Psychiatry, 39,* 1–18.

Lindeman, E. (1944). Symptomatology and management of acute grief. *American Journal of Psychiatry, 101,* 141–148.

Linehan, M. M., Goodstein, J. L., Nielsen, S. L., & Chiles, J. A. (1983). Reasons for staying alive when you are thinking of killing yourself: The Reasons for Living Inventory. *Journal of Consulting and Clinical Psychology, 51,* 276–286.

Linville, P. W. (1987). Self-complexity as a cognitive buffer against stress-related illness and depression. *Journal of Personality and Social Psychology, 52,* 663–676.

Lipkus, I. (1991). The construction and preliminary validation of a Global Belief in a Just World Scale and the exploratory analysis of the Multidimensional Belief in a Just World Scale. *Personality and Individual Differences, 12,* 1171–1178.

Litt, M. D. (1988). Self-efficacy and perceived control: Cognitive mediators of pain tolerance. *Journal of Personality and Social Psychology, 54,* 149–160.

Litt, M. D., Nye, C., & Shafer, D. (1995). Preparation for oral surgery: Evaluating elements of coping. *Journal of Behavioral Medicine, 18,* 435–459.

Lohr, J. M., Hamberger, L. K., & Bonge, D. (1988). The relationship of factorially validated measures of anger-proneness and irrational beliefs. *Motivation and Emotion, 12,* 171–183.

Long, B. C. (1984). Aerobic conditioning and stress inoculation: A comparison of stress-management interventions. *Cognitive Therapy and Research, 8,* 517–542.

Long, B. C., & Haney, C. J. (1988). Coping strategies for working women: Aerobic exercise and relaxation interventions. *Behavior Therapy, 19,* 75–83.

Long, B. C., & Sangster, J. I. (1993). Dispositional optimism/pessimism and coping strategies: Predictors of psychosocial adjustment of rheumatoid and osteoarthritis patients. *Journal of Applied Social Psychology, 23,* 1069–1091.

Lyubomirsky, S., & Nolen-Hoeksema, S. (1993). Self-perpetuating properties of dysphoric rumination. *Journal of Personality and Social Psychology, 65,* 339–349.

Lyubomirsky, S., & Nolen-Hoeksema, S. (1995). Effects of self-focused rumination on negative thinking and interpersonal problem solving. *Journal of Personality and Social Psychology, 69,* 176–190.

Mabel, S. (1994). Empirical determination of anger provoking characteristics intrinsic to anger provoking circumstances. *Journal of Social and Clinical Psychology, 13,* 174–188.

MacPherson, M. (1984). *Long time passing: Vietnam and the haunted generation.* Garden City, NY: Doubleday.

Maddi, S. R., Bartone, P. T., & Puccetti, M. C. (1987). Stressful events are indeed a factor in physical illness: Reply to Schroeder and Costa (1984). *Journal of Personality and Social Psychology, 52,* 833–843.

Maddux, J. E. (1991). Self-efficacy. In C. R. Snyder & D. R. Forsyth (Eds.), *Handbook of social and clinical psychology* (pp. 57–78). New York: Pergamon.

Manne, S., & Sandler, I. (1984). Coping and adjustment to genital herpes. *Journal of Behavioral Medicine, 7,* 391–410.

Manne, S. L., & Zautra, A. J. (1989). Spouse criticism and support: Their association with coping and psychological adjustment among women with rheumatoid arthritis. *Journal of Personality and Social Psychology, 56,* 608–617.

Marcus, B. H., & Owen, N. (1992). Motivational readiness, self-efficacy, and decision-making for exercise. *Journal of Applied Social Psychology, 22,* 3–16.

Margolin, G., Talovic, S., & Weinstein, C. D. (1983). Areas of Change Questionnaire: A practical approach to marital assessment. *Journal of Consulting and Clinical Psychology, 51,* 920–931.

Markman, H. J. (1981). Prediction of marital distress: A 5-year follow-up. *Journal of Consulting and Clinical Psychology, 49,* 760–762.

Markman, H. J., Floyd, F. J., Stanley, S. M., & Lewis, H. C. (1986). Prevention. In N. S. Jacobson & A. S. Gurman (Eds.), *Clinical handbook of marital therapy* (pp. 173–195). New York: Guilford.

Markman, H. J., Floyd, F. J., Stanley, S. M., & Storaasli, R. D. (1988). Prevention of marital distress: A longitudinal investigation. *Journal of Consulting and Clinical Psychology, 56,* 210–217.

Markman, H. J., & Hahlweg, K. (1993). The prediction and prevention of marital distress: An international perspective. *Clinical Psychology Review, 13*, 29–43.

Markman, H. J., Renick, M. J., Floyd, F. J., Stanley, S. M., & Clements, M. (1993). Preventing marital distress through communication and conflict management training: A 4- and 5-year follow-up. *Journal of Consulting and Clinical Psychology, 61*, 70–77.

Markus, H., & Nurius, P. (1986). Possible selves. *American Psychologist, 41*, 954–969.

Marmar, C. R., & Horowitz, M. J. (1988). Diagnosis and phase-oriented treatment of posttraumatic stress disorder. In J. P. Wilson, Z. Harel, & B. Kahana (Eds.), *Human adaptation to extreme stress: From the Holocaust to Vietnam* (pp. 81–103). New York: Plenum.

Marshall, G. N. (1991). A multidimensional analysis of internal health locus of control beliefs: Separating the wheat from the chaff? *Journal of Personality and Social Psychology, 61*, 483–491.

Marshall, G. N., & Lang, E. L. (1990). Optimism, self-mastery, and symptoms of depression in women professionals. *Journal of Personality and Social Psychology, 59*, 132–139.

Marshall, G. N., Wortman, C. B., Vickers, R. R., Kusulas, J. W., & Hervig, L. K. (1994). The five-factor model of personality as a framework for personality-health research. *Journal of Personality and Social Psychology, 67*, 278–286.

Martin, J. E., & Dubbert, P. M. (1982). Exercise applications and promotion in behavioral medicine: Current status and future directions. *Journal of Consulting and Clinical Psychology, 50*, 1004–1017.

Martin, R. A., & Lefcourt, H. M. (1983). Sense of humor as a moderator of the relation between stress and moods. *Journal of Personality and Social Psychology, 45*, 1313–1324.

Matarazzo, J. D. (1980). Behavioral health and behavioral medicine: Frontiers for a new health psychology. *American Psychologist, 35*, 807–817.

Matarazzo, J. D. (1984). Behavioral immunogens. In B. L. Hammonds & C. J. Scheirer (Eds.), *Psychology and health* (pp. 9–43). Washington, DC: American Psychological Association.

Mayerson, N. H., & Rhodewalt, F. (1988). The role of self-protective attributions in the experience of pain. *Journal of Social and Clinical Psychology, 6*, 203–218.

Mawson, D., Marks, I. M., Ramm, L., & Stern, R. S. (1981). Guided mourning for morbid grief: A controlled outcome study. *British Journal of Psychiatry, 138*, 185–193.

McArthur, D. L., Cohen, M. J., Gottlieb, H. J., Naliboff, B. D., & Schandler, S. L. (1987a). Treating chronic low back pain: I. Admissions to initial follow-up. *Pain, 29*, 1–22.

McArthur, D. L., Cohen, M. J., Gottlieb, H. J., Naliboff, B. D., & Schandler, S. L. (1987b). Treating chronic low back pain: II. Long-term follow-up. *Pain, 29*, 23–38.

McCaul, K. D., & Malott, J. M. (1984). Distraction and coping with pain. *Psychological Bulletin, 95*, 516–533.

McCrae, R. R. (1991). The five-factor model and its assessment in clinical settings. *Journal of Personality Assessment, 5*, 399–414.

McCrae, R. R. (1993). Moderated analyses of longitudinal personality stability. *Journal of Personality and Social Psychology, 65*, 577–585.

McCrae, R. R., & Costa, P. T. (1986). Personality, coping, and coping effectiveness in an adult sample. *Journal of Personality, 54*, 385–405.

McCrae, R. R., & Costa, P. T. (1991). Adding *liebe und arbeit*: The full five-factor model and well-being. *Personality and Social Psychology Bulletin, 17*, 227–232.

McCrae, R. R., & John, O. P. (1992). An introduction to the five-factor model and its applications. *Journal of Personality, 60*, 175–215.

McGoldrick, M., Almeida, R., Moore-Hines, P., Rosen, E., Garcia-Preto, N., & Lee, E. (1991). Mourning in different cultures. In F. Walsh & M. McGoldrick (Eds.), *Living beyond loss: Death in the family* (pp. 176–206). New York: Norton.

McIntosh, D. N., Silver, R. C., & Wortman, C. B. (1993). Religion's role in adjustment to a negative life event: Coping with the loss of a child. *Journal of Personality and Social Psychology, 65*, 812–821.

McKay, M., Rogers, P. D., & McKay, J. (1989). *When anger hurts: Quieting the storm within.* Oakland, CA: New Harbinger.

McKusick, L. (1988). The impact of AIDS on practitioner and client: Notes for the therapeutic relationship. *American Psychologist, 43*, 935–940.

McMullin, R. E. (1986). *Handbook of cognitive therapy techniques.* New York: Norton.

Mead, M. (1986). Jealousy: Primitive and civilised. In G. Clanton & L. G. Smith (Eds.), *Jealousy* (pp. 115–126). Lanham, MD: University Press of America.

Meer, J. (1986, June). The reason of age. *Psychology Today, 20,* 60–64.

Meichenbaum, D. (1977). *Cognitive-behavior modification.* New York: Plenum.

Meichenbaum, D. (1985). *Stress inoculation training.* New York: Pergamon.

Melamed, B. G. (1984). Health intervention: Collaboration for health and science. In B. L. Hammonds & C. J. Scheier (Eds.), *Psychology and health* (pp. 49–119). Washington, DC: American Psychological Association.

Melchior, L. A., & Cheek, J. M. (1990). Shyness and anxious self-preoccupation during a social interaction. *Journal of Social Behavior and Personality, 5,* 117–130.

Melzack, R. (1975). The McGill Pain Questionnaire: Major properties and scoring methods. *Pain, 1,* 277–299.

Melzack, R., Jeans, M. E., Stratford, J. G., & Monks, R. C. (1980). Ice massage and transcutaneous electrical stimulation: Comparison of treatment for low-back pain. *Pain, 9,* 209–217.

Menaghan, E. (1982). Measuring coping effectiveness: A panel analysis of marital problems and coping efforts. *Journal of Health and Social Behavior, 23,* 220–234.

Meyer, C. B., & Taylor, S. E. (1986). Adjustment to rape. *Journal of Personality and Social Psychology, 50,* 1226–1234.

Meyer, T. J., & Mark, M. M. (1995). Effects of psychosocial interventions with adult cancer patients: A meta-analysis of randomized experiments. *Health Psychology, 14,* 101–108.

Michela, J. L., Peplau, L. A., & Weeks, D. G. (1982). Perceived dimensions of attributions for loneliness. *Journal of Personality and Social Psychology, 43,* 929–936.

Mikulincer, M., & Segal, J. (1990). A multidimensional analysis of the experience of loneliness. *Journal of Social and Personal Relationships, 7,* 209–230.

Miller, G. E., & Bradbury, T. N. (1995). Refining the association between attributions and behavior in marital interaction. *Journal of Family Psychology, 9,* 196–208.

Miller, L. C., Berg, J. H., & Archer, R. L. (1983). Openers: Individuals who elicit intimate self-disclosure. *Journal of Personality and Social Psychology, 44,* 1234–1244.

Miller, S. M. (1987). Monitoring and blunting: Validation of a questionnaire to assess styles of information seeking under threat. *Journal of Personality and Social Psychology, 52,* 345–353.

Miller, S. M., & Birnbaum, A. (1988). Putting the life back into 'life events': Toward a cognitive social learning analysis of the coping process. In S. Fisher & J. Reason (Eds.), *Handbook of life stress, cognition, and health* (pp. 499–511). New York: Wiley.

Miller, S. M., Brody, D. S., & Summerton, J. (1988). Styles of coping with threat: Implications for health. *Journal of Personality and Social Psychology, 54,* 142–148.

Miller, S. M., Combs, C., & Stoddard, E. (1989). Information, coping and control in patients undergoing surgery and stressful medical procedures. In A. Steptoe & A. Appels (Eds.), *Stress, personal control, and health* (pp. 107–130). New York: Wiley.

Miller, S. M., Leinbach, A., & Brody, D. S. (1989). Coping style in hypertensive patients: Nature and consequences. *Journal of Consulting and Clinical Psychology, 57,* 142–148.

Miller, S. M., Roussi, P., Caputo, C. G., & Kruus, L. (1995). Patterns of children's coping with an aversive dental treatment. *Health Psychology, 14,* 236–246.

Mills, R. T., & Krantz, D. S. (1979). Information, choice, and reactions to stress: A field experiment in a blood bank with laboratory analogue. *Journal of Personality and Social Psychology, 37,* 608–620.

Mitchell, R. E., Billings, A. G., & Moos, R. H. (1982). Social support and well-being: Implications for prevention programs. *Journal of Primary Prevention, 3,* 77–98.

Mitchell, R. E., Cronkite, R. C., & Moos, R. H. (1983). Stress, coping, and depression among married couples. *Journal of Abnormal Psychology, 92,* 433–448.

Monroe, S. (1982). Life events and disorder: Event-symptom associations and the course of disorder. *Journal of Abnormal Psychology, 91,* 14–24.

Monroe, S. (1983). Major and minor life events as predictors of psychological distress: Further issues and findings. *Journal of Behavioral Medicine, 6,* 189–205.

Monroe, S., Bellack, A. S., Hersen, M., & Himmelhoch, J. M. (1983). Life events, symptom course, and treatment outcome in unipolar depressed women. *Journal of Consulting and Clinical Psychology, 51,* 604–615.

Monroe, S., Bromet, E. J., Connell, M. M., & Steiner, S. C. (1986). Social support, life events, and depressive symptoms: A 1-year prospective study. *Journal of Consulting and Clinical Psychology, 54,* 424–431.

Moos, R. H., & Lemke, S. (1994). *Group residences for older adults: Physical features, policies, and social climate.* New York: Oxford University Press.

Morin, S. F. (1988). AIDS: The challenge to psychology. *American Psychologist, 43,* 838–842.

Moustakas, C. E. (1961). *Loneliness.* Englewood Cliffs, NJ: Prentice-Hall.

Mullen, P. E., & Martin, J. (1994). Jealousy: A community study. *British Journal of Psychiatry, 164,* 35–43.

Murray, C. B., & Warden, M. R. (1992). Implications of self-handicapping strategies for academic achievement: A reconceptualization. *Journal of Social Psychology, 132,* 23–37.

Naveh-Benjamin, M. (1991). A comparison of training programs intended for different types of test-anxious students: Further support for an information-processing model. *Journal of Educational Psychology, 83,* 134–139.

Newquist, D. (1985). Voodoo death in the American aged. In J. E. Birren & J. Livingston (Eds.), *Cognition, stress, and aging* (pp. 111–133). Englewood Cliffs, NJ: Prentice-Hall.

Nezu, A. M. (1986). Efficacy of a social-problem therapy approach for unipolar depression. *Journal of Consulting and Clinical Psychology, 54,* 196–202.

Nezu, A. M., Nezu, C. M., & Blissett, S. E. (1988). Sense of humor as a moderator of the relation between stressful events and psychological distress: A prospective analysis. *Journal of Personality and Social Psychology, 54,* 520–525.

Nezu, A. M., Nezu, C. M., Saraydarian, L., Kalmar, K., & Ronan, G. F. (1986). Social problem solving as a moderating variable between negative life stress and depressive symptoms. *Cognitive Therapy and Research, 10,* 489–498.

Nicholls, J. G. (1984). Achievement motivation: Conceptions of ability, subjective experience, task choice, and performance. *Psychological Review, 91,* 328–346.

Nielson, W. R., & MacDonald, M. R. (1988). Attributions of blame and coping following spinal cord injury: Is self-blame adaptive? *Journal of Social and Clinical Psychology, 7,* 163–175.

Nix, G., Watson, C., Pyszczynski, T., & Greenberg, J. (1995). Reducing depressive affect through external focus of attention. *Journal of Social and Clinical Psychology, 14,* 36–52.

Nolen-Hoeksema, S. (1991). Responses to depression and their effects on the duration of depressive episodes. *Journal of Abnormal Psychology, 100,* 569–582.

Nolen-Hoeksema, S., & Morrow, J. (1991). A prospective study of depression and posttraumatic stress symptoms after a natural disaster: The 1989 Loma Prieta Earthquake. *Journal of Personality and Social Psychology, 61,* 115–121.

Nolen-Hoeksema, S., & Morrow, J. (1993). Effects of rumination and distraction on naturally occurring depressed mood. *Cognition and Emotion, 7,* 561–570.

Nolen-Hoeksema, S., Morrow, J., & Fredrickson, B. L. (1993). Response styles and the duration of episodes of depressed mood. *Journal of Abnormal Psychology, 102,* 20–28.

Nolen-Hoeksema, S., Parker, L. E., & Larson, J. (1994). Ruminative coping with depressed mood following loss. *Journal of Personality and Social Psychology, 67,* 92–104.

Norem, J. K., & Cantor, N. (1986a). Anticipatory and post-hoc cushioning strategies: Optimism and defensive pessimism in "risky" situations. *Cognitive Therapy and Research, 10,* 347–362.

Norem, J. K., & Cantor, N. (1986b). Defensive pessimism: Harnessing anxiety as motivation. *Journal of Personality and Social Psychology, 51,* 1208–1217.

Norris, F. H., Kaniasty, K. Z., & Scheer, D. A (1990). Use of mental health services among victims of crime: Frequency, correlates, and subsequent recovery. *Journal of Consulting and Clinical Psychology, 58,* 538–547.

Novaco, R. W. (1975). *Anger control.* Lexington, MA: Heath.

Novaco, R. W. (1976). Treatment of chronic anger through cognitive and relaxation controls. *Journal of Consulting and Clinical Psychology, 44,* 681.

Novaco, R. W. (1980). Training of probation counselors for anger problems. *Journal of Counseling Psychology, 27,* 385–390.

Novaco, R. W. (1985). Anger and its therapeutic regulation. In M. Chesney & R. Roseman (Eds.), *Anger and hostility in cardiovascular disorders* (pp. 203–226). Washington, DC: Hemisphere.

Novaco, R. W. (1986). Anger control as a clinical and social problem. In R. J. Blanchard & D. C. Blanchard (Eds.), *Advances in the study of aggression* (Vol. 3, pp. 1–67). New York: Academic Press.

Novy, D. M., Nelson, D. V., Francis, D. J., & Turk, D. C. (1995). Perspectives of chronic pain: An evaluative comparison of restrictive and comprehensive models. *Psychological Bulletin, 118,* 238–247.

Nowack, K. M. (1989). Coping style, cognitive hardiness, and health status. *Journal of Behavioral Medicine, 12,* 145–158.

Orvis, B. R., Kelley, H. H., & Butler, D. (1976). Attributional conflict in young couples. In J. H. Harvey, W. J. Ickes, & R. F. Kidd (Eds.), *New directions in attribution research* (Vol. 1, pp. 353–386). Hillsdale, NJ: Erlbaum.

Parkes, K. R. (1984). Locus of control, cognitive appraisal, and coping in stressful episodes. *Journal of Personality and Social Psychology, 46,* 655–668.

Paulhus, D. L., & Martin, C. L. (1988). Functional flexibility: A new conception of interpersonal flexibility. *Journal of Personality and Social Psychology, 55,* 88–101.

Paulus, P. B., McCain, G., & Cox, V. C. (1978). Death rates, psychiatric commitments, blood pressure and perceived crowding. *Environmental Psychology and Nonverbal Behavior, 3,* 107–116.

Pavot, W., & Diener, E. (1993). Review of the Satisfaction with Life Scale. *Psychological Assessment, 5,* 164–172.

Peacock, E. J., & Wong, P. T. P. (1990). The Stress Appraisal Measure (SAM): A multidimensional approach to cognitive appraisal. *Stress Medicine, 6,* 227–236.

Pearlin, I., & Schooler, C. (1978). The structure of coping. *Journal of Health and Social Behavior, 19,* 2–21.

Peck, R. C. (1968). Psychological developments in the second half of life. In B. L. Neugarten (Ed.), *Middle age and aging: A reader in social psychology* (pp. 88–92). Chicago: University of Chicago Press.

Pegalis, L. J., Shaffer, D. R., Bazinni, D. G., & Greenier, K. (1994). On the ability to elicit self-disclosure: Are there gender-based and contextual limitations on the opener effect? *Personality and Social Psychology Bulletin, 20,* 412–420.

Pennebaker, J. W. (1989). Confession, inhibition, and disease. In L. Berkowitz (Ed.), *Advances in experimental social psychology* (Vol. 22, pp. 211–241). New York: Academic Press.

Pennebaker, J. W., Colder, M., & Sharp, L. K. (1990). Accelerating the coping process. *Journal of Personality and Social Psychology, 58,* 528–537.

Pennebaker, J. W., Hughes, C. F., & O'Heeron, C. (1987). The psychophysiology of confession: Linking inhibitory and psychosomatic processes. *Journal of Personality and Social Psychology, 52,* 781–793.

Pennebaker, J. W., Kiecolt-Glaser, J. K., & Glaser, R. (1988). Disclosure of traumas and immune function: Health implications for psychotherapy. *Journal of Personality and Social Psychology, 56,* 239–245.

Pennebaker, J. W., & O'Heeron, R. C. (1984). Confiding in others and illness rate among spouses of suicide and accidental death victims. *Journal of Abnormal Psychology, 93,* 473–476.

Pennebaker, J. W., & Susman, J. R. (1988). Disclosure of traumas and psychosomatic processes. *Social Science and Medicine, 26,* 327–332.

Peplau, L. A., Russell, D., & Heim, M. (1979). The experience of loneliness. In I. H. Frieze, D. Bar-Tal, & J. S. Carroll (Eds.), *New approaches to social problems: Applications of attribution theory* (pp. 53–78). San Francisco: Jossey-Bass.

Perdue, C. W., & Gurtman, M. B. (1990). Evidence for the automaticity of ageism. *Journal of Experimental Social Psychology, 26,* 199–216.

Perlman, D., & Peplau, L. A. (1981). Toward a social psychology of loneliness. In S. Duck & R. Gilmour (Eds.), *Personal relationships in disorder* (pp. 31–56). London: Academic Press.

Perlmuter, L. C., & Langer, E. J. (1983). The effects of behavioral monitoring on the perception of control. *Clinical Gerontologist, 1,* 37–43.

Perloff, L. (1987). Social comparison and illusions of invulnerability to negative life events. In C. R. Snyder & C. E. Ford (Eds.), *Coping with negative life events* (pp. 217–242). New York: Plenum.

Persons, J. (1995). Two acceptance vignettes. *The Behavior Therapist, 18,* 153.

Peterson, C. (1988). Explanatory style as a risk factor for illness. *Cognitive Therapy and Research, 12,* 117–130.

Peterson, C., & Barrett, L. C. (1987). Explanatory style and academic performance among university freshmen. *Journal of Personality and Social Psychology, 53,* 603–607.

Peterson, C., & Seligman, M. E. P. (1987). Explanatory style and illness. *Journal of Personality, 55,* 237–265.

Peterson, C., Seligman, M. E. P., & Vaillant, G. E. (1988). Pessimistic explanatory style is a risk factor for physical illness: A thirty-five-year longitudinal study. *Journal of Personality and Social Psychology, 55,* 23–27.

Pfeiffer, S. M., & Wong, P. T. P. (1989). Multidimensional jealousy. *Journal of Social and Personal Relationships, 6,* 81–196.

Phares, E. J. (1976). *Locus of control in personality.* Morristown, NJ: General Learning Press.

Pierce, G. R., Sarason, I. G., & Sarason, B. R. (1991). General and relationship-based perceptions of social support: Are two constructs better than one? *Journal of Personality and Social Psychology, 61,* 1028–1039.

Pietromonaco, P. R., & Markus, H. (1985). The nature of negative thoughts in depression. *Journal of Personality and Social Psychology, 48,* 799–807.

Pilkonis, P. A. (1977). The behavioral consequences of shyness. *Journal of Personality, 45,* 596–611.

Piper, A. I., & Langer, E. J. (1987). Aging and mindful control. In M. Baltes & P. Baltes (Eds.), *Aging and mindful control.* Hillsdale, NJ: Erlbaum.

Pomerleau, O. F., & Rodin, J. (1986). Behavioral medicine and health psychology. In S. L. Garfield & A. E. Bergin (Eds.), *Handbook of psychotherapy and behavior change* (pp. 483–522). New York: Wiley.

Ptacek, J. T., & Dodge, K. L. (1995). Coping strategies and relationship satisfaction in couples. *Personality and Social Psychology Bulletin, 21,* 76–84.

Pyszczynski, T., & Greenberg, J. (1983). Determinants of reductions in intended effort as a strategy for coping with anticipated failure. *Journal of Research in Personality, 17,* 412–422.

Pyszczynski, T., & Greenberg, J. (1986). Evidence for a depressive self-focusing style. *Journal of Research in Personality, 20,* 95–106.

Pyszczynski, T., & Greenberg, J. (1987a). Depression, self-focused attention, and self-regulatory perseveration. In C. R. Snyder & C. E. Ford (Eds.), *Coping with negative life events* (pp. 105–129). New York: Plenum.

Pyszczynski, T., & Greenberg, J. (1987b). Self-regulatory perseveration and the depressive self-focusing style: A self-awareness theory of reactive depression. *Psychological Bulletin, 102,* 122–138.

Pyszczynski, T., Hamilton, J. C., Herring, F. H., & Greenberg, J. (1989). Depression, self-focused attention, and the negative memory bias. *Journal of Personality and Social Psychology, 57,* 351–357.

Pyszczynski, T., Holt, K., & Greenberg, J. (1987). Depression, self-focused attention, and expectancies for positive and negative-future life events for self and others. *Journal of Personality and Social Psychology, 52,* 994–1001.

Radloff, L. S. (1977). The CES-D Scale: A self-report depression scale for research in the general population. *Applied Psychological Measurement, 1,* 385–401.

Rando, T. A. (1984). *Grief, dying, and death.* Champaign, IL: Research Press.

Raps, C. S., Peterson, C., Reinhard, K. E., Abramson, L. Y., & Seligman, M. E. P. (1982). Attributional style among depressed patients. *Journal of Abnormal Psychology, 91,* 102–108.

Raps, C. S., Reinhard, K. E., & Seligman, M. E. P. (1980). Reversal of cognitive and affective deficits associated with depression and learned helplessness by mood elevation in patients. *Journal of Abnormal Psychology, 89,* 342–349.

Reed, G. M., Kemeny, M. E., Taylor, S. E., Wang, H. J., & Visscher, B. R. (1994). Realistic acceptance as a predictor of decreased survival time in gay men with AIDS. *Health Psychology, 13,* 299–307.

Reed, G. M., Taylor, S. E., & Kemeny, M. E. (1993). Perceived control and psychological adjustment in gay men with AIDS. *Journal of Applied Social Psychology, 23,* 791–824.

Reich, J. W., & Zautra, A. J. (1991). Experimental and measurement approaches to internal control in at-risk older adults. *Journal of Social Issues, 47,* 143–158.

Reich, J. W., & Zautra, A. J. (1995a). Other-reliance encouragement effects in female rheumatoid arthritis patients. *Journal of Social and Clinical Psychology, 14,* 119–133.

Reich, J. W., & Zautra, A. J. (1995b). Spouse encouragement of self-reliance and other-reliance in rheumatoid arthritis couples. *Journal of Behavioral Medicine, 18,* 249–260.

Reis, H. T., Wheeler, L., Nezlek, J., Kernis, M. H., & Spiegel, N. (1985). On specificity in the impact of social participation on physical and psychological health. *Journal of Personality and Social Psychology, 48,* 456–471.

Reker, G. T. (1985). Toward a holistic model of health, behavior, and aging. In J. E. Birren & J. Livingston (Eds.), *Cognition, stress, and aging* (pp. 143–173). Englewood Cliffs, NJ: Prentice-Hall.

Reker, G. T., & Wong, P. T. P. (1985). Personal optimism, physical and mental health. In J. E. Birren & J. Livingston (Eds.), *Cognition, stress, and aging* (pp. 134–173). Englewood Cliffs, NJ: Prentice-Hall.

Revenson, T. A., & Felton, B. J. (1989). Disability and coping as predictors of psychological adjustment to rheumatoid arthritis. *Journal of Consulting and Clinical Psychology, 57,* 344–348.

Rhodewalt, F. (1990). Self-handicappers: Individual differences in the preference for anticipatory self-protective acts. In R. L. Higgins, C. R. Snyder, & S. Berglas (Eds.), *Self-handicapping: The paradox that isn't* (pp. 69–106). New York: Plenum.

Rhodewalt, F. (1994). Conceptions of ability, achievement goals, and individual differences in self-handicapping behavior: On the application of implicit theories. *Journal of Personality, 62,* 67–85.

Rhodewalt, F., & Davison, J. (1986). Self-handicapping and subsequent performance: Role of outcome valence and attributional certainty. *Basic and Applied Social Psychology, 7,* 307–323.

Rhodewalt, F., & Fairfield, M. (1991). Claimed self-handicaps and the self-handicapper: The relation of reduction in intended effort to performance. *Journal of Research in Personality, 25,* 402–417.

Rhodewalt, F., Morf, C., Hazlett, S., & Fairfield, M. (1991). Self-handicapping: The role of discounting and augmentation in the preservation of self-esteem. *Journal of Personality and Social Psychology, 61,* 122–131.

Rhodewalt, F., Saltzman, A. T., & Wittmer, J. (1984). Self-handicapping among competitive athletes: The role of practice in self-esteem protection. *Basic and Applied Social Psychology, 5,* 197–209.

Rhodewalt, F., Sanbonmatsu, D. M., Tschanz, B., Feick, D. L., & Waller, A. (1995). Self-handicapping and interpersonal trade-offs: The effects of claimed self-handicaps on observers' performance evaluations and feedback. *Personality and Social Psychology Bulletin, 21,* 1042–1050.

Rhodewalt, F., & Zone, J. B. (1989). Appraisal of life change, depression and illness in hardy and nonhardy women. *Journal of Personality and Social Psychology, 56,* 81–88.

Richter, C. P. (1957). On the phenomenon of sudden-death in animals and man. *Psychosomatic Medicine, 19,* 191–198.

Riesman, D., Denny, R., & Glazer, N. (1961). *The lonely crowd.* New Haven, CT: Yale University Press.

Robinson, L. A., Berman, J. S., & Neimeyer, R. A. (1990). Psychotherapy for the treatment of depression: A comprehensive review of controlled outcome research. *Psychological Bulletin, 108,* 30–49.

Rochford, E. B., Jr., & Blocker, T. J. (1991). Coping with "natural" hazards as stressors: The predictions of activism in a flood disaster. *Environment and Behavior, 23,* 171–194.

Rodin, J., & Baum, A. (1978). Crowding and helplessness: Potential consequences of density and loss of control. In A. Baum & Y. M. Epstein (Eds.), *Human response to crowding.* Hillsdale, NJ: Erlbaum.

Rodin, J., & Langer, E. J. (1977). Long-term effects of a control-relevant intervention with the institutionalized aged. *Journal of Personality and Social Psychology, 35,* 897–902.

Rodin, J., & Salovey, P. (1989). Health psychology. *Annual Review of Psychology, 40,* 533–579.

Rogers, C. R. (1961). *On becoming a person.* Boston: Houghton Mifflin.

Rook, K. S. (1984). Promoting social bonding. *American Psychologist, 39,* 1389–1407.

Rook, K. S. (1987). Social support versus companionship: Effects on life stress, loneliness, and evaluation by others. *Journal of Personality and Social Psychology, 52,* 1132–1147.

Rosenman, R. H. (1978). The interview method of assessment of the coronary-prone behavior pattern. In T. M. Dembroski, S. M. Weiss, J. L. Shields, S. G. Haynes, & M. Feinleib (Eds.), *Coronary-prone behavior* (pp. 55–69). New York: Springer-Verlag.

Rosenstiel, A. K., & Keefe, F. J. (1983). The use of coping strategies in chronic low back pain patients: Relationship to patient characteristics and current adjustment. *Pain, 17,* 33–44.

Roskies, E., Seraganian, P., Oseasohn, R., Hanley, J. A., Collu, R., Martin, N., & Smilga, C. (1986). The Montreal Type A Intervention Project: Major findings. *Health Psychology, 5,* 45–69.

Ross, S. M., Gottfredson, D. K., Christensen, P., & Weaver, R. (1986). Cognitive self-statements in depression: Findings across clinical populations. *Cognitive Therapy and Research, 10,* 159–166.

Rotenberg, K. J. (1994). Loneliness and interpersonal trust. *Journal of Social and Clinical Psychology, 13,* 152–173.

Rothbaum, F., Weisz, J. R., & Snyder, S. S. (1982). Changing the world and changing the self: A two-process model of perceived control. *Journal of Personality and Social Psychology, 42,* 5–37.

Rotter, J. B. (1966). Generalized expectancies for internal versus external control of reinforcement [Special Issue]. *Psychological Monographs, 80*(1).

Roy, R. (1984). Pain clinics: Reassessment of objectives and outcomes. *Archives of Physical Medicine and Rehabilitation, 65,* 448–451.

Rubenstein, C. M., & Shaver, P. (1980). Loneliness in two northeastern cities. In J. Hartog, J. R. Audry, & Y. A. Cohen (Eds.), *The anatomy of loneliness* (pp. 319–337). New York: International Universities Press.

Rubenstein, C. M., & Shaver, P. (1982). The experience of loneliness. In L. A. Peplau & D. Perlman (Eds.), *Loneliness: A sourcebook of theory, research and therapy* (pp. 206–223). New York: Wiley-Interscience.

Rubonis, A. V., & Bickman, L. (1991). Psychological impairment in the wake of disaster: The disaster-psychopathology relationship. *Psychological Bulletin, 109,* 384–399.

Russell, C. H. (1989). *Good news about aging.* New York: Wiley.

Russell, D. (1982). The Causal Dimension Scale: A measure of how individuals perceive causes. *Journal of Personality and Social Psychology, 42,* 1137–1145.

Russell, D., Cutrona, C. E., Rose, J., & Yurko, K. (1984). Social and emotional loneliness: An examination of Weiss's typology of loneliness. *Journal of Personality and Social Psychology, 46,* 1313–1321.

Russell, D., & Fehr, B. (1990). Fuzzy concepts in a fuzzy hierarchy: Varieties of anger. *Journal of Personality and Social Psychology, 67,* 186–205.

Russell, D., & McAuley, E. (1986). Causal attributions, causal dimensions, and affective reactions to success and failure. *Journal of Personality and Social Psychology, 50,* 1174–1185.

Russell, D., Peplau, L. A., & Cutrona, C. E. (1980). The Revised UCLA Loneliness Scale: Concurrent and discriminant validity evidence. *Journal of Personality and Social Psychology, 39,* 472–480.

Ryan, W. (1971). *Blaming the victim.* New York: Random House.

Ryff, C. D. (1989a). Happiness is everything, or is it? Explorations on the meaning of psychological well-being. *Journal of Personality and Social Psychology, 57,* 1069–1081.

Ryff, C. D. (1989b). In the eye of the beholder: Views of psychological well-being among middle-aged and older adults. *Psychology and Aging, 4,* 195–210.

Ryff, C. D. (1991). Possible selves in adulthood and old age: A tale of shifting horizons. *Psychology and Aging, 6,* 286–295.

Salovey, P., & Rodin, J. (1988). Coping with envy and jealousy. *Journal of Social and Clinical Psychology, 7,* 15–33.

Sarason, B. R., Shearin, E. N., Pierce, G. R., & Sarason, I. G. (1987). Interrelations of social support measures: Theoretical and practical implications. *Journal of Personality and Social Psychology, 52,* 813–832.

Sarason, I. G. (1984). Stress, anxiety, and cognitive interference: Reactions to tests. *Journal of Personality and Social Psychology, 46,* 929–938.

Sarason, I. G., Sarason, B. G., & Pierce, G. R. (1995). Cognitive interference: At the intelligence-personality crossroads. In D. H. Saklofske & M. Zeidner (Eds.), *International handbook of personality and intelligence: Perspectives on individual differences* (pp. 285–296). New York: Plenum.

Sarason, I. G., Levine, H. M., Basham, R. B., & Sarason, B. R. (1983). Assessing social support: The Social Support Questionnaire. *Journal of Personality and Social Psychology, 44,* 127–139.

Sarason, I. G., Sarason, B. R., Shearin, E. N., & Pierce, G. R. (1987). A brief measure of social support: Practical and theoretical implications. *Journal of Social and Personal Relationships, 4,* 497–510.

Schaefer, C., Coyne, J. C., & Lazarus, R. S. (1981). The health-related function of social support. *Journal of Behavioral Medicine, 4,* 381–406.

Scheier, M. F., & Carver, C. S. (1985). Optimism, coping, and health: Assessment and implications of generalized outcome expectancies. *Health Psychology, 4,* 219–247.

Scheier, M. F., & Carver, C. S. (1992). Effects of optimism on psychological and physical well-being: Theoretical overview and empirical update. *Cognitive Therapy and Research, 16,* 201–228.

Scheier, M. F., Matthews, K. A., Owens, J. F., Magovern, G. J., Sr., Lefebvre, R. C., Abbott, R. A., & Carver, C. S. (1989). Dispositional optimism and recovery from coronary artery bypass surgery: The beneficial effects on physical and psychological well-being. *Journal of Personality and Social Psychology, 57,* 1024–1040.

Scheier, M. F., Weintraub, J. K., & Carver, C. S. (1986). Coping with stress: Divergent strategies of optimists and pessimists. *Journal of Personality and Social Psychology, 51,* 1257–1264.

Scherer, M., & Adams, C. H. (1983). Construct validation of the Self-Efficacy Scale. *Psychological Reports, 53,* 899–902.

Scherer, M., Maddux, J. E., Mercandante, B., Prentice-Dunn, S., Jacobs, B., & Rogers, R. R. (1982). The Self-Efficacy Scale: Construction and validation. *Psychological Reports, 51,* 663–671.

Schlichter, K. J., & Horan, J. J. (1981). Effects of stress inoculation on the anger and aggression management skills of institutionalized juvenile delinquents. *Cognitive Therapy and Research, 5,* 359–365.

Schmidt, N. B. (1994, April). The Schema Questionnaire and the Schema Avoidance Questionnaire. *The Behavior Therapist,* 90–92.

Schmidt, N. B., Joiner, T. E., Jr., Young, J. E., & Telch, M. J. (1995). The Schema Questionnaire: Investigation of psychometric properties and the hierarchical structure of a measure of maladaptive schemas. *Cognitive Therapy and Research, 19,* 295–321.

Schmolling, P. (1984). Human reactions to the Nazi concentration camps: A summing up. *Journal of Human Stress, 10,* 108–120.

Schoenberg, B. M. (Ed.). (1980). *Bereavement counseling: A multidisciplinary handbook.* Westport, CT: Greenwood Press.

Schulz, R., & Decker, S. (1985). Long-term adjustment to physical disability: The role of social support, perceived control, and self-blame. *Journal of Personality and Social Psychology, 48,* 1162–1172.

Schulz, R., Heckhausen, J., & Locher, J. L. (1991). Adult development, control, and adaptive functioning. *Journal of Social Issues, 47,* 177–196.

Schunk, D. H. (1982). Effects of effort attributional feedback on children's perceived self-efficacy and achievement. *Journal of Educational Psychology, 74,* 548–556.

Schunk, D. H. (1983). Ability versus effort attributional feedback: Differential effects on self-efficacy and achievement. *Journal of Educational Psychology, 75,* 848–856.

Schunk, D. H. (1984). Sequential attributional feedback and children's achievement behaviors. *Journal of Educational Psychology, 76,* 1159–1169.

Schunk, D. H., & Hanson, A. R. (1985). Peer models: Influence on children's self-efficacy and achievement. *Journal of Educational Psychology, 77,* 313–322.

Schunk, D. H., Hanson, A. R., & Cox, P. D. (1987). Peer-model attributes and children's achievement behaviors. *Journal of Educational Psychology, 79,* 54–61.

Schwartz, M. D., Lerman, C., Miller, S. M., Daly, M., & Masny, A. (1995). Coping disposition, perceived risk, and psychological distress among women at increased risk for ovarian cancer. *Health Psychology, 14,* 232–235.

Schwartzberg, S. S., & Janoff-Bulman, R. (1991). Grief and the search for meaning: Exploring the assumptive worlds of bereaved college students. *Journal of Social and Clinical Psychology, 10,* 270–288.

Schwarz, R. A., & Prout, M. F. (1991). Integrative approaches in the treatment of post-traumatic stress disorder. *Psychotherapy, 28,* 364–373.

Scott, D. S., & Barber, T. X. (1977). Cognitive control of pain: Effects of multiple cognitive strategies *Psychological Record, 27,* 373–383.

Sedikides, C. (1992). Mood as a determinant of attentional focus. *Cognition and Emotion, 6,* 129–148.

Segrin, C. (1990). A meta-analytic review of social skill deficits in depression. *Communication Monographs, 57,* 292–308.

Segrin, C., & Abramson, L. Y. (1994). Negative reactions to depressive behaviors: A communication theories analysis. *Journal of Abnormal Psychology, 103,* 655–668.

Segrin, C., & Dillard, J. P. (1992). The interactional theory of depression: A meta-analysis of the research literature. *Journal of Social and Clinical Psychology, 11,* 43–70.

Seligman, M. E. P. (1975). *Helplessness: On depression, development, and death.* New York: W. H. Freeman.

Shaver, P., & Rubenstein, C. M. (1980). Childhood attachment experience and adult loneliness. In L. Wheeler (Ed.), *Review of personality and social psychology* (Vol. 1, pp. 42–73). Newbury Park, CA: Sage.

Shaver, P., Schwartz, J., Kirson, D., & O'Connor, C. (1987). Emotion and emotion knowledge: Further explorations of a prototype approach. *Journal of Personality and Social Psychology, 52,* 1061–1086.

Shepperd, J. A., & Arkin, R. M. (1989). Determinants of self-handicapping: Task importance and effects of pre-existing handicaps on self-generated handicaps. *Personality and Social Psychology Bulletin, 15,* 101–112.

Sherman, S. J., Skov, R. B., Hervitz, E. F., & Stock, C. B. (1981). The effects of explaining hypothetical future events: From possibility to probability to actuality and beyond. *Journal of Experimental Social Psychology, 17,* 142–158.

Shotland, R. L., & Craig, J. M. (1988). Can men and women differentiate between friendly and sexually interested behavior? *Social Psychology Quarterly, 51,* 66–73.

Showers, C. (1992). The motivational and emotional consequences of considering positive or negative possibilities for an upcoming event. *Journal of Personality and Social Psychology, 63,* 474–484.

Shupe, D. R. (1985). Perceived control, helplessness, and choice. In J. E. Birren & J. Livingston (Eds.), *Cognition, stress, and aging* (pp. 174–197). Englewood Cliffs, NJ: Prentice-Hall.

Sibicky, M., & Dovidio, J. F. (1986). Stigma of psychological therapy: Stereotypes, interpersonal reactions, and the self-fulfilling prophecy. *Journal of Counseling Psychology, 33,* 148–154.

Siegel, J. M. (1986). The Multidimensional Anger Inventory. *Journal of Personality and Social Psychology, 51,* 191–200.

Sillars, A. L. (1981). Attributions and interpersonal conflict resolution. In J. H. Harvey, W. J. Ickes, & R. L. Kidd (Eds.), *New directions in attribution research* (Vol. 3, pp. 279–305). Hillsdale, NJ: Erlbaum.

Silver, R. C., Wortman, C. B., & Crofton, C. (1990). The role of coping in support provision: The self-presentational dilemma of victims of life crises. In B. R. Sarason, I. G. Sarason, & G. R. Pierce (Eds.), *Social support: An interactional view* (pp. 397–426). New York: Wiley.

Simon, C. (1987, December). Age-proofing the home. *Psychology Today, 21,* 52–53.

Simons, A. D., McGowan, C. R., Epstein, L. H., Kupfer, D. J., & Robertson, R. J. (1985). Exercise as a treatment for depression: An update. *Clinical Psychology Review, 5,* 553–568.

Simpson, J. A. (1990). Influence of attachment styles on romantic relationships. *Journal of Personality and Social Psychology, 59,* 971–980.

Singer, J. L. (1974). *Imagery and daydream methods in psychotherapy and behavior modification.* New York: Academic Press.

Skinner, B. F. (1986). What's wrong with daily life in the western world. *American Psychologist, 41,* 568–574.

Skinner, B. F., & Vaughan, M. E. (1983). *Enjoy old age.* New York: Norton.

Slater, P. (1970). *The pursuit of loneliness.* Boston: Beacon Press.

Smith, C. A., Dobbins, C. J., & Wallston, K. A. (1991). The mediational role of perceived competence in psychological adjustment to rheumatoid arthritis. *Journal of Applied Social Psychology, 21,* 1218–1247.

Smith, C. A., Haynes, K. N., Lazarus, R. S., & Pope, L. K. (1993). In search of the "hot" cognitions: Attributions, appraisals, and their relation to emotion. *Journal of Personality and Social Psychology, 65,* 916–929.

Smith, C. A., & Lazarus, R. S. (1993). Appraisal components, core relational themes, and the emotions. *Cognition and Emotion, 7,* 233–269.

Smith, D. S., & Strube, M. J. (1991). Self-protective tendencies as moderators of self-handicapping impressions. *Basic and Applied Social Psychology, 12,* 63–80.

Smith, T. W. (1992). Hostility and health: Current status of a psychosomatic hypothesis. *Health Psychology, 11,* 139–150.

Smith, T. W., Peck, J. R., Milano, R. A., & Ward, J. R. (1988). Cognitive distortion in rheumatoid arthritis: Relation to depression and disability. *Journal of Consulting and Clinical Psychology, 56,* 412–416.

Smith, T. W., Peck, J. R., & Ward, J. R. (1990). Helplessness and depression in rheumatoid arthritis. *Health Psychology, 9,* 377–389.

Smith, T. W., Snyder, C. R., & Handlesman, M. M. (1982). On the self-serving of an academic wooden leg: Test anxiety as a self-handicapping strategy. *Journal of Personality and Social Psychology, 42,* 314–321.

Smith, T. W., Snyder, C. R., & Perkins, S. C. (1983). The self-serving function of hypochondriacal complaints: Physical symptoms as self-handicapping strategies. *Journal of Personality and Social Psychology, 44,* 787–797.

Snyder, C. R. (1989). Reality negotiation: From excuses to hope and beyond. *Journal of Social and Clinical Psychology, 8,* 130–157.

Snyder, C. R. (1990). Self-handicapping process and sequelae: On the taking of a psychological dive. In R. L. Higgins, C. R. Snyder, & S. Berglas (Eds.), *Self-handicapping: The paradox that isn't* (pp. 107–150). New York: Plenum.

Snyder, C. R., & Higgins, R. L. (1988a). Excuses: Their effective role in the negotiation of reality. *Psychological Bulletin, 104*, 23–35.

Snyder, C. R., & Higgins, R. L. (1988b). From making to being the excuse: An analysis of deception and verbal/nonverbal issues. *Journal of Nonverbal Behavior, 12*, 237–252.

Snyder, C. R., Irving, L. M., & Anderson, J. R. (1991). Hope and health. In C. R. Snyder & D. R. Forsyth (Eds.), *Handbook of social and clinical psychology* (pp. 285–305). New York: Pergamon.

Snyder, C. R., & Smith, T. W. (1982). Symptoms as self-handicapping strategies: On the virtues of new wine in an old bottle. In G. Weary & H. L. Mirels (Eds.), *Integration of clinical and social psychology* (pp. 104–127). New York: Oxford University Press.

Snyder, C. R., & Smith, T. W. (1986). On being "shy like a fox": A self-handicapping analysis. In W. H. Jones, J. M. Cheek, & S. R. Briggs (Eds.), *Shyness: Perspectives on research and treatment* (pp. 161–172). New York: Plenum.

Snyder, C. R., Smith, T. W., Augelli, R. W., & Ingram, R. E. (1985). On the self-serving function of social anxiety: Shyness as a self-handicapping strategy. *Journal of Personality and Social Psychology, 48*, 970–980.

Solano, C. H. (1989). Loneliness and perceptions of control: General traits versus specific attributions. In M. Hojat & R. Crandall (Eds.), *Loneliness: Theory, research, and applications* (pp. 201–214). Newbury Park, CA: Sage.

Solano, C. H., Batten, P. G., & Parish, E. A. (1982). Loneliness and patterns of self-disclosure. *Journal of Personality and Social Psychology, 43*, 524–531.

Solomon, S. D., Regier, D. A., & Burke, J. D. (1989). Role of perceived control in coping with disaster. *Journal of Social and Clinical Psychology, 8*, 376–392.

Spanos, N. P., Brown, J. M., Jones, B., & Horner, D. (1981). Cognitive activity and suggestions for analgesia in the reduction of reported pain. *Journal of Abnormal Psychology, 90*, 554–561.

Spanos, N. P., Horton, C., & Chaves, J. F. (1975). The effects of two cognitive strategies on pain threshold. *Journal of Abnormal Psychology, 84*, 677–681.

Spanos, N. P., Radtke-Bodorik, H. L., Ferguson, J. D., & Jones, B. (1979). The effects of hypnotic susceptibility, suggestions for analgesia, and the utilization of cognitive strategies on the reduction of pain. *Journal of Abnormal Psychology, 88*, 282–292.

Spanos, N. P., Stam, H. J., & Brazil, K. (1981). The effects of suggestion and distraction on coping ideation and reported pain. *Journal of Mental Imagery, 5*, 75–90.

Sprecher, S., & Duck, S. (1994). Sweet talk: The importance of perceived communication for romantic and friendship attraction experienced during a get-acquainted date. *Personality and Social Psychology Bulletin, 20*, 391–400.

Stall, R. D., Coates, T. J., & Hoff, C. (1988). Behavioral risk reduction for HIV infection among gay and bisexual men: A review of results from the United States. *American Psychologist, 43*, 878–885.

Stam, H. J., & Spanos, N. P. (1980). Experimental designs, expectancy effects, and hypnotic analgesia. *Journal of Abnormal Psychology, 89*, 751–762.

Stampfl, T., & Lewis, D. (1967). Essentials of implosive therapy: A learning-theory-based psychodynamic behavioral therapy. *Journal of Abnormal Psychology, 72*, 496–503.

Staneski, R. A., Kleinke, C. L., & Meeker, F. B. (1977). Effects of ingratiation, touch, and use of name on evaluation of job applicants and interviewers. *Social Behavior and Personality, 5*, 13–19.

Stanton, A. L., & Snider, P. R. (1993). Coping with a breast cancer diagnosis: A prospective study. *Health Psychology, 12*, 16–23.

Staples, S. L. (1996). Human response to environmental noise. *American Psychologist, 51*, 143–150.

Stearns, C. Z., & Stearns, P. N. (1986). *Anger: The struggle for emotional control in American history.* Chicago: University of Chicago Press.

Steinglass, P., & Gerrity, E. (1990). Natural disasters and post-traumatic stress disorder: Short-term versus long-term recovery in two disaster-affected communities. *Journal of Applied Social Psychology, 20*, 1746–1765.

Steinmetz, J. L., Lewinsohn, P. M., & Antonuccio, D. O. (1983). Prediction of individual outcome in a group intervention for depression. *Journal of Consulting and Clinical Psychology, 51*, 331–337.

Sternberg, R. J. (1986). A triangular theory of love. *Psychological Review, 93,* 119–135.

Sternberg, R. J., & Grajeck, S. (1984). The nature of love. *Journal of Personality and Social Psychology, 47,* 312–329.

Stone, A. A., Kennedy-Moore, E., & Neale, J. M. (1995). Association between daily coping and end-of-day mood. *Health Psychology, 14,* 341–349.

Storr, A. (1988). *Solitude: A return to the self.* New York: Free Press.

Stroebe, M., & Stroebe, W. (1991). Does "grief work" work? *Journal of Consulting and Clinical Psychology, 59,* 479–482.

Stuart, R. B. (1980). *Helping couples change.* New York: Guilford.

Suedfeld, P. (1982). Aloneness as a healing experience. In L. A. Peplau & D. Perlman (Eds.), *Loneliness: A sourcebook of current theory, research and therapy* (pp. 54–67). New York: Wiley-Interscience.

Sullivan, H. S. (1970). *The psychiatric interview.* New York: Norton.

Sullivan, M. J. L., Bishop, S. R., & Pivik, J. (1995). The pain catastrophizing scale: Development and validation. *Psychological Assessment, 7,* 524–532.

Suls, J. (1982). Social support, interpersonal relations, and health: Benefits and liabilities. In G. Sanders & J. Suls (Eds.), *Social psychology of health and illness.* Hillsdale, NJ: Erlbaum.

Suls, J., & Fletcher, B. (1985). The relative efficacy of avoidant and nonavoidant coping strategies: A meta-analysis. *Health Psychology, 4,* 249–288.

Suter, A. H. (1991). *Noise and its effects.* Washington, DC: Administrative Conference of the United States.

Sweeney, P. D., Anderson, K., & Bailey, S. (1986). Attributional style in depression: A meta-analytic review. *Psychological Bulletin, 50,* 974–991.

Swinkels, A., & Giuliano, T. A. (1995). The measurement and conceptualization of mood awareness: Monitoring and labeling one's mood states. *Personality and Social Psychology Bulletin, 21,* 934–949.

Szasz, T. S. (1987). *Insanity: The idea and its consequences.* New York: Wiley.

Szasz, T. S. (1990). *Conversation hour.* Audiotape (C289–CH13) from the Evolution of Psychotherapy Conference, Anaheim, CA. Phoenix, AZ: Milton Erickson Foundation.

Tabachnik, N., Crocker, J., & Alloy, L. B. (1983). Depression, social comparison, and the false-consensus effect. *Journal of Personality and Social Psychology, 45,* 688–699.

Tait, R., & Silver, R. C. (1989). Coming to terms with major negative life events. In J. S. Uleman & J. A. Bargh (Eds.), *Unintended thought* (pp. 351–382). New York: Guilford.

Taylor, C. J., & Scogin, F. (1992). Dysphoria and coping in women: The effect of threat and challenge appraisals. *Journal of Social and Clinical Psychology, 11,* 26–42.

Taylor, S. E. (1979). Hospital patient behavior: Reactance, helplessness, or control? *Journal of Social Issues, 35,* 156–184.

Taylor, S. E. (1983). Adjustment to threatening events: A theory of cognitive adaptation. *American Psychologist, 38,* 1161–1173.

Taylor, S. E. (1987). The progress and prospects of health psychology: Tasks of a maturing discipline. *Health Psychology, 6,* 73–87.

Taylor, S. E. (1989). *Positive illusions: Creative self-deception and the healthy mind.* New York: Basic Books.

Taylor, S. E. (1994). *Health psychology* (3rd ed.). New York: McGraw-Hill.

Taylor, S. E., Aspinwall, L. G., Giuliano, T. A., Dakof, G., & Reardon, K. K. (1993). Storytelling and coping with stressful events. *Journal of Applied Social Psychology, 23,* 703–733.

Taylor, S. E., & Brown, J. D. (1988). Illusion and well-being: A social psychological perspective on mental health. *Psychological Bulletin, 103,* 193–210.

Taylor, S. E., & Clark, L. F. (1986). Does information improve adjustment to noxious medical procedures? In M. J. Saks & L. Saks (Eds.), *Advances in applied social psychology* (Vol. 3, pp. 1–28). Hillsdale, NJ: Erlbaum.

Taylor, S. E., Falke, R. L., Shoptaw, S. J., & Lichtman, R. R. (1986). Social support, support groups, and the cancer patient. *Journal of Consulting and Clinical Psychology, 54,* 608–615.

Taylor, S. E., Helgeson, V. S., Reed, G. M., & Skokan, L. A. (1991). Self-generated feelings of control and adjustment to physical illness. *Journal of Social Issues, 47,* 91–109.

Taylor, S. E., Kemeny, M. E., Aspinwall, L. G., Schneider, S. G., Rodriguez, R., & Herbert, M. (1992). Optimism, coping, psychological distress, and high-risk sexual behavior among men at risk for acquired immunodeficiency syndrome (AIDS). *Journal of Personality and Social Psychology, 63,* 460–473.

Taylor, S. E., Lichtman, R. R., & Wood, J. V. (1984). Attributions, beliefs about control, and adjustment to breast cancer. *Journal of Personality and Social Psychology, 46,* 489–502.

Taylor, S. E., & Lobel, M. (1989). Social comparison activity under threat: Downward evaluation and upward contacts. *Psychological Review, 96,* 569–575.

Taylor, S. E., Wood, J. V., & Lichtman, R. R. (1983). It could be worse: Selective evaluation as a response to victimization. *Journal of Social Issues, 39,* 19–40.

Teglasi, H., & Hoffman, M. A. (1982). Causal attributions of shy subjects. *Journal of Research in Personality, 16,* 376–385.

Teitelman, J. L., & Priddy, J. M. (1988). From psychological theory to practice: Improving frail elders' quality of life through control-enhancing interventions. *Journal of Applied Gerontology, 7,* 298–315.

Terry, D. J. (1994). Determinants of coping: The role of stable and situational factors. *Journal of Personality and Social Psychology, 66,* 895–910.

Thoits, P. A. (1986). Social support as coping assistance. *Journal of Consulting and Clinical Psychology, 54,* 416–423.

Thompson, S. C., & Kelley, H. H. (1981). Judgments of responsibility for activities in close relationships. *Journal of Personality and Social Psychology, 41,* 469–477.

Thompson, S. C., Sobolew-Shubin, Galbraith, M. E., Schwankovsky, L., & Cruzen, D. (1993). Maintaining perceptions of control: Finding perceived control in low-control circumstances. *Journal of Personality and Social Psychology, 64,* 293–304.

Thorne, A. (1987). The press of personality: A study of conversations between introverts and extraverts. *Journal of Personality and Social Psychology, 53,* 718–726.

Tice, D. M. (1991). Esteem protection or enhancement? Self-handicapping motives and attributions differ by trait self-esteem. *Journal of Personality and Social Psychology, 60,* 711–725.

Timko, C., & Moos, R. H. (1989). Choice, control, and adaptation among elderly residents of sheltered care settings. *Journal of Applied Social Psychology, 19,* 636–655.

Titchener, J. L., & Kapp, F. T. (1976). Family and character change at Buffalo Creek. *American Journal of Psychiatry, 133,* 295–299.

Trimble, M. R. (1985). Post-traumatic stress disorder:History of a concept. In C. R. Figley (Ed.), *Trauma and its wake* (pp. 5–14). New York: Brunner/Mazel.

Tross, S., & Hirsch, D. A. (1988). Psychological distress and neuropsychological complications of HIV infections and AIDS. *American Psychologist, 43,* 929–934.

Trull, T. J. (1992). *DSM-III-R* personality disorders and the five-factor model of personality: An empirical comparison. *Journal of Abnormal Psychology, 101,* 553–560.

Tucker, J. A., Vuchinich, R. E., & Sobell, M. B. (1981). Alcohol consumption as a self-handicapping strategy. *Journal of Abnormal Psychology, 90,* 220–230.

Turk, D. C., Holzman, A. D., & Kerns, R. D. (1986). Chronic pain. In K. A. Holroyd & T. L. Creer (Eds.), *Self-management of chronic disease* (pp. 441–472). New York: Academic Press.

Turk, D. C., Meichenbaum, D., & Genest, M. (1983). *Pain and behavioral medicine.* New York: Guilford.

Turk, D. C., Rudy, T. E., & Salovey, P. (1985). The McGill Pain Questionnaire reconsidered: Confirming the factor structure and examining appropriate uses. *Pain, 21,* 385–397.

Turner, J. A., & Clancy, S. (1986). Strategies for coping with chronic low back pain: Relationship to pain and disability. *Pain, 24,* 355–364.

Turner, J. A., Clancy, S., & Vitaliano, P. P. (1987). Relationships of stress, appraisal, and coping to chronic low back pain. *Behavior Research and Therapy, 25,* 281–288.

U.S. News & World Report. (1987, June 29). Taking the pain out of pain. 50–57.

Van der Velde, F. W., & Van der Pligt, J. (1991). AIDS-related health behavior: Coping, protection motivation, and previous behavior. *Journal of Behavioral Medicine, 14,* 429–451.

Vasey, M. W., & Borkovec, T. D..(1992). A catastrophizing assessment of worrisome thoughts. *Cognitive Therapy and Research, 16,* 1–15.

Velten, E. (1968). A laboratory task for induction of mood states. *Behavior Research and Therapy, 6,* 473–482.

Vickio, C. J., Cavanaugh, J. C., & Attig, T. W. (1990). Perceptions of grief among university students. *Death Studies, 14,* 231–240.

Vinokur, A., Schul, Y., & Caplan, R. D. (1987). Determinants of perceived social support: Interpersonal transactions, personal outlook, and transient affective states. *Journal of Personality and Social Psychology, 53,* 1137–1145.

Vitaliano, P. P. (1988). *ADS and WCCL manual.* Seattle: University of Washington Press.

Vitaliano, P. P., DeWolfe, D. J., Maiuro, R. D., Russo, J., & Katon, W. (1990). Appraised changeability of a stressor as a modifier of the relationship between coping and depression: A test of the hypothesis of fit. *Journal of Personality and Social Psychology, 59,* 582–592.

Vitaliano, P. P., Katon, W., Maiuro, R. D., & Russo, J. (1989). Coping in chest pain patients with and without psychiatric disorders. *Journal of Consulting and Clinical Psychology, 57,* 338–343.

Vitaliano, P. P., Russo, J., Weber, L., & Celum, C. (1993). The Dimensions of Stress Scale: Psychometric Properties. *Journal of Applied Social Psychology, 23,* 1847–1878.

Vitkus, J., & Horowitz, L. M. (1987). Poor social performance of lonely people: Lacking a skill or adopting a role? *Journal of Personality and Social Psychology, 52,* 1266–1273.

Wallis, R., & Kleinke, C. L. (1995). Acceptance of external versus internal excuses by an externally or internally oriented audience. *Basic and Applied Social Psychology, 17,* 411–420.

Wallston, B. S., Alagna, S. W., DeVillis, B. M., & DeVillis, R. F. (1983). Social support and physical health. *Health Psychology, 2,* 367–391.

Wallston, B. S., Wallston, K. A., Kaplan, G. D., & Maides, S. A. (1976). Development and validation of the Health Locus of Control (HLC) Scale. *Journal of Consulting and Clinical Psychology, 44,* 580–585.

Walster, E. (1966). Assignment of responsibility for an accident. *Journal of Personality and Social Psychology, 3,* 73–79.

Wanderer, Z., & Cabot, T. (1978). *Letting go.* New York: Warner Books.

Ward, C. (1988). The Attitude Toward Rape Victims Scale. *Psychology of Women Quarterly, 12,* 127–146.

Waterman, A. S. (1993). Two conceptions of happiness: Contrasts of personal expressiveness (eudaimonia) and hedonic enjoyment. *Journal of Personality and Social Psychology, 64,* 678–691.

Watzlawick, P. (1983). *The situation is hopeless, but not serious: The pursuit of unhappiness.* New York: Norton.

Watzlawick, P. (1988). *Ultra-solutions.* New York: Norton.

Watzlawick, P., Weakland, J., & Fisch, R. (1974). *Change: Principles of problem formation and problem resolution.* New York: Norton.

Weary, G., & Williams, J. P. (1990). Depressive self-presentation: Beyond self-handicapping. *Journal of Personality and Social Psychology, 58,* 892–898.

Weeks, D. G., Michela, J. L., Peplau, L. A., & Bragg, M. E. (1980). The relation between loneliness and depression: A structural equation analysis. *Journal of Personality and Social Psychology, 39,* 1238–1244.

Weinberger, D. A., & Davidson, M. N. (1994). Styles of inhibiting emotional expression: Distinguishing repressive coping from impression management. *Journal of Personality, 62,* 587–613.

Weinberger, D. A., & Schwartz, G. E. (1990). Distress and restraint as superordinate dimensions of self-reported adjustment. *Journal of Personality, 58,* 381–417.

Weiner, B. (1979). A theory of motivation for some classroom experiences. *Journal of Educational Psychology, 71,* 3–25.

Weiner, B. (1985). An attributional theory of achievement motivation and emotion. *Psychological Review, 92,* 548–573.

Weiner, B., Frieze, I., Kukla, A., Reed, L., Rest, S., & Rosenbaum, R. M. (1971). *Perceiving the causes of success and failure.* Morristown, NJ: General Learning Press.

Weiner, B., Perry, R. P., & Magnusson, J. (1988). An attributional analysis of reactions to stigmas. *Journal of Personality and Social Psychology, 55,* 738–748.

Weiner, B., Russell, D., & Lerman, D. (1979). The cognition-emotion process in achievement-related contexts. *Journal of Personality and Social Psychology, 37,* 1211–1220.

Weiss, J. C. (1995a). Cognitive therapy and life review therapy: Theoretical and therapeutic implications for mental health counselors. *Journal of Mental Health Counseling, 17,* 157–172.

Weiss, J. C. (1995b). Universities for the second phase of life: Counseling, wellness, and senior citizen programs. *Journal of Gerontological Social Work, 23,* 3–24.

Weiss, R. S. (1973). *Loneliness: The experience of emotional and social isolation.* Cambridge, MA: MIT Press.

Weiss, R. S. (1974). The provisions of social relationships. In Z. Rubin (Ed.), *Doing unto others.* Englewood Cliffs, NJ: Prentice-Hall.

Wertheim, E. H., & Schwartz, J. C. (1983). Depression, guilt, and self-management of pleasant and unpleasant events. *Journal of Personality and Social Psychology, 45,* 884–889.

Westra, H. A., & Kuiper, N. A. (1992). Type A, irrational cognitions, and situational factors relating to stress. *Journal of Research in Personality, 26,* 1–20.

Wethington, E., & Kessler, R. C. (1986). Perceived support, received support, and adjustment to stressful life events. *Journal of Health and Social Behavior, 27,* 78–89.

White, J. (1982). *Rejection.* Reading, MA: Addison-Wesley.

White, R. W. (1959). Motivation reconsidered. *Psychological Review, 66,* 297–333.

Wideman, M. V., & Singer, J. L. (1984). The role of psychological mechanisms in preparation for child-birth. *American Psychologist, 39,* 1357–1371.

Wiener, M., & Mehrabian, A. (1968). *Language within language: Immediacy, a channel in communication.* New York: Appleton-Century-Crofts.

Wilfley D., & Kunce, J. (1986). Differential physical and psychological effects of exercise. *Journal of Counseling Psychology, 33,* 337–342.

Williams, D. A., & Keefe, F. J. (1991). Pain beliefs and the use of cognitive-behavioral coping strategies. *Pain, 46,* 185–190.

Williams, P. G., Wiebe, D. J., & Smith, T. W. (1992). Coping processes as mediators of the relationship between hardiness and health. *Journal of Behavioral Medicine, 15,* 237–255.

Wills, T. A. (1987). Help-seeking as a coping mechanism. In C. R. Snyder & C. E. Ford (Eds.), *Coping with negative life events* (pp. 19–50). New York: Plenum.

Wills, T. A., & DePaulo, B. M. (1991). Interpersonal analysis of the help-seeking process. In C. R. Snyder & D. R. Forsyth (Eds.), *Handbook of social and clinical psychology* (pp. 350–375). New York: Pergamon.

Wilson, J. P., Smith, W. K., & Johnson, S. K. (1985). A comparative analysis of PTSD among various survivor groups. In C. R. Figley (Ed.), *Trauma and its wake* (pp. 142–172). New York: Brunner/Mazel.

Wilson, T. D., & Linville, P. W. (1982). Improving the academic performance of college freshmen: Attribution theory revisited. *Journal of Personality and Social Psychology, 42,* 367–376.

Wilson, T. D., & Linville, P. W. (1985). Improving the performance of college freshmen with attributional techniques. *Journal of Personality and Social Psychology, 49,* 287–293.

Wolpe, J. (1958). *Psychotherapy by reciprocal inhibition.* Palo Alto, CA: Stanford University Press.

Wolpe, J. (1982). *The practice of behavior therapy* (3rd ed.). Elmsford, NY: Pergamon.

Wood, J. V., Taylor, S. E., & Lichtman, R. R. (1985). Social comparison in adjustment to breast cancer. *Journal of Personality and Social Psychology, 49,* 1169–1183.

Worden, J. W. (1982). *Grief counseling and grief therapy.* New York: Springer.

Worthington, E. L., & Shumate, M. (1981). Imagery and verbal counseling methods in stress inoculation training for pain control. *Journal of Counseling Psychology, 28,* 1–6.

Wortman, C. B., Carnelley, K. B., Lehman, D. R., Davis, C. G., & Exline, J. J. (1995). Coping with the loss of a family member: Implications for community-level research and intervention. In S. E. Hobfoll & M. W. deVries (Eds.), *Extreme stress and communities: Impact and intervention* (pp. 83–103). Dordrecht, the Netherlands: Kluwer.

Wortman, C. B., & Silver, R. C. (1987). Coping with irrevocable loss. In G. R. VandenBos & B. K. Bryant (Eds.), *Cataclysms, crises, and catastrophies: Psychology in action* (Vol. 6, pp. 189–235). Washington, DC: American Psychological Association.

Wortman, C. B., & Silver, R. C. (1989). The myths of coping with loss. *Journal of Consulting and Clinical Psychology, 57,* 349–357.

Wright, L., Bussmann, K., Freidman, A., Khoury, M., Owens, F., & Paris, W. (1990). Exaggerated social control and its relationship to the Type A behavior pattern. *Journal of Research in Personality, 24,* 258–269.

Yelin, E., Meenan, R., Nevitt, M., & Epstein, W. (1980). Effects of disease, social and work factors. *Annals of Internal Medicine, 93,* 551–556.

Young, J. E. (1982). Loneliness, depression, and cognitive therapy: Theory and application. In L. A. Peplau & D. Perlman (Eds.), *Loneliness: A sourcebook of current theory, research, and therapy* (pp. 379–405). New York: Wiley-Interscience.

Young, J. E. (1994). *Cognitive therapy for personality disorders: A schema-focused approach* (2nd ed.). New York: Cognitive Therapy Center of New York.

Zautra, A. J., & Manne, S. L. (1992). Coping with rheumatoid arthritis: A review of a decade of research. *Annals of Behavioral Medicine, 14,* 31–39.

Zautra, A. J., Reich, J. W., & Guarnaccia, C. A. (1990). Some everyday life consequences of disability and bereavement for older adults. *Journal of Personality and Social Psychology, 59,* 550–561.

Zautra, A. J., Reich, J. W., & Newsom, J. T. (1995). Autonomy and sense of control among older adults: An examination of their effects on mental health. In L. Bond, S. Cutler, & A. Grams (Eds.), *Promoting successful and productive aging.* Newbury Park, CA: Sage.

Zautra, A. J., & Wrabetz, A. B. (1991). Coping success and its relationship to psychological distress for older adults. *Journal of Personality and Social Psychology, 61,* 801–810.

Zborowski, M. (1969). *People in pain.* San Francisco: Jossey-Bass.

Zeiss, A. M., Lewinsohn, P. M., & Munoz, R. F. (1979). Nonspecific improvement effects in depression using interpersonal skills training. *Journal of Consulting and Clinical Psychology, 47,* 427–439.

Zevon, M. A., Karuza, J., & Brickman, P. (1982). Responsibility and the elderly: Applications to psychotherapy. *Psychotherapy: Theory, Research, and Practice, 4,* 405–411.

Zimbardo, P. G. (1977). *Shyness: What it is, what to do about it.* Reading, MA: Addison-Wesley.

Zimbardo, P. G., Cohen, A., Weisenberg, M., Dworkin, L., & Firestone, I. (1969). The control of experimental pain. In P. G. Zimbardo (Ed.), *The cognitive control of motivation* (pp. 100–122). Glenview, IL: Scott, Foresman.

Zung, W. W. K. (1965). A self-rating depression scale. *Archives of General Psychiatry, 12,* 63–70.

INDEX

TO THE OWNER OF THIS BOOK:

I hope that you have found *Coping with Life Challenges,* Second Edition, useful. So that this book can be improved in a future edition, would you take the time to complete this sheet and return it? Thank you.

School and address: ———————————————————————————

Department: ———————————————————————————

Instructor's name: ———————————————————————————

1. What I like most about this book is: ———————————————————

———————————————————————————————

———————————————————————————————

2. What I like least about this book is: ———————————————————

———————————————————————————————

———————————————————————————————

3. My general reaction to this book is: ———————————————————

———————————————————————————————

4. The name of the course in which I used this book is: ————————————

———————————————————————————————

5. Were all of the chapters of the book assigned for you to read? ——————————

　　If not, which ones weren't? ———————————————————————

6. In the space below, or on a separate sheet of paper, please write specific suggestions for improving this book and anything else you'd care to share about your experience in using the book.

———————————————————————————————

———————————————————————————————

———————————————————————————————

———————————————————————————————

———————————————————————————————

Optional:

Your name: _____ Date: _____

May Brooks/Cole quote you, either in promotion for *Coping with Life Challenges,* Second Edition, or in future publishing ventures?

Yes: _____ No: _____

Sincerely,

Chris L. Kleinke

FOLD HERE

NO POSTAGE
NECESSARY
IF MAILED
IN THE
UNITED STATES

BUSINESS REPLY MAIL

FIRST CLASS   PERMIT NO. 358   PACIFIC GROVE, CA

POSTAGE WILL BE PAID BY ADDRESSEE

ATT: *Chris L. Kleinke*

**Brooks/Cole Publishing Company
511 Forest Lodge Road
Pacific Grove, California 93950-9968**

FOLD HERE